Misrepresentations

Graham Bradshaw

Misrepresentations

Shakespeare and the Materialists

Cornell University Press

ITHACA AND LONDON

First published 1993 by Cornell University Press.

Library of Congress Cataloging-in-Publication Data

Bradshaw, Graham.
    Misrepresentations : Shakespeare and the materialists / Graham Bradshaw.
      p. cm.
    Includes bibliographical references (p.) and index.
    ISBN 0-8014-2890-4 (cloth : alk. paper).—ISBN 0-8014-8129-5
(paper : alk. paper)
    1. Shakespeare, William, 1564–1616—Criticism and interpretation—
History—20th century. 2. Historical criticism (Literature)
3. Criticism—History—20th century. 4. Literature and
anthropology. 5. Materialism. I. Title.
PR2970.B73 1993
822.3'3—dc20   93-30897

Printed in the United States of America

⊚ The paper in this book meets the minimum requirements of the
American National Standard for Information Sciences—Permanence
of Paper for Printed Library Materials, ANSI Z39.48-1984.

For Jonas and Millie

I have arrived at the rock bottom of my convictions.
And one might almost say that these foundation-walls are
  carried by the whole house.
One gives a false picture of doubt.

—Ludwig Wittgenstein, *On Certainty*

Contents

Acknowledgments   ix

A Note on the Text   xi

PROLOGUE
Is Shakespeare Evil?   1

Reviving Tillyard	1
Buddies	8
Chaotic Sites	18
The E-Effect	26

CHAPTER ONE
Being Oneself: New Historicists,
Cultural Materialists, and *Henry V*   34

The Trouble with Harry	34
The Historiographical Challenge	46
Dramatic "Rhyming"	63
Who Them? Where Us?	80
Systems in Force	98
Being Oneself	112

CHAPTER TWO

Dramatic Intentions:
Two-Timing in Shakespeare's Venice 125

Jessica's Lie   125
Complex Designs   139
Obeying the Time   148
Fashioning *Othello*   168
A Choice of Delusions   190
"A Horrible Conceite"   201

EPILOGUE

The New Historicist as Iago 223

Seeing Through Seeing Through   223
The Fear of Being Taken In   227
The Riverbed   232
Othello 1980   245

APPENDIX

Dashing Othello's Spirits 258

Notes 283

Index 315

Acknowledgments

Much of this book was written at the National Humanities Center in North Carolina, where what seemed like the happiest and most productive year of my academic life passed all too quickly. I am most grateful to the staff and librarians of that magnificent institution, and to the various NHC Fellows, among them Mark Turner, Stan Chojnicki, Mel Richter, and Dick Lewis, who contributed more to this book than they realized. As ever, the University of St. Andrews was generous in providing leave and assistance. I also thank the British Academy and the Carnegie Trust for help at various times.

Some material in this book first appeared, usually in a very different form, in *English Studies, Poetica, Meridian,* the *Times Literary Supplement,* the *Age Monthly Review,* and the *London Review of Books;* I am grateful to the editors of these journals for permission to recycle and rework or restore this material.

I thank the British Council and Kyoto University for inviting me to Japan to lecture on some of the topics treated in this book; the discussions that followed were especially helpful when I was making the final revisions. I also thank the readers for Cornell University Press for sending reports that were helpfully detailed and encouraging; Carol Betsch and Valerie Haskins for their patient, instructive editing; and the University of Queensland for (yet again) providing hospitality, in the summer of 1992 when I was finishing this book.

[ix]

I am especially grateful to Tony Nuttall for going through a lengthy first draft of this book and of a companion volume on Donne and Jonson (which may yet appear), and for offering numerous helpful suggestions. All the other friends and colleagues who have helped, in ways I could never properly acknowledge here, know who they are and, I hope, know how grateful I am.

Finally, some special words of thanks to Stephen Greenblatt, whose readings of Shakespeare I criticize at great length in this book. I admire Greenblatt but love Shakespeare, and think that new historicist readings—even his—diminish the plays; at the same time I find his conception of "cultural poetics" profoundly helpful, above all because it seems to me at odds with the estranging effect of those readings. Some of these points were also developed in a lecture at Berkeley which Greenblatt, very characteristically, took some trouble to arrange. That welcoming response to an attempt at critical dialogue was especially encouraging, and exemplary; I can only hope that this book lives up to it.

G. B.

A Note on the Text

I have quoted from the First Folio, while giving act, scene, and line references from *The Riverside Shakespeare*, ed. G. Blakemore Evans et al., 2 vols. (Boston: Houghton Mifflin, 1974); I substitute the modern *u*, *v*, and *s* in all cases. Apart from correcting undisputed misprints, adjusting the Folio lineation, and noting some significant Quarto variants in square brackets, I have very occasionally modernized a Folio spelling that might mislead or baffle readers who always read Shakespeare in modernized editions.

The opposed view, that it is more considerate to use a good modernized edition, is often put by critics who would never dream of quoting Donne, Jonson, or Milton in a modernized text; the arguments on either side tend to rationalize established preferences or vested interests. It is true that we cannot know when the Folio spelling and punctuation is Shakespeare's, but we can be sure that a modernized edition is not. My appendix, "Dashing Othello's Spirits," suggests some positive reasons for my own preference, but the strongest reason may well be negative: I dislike reading Shakespeare in modernized texts because I am distracted by the sense that what I am reading could never have been written at any time. It isn't Shakespeare's English, and it isn't modern English; you know not where to have it. This evidently doesn't trouble many critics whose scholarly knowledge of textual and linguistic matters far surpasses my own, and may not matter very much very often; yet in reading a modernized text one is in no position to see when or how it might matter.

After gloomily resolving to quote from a modernized text and writing about half of this book, I found that self-imposed ordinance too painful and reflected that it was, after all, my book. Perhaps some readers who always read Shakespeare in modernized texts will be happily surprised, and find that (to adapt Ben Jonson) they prefer to read a language such as men once used.

Misrepresentations

Is Shakespeare Evil?

ISM (i′ z'm), *quasi-sb.* [The prec. suffix *-ism* used generically
as an independent word.] A form of doctrine, theory, or
practice having, or claiming to have, a distinctive character
or relation: chiefly used disparagingly, and sometimes with
implied reference to *schism.*

— *New English Dictionary*

Reviving Tillyard

In my book *Shakespeare's Scepticism*[1] I offered an account of Shakespeare's dramatic perspectivism and supposed that readers who
found my approach persuasive could draw certain conclusions.
There seemed no need to enter into any sustained disagreement with
other very different and more influential approaches. I was pleased
when the conclusions I had in mind were drawn by some American
and British reviewers, and bemused when others made up for my
own unwillingness to "situate" my "approach" among the various
competing "isms" by explaining that my book was the work of a "deconstructionist" who wouldn't come clean, or of a "wily Leavisite," or
of a "radical humanist." Such "ismic" tagging is a familiar but anticriti-
cal feature of contemporary academic criticism; "isms" are for us
what "ologies" were for Mrs. Gradgrind. In critical terms, learning
that Stephen Greenblatt and Leonard Tennenhouse are New Historicists, or that Graham Holderness and Jonathan Dollimore are Cultural Materialists, or that A. P. Rossiter and E. M. W. Tillyard were
Essentialist Humanists is far less important than seeing how

[1]

Greenblatt's superiority to Tennenhouse, Holderness's to Dollimore, and Rossiter's to Tillyard depend on differences in critical acumen, not on Good Ideological Housekeeping Seals of Approval. Indeed, the "ismic" tagging is not merely less important but actively misleading, if, as this book argues, the "Essentialist Humanist" is an ideological fiction, and if we see that the current tendency to treat and explain critical differences as ideological conflicts, or "ismic" cockfights, is something to be opposed by those who care about literature and criticism.

Hence this book's double subject. Although (I scarce can think it, but am told) it is more polemical than its predecessor, my hope and aim in writing it has been that its polemical parts would be seen to take their place in a positive argument. It follows from the earlier book in its concern with Shakespeare's perspectivism, and with the challenging intricacy and complexity of the plays' dramatic thinking; but it also considers *Henry V* and *Othello* as test cases that provide a vantage point from which to appraise our present critical situation. So, for example, those prematurely politicized readings of *Henry V* which I consider in Chapter 1 all sample that play in a dismayingly partial way, while using it to "instantiate" whatever theory underlies the reading. Yet it is still open to us to do what these readings do not do, and allow the play to test, not merely "instantiate," the theory. Moreover, collecting and weighing our responses to what different readings demonstrably block out or take for granted can both illuminate Shakespeare's complex design and help us to isolate—and even historicize—some significant differences between American "new historicism" and British "cultural materialism." W. H. Auden once remarked that a work of art reads us; if the plays do read us, they can help us to historicize our present.

To see better what is at issue, and how "ideological critique" presents itself as some kind of advance on "criticism," we might consider what Hugh Grady's *Modernist Shakespeare* calls "The Case of E. M. W. Tillyard."[2] Grady refers to Tillyard's "meteoric" fall into "disfavor," and it is true enough that "Tillyardian" is now a pejorative term. Yet I well remember how, as a Cambridge undergraduate in the mid-sixties, I seldom heard Tillyard's name without the critical equivalent of a mental health warning. Meteors travel faster than that, and if we ask when the great assault on Tillyard took place, the historical answer is—twice.

The *critical* dismantling of Tillyard's representative assumptions began in the 1940s as his books appeared, and then continued on both
sides of the Atlantic through the fifties and sixties. To recall some
landmarks: Don Cameron Allen's devastating discussion of *The Elizabethan World Picture* appeared in 1945; Rossiter's lectures in Cambridge and Stratford were widely influential in the fifties, even before
they were posthumously collected in *Angel with Horns* in 1961; Norman Rabkin's *Shakespeare and the Common Understanding* appeared in
1967, and was followed in 1968 by Wilbur Sanders's *Dramatist and the
Received Idea* and Sigurd Burckhardt's *Shakespearian Meanings*.[3] What
was being called into question—through Rossiter's emphasis on "ambivalence" and "two-eyed vision" or Rabkin's account of "complemen-
tarity"—was not merely Tillyard's own undertaking to explain what
Shakespeare "really" believed and what the plays "really" mean, but
any such search for a single, authentic, and authoritative "meaning."
As Stephen Booth mischievously put it in his 1969 essay "On the
Value of Hamlet": "The history of criticism shows us too ready to
indulge a not wholly inexplicable fancy that in *Hamlet* we behold the
frustrated and inarticulate Shakespeare furiously wagging his tail in
an effort to tell us something."[4] Although it was obvious enough that
these critics found Tillyard's authoritarianism uncongenial, the burden of their critical disagreements with Tillyard was not that his readings were ideologically or politically unacceptable, or evil, but that
they were critically inadequate and reductive.

Of course this is not to deny that Tillyard's books were very influential throughout the fifties and sixties; but in the same period the
critical and historical issues were being vigorously debated and alternatives presented—years and even decades before the materialists ma-
terialized and presented their *ideological* "critiques" in the seventies
and eighties. So what was new? In his 1985 essay "Shakespeare, Cultural Materialism and the New Historicism," Jonathan Dollimore explains what, above all, made the materialist critique of Tillyard's
"error" so powerfully original and searching: "The error, from a materialist perspective, is falsely to unify history and social process in
the name of 'the collective mind of the people.' . . . In other words,
the didactic stress on order was in part an anxious reaction to emergent and (in)-subordinate social forces which were perceived as
threatening. Tillyard's world picture, to the extent that it did still exist,
was not shared by all."[5] In other words, there can be no convincing

presentation of the Elizabethan world picture until we "learn to read the unprinted works of the suppressed majorities"—but that is how D. C. Allen put it in 1945.

A trend or tendency is in question, and for an instructive parallel we might recall William Empson's splendidly vigorous dismantling of Derek Traversi's reading of *The Tempest:*

> Caliban has to be viewed gravely because in his case there is Symbolism at work. Sentimental critics have given Caliban credit for a poetical nature, but Traversi has an answer: "the poetry which we admire in Caliban was given him, at least in part, by Prospero ("You taught me language; and my profit on't / Is, I know how to curse"). We know that Caliban is beyond redemption because when boasting he threatens to inflict on Prospero "unrestrained physical cruelty"; whereas when Prospero makes Caliban scream with pain all night that is spiritual power. Indeed "Caliban is bound by his nature to service"; please notice that Traversi is expressing here the pure milk of the master-race doctrine, and it is presented with the usual glum sanctimoniousness as a traditional Christian moral, with no sign that it has ever been questioned. Before the first entry of Caliban, Miranda expresses distaste for him and Prospero answers:
>
> > But, as 'tis,
> > We cannot miss him: he does make our fire,
> > Fetch in our wood; and serves in offices,
> > That profit us.
>
> The kind of life that Prospero has established in his retreat assumes, in fact, the submission of Caliban as a necessary condition. That this submission requires an effort, indicates once more that the island is a reflection of the outer world.
>
> It appears that, if you have to pinch Caliban black and blue as soon as he stops chopping wood, that is rather like keeping a vow of chastity. I must say, I wouldn't like to run into a Moral Critic on a dark night; there is something very shambling and subhuman about the whole movement.[6]

Empson next turned to, and on, Frank Kermode's edition of *The Tempest,* challenging the idea that "the description of Caliban in the List of Names as 'a savage and deformed slave' means that Shakespeare considered him inherently a slave, much as Aristotle would have done": "Caliban simply *is* a slave of Prospero, who first addresses him as 'slave!'; this is not in itself proof that Shakespeare approved of slavery. You might as well say that to write 'a prostitute' in the dramatis personae would mean approval of prostitution. When Kermode assumes it he is accepting a formula: 'Way back in early times they didn't have advanced ideas, like we have; they just had moral ideas, and that was much better'" (239–40).

Some jokes improve with time. Empson's essay was written in 1964, and it anticipates familiar contemporary preoccupations—although we should also notice how few of the currently proliferating discussions of colonial discourse in *The Tempest* share Empson's complementary interest in the practices and conventions of Shakespearean poetic drama. We can be sure that the simple but important question of why Caliban speaks in verse is *not* what Terry Eagleton has in mind when he calls for a "Caliban school of criticism"; nor does Eagleton mention Empson's challenge to Traversi and Kermode (or the anti-Prospero readings of writers like Robert Graves and Ted Hughes, or of critics like Clifford Leech and Harry Berger Jr.).[7] Malcolm Evans doesn't mention Empson either, in entering his own more extended quarrel with Kermode's edition in *Signifying Nothing;* but then recognizing how Empson's dissection of the "master-race doctrine" anticipated his own would have interfered with his unremittingly hostile characterization of the "humanist."[8] Empson's complaint, in 1964, about presenting a "traditional" point of view "with no sign that it has even been questioned" now seems more than ever justified.

So, today's undergraduates might be forgiven for supposing that the assault on Tillyard was a more recent achievement, since that is the impression given by books such as *Signifying Nothing,* Dollimore's *Radical Tragedy,*[9] or (to return to the most recent of my instances) Grady's *Modernist Shakespeare.* In devoting one of his five chapters to "The Case of E. M. W. Tillyard," Grady emphasizes "the centrality of Tillyard's work in the Shakespeare studies of the period 1940–70" and attributes the current "reversal" to the "major revisionist effort" of materialist critics like Graham Holderness, Jonathan Dollimore, Alan Sinfield, and John Drakakis during "the last twenty years":

> Ironically few books of such influence in a given literary field are now in such disfavour among that field's specialists as are Tillyard's works at

present among Renaissance scholars. Tillyard's works have in the last twenty years suffered a reversal of fortune in influence more meteoric and startling than their original climb to pre-eminent influence, and they have become the target of a major revisionist effort.[10]

Grady's omissions continue that "major revisionist effort." That he should altogether ignore skeptical or hostile contemporary responses to Tillyard, like D. C. Allen's, would be disquieting enough in an allegedly historical study. But then Wilbur Sanders's *Dramatist and the Received Idea* and Sigurd Burckhardt's *Shakespearian Meanings* are mentioned only in passing: Sanders is acknowledged in one sentence, while the brief reference to Burckhardt suggests that his untimely suicide still left the essential work to be done in the seventies and eighties.[11] Astonishingly, Rossiter's *Angel with Horns* and Rabkin's *Shakespeare and the Common Understanding* are not discussed at all; they don't even find a place in Grady's copious footnotes or very lengthy bibliography. Rabkin's important later work *Shakespeare and the Problem of Meaning* isn't mentioned either; and when Grady argues that Kuhn's concept of "paradigm" has an unexpectedly fruitful application to literary history, he doesn't mention that Rabkin was making this point in his 1969 foreword to *Reinterpretations of Elizabethan Drama*.[12]

Such remarkable omissions can seem strategic: in clearing the path for the Radiant Future of ideological critique, they are all too reminiscent of that air-brush technique which is familiar to readers of Milan Kundera's *Book of Laughter and Forgetting*. As Keith Brown wryly complained in reviewing Terence Hawkes's *That Shakespeherian Rag*, Hawkes doesn't want the past to be intelligent, since the materialist cavalry could not ride so excitingly to the rescue.[13] And a similar explanation might be offered for the resurrection of Tillyard in the seventies and eighties as an oppositional caricature of the "essential humanist." As "liberal humanists" go, Tillyard was markedly illiberal and politically reactionary; those "humanists" who had already done the critical demolition work would not spring to his defense, and Tillyard could not defend himself since he was dead—the perfect candidate. He had only to be exhumed, propped on his horse like El Cid, and sent back into the field.

The trouble with this kind of explanation is that it answers one cultural conspiracy theory with another, and so, in its protesting way, renders more plausible what it should be resisting—the attempt to represent critical disagreement as ideological disputes or "ismic" conflicts. Certainly, any claim that the reaction against Tillyard (or against imperialist readings of *The Tempest*) didn't take place until the seventies and eighties is historically untrue, and in that sense a demonstrable misrepresentation. But insofar as Dollimore or Grady would countenance my own distinction between the earlier, critical assault on Tillyard and the later ideological assault, it would be to argue that the earlier, "humanist" assault did not accomplish, or even attempt, what was needed—namely, the ideological critique. To accuse Dollimore or Grady of strategic omissions or deliberate misrepresentation is as unfair and unclarifying as Stephen Greenblatt's description of the soliloquizing Henry IV and Henry V as "hypocrites":[14] there is no good reason, and no need, to suppose that Dollimore and Grady do not believe what they say, like the Shakespearean monarchs. Whether *we* should believe it is another matter.

There is indeed an important difference between the earlier critical assault on Tillyard and the later, ideological critique. But one consequence of that difference is that we cannot now very well say what it was without either approving or challenging the oppositionally abstract terms of the ideological critique. To ask why "essentialist humanism" is so unacceptable to what Graham Holderness conflatingly calls "the 'new historicism' of cultural materialism"[15] is preemptive: putting the question in these terms already implies that ideological critique represents an advance on criticism, not an alternative to criticism.

The target of the ideological critique is an "essentialist," quasi-theological concern with "man"; yet identifying the target in this way is a theologizing move, which creates and demonizes the "humanist" Other whose existence is necessary to what might be called essentialist materialism. This is very like the problem that exasperates John Ellis in *Against Deconstruction,* where, for example, he observes that Derrida attacks "universal" misconceptions in the theory of language while appearing to know nothing of the work of writers like Wittgenstein or Firth.[16] If somebody rushes about protesting against the universal belief that the world is flat, to reply "But that's not true" is not to argue that the world is flat. More than a century has passed since Nietzsche wrote of "the prison-house of language" and argued that we interpret the world as we interpret a text. So-called humanist critics—not all, but some—have been engaged with these problems for as long as they have been engaged with *Nostromo, Ulysses,* or indeed with Nietzsche. Yet we are to believe that blind essentialist mammoths roamed and ruled the literary landscape until the late sixties, and that the force of the Nietzschean challenge went unrecognized until then. To believe such things is to demonstrate the force of Nietzsche's acrid little maxim, "Belief is a form of not wanting to know." As for believing that Tillyard's "pre-eminent influence" was effectively challenged only in "the last twenty years," those who can swallow ostriches will not strain at that gnat.

The real interest of "The Case of E. M. W. Tillyard" is that it suggests how the advance into the Radiant Future of ideological critique can also be seen as a return to the critical Dark Ages. So, in the materialist, avowedly anti-humanist terms of Dollimore and Sinfield's essay "History and Ideology: The Instance of *Henry V,*" what a critic like Wilbur Sanders has in common with Tillyard, ideologically, is far more important than their momentous, but merely critical, differences.[17] In critical terms, what Dollimore and Sinfield have in common with Tillyard is far more important than their momentous, but merely ideological, differences. Nor is it surprising that they don't attach much importance to the earlier, critical attacks on Tillyard's critical and interpretative method: today, Tillyard's critical grandchildren—the most able and influential exponents of one-eyed "What Shakespeare 'really' means" readings—are to be found on the Left rather than the Right, speaking of epistemes rather than world pictures.

Examining a few more preliminary examples now, in this prologue, will involve some repetition later; but the examples should show why this book has a double subject—and why asking the question "Is Shakespeare Evil?" is not merely a melodramatic way of pepping and propping up the old piety that Shakespeare is really very Good.

Buddies

It is clear that Tillyard's Shakespeare is so authoritarian and repressive as to be ideologically Evil to a critic like Jonathan Dollimore, whose *Radical Tragedy* then rescues, or "reappropriates," Shakespeare by emphasizing the plays' "materialist perspective" in a no less single-minded fashion—producing a Good "Shakespeare" whom Tillyard would have found wicked, and even bolshy. The ideological disagreement between Tillyard and Dollimore could hardly be more extreme, but we see what is at issue in critical terms when we see how closely these critics resemble each other in their critical and interpretative method.

Radical Tragedy carries on the old bad Tillyardian habit of giving particular characters and speeches a supradramatic significance, which is then identified with what the play or the dramatist "really" thinks, and usually coincides with what the critic thinks. "In fact," the pleased Dollimore observes of *King Lear,* "the play repudiates the essentialism which the humanist reading of it presupposes": in *"Lear,* as in *Troilus,* man is decentred not through misanthropy but in order to make visible social process and its forms of ideological misrecognition."[18] Here, the words "in order to" confidently and unequivocally attribute to Shakespeare an intention that happily corresponds with the critic's own "materialist perspective": apparently Shakespeare *intended* to "repudiate" essentialist humanism, and the play "in fact" does this, although it has been persistently misrepresented within an idealist culture. This is the other side, ideologically, of the same bad methodological penny: where Tillyard was delighted to hear His Master's Voice in any invocation of law and order, and associated the "radical" with something nasty, the British cultural materialist knows that the "radical," "subversive," "marginal," or (I am trying to keep pace) "dissident" perspective is always superior. So, Dollimore's thoroughly Tillyardian inversion of Tillyard presents a Shakespeare who was *really* a crypto-materialist, and whose *true* subversiveness has been appropriated and misrepresented by the "humanist" Enemy.

Naturally, Shakespeare was not the only dramatist victim of this sensationally massive cultural conspiracy: although the Truth has for so long been suppressed by "humanists," other Elizabethan and Jacobean dramatists were also crypto-materialists. To take just one instance, Dollimore's reading of Chapman's *Bussy d'Ambois* (186–88) shows how uncannily close that play's materialist insights are to those in *King Lear.* Did not Marx insist that "it is not the consciousness of men that determines their being, but, on the contrary, their social being that determines their consciousness"? We are accordingly told, in equivalent not-but terms, that Bussy's taunting of Maffé in the first scene illustrates "the recurring emphasis of this play: identity is shown to be constituted not essentially but socially." Then, wielding another ideologically firm *not-but* like Truth's broadsword, Dollimore observes that Bussy's "*virtus* is shown to be not innate but the effect—and thus the vehicle—of court power": here we see Chapman's remarkable anticipation of Foucault's perception that "the individual is an effect of power, and at the same time, or precisely to the extent to which it is that effect, it is . . . its vehicle." As for Bussy's last speech, it includes a breathtakingly radical assertion that "the idea of substantial essence is an illusion." Since Dollimore doesn't notice that Chapman had based the lines in question on a passage in Erasmus's *Adagia* ("Homo Bulla"), where Erasmus was developing an idea he had found in Plutarch, he isn't troubled by the question, if Erasmus delved and Chapman span, who was then the radical man?[19]

Radical Tragedy appeared, with Orwellian timeliness, in 1984. A year later Dollimore and Alan Sinfield's essay "History and Ideology: The Instance of *Henry V*" appeared in John Drakakis's collection, *Alternative Shakespeares.* I consider this essay in some detail in Chapter 1; the point to notice here is that the alternative "Shakespeare" this essay presents could not be more unlike the crypto-materialist "Shakespeare" of *Radical Tragedy* and is a more alarming version of Tillyard's authoritarian hero. Indeed, Tillyard himself might have shuddered on being told how Henry's speech outside the walls of Harfleur represents Shakespeare's fervently patriotic fantasy about the proper solution to the Irish problem: the solution is so reminiscent of Conrad's Kurtz ("Exterminate the brutes") as to suggest that Shakespeare really was evil. Dollimore and Sinfield are entirely untroubled by the difficulty, or impossibility, of reconciling this "Shakespeare" with the crypto-materialist "Shakespeare" of *Radical Tragedy;* indeed, that glaring contradiction still isn't acknowledged, let alone explained, in the much longer version of "History and Ideology" that appears in Sinfield's collection, *Faultlines*—where we are told that Shakespeare, Bath, and Chartres are all "instruments of domination."[20]

It would be implausible, as well as insulting, to suppose that Sinfield was forcing Dollimore to put his name to a slander on his own crypto-materialist hero; nor do we need to suppose that both critics believe, but somehow just forgot to mention, that other Shakespeare plays are less wicked than *Henry V.* The more plausible explanation is that these critics just aren't troubled by the contradiction between these alarmingly different "Shakespeares," since either "Shakespeare" will serve their "declared objective," which is constant. In the final section of *Radical Tragedy*—where the title, "Beyond Essentialist Humanism," suggests some kind of ideological Star Trek rather than a trip down memory lane—Dollimore explains: "Anti-humanism and its declared objective—the decentring of man—is probably the most controversial aspect of Marxist, structuralist and post-structuralist theory" (249). Although scrupulous readers might be startled by that conflating reference to "theory"—where different, and frequently conflicting theories are in question—it evidently matters very little which way the "humanist" cat is skinned, so long as it is; neither does it seem to matter which "Shakespeare" is deployed in the anti-humanist crusade. The Tillyardian method can call either one from the vasty interpretative deep, and in the *Henry V* essay the critical method is still thoroughly Tillyardian; it's just that in this case we are to suppose that the "real" Shakespeare is ventriloquizing through Henry and the Chorus, and not, for example, through Michael Williams. Since the target is still "essentialist humanism," the critical inconsistency remains ideologically consistent, politically correct, and—for Dollimore and Sinfield—untroubling.

This explanation also suggests how to unravel, or genealogize, the related contradiction in Dollimore and Sinfield's foreword to their 1985 collection, *Political Shakespeare: New Essays in Cultural Materialism.* The foreword, which is simply called "Cultural Materialism," concludes: "Cultural materialism does not, like much established literary criticism, attempt to mystify its perspective as the natural or obvious interpretation of an allegedly given textual fact. On the contrary, it registers its commitment to the transformation of a social order that exploits people on grounds of race, gender, sexuality and class."[21] I hope I shall not be thought to be in favor of exploiting people on grounds of race, gender, sexuality, and class if I remark that "On the contrary" is inconsequential and also strikingly at odds with Dollimore's earlier account of a massive cultural conspiracy to misrepresent the Truth about what Shakespeare was really ("in fact") saying and intending. Consider the earlier claim that Shakespeare writes plays like *King Lear* or *Troilus and Cressida* "in order to make visible social process and the forms of social recognition," and that he "repudiates the essentialism which the humanist reading . . . presupposes";

doesn't this claim "mystify" the "materialist perspective" as the "natural" interpretation of an "allegedly given textual fact"? Well yes, of course it does; but once again these critics are entirely untroubled by critical and logical inconsistencies, so long as they are consistent with the ideological, anti-humanist objectives. Even the jarring inconsequentiality of that "On the contrary" falls into place, with a little click, once we see how the sense it makes is ideological, not logical: the controlling assumption in the foreword's penultimate sentence is that the materialist critic doesn't *need* to "mystify" *his* "perspective," because the "materialist perspective" is True.

Conversely, the "essentialist humanist" can only "attempt to mystify" his "perspective," because it's false and evil—part of a social order that exploits people. There are only two perspectives, one true, the other false. It's a wonderfully simple argument, and, if one ponders the analogy with Britain's archaic and indefensible two-party system, wonderfully British. Consider the logical structure of the argument in the accusatory finale of Sinfield's *Faultlines.* The closing pages revive the claim that *The Merchant of Venice* is "really" an anti-Semitic play and at the same time show how ideological critique reduces the interpretative options. "The liberal reading," which makes "the standard liberal move" and furthers oppression, is opposed to "the dissident reading," which sides with "subordinated groups." The "standard liberal move" is, plausibly enough, that of affirming Shylock's "humanity," and it isn't obviously wicked; to show how sinister the move really is, Sinfield recycles Arnold Wesker's argument that no matter how the play is produced, "the image comes through inescapably: the Jew is mercenary and revengeful, sadistic, without pity"—after which any affirmation of Shylock's "humanity" merely "adds insult to injury."[22]

Suppose we ask, what could be the *point* of arguing that this play is "really" anti-Semitic, and that any affirmation of Shylock's humanity only adds insult to injury? After all, such an argument would have no point where it was already taken for granted that the play was anti-Semitic and that this was one of its admirable features. In that notorious production for which Werner Krauss, an actor who frequently appeared in anti-Semitic Nazi propaganda films, was personally selected by Goebbels to play the role of Shylock, there was a clear intention to insult and injure; but it seems most unlikely that anybody thought this end would be achieved, and given a brutally effective twist, by affirming Shylock's humanity.[23] Neither would the argument have any more point in Israel, where Shylock's humanity and the wickedness of anti-Semitism are taken for granted, but *The Merchant of Venice* is (according to Michael Handelsatz) "the most performed Shakespearian play": indeed, those who are persuaded by Erich Fried's distressed explanation that "it is quite obvious that the play is being used as a partial justification for Zionism, which is quite as much of a distortion as the Nazis' use of it" might think it is the humanity of the non-Jewish Semite that needs to be affirmed, for example, by having a good Palestinian actor play Shylock.[24] But then Sinfield's argument would have no more point in a society that took the play's anti-Semitism for granted, but for that reason did not admire or perform the play—as in the Hungary described by Anna Földes:

> I belong to a generation in Hungary which had never seen *The Merchant of Venice* on stage until last season, because we felt that after the holocaust, we could not produce that play. Last year, after a lot of discussion, we decided that it need not necessarily be just a tool for antisemitism but could show how Shylock came to the crime. Shylock was presented as a man isolated from society, insulted and injured, so that the play was against discrimination and against inhuman behaviour on all sides. It was not against the Jews but against all brutality. (Elsom, 177)

Whatever point Sinfield's argument *could* have depends upon its being advanced in a "liberal" society where it is usual for people to think that anti-Semitism is evil *and* that Shakespeare's play is good, and not self-evidently anti-Semitic. In such circumstances—our circumstances—a critic who was convinced that admiring this work is playing with fire might think it urgently necessary to make "liberals" see that this is what they are doing: Chinua Achebe's attack on *Heart of Darkness* would be a comparable instance.[25] But of course Sinfield isn't attempting that, since any such attempt would require both some willingness to engage in critical dialogue and an extended commentary. The point of Sinfield's conspicuously perfunctory argument is not to convince but to abuse the "liberal," by claiming that the play the "liberal" likes is really evil. Yet the smearing insinuation that the "liberal" connives with anti-Semitism, by failing to recognize and repudiate it, is awkwardly at odds with the conditions that are necessary for the argument to have any critical point.

One obvious objection to the Sinfield-Wesker line is that the play's
Christians are presented critically, and in the trial scene show themselves capable of acting in a way that is "mercenary and revengeful,
sadistic, without pity."[26] Of course not everybody feels that, or feels it
to the same degree: there are more than two ways of responding
to *Merchant of Venice*—especially to that difficult moment when the
Christian knife is given a final vengeful twist in a parody of "mercie":

Duke.	He shall doe this, or else I doe recant
	The pardon that I late pronounced heere.
Portia.	Art thou contented Jew? what dost thou say?
Shylock.	I am contented.

(4.1.391–94)

That responses to this will vary, and vary more significantly than
responses to *Jew Süss*, is one of the effects of the play's intricate and
complex design. So, somebody who is troubled by Portia's repeated
use of "Jew" might reflect on the intelligently proleptic irony of intro-
ducing her with a speech where she reflects, "If to doe were as easie
as to know what were good to doe, Chappels had been Churches, and
poore mens cottages Princely Pallaces: it is a good Divine that followes
his owne instructions; I can easier teach twentie what were good to
be done, then be one of the twentie to follow mine owne teaching"
(1.2.12–17). Since Portia is thinking about her father's will and knows
nothing of the bond, this might in turn suggest why Shakespeare has
yoked together the story of the bond and the story of the caskets—
and why it is dangerous to suppose that the directing intelligence at
work within the work is ventriloquizing through any of its characters.
We similarly hear the embittered Shylock determining to follow
"Christian example" rather than Christian principles: "If a Jew wrong
a Christian, what is his humility, revenge? If a Christian wrong a Jew,
what should his sufferance be by Christian example, why revenge?"
(3.1.57–60). Yet these highly organized perspectival ironies will not
tell us *what* to think of Shylock (or Portia): rather, they show different
ways of thinking about Shylock which reflect on one another, and in
that way also show how a work of art reads us. People can and plainly
do respond very differently to these highly organized perspectival
ironies within the text, for reasons that are not solely determined by
the text: much depends on the dispositions and abilities of individual

spectators, and on when, where, and how the play is being performed—Portia and Shylock may be played in very different ways,
and so on.

This is why we should think of the play not as an encoded message
but as a highly organized and powerfully generative matrix of meanings, or field of forces. The latter metaphor can be helpful if it suggests what is and is not determinable. The effect of the "forces" that
are being released in the trial scene is not determinable: for example,
the effect of Portia's insistent use of the word "Jew" while appealing
to Shylock to show mercy will always shock some spectators more than
others, will be more or less obviously jarring depending on the actress's delivery, Shylock's response, and so on. But the "field" within
which these forces are released and set against each other is highly
organized and in that sense determined. To suppose that this play or
any Shakespearean poetic drama is trying and then—to judge from
the interpretative disagreements—all too evidently failing to deliver
a single, reductive "meaning" is to be inadequate to the directing
intelligence at work within the work, and unresponsive to its intricate
and complex process of dramatic thinking. When David Thacker, the
artistic director of the Young Vic, solemnly opines that "as an artist,
you have to face up to your responsibility to show to an audience what
in your view these plays are trying to communicate," he is assuming
that the audience cannot think and that the semi-articulate dramatist
cannot "communicate": the play becomes a wall on which the authoritarian director scrawls some trite graffito.[27] The intricate process of
Shakespeare's poetic-dramatic thinking is similarly short-circuited
whenever Tillyardian historicists and anti-Tillyardian, neo-Tillyardian
materialists undertake to tell us what the play is "really" saying, or
what the dramatist "really" thinks. What is remarkable in Sinfield's
perfunctorily provocative account is its complete indifference to how
the play does its thinking.

So, for example, since Sinfield finds Shylock's Christian "persecu-
tors" hateful (301) we might have expected him to be alert to dramatic
or perspectival ironies. Yet what is most curious about Sinfield's view
of the play's Christians is not so much its vehemence (where being
anti-Christian is presumably not like being anti-Semitic, so long as one
is being vehemently anti–anti-Semitic) as his altogether unquestioning
assumption that the anti-Semitic Shakespeare couldn't possibly have
intended to show his Christians in an ironic or critical light. Prac-

titioners of the Tillyardian method always just know, or divine, osmoti-
cally, which of the attitudes expressed by characters are condemned
or condoned by "the play" or its author. That Portia's first extended
speech reflects on the difficulty of practicing what one preaches must
be ascribed, like Shylock's own bitter reflections on the gulf between
Christian principles and Christian practice, to inadvertence on Shakespeare's part. But here the very perfunctoriness of the argument
shows how it is merely reactive and instrumental, entirely subordinate
to the anti-humanist obsession.

The basic strategy here, as in the essay on *Henry V*, is to unmask
"humanism" by associating the humanists' beloved Bard with hor-
rifying inhumanities—the Nazis' "final solution" to the Jewish problem in the one case, and in the other the no less obscene, genocidal
"fantasy" of a final solution to the Irish problem. At this point we
might notice that Dollimore's essay "Transgression and Surveillance
in *Measure for Measure*" appeared in 1985—the same year as the essay
on *Henry V* and only a year after *Radical Tragedy*—and discovers yet
another "reactionary fantasy, neither radical nor liberating": the closing scene of *Measure for Measure* "is not a cancelling of authoritarianism so much as a fantasy resolution of the very fears from which
authoritarianism partly grows . . . a redemptive wish-fulfillment of
the status quo."[28] In this solo flight Dollimore himself substitutes an
evil, reactionary, and repressively authoritarian Shakespeare for the
good crypto-materialist Shakespeare whose true contents and intentions were allegedly misrepresented and suppressed by the essential-
ist-idealist-liberal-humanist Enemy. As ever, the contradiction doesn't
matter, as long as the critically contradictory readings advance the
ideological "objective."

But of course it matters, very much, and not only to anyone who
is concerned with Shakespeare but also to anyone who *thinks* about
what is involved in believing that values are culturally specific and
historically contingent. That is what cultural materialists repeatedly
say they believe, and presumably believe they believe; but these contradictory accounts of Shakespeare show why we need to distinguish,
like Portia, between theory and practice. Dollimore and Sinfield's neo-
Tillyardian readings are constantly reactive and oppositional, but
never reflexive. They take for granted that "humanist" values and
perceptions are culturally specific and historically contingent, and

therefore (which does not follow) false, and that their own values and perceptions are not culturally and historically bounded, but true.

This theologizes what is at issue, and reveals ideological priests in mufti. It also exposes an ideological faultline—just the kind of thing that ideological critique professes to uncover, but here Dollimore and Sinfield are protected not only by their unreflexive assumption that ideology is what other people have but also by a striking absence of significant internal disagreement within the ranks. Such disagreements are not so rare in other, non-Shakespearean contexts: for example, deconstruction has helped to expose what Christopher Norris calls "the perceived failure of Althusserian Marxism to make good its claims for a 'scientific' discourse of ideological critique."[29] Yet collections such as *Political Shakespeare, Alternative Shakespeares,* and *The Shakespeare Myth* present a united front, in always concentrating their attack on the "essentialist humanist" Enemy. Of course, if a so-called humanist seems to "elide cultural materialism and post-structuralism" that only shows how the "same misconceptions keep churning on," as Alan Sinfield angrily complains;[30] but when Dollimore explains that "anti-humanism" is the "declared objective" of "Marxist, structuralist and post-structuralist theory" that is alright, and in that sense right, though not all right.

When Dollimore and Sinfield assert that cultural meanings are "always, finally, political," they are not challenged from within the ranks to explain why political meanings are not always, finally, cultural meanings.[31] Those anti-humanist critics who also maintain, like Terence Eagleton, Terence Hawkes, and Christopher Norris, that there is no Shakespeare, only "Shakespeares," could be—and in theory ought to be—as ready to "demystify" neo-Tillyardian materialist accounts of what Shakespeare is "in fact" saying, or to "critique" the transparent tendentiousness of Graham Holderness's suggestion that "a reactionary or liberal-humanist appropriation of a text can be revealed as demonstrably inferior, less truthful, less accurate, less convincing than a progressive and materialist reading."[32] Yet of course this is what doesn't happen, in practice; the anti-humanist front holds. One explanation is that these critics sink their family differences in order to address the more important anti-humanist objective; but another, which is all too compatible with the quasi-theological demonizing of the "humanist" Other, is that these critics do not practice what they preach. If we compare what Hawkes has to say of

Henry V in "Wittgenstein's Shakespeare" with Christopher Norris's discussion of *Othello* in "Post-Structuralist Shakespeare," we can see how the failure to engage seriously with Shakespeare's irreducibly complex designs runs hand in hand with the failure to engage seriously with their professed belief (with which I have no quarrel) that values are culturally and historically specific.

Chaotic Sites

The question "Is Shakespeare Evil?" would be dismissed by Terence Hawkes, not because he thinks Shakespeare Good but because he regards the Shakespearean text as nothing more than the chaotic site for a frivolous and boring ideological free-for-all. After an extended, characteristically exuberant party piece in which he parodies the Olivier *Henry V* by imagining an anti-Henry Nazi production, "dedicated to the Wehrmacht," Hawkes concludes by explaining that his "case is a simple one": "If Shakespeare can be made to support causes as opposed as [these], then his plays are neither good nor bad in themselves, and beyond the various readings to which they may be subjected there lies no final, authoritative, coherent, or essential meaning to which we can ultimately and gratefully turn."[33] Indeed this is "simple"; those references to causes Shakespeare can "be *made to* support" and readings to which the plays "may be *subjected*" give the game away. One thing the Shakespearean text of *Henry V* does indeed demonstrate in a "final, authoritative" fashion is that Olivier could only produce his uncomplicated pro-Henry reading by suppressing more than half the play; Hawkes's imaginary anti-British production would have to do the same, or worse. But for Hawkes all readings are partial, so who is to say whether some are better or worse than others? Well, nobody, in this pop-anarchic account of what is at issue. Yet his essay only attacks "humanist" readings: there is some undeclared mental baggage.

Hawkes's argument brings him to a point where the proper next step is obvious, although he won't take it. This would be to examine *Henry V* more closely to see how it organizes or frames discrepant or opposed views of Henry, and in this way produces, and orchestrates, that familiar twentieth-century debate about whether Henry is a

Machiavellian hypocrite or the mirror of Christian kings (in a non-ironic sense). To establish that the play won't tell us how to regard Henry, or whether he is right or wrong to go to war with France, and so on, does not establish that it is a chaotic site; we may even think the play the more intelligent because it shows how differently such issues appear when seen from the point of view of, say, Henry, the Chorus, Williams, Mistress Quickly, and the King of France. But here Hawkes's argument that there is no "final, authoritative, coherent, or essential meaning to which we can ultimately and gratefully turn" is less remarkable than his assumption that we should want, let alone be "grateful" for, a "final, authoritative" meaning—instead of feeling grateful when a great work of art seems inexhaustibly meaningful. That assumption is alarmingly authoritarian, betraying a strong prescriptive impulse and some wish to be an ultimate "authority" and dispenser of "final" meanings. Words like "ultimate" and "final" don't suggest any kind of experience you would want to go on repeating: such language could not be more remote from the experience of frequenting a loved work of art, or of becoming imaginatively inward with modes of feeling and perception different from our own. But then, for all its gloss of modernity, Hawkes's poststructuralist fireworks display is predicated on that misplaced, thoroughly Tillyardian expectation of a "final, authoritative" meaning. He sees that there is no Authorized Version; but he doesn't see how the frustration of that expectation represents nothing more than the loss of an illusion not worth having. Instead, he leaps to the conclusion that if the play does not mean One Thing it means anything, or nothing.

This Tillyardian remnant prevents him from seeing how he is confusing different senses of "partial." My reading of *Henry V* is, like any other reading, "partial," because it cannot exhaust the play's meanings. Olivier's wartime effort and Hawkes's own flamboyant counterinstance are partial in that inevitable sense, but also in another: in each case the "reading" depends upon a very partial sampling of the text, which suppresses or disregards all those parts of the text which show why—although there is no final, authoritative reading—this particular "reading" is simplistic and impossible to sustain. Suppose that a pianist's announced performance of a Beethoven sonata lasted only three minutes, because he had left out whatever he couldn't play or make sense of, and that the pianist then sought to justify this by arguing that all "readings" are "partial," that there is no basis for preferring Edwin Fischer's reading to his own, and that the search for "unity" or "imaginary coherence" is a humanist illusion. We would be hearing another version of Hawkes's argument, but in a context where it would be obviously sufficient to reply that Fischer's reading is "partial" only in the unavoidable sense, which is compatible with its being "authoritative" though not final or definitive, whereas the travesty was neither a performance nor a reading, because it was also "partial" in the avoidable, so critically damaging, sense. In slithering between these senses of "partial" Hawkes is helped by the way in which the idea of a "reading" (as commentary or interpretation) customarily takes for granted the prior activity of reading (as performance). We don't expect a "reading" of a play to go through a text as a performance does, but we expect the "reading" to have been preceded by, and tested against, a reading that attempts to make sense of the work as a whole.

More surprisingly, Hawkes's derridative choplogic reappears in Norris's more complicated argument, and delivers Norris's Hawkesean conclusion: "All we have are the readings which inevitably tell the various partial and complicated stories of their own devising."[34] Norris's discussion of *Othello* turns on his somewhat belated discovery that Leavis's view of Othello resembles Iago's, while Bradley's view of Othello resembles Othello's view of himself: as Norris puts it, the "difference of views between Bradley and Leavis becomes oddly intertwined with the drama played out between Othello and Iago," since "Othello's romanticized self-image finds an echo and analogue" in "Bradley's reading," and a "further twist of the same interpretative logic" only shows how "Leavis plays an Iago-like role in destroying the illusion of Othello's nobly suffering innocence" (118–19). This is true, and it's important; but it's well known to anyone familiar with the "liberal humanist" criticism Norris attacks: it has been searchingly discussed by several "humanist" critics, notably John Bayley and Jane Adamson.[35] Here is Bayley, commenting in 1960 on what lies behind "the odd irony that those who decline to be taken in by Othello find themselves in the company of Iago" (129):

> The initial fallacy of so much *Othello* criticism is the assumption that it is a simple clear-cut affair, and that the task of the critic is to determine what kind of simplicity, so to speak, is involved. . . . But if we rather assume, from the nature of the subject and of the response we give to

it, that the play is likely to be a highly complex affair, with a Shakespearean variety of perceptions and significances, then we shall cease to be
merely pro- or anti-Othello. (145)

That comment sends us back to, and further into, the play to see
how its complex design opposes what Bayley calls the "Iago viewpoint"
to the "Othello viewpoint." Seeing that design provides the best vantage point from which to account for what is so unsatisfactory in
Leavis's account of Othello as a deluded egotist: despite his vigorous
repudiation of Bradley's preoccupation with "character," Leavis's own
reading is more narrowly characterological, depends upon a very partial sampling of the Shakespearean text, and presents one term of the
Othello-"problem" as its solution without considering how the play
produces the "problem."

We cannot know whether Norris knows how many "humanist" critics had anticipated his own interest in Leavis-as-Iago, since his own
scornful account of "humanist" readings never takes him (or us) past
Leavis's 1937 essay.[36] Cutting out more than half a century of critical
thinking about Othello makes it easier for him to claim that nobody
could "acknowledge" the interpretative "predicament" until the ad-
vent of "post-structuralism," but now Norris's case becomes as "simple" as Hawkes's: what Bradley and Leavis do with the play shows how
their readings are controlled by "pressing ideological imperatives."
Just as Dr. Johnson's mistake was to believe in the "joint accountability
of language, reason and truth," the deluded Leavis's "effort of ideological containment" inevitably "founders" because it stakes "its authority on presupposed absolute values of language, morality and
truth": "At the close, Leavis writes, 'he is still the same Othello in
whose essential make-up the tragedy lay.' It is on this notion of 'essential' human nature, both as norm and as measure of 'tragic' deviation,
that Leavis's essay splinters into so many diverse and conflicting
claims" (123). As usual, benighted humanists are chastized for failing
to see how what they take for "truth" is "an imposition of meanings
and values as conceived by the dominant ideology," whereas "post-
structuralism affords an understanding of the ideological compulsions at work in this persistent allegory of errors." The text can produce only a "casebook of endlessly dissenting views" (124).

Norris's difficulty in accounting for the unsatisfactoriness of Leavis's
reading is that his theory won't allow him to make the kind of appeal

Bayley (and Rossiter and Adamson) makes to the play as a complex design (or "highly complex affair"). In practice he is making it, of course, as soon as he observes that the contrast between "Bradley's blinkered idealism" and Leavis's "ruthless debunking approach" reworks the opposition between Othello and Iago. But to think that through, by attending more closely to the play's complex design, would threaten his own Hawkesean conclusion. Instead, his interest in the relationship between Leavis/Bradley and Iago/Othello is merely strategic, a means of arguing that "Leavis has invented his own Othello in pursuit of an imaginary coherence required by certain pressing ideological imperatives" (122). To speak of "imaginary coherence" at least implies that not all "coherence" is imaginary. "All we have are the readings which inevitably tell the various partial and complicated stories of their own devising"; yet these "endlessly dissenting" and "partial" readings are readings of a play we also have before us, and they retell a complicated story of Shakespeare's devising. Once again the language reveals a controlling assumption, which in this case corresponds with Bayley's "initial fallacy." If we ask why Norris speaks of "errors" or why the inevitably "partial" character of different readings is taken to be invalidating—Norris speaks scornfully of "endlessly dissenting views" without allowing that different readings can illuminate an inexhaustible play—the answer is that he, like Hawkes, predicates his argument on the disappointment of the thoroughly Tillyardian expectation of finding the one Authorized Version. On discovering that this is not available—and reading the critics is enough to show that, though we must read the play more intelligently to see why it isn't available—Norris concludes, like Hawkes, that the play is a merely chaotic site for ideological contestation. We glimpse the path that is not taken when Norris observes that "Shakespeare's meaning can no more be reduced to the currency of liberal-humanist faith than his text to the wished-for condition of pristine authority": sadly, his point is not that attempts to "reduce" the play to a single, "pristine" and authoritative "Shakespearean meaning" are misconceived, but that the "liberal-humanist faith" is merely "an imposition of meanings and values as conceived by the dominant ideology."

We are assured that "post-structuralism affords an understanding of the ideological compulsions at work"—that is, an understanding of the liberal-humanist errors, not of the play—just as we are assured that the interpretative "predicament" had never before been "acknowledged." But at this point we might notice how Bayley's account of that "predicament" extends to Norris's analysis. Another, and fairly uncontroversial, way of putting Bayley's point about the way in which *Othello* opposes the "Iago viewpoint" to the "Othello" viewpoint would be to say that the play is opposing materialist and idealist viewpoints. In that case, Norris's own repudiation of Leavis's allegedly "essentialist" concern with allegedly "absolute values of language, morality and truth" reworks the narrowly characterological debate about *Othello* in ideological terms and does so in a way that brings Norris himself down, willy-nilly, into the Iago camp. Here *Othello* is reading Norris.

These representative cases suggest that, instead of believing the story about materialism's war on the Great Satan of "essentialist humanism," we should notice how we are being offered primitive and sophisticated versions of that Tillyardian search for an Authorized Version. Primitive neo-Tillyardian materialists like Dollimore and Sinfield assume, like Tillyard, that *the* Shakespearean Meaning exists, but also assume, since Tillyard is the ideological Enemy, that the Meaning must be somewhere else, or something else. So, this approach delivers either the good, subversive crypto-materialist Shakespeare, whom the "essentialist humanists" appropriate, misrepresent, and suppress, because They are Evil; or the evil, authoritarian Bard whom "essentialist humanists" take to be Good, again because They are Evil. Sophisticated neo-Tillyardian materialists like Hawkes and Norris know that the Shakespearean Meaning is not to be found—Shakespeare will not tell us what to think, or what he "really" thinks, of Henry V or Othello—but assume that its absence proves that the play is a chaotic site; this assumption provides the basis for their own arbitrarily selective assault on "essentialist humanism," in which the accounts of Shakespeare are still subordinate to the anti-humanist "objective." The primitives invert, and the sophisticates pervert, the Tillyardian assumption; both variants are "anti-humanist" and ineradicably authoritarian.

For an American version of the primitive neo-Tillyardian approach, one might turn to Jean E. Howard's much admired 1986 essay "The New Historicism in Renaissance Studies," where the "Renaissance" is characterized, in breezily unhistorical fashion, as "a boundary or liminal space between two more monolithic periods where one can see acted out a clash of paradigms and ideologies."[37] After acknowledging her debt to Dollimore for this world-pictures sandwich, or historicist Dagwood, Howard happily expands on it: we must "reunderstand" the "Renaissance" as she understands it, that is, by seeing it as a "transitional position between the Middle Ages—held to be encumbered with a monolithic Christian ideology and a static and essentially unhistorical view of itself—and the modern era—marked by the rise of capitalism with its attendant bourgeois ideology of humanism, progress and the all-important interiority and self-presence of the individual" (15). Such world pictures combine contempt for the particular case with an incapacitating lack of critical interest in whatever lies on either side of the critic's chosen "field" of professional specialisation; Stephen L. Collins pointedly concludes in "Where's the History in the New Literary Historicism?" that such generalizations are fundamentally "ahistorical and might even be considered ahistoricist."[38]

Similarly, the sophisticated—newer, nower!—version resurfaces in an American study like Grady's *Modernist Shakespeare.* The very first sentence tells us, in a would-be engaging confessional manner, that "Shakespearian criticism has long been in search of the authentic Shakespearian meaning, and almost every critic, including this one, writes as if s/he had come to be in possession of it." Those little words "the" and "it" carry the disabling Tillyardian expectation that the "meaning" in question will be single, fixed, and final. It doesn't occur to Grady that to talk of *the* "authentic Shakespearean meaning" is critically reactionary and contrasts sadly with Rabkin's optimistic sense, in 1969, that Shakespeare criticism was at last "freed from the increasingly deadening obligation to an old paradigm to reduce works to meanings."[39] Once it becomes apparent that this fantasy of a fixed and final Meaning is disappointed Grady concludes that there is no "authentic" Shakespeare, only differently constituted "Shakespeares": "We can take off those older lenses; we are manifestly now in the process of doing so. . . . But there is no 'authentic' Shakespeare there for the picking. After the Modernist Shakespeare there comes—the Postmodernist Shakespeare. There is, simply, no other alternative—unless it is to revive an older Shakespeare" (4). This un-radiant Future offers a succession of "ismic" approaches to "Shakespeare" that can never be appraised as approaches to *Shakespeare* by considering whether and how they bring us nearer to their ostensible subject. The result is a nonteleological process that moves (in the Kuhnian terms Grady favors) "steadily *from* primitive beginnings but *toward* no goal,"[40] surrenders Shakespeare, and, if we take a larger view, surrenders critical and human responsibility as well.

For if we do seriously believe that values are culturally and historically specific—including our own values: that is the force of the word "seriously"—and that our perceptions are always culturally and historically bounded, the most pressing problem is that of knowing how to affirm whatever values we continue to hold. Showing that "humanist" values are contingent doesn't help much, if that is just what values are, and showing that a "humanist" reading treats particular values as "absolute" will not of itself establish that the reading is false or inferior. The word "absolute" is often used too clinically or polemically. When Sinfield assumes that anti-Semitism is evil and when Malcolm Evans assumes that slavery is evil, they are of course affirming values. They don't pause to make clear that they are talking about values they think it (absolutely) necessary to affirm in any world we would want to live in; but in their own terms they necessarily cannot assume that these values are (in Wittgenstein's sense) *in the world,* as part of its fabric and furniture. To regard this inconsistency as self-refuting, and incompatible with believing that values are contingent, would be like arguing that a philosopher who arrives punctually to give his lecture on the unreality of time has no subject: the knock-down argument merely dismisses the problem.

Norris tries to clinch his case against Leavis's reading by pouncing on Leavis's reference to Othello's "essential make-up." For Norris this shows how Leavis's reading is unsatisfactory *because* it "stakes its authority on presupposed absolute values of language, morality and truth." But Leavis's use of the word "essential" *doesn't* establish that he is an essentialist "liberal humanist" in Norris's more comprehensive—and more essentialist—sense. Suppose we set aside the word "absolute," and also the word "presupposed," with its slurring assumption that "essentialist humanists" just won't think about the (different) values they affirm and so are defenseless against the "imposition of meanings and values as conceived by the dominant ideology." We must then ask: what is our outlook if, after recognizing that our own values are historically and culturally specific, we surrender the concern with "values of language, morality and truth"? For a powerful answer to that question we cannot do better than turn to Christopher Norris.

We cannot do better, that is, when Norris is thinking seriously. His

essay "Post-Structuralist Shakespeare" originally appeared in John
Drakakis's 1985 collection, *Alternative Shakespeares*, with Dollimore and
Sinfield's essay on *Henry V* and other essentialist assaults on "essentialist humanism." It kept bad company. Now that it is reprinted in Norris's *Deconstruction and the Interests of Theory*, it seems out of place—
which is to Norris's credit. Most of the other essays in this collection
show how differently and how powerfully Norris writes whenever he
is confronting what he evidently regards as more important and urgent matters: Stanley Fish's "line of knock-down polemical response";
the scorn for "truth" displayed by Lyotard or Baudrillard; Gillian
Rose's attack on the nihilistic aspects of poststructuralism; the
"sceptical historiography that regards truth as entirely a product of
rhetorical or narrative contrivance"; or the devil-take-the-hindmost
Mammonism of Thatcher's Britain:

> After all, we in Britain are living through a period when it is especially
> vital to maintain a due sense of the difference between fact and fiction,
> historical truth and the various kinds of state-sponsored myth that cur-
> rently pass for truth. It is not a good time to be telling students that
> history is only what counts as such according to some present consensus-
> view, and that finally it all comes down to a struggle for power between
> various, more or less plausible narrative fictions. (15–16)

Well, yes. Some things (if not Shakespeare) concentrate the mind,
and make Norris himself insist that it is now more than ever necessary
to teach students how to *oppose* that "will to undermine truth and
reason by way of a thoroughgoing 'textualist' critique that reduces
such values to so many ultimately groundless metaphors and fictions."
He is careful to rescue Derrida, or late Derrida, from any such charge,
though he doesn't think Nietzsche worth that trouble;[41] but then he
doesn't even notice the contrast between his morally and intellectually
urgent response to Thatcher's Britain and the pococurantist,
Hawkesean patter of his essay "Post-Structuralist Shakespeare," in
which Leavis is taken to task for his concern with "values of language,
morality and truth."

The E-Effect

Crossing the Atlantic again, we find an equivalent problem surfacing in Greenblatt's contribution to H. Aram Veeser's excellent collec-

tion, *The New Historicism.*[42] Greenblatt's essay includes an impassioned, witty, and devastating assault on Ronald Reagan's well-documented inability to distinguish fact from fiction (or film). But suppose Reagan wanted to repair this deficiency and asked what he should read: would anybody suggest that reading the new historicists would help? One effect of the Foucauldian component in new historicism is that whatever line separates historical fact from narrative fiction can become so thin and uncertain as to be indecipherable. Greenblatt sees the danger in this, just as Norris is horrified both by Thatcher's Britain and by the danger that deconstructionist theories may have a paralyzing rather than mobilizing effect. That Norris and Greenblatt both see how their own arguments might seem to promote what they rightly deplore is admirable: the dilemma they confront is very real. There are contexts in which it is necessary to argue that history and truth are constructed, just as there are occasions when it is necessary to insist, like Clifford Geertz, that making things out is not the same as making them up, and that some things, once seen, cannot be unseen.[43]

Greenblatt is not only far more perceptively concerned with Shakespeare than Dollimore and Sinfield or Hawkes and Norris, his own critical practice is informed with a *genuine,* compellingly urgent sense of what is involved in believing that values—including one's own—are culturally and historically specific. That he prefers the term "cultural poetics" to "new historicism" is not surprising, given this keen awareness of what (in a different though not unrelated context) the American musicologist Richard Taruskin calls "the pastness of our present."[44] Nonetheless, a curious problem appears if, once again using that question "Is Shakespeare Evil?" as a probe, we ask where and how Greenblatt's Shakespeare differs from the nasty creature described in Leonard Tennenhouse's *Power on Display.*[45]

Tennenhouse's Shakespeare is a sycophantic court toady whose plays were "a vehicle for disseminating court ideology," and who stopped at nothing in his determination "to idealize political authority." *Richard II* shows how Richard's mistake was not that of using his power improperly but that of not exercising it forcefully enough (77); the "comedic ending" of *Henry V* shows how "the English line should dominate the French just as the husband should dominate the wife and the sovereign should rule over the subject" (71); Cordelia dies to ensure the male succession and preserve the "patriarchal principle" (142)—and so on. Like Dollimore and Sinfield in their essay on *Henry V,* Tennenhouse presents an authoritarian and markedly patriarchal

Shakespeare who "understands power as the inevitable unfolding of order" (82). The chief difference between this Shakespeare and Till-yard's is that Tillyard expected his readers to approve of, and take heart from, an age when the idea of cosmic order was "so taken for granted, so much part of the collective mind of the people,"[46] whereas Tennenhouse expects his readers to know better.

The difference between Tennenhouse's readings and those of Dolli-more and Sinfield is more interesting, and helps us to make out the less obvious resemblance between Tennenhouse's Shakespeare and Greenblatt's. All these British and American readings present con-trasts between Them and Us; but the contrasts work differently be-cause there are two different versions of Them and Us. For Dollimore and Sinfield *They* are always the "essentialist humanist" Enemy, past and present; because this antagonism generates a series of opposi-tional accounts of what the plays "really" mean, there is no possibility of any more challenging encounter with Shakespeare's poetic-dra-matic perspectivism as an exploratory or interrogative mode of dra-matic thinking. For Tennenhouse, and also for Greenblatt, *They* are Shakespeare and his audiences, and the contrast that matters most is that between what They believed and what we know to be True (Tennenhouse) or now take to be True (the warier Greenblatt).

That willingness to think of the Elizabethan or Jacobean audience as a "collectivity" (Greenblatt's term) suggests another variant of Till-yardian historicism; I return to this later. But the difference between these versions of Them and Us points to another more fundamental contrast, since the usual effect of the British version is to rally the troops in an ongoing struggle, whereas the usual effect of the Ameri-can version is to *estrange* Shakespeare and the Renaissance. The Brit-ish cultural materialists' readings are constantly reactive. Sometimes they present a suppressed, subversive Shakespeare, at other times they present a repressively authoritarian Shakespeare, but this reflects the difficulty of determining what, after decades of Anglo-American plu-ralism, is to be selected and opposed as *the* "humanist reading;" once that decision has been made, what follows is predictable. The results may also overlap with American new historicist readings, prompting talk of "the 'new historicism' of cultural materialism," but here we need to notice how what constantly governs the new historicist read-ings, in practice, if not theory, is what might be called the new histori-cist E-effect, or estrangement-effect: even when there is (and there often isn't) some moderating emphasis on the complexity and reciprocity of cultural "negotiations" with the past, the effect of the *readings* is always to emphasize cultural difference and discontinuity. On this highly professionalized view, whatever separates "us" from Shakespeare and the Renaissance is more important than what joins us, so that anybody who thinks Shakespeare our contemporary is showing how little he or she understands.

Or that is the tendency. It is sufficiently marked to help explain why and how Greenblatt's celebrated essay "Invisible Bullets" gives a characteristically deft but evasive twist to the question "Is Shakespeare Evil?"[47] Greenblatt is quite unequivocal in ascribing all those "subversive doubts" that the second tetralogy "continually awakens" to "Shakespeare": to this extent his Shakespeare seems reassuringly unlike Tennenhouse's toady. But the essay also insists on a "carefully plotted official strategy" which ensured that all such doubts would only "serve paradoxically to intensify the power of the king." Here "Shakespeare" suddenly drops from sight, at the very moment when we might very much want to know whether the apparently "subversive" dramatist was a helpless victim of this mysteriously inexorable process, or a willing, alarmingly crafty accomplice whose "subversive doubts" were stagily introduced to ensure that "power" contains "subversion." The discussion of *Othello* in *Renaissance Self-Fashioning* produces an equivalent problem.[48] Greenblatt's Othello is a deluded Christian convert, whose acceptance of a markedly antisexual but "orthodox" Christian (or Pauline) doctrine unhinges him and finally drives him to murder. To be sure, this is a crude summary of a subtly ramified thesis, but it is sufficient to suggest the problem Greenblatt's discussion never directly addresses. Greenblatt makes clear that he thinks the "orthodox doctrine" perverted and perverting; because it is so alien (watch out for Them and Us!), he spends some time explaining it—but that delivers the problem. For suppose the doctrine is as important to our understanding of the play as Greenblatt maintains. Then, if Shakespeare's play accepts or condones the doctrine without seeing how it is perverted and perverting, the play becomes far more alien than readers and spectators have taken it to be; enthralled modern audiences are merely betraying their lack of historical understanding. If, on the other hand, Shakespeare's play is diagnosing the neurotic-making dynamics of the Christian (or Pauline) doctrine, then it is a far more extraordinary and revolutionary document than Greenblatt's own reading ever suggests. As soon as we attend to the inner logic of Greenblatt's argument, it becomes clear which of these alternatives he implicitly, though never explicitly, endorses—clear that his Shakespeare is a tamer, less subversive dramatist than his Marlowe; and clear too that, although he so evidently loves Shakespeare, the logic of his readings is reductive and curiously masochistic. *Othello* is being seen, like *Henry V,* as another museum piece.

If this claim suggests how Greenblatt is a uniquely complicated case, as we expect a major critic to be—and he is that—it nonetheless allows me to pull together a nexus of related issues, not to conclude, but to bring this book to the starting line. So, one feature of Greenblatt's readings that is generally representative, whether or not we would quarrel with conflating references to "the 'new historicism' of cultural materialism," is the way in which they depend upon a very partial sampling of the text. Greenblatt's account of *Othello* is being provided with a cultural-historical context, but not a dramatic context; it is related to the complex design of the critic's argument, not to that of Shakespeare's play.

This conclusion also suggests why the issue of intention is like the Bad Fairy in Grimm: if you don't invite her to the interpretative feast she comes anyway, with a curse. Many materialist critics dismiss any concern with dramatic intentions: the search for "imaginary coherence" or "unity" is derided as a "humanist" illusion, or as part of the cultural conspiracy to conceal ideological inconsistencies within the text. Yet as soon as we attend with any closeness to their readings and their language, we find them all implying or assuming some intention—usually a single intention, and often an ugly intention that makes the question "Is Shakespeare Evil?" far more ominous than it should be.

This tendency can be obvious: to suppose, like Tennenhouse, that Shakespeare's plays were "a vehicle for disseminating court ideology"[49] is like supposing that the stuff that floats on the top of our polluted rivers directs their flow. But the tendency also appears in very good books, like Phyllis Rackin's *Stages of History,* where she explains "the long-standing preference of conservative critics for Richard III and the plays of the second tetralogy and their superior canonical status to King John and the Henry VI plays": "Set in a providential universe, graced with aesthetic unity, these plays construct a world where the authority of the playwright as well as that of God is clearly manifest."[50] "Conservative critics" preferred that world, whereas the "radical criticism of the present" is more drawn to the "Machiavellian universe" of the earlier plays where "the principle of causation becomes inscrutable, and the audience has no guidance to help them discover significance or assign value as they watch the action unfold" (55). If our response is so far determined by what "conservative" or "radical" prejudices we bring to the show, before we have even seen it, it is not obvious what studying literature and drama can ever teach us.

Rackin herself later qualifies this suggestion that Shakespeare's intention in the second tetralogy is more "visible" and authoritarian by arguing that it "replaces the teleological, providential narrative of Tudor propaganda with a self-referential cycle that ends by interrogating the entire project of historical mythmaking" (60–61). But we should notice that this more subtle argument about what is "increasingly self-conscious and skeptical" is also characterizing a (more complicated) dramatic intention, or "double agenda." My own concern is with Shakespeare as the directing intelligence at work within the work, not with the Shakespeare who had laundry lists or prior intentions. The sequence of speeches and scenes in a Shakespearean poetic drama is not random; a play doesn't "emerge from fields of discourse" like a poppy, and one of the reasons we don't interpret and argue about poppies is that they're not *meant*. But, as I wish to emphasize at the outset, to be concerned with dramatic intentions in this sense— with the play as a highly organized matrix of potential meanings, rather than as a chaotic site—is to be concerned with how the play thinks or sets us thinking, not with what the play "really" thinks or tells "us" to think.

Indeed, we are not seriously engaging with the drama as a complex design if we won't ask questions such as these: Why does Shakespeare bring together the story of the caskets and the story of the bond? Why does Shakespeare make it so difficult to decide whether Henry is right or wrong to go to war with France? and Why does Shakespeare make his Moor and Desdemona a newly married couple, set Desdemona alongside a crypto-feminist Emilia, and then invent Bianca to round out the female trio? In each case the "why?" involves a "how?" and sends us further into the play, not off on a giddy wild-goose chase after prior intentions. As it happens, all these questions also involve strikingly purposive—creatively purposeful—departures from what Shakespeare found in his sources. Noticing such departures can alert us to things in the play we had not noticed, and common sense suggests that they can provide a guide to dramatic intentions—again, not to what we must think, but to what we are being given to think about. There is nothing wrong with reading the "Henriad" with an "interpretive model" provided by a reading of Harriot, if the model works; but it is odd to show no interest in what Shakespeare did with Holinshed and Hall. Greenblatt himself once referred to the study of sources as the elephants' graveyard of Shakespeare criticism, and such irritation might seem justifiable if we recall how often that study has been prompted by the wish to settle debates—to tell us what Shakespeare and/or his monolithic audience *must* have thought about Jews, Moors, the Irish, or whatever. My own impression—and argument, in the relevant stretches of the two essays that follow—is that Shakespeare's purposive departures from his sources are more consistent with a wish to start, not settle, debate. Here it is a mistake, in historical as well as critical terms, not to remember that Emilia and Michael Williams, or spectators with views like theirs, were to be found offstage as well as onstage, sitting in audiences that were no more to be regarded as monolithic entities than are today's audiences. Shakespeare belonged to that first generation of English dramatists whose livings depended on pleasing a mixed audience. He peopled his stage with Elizabethans who think and feel differently about different matters—like their counterparts in the audience, whose disagreements about matters large and small produced so many violent quarrels, litigation on the scale of a national epidemic, and frequent fatalities. To forget these facts is another neo-Tillyardian way of ironing out whatever conflicts with the critic's Authorized Version.

Hence this book's double subject, and my wish to allow the plays to test, and not merely "instantiate," the theoretical or assumptive basis for currently influential readings. Of course the danger in this notion of "testing" is that of deifying one's own reading as "the play," and then representing opposed readings as "misrepresentations." Yet where that happens—and the best efforts will never ensure that it never happens—it is best that it happen in the open, with a lively and specific sense of what is at issue, and of the need for *dialogue*. It is obvious enough that my own account of what I take to be the historiographical challenge in *Henry V* will not convince those already convinced that the play shows how Henry really is the "mirror of Christian Kings," or a Machiavellian hypocrite. But examining the particular case helps us to clarify the more fundamental and extensive difference between undertaking to explain what the play "really" means and thinking of a Shakespearean poetic drama as a powerfully generative matrix of multiple meanings, or field of forces.

As one would expect, given the combatively theoretical nature of contemporary criticism, there are already many notable accounts of "the 'new historicism' of cultural materialism"; some of the best are by now assembled in collections like H. Aram Veeser's *New Historicism* and Jean E. Howard and Marion F. O'Connor's *Shakespeare Reproduced.*[51] But to find an extended examination of a Shakespeare play in any of these accounts would be rather startling, since their focus tends to be political, theoretical, or methodological. Readers whose interests are chiefly of that kind may find this book disappointing, since so much of it is given over to discussions of *Henry V* and *Othello;* but then, as we have already seen, the readings can expose ideological "faultlines" and a significant rift between theory and practice. As for the argument that there is no Shakespeare, only "Shakespeares," this book presents a lengthy reply; a short answer would be that "Shakespeares" is interesting but Shakespeare are better.

Being Oneself: New Historicists, Cultural Materialists, and *Henry V*

The Trouble with Harry

One problem with historicist readings, old and "New," is their unhistorical readiness to think of the Original Audience as some fabulous beast with many bodies but one obediently loyal heart, and one unimpressive mind. As Stephen Greenblatt explains in the opening pages of *Shakespearean Negotiations*, the "Shakespearean theater" is "the product of collective intentions" and "manifestly addresses its audience as collectivity": it "depends upon a felt community"; there is "no attempt to isolate and awaken the sensibilities of each individual member of the audience, no sense of the disappearance of the crowd."[1] On this view "Shakespearean theater" was altogether remote from the kind of theater Brecht envisaged when he urged his company not to regard, and play to, the audience as a monolithic entity: "He asked them to think of their audience as a divided group of friends and enemies, rich and poor, and to *divide* their audience accordingly by addressing themselves to one part of the audience now, to another part the next moment."[2] Similarly, the interests of the homogeneous audience described in Ann Jennalie Cook's *Privileged Playgoers of Shakespeare's London* were so nearly identified with those of the queen as to make the elaborate apparatus of state and censorship seem curiously excessive; nor is this difficulty resolved when it is explained that "the entire rationale for the existence of dramatic companies was that they provided essential recreation for the sovereign."[3] "In theory," she adds—but whose theory is it?—"public performances merely provided an opportunity for rehearsal and perfection of plays before they were presented at Court." In *Power on Display*, Leonard Tennenhouse's chief reservation about Cook's thesis is that it isn't pressed harder: "I simply want to take this notion more literally than Cook does."[4] This he does, with predictable results, and he sets out the controlling assumptions that produce his readings: *since* "the audience was always implicitly the queen, . . . we *have to* consider the drama as a forum for staging symbolic shows of state power and as a vehicle for disseminating court ideology," just as "we *have to* assume these *had to be* presented without challenging her policies or demeaning her person" (39, my italics).

What is less obvious, though still predictable, is the relation between these assumptions about Elizabethan audiences and the assumption of so many modern directors that their business in interpreting a play is to tell contemporary audiences what to think. When Greenblatt firmly rejects the arguments of all those critics "since Hazlitt" who think that the apparent glorification of the monarch in *Henry V* is "bitterly ironic," he explains that "even today, and in the wake of full-scale ironic readings and at a time when it no longer seems to matter very much, it is not at all clear that *Henry V* can be successfully performed as subversive" (63). *Shakespearean Negotiations* appeared when the English Shakespeare Company was traveling the world with its marathon production of the two historical tetralogies; those who saw the ESC's markedly anti-Henry *Henry V* and felt it didn't work might, like those who are unconvinced by anti-Henry critical readings, find Greenblatt's appeal to the conditions for a successful performance all the more persuasive. Yet it's important to see why Greenblatt's point is so sharply at odds with that made by the actor Alan Howard, after playing Henry in the Royal Shakespeare Company's 1982 production: "People have tried to do *Henry V* as a play glorifying war, and a play condemning war; but by allowing the text to be free, without preconceptions, one discovers that the play does both these things and many others besides."[5] Howard speaks of "allowing the text to be free," but Greenblatt is imagining, and endorsing, that kind of production which will neither trust the play nor allow the audience— now a contemporary audience, but no less homogeneous—to think for itself. The director decides whether the play is or is not to be "performed as subversive"; it is taken for granted that any audience which was allowed or encouraged to think for itself would be as helpless as the would-be apostles in the Monty Python film *Life of Brian;* when told to "fuck off," they ask, in painful bewilderment, "How shall we fuck off, O Lord?" Greenblatt next registers his disagreement with readings which argue that "Shakespeare's depiction of Henry V" is not "subversive" but "radically ambiguous." But if a "subversive" reading won't work, "even today," and "ambiguous" readings are unconvincing, little room is left for maneuver—indeed none, in Greenblatt's terms, since his own reading doesn't suggest that a pro-Henry reading could be any more "successfully performed" today. Although he refrains from drawing the evident conclusion, the play belongs in a museum.

The ESC *Henry V* was modern and streetwise, since the production emphasized—or insisted on—its topicality. And there was more than that—or much despite that—to be grateful for, including the chance (which Elizabethan audiences perhaps never had) to test our sense of whether the "tetralogies" work as tetralogies: to be reminded of the continuities as well as the shifts or redirections within each cycle is always valuable, but rarely possible, in the theater. So, for example, there was an admirable emphasis on the plays' *regional* contrasts. Having Hotspur, the "northern youth," speak in a very thick northern accent extended the contrasts with Hal, the fluent, southern, metropolitan prince; the "Henriad" explores various cultural fictions, including this mythopeic (rather than historical) contrast between concepts of "Englishness." That Shakespeare took pains to introduce Hotspur in *Richard II,* without finding much for him to do, suggests that he was thinking ahead but doesn't prepare us for one crucial poetic-dramatic shift: how Hotspur's namesake in *Richard II* talks doesn't matter much, since the verse he speaks never sounds like the exuberantly eruptive, uncourtly, and anticourtly verse that speaks "Hotspur" in the play that followed. But then it was also clear that the ESC's intention in emphasizing regional differences was to "make a statement" about contemporary regional and political divisions in a far-from-united Kingdom; and this topicality was underscored by a lot of interpolated stage business, like having "Hal's Angels" going off to bash the French Argies and (in case we still missed the analogy) waving a banner saying "Gotcha!" An American director who was similarly concerned with Shakespeare's contemporaneity might have shown the troops leaving to deal with the Noriega "thing," and carrying ghetto- or embassy-blasters along with their other weapons.

The present eminence of the director, like that of the conductor, is a peculiar and significantly modern development. Both are expected to function as the custodians and interpreters of a cultural museum. Michael Bogdanov and Michael Pennington, the ESC's joint directors, explained that their chief concern was to "repoliticize" the tetralogies by emphasizing what Bogdanov referred to as "the sordid immorality masquerading underneath all the stuff about divine right," and what Pennington succinctly called the "alternative narrative"—in which Shakespeare, "the humanist and poet," was "subtly at work," undermining the "superficially orthodox tub-thumping and blatant nationalism."[6] In other words, the "alternative narrative" told the Right Story, that is, the Left Story. Olivier, Tillyard, and other reactionaries, including Shakespeare's Chorus, had told the Wrong Story. One might agree, at least in seeing Olivier's markedly pro-Henry 1944 film as a wartime effort, with significant critical parallels in Tillyard's *Shakespeare's History Plays* (1944) and Dover Wilson's *Fortunes of Falstaff* (1943).[7] Times change, though we should try not to confuse evolution with progress. The way in which the ESC's markedly anti-Henry production inverted that of Olivier has a no less striking, and methodologically exact, critical parallel in those contemporary British cultural materialist readings of Shakespeare which, like Jonathan Dollimore's *Radical Tragedy*, invert Tillyard's political views while continuing Tillyard's bad critical habit of giving particular characters or speeches a privileged, supradramatic significance.[8] In each case—Olivier *and* the ESC, Tillyard *and* the cultural materialists—there is an unexamined assumption that what is being privileged corresponds with the ideological viewpoint that we are to think "the play" (Shakespeare in scare-quotes) really promotes but that far more obviously corresponds with the critic's or director's own ideological inclinations. Those uncertainties which the play provokes are regarded, or at any rate treated, as though they were some kind of obscuring overlay or static.

Here it is worth remembering how Elizabethan actors were given parts and cues, not complete texts, and were not burdened with the knowledge that they were interpreting our national classics. Today, "good theatre" is great drama's most treacherous friend; it betrays with a kiss. The greatest danger for the actor, especially an intelligently analytical modern actor, is that his sense of the play will prevent him from being loyal to his part. The greatest danger for the director, especially the custodian-interpreter with a passionately committed sense of Shakespeare's "relevance" outside the cultural museum, is that he will proceed as though allowing an audience to think for itself would be a dereliction of duty. Since I am objecting to both the Tillyardian and the cultural materialist view—so that I can expect, as Erasmus politely put it, to be pissed on from both sides—it should at least be clear that my objection is not "primarily" political (as Stanley Fish would say) or "ultimately" political (as the cultural materialists say). Words like "ultimately" or "primarily" mean much the same at this level of discourse; "cultural meanings" are, as Jonathan Dollimore and Alan Sinfield insist in their "Cultural Politics" series, "always, finally, political meanings,"[9] but food is always, finally, something else. I am not denying that all readings are in *some* sense political, since there are no purely literary values or neutral readings, only readings-for. But I am objecting to prematurely politicized readings that short-circuit the genuinely exploratory process of Shakespeare's dramatic thinking.

Although I didn't discuss *Henry V* in *Shakespeare's Scepticism,* I did characterize this process of Shakespearean dramatic thinking and try to explain why it goes much further than talk of mixed drama readily suggests. I argued that the process is essentially experiential and per-spectival: that is, it depends on the way in which the plays unfold discrepant or sharply opposed perspectives on characters and on problematic issues such as "love" and "honor" or the divine right of kings. I used the term "framing" to emphasize the way in which these perspectival conflicts are not isolated flare-ups, but are developed and articulated through the play's structural dynamics. Often, this issues in some powerfully organized collisional moment, a poetic-dramatic configuration or gestalt,[10] in which we find ourselves *simultaneously* apprehending opposed potentialities of meaning, as we try to collect and make sense of our own startlingly divided responses. Here Keats's concept of negative capability is indispensable, even though Keats was never concerned with the plays' dramatic organization: his fragmen-tary comments suggest that he always approached the plays (and son-nets) as Jack Horner approached pies, for isolatable plums. Yet Keats saw how Shakespeare goes inside, or imaginatively inhabits, an Iago or Imogen; the gestalt-experience of being drawn in contrary directions is usually precipitated when we find ourselves recognizing something challengingly and irreducibly different in a character's way of seeing and feeling his or her situation. This also explains why "either/or" disputes are rife in Shakespeare criticism—about whether Othello is a noble hero or a deluded egotist; whether Shylock is a comic villain or a tragic victim; whether we see with Macbeth or merely see through him; whether Caliban is a savage on whose nature nurture will not stick or Shakespeare's first American and a victim of colonialism; whether Henry V is an ideal king or a Machiavellian hypocrite, and so on. In such cases the poetic-dramatic framing of discrepant perspectives *produces* the interpretative disagreement, which in turn suggests why "either/or" disputes should be approached with caution: for if the play's engrossing interest and power to disturb depend in part on our being pulled in contrary directions, interpretative attempts to *resolve* that conflict both testify to and, in a paradoxical way, attempt to defeat those energies which make the play *work*. We need ways of speaking to the play that better acknowledge its power to read us. And if, as I believe, *Henry V* is the most underrated play in the Works, one reason for this is that directors usually refuse to stage Shakespeare's play.

Certainly, different stagings can illuminate what Stephen Orgel calls the "areas of ambiguity" in a Shakespearean text, and it is true that the text of a drama is not the play until it is *expanded* into a performance; but then, to balance one truism with another, any particular performance (or reading) is also a *contraction* of the text's potentialities.[11] We too often confuse that kind of contraction, which follows inevitably from the need to make interpretative choices, with the chainsaw massacre that occurs when cuts altogether destroy a play's structural dynamics, which is what happened in Olivier's *Henry V*. All in all, Olivier's version cuts just under, and Kenneth Branagh's recent film just over, 53 percent of Shakespeare's text.[12] But although they are still fatal to Shakespeare, Branagh's cuts often seem clueless and recall Edgar Allan Poe's orangutan with a razor. The Olivier cuts are intensely, relentlessly purposeful. What remains is an uplifting anthology, partial in both senses, and all too representative of the way in which so many critics and directors repeatedly respond to this play's interrogative energies by working to suppress them. For this very reason Olivier the director and editor is a quite wonderfully astute guide, even in matters of fine detail, to those complicating perspectives which Shakespeare's neglected play so challengingly frames: we have only to pick through the surgical bin to see what was cut out.

Indeed there are moments when Olivier the director actually recalls, by translating into visual images, some of the play's disconcertingly critical perspectives. After the King's (or Olivier/Burbage's) ringing delivery of the tennis-balls speech we see and hear the Globe audience erupting in jingoistic applause; the effect, whether or not this was Olivier's intention, includes a Brechtian reminder that we have just heard a performance making that kind of appeal. A suddenly disconcerting close-up in the final scene shows Katherine's small hand ambiguously clenched in the King's powerful fist.[13] Yet such moments are at best fleeting visual souvenirs of what has been lost: wherever the play's adversely critical perspectives threaten Henry in any serious or sustained way, they are cut. Rather than have Henry give the order to cut the French prisoners' throats, Olivier cuts the text instead and interpolates a scene in which the French butcher English boys in technicolor; yet, as Gary Taylor pertinently suggests in his Oxford edition, the only reason for the stage direction specifying that some French prisoners are on stage is that they are to be butchered before our eyes.[14] Similarly, we aren't allowed to hear Henry's speech at Harfleur threatening a havoc of rape and slaughter in which naked infants will be "spitted upon Pykes"; and, although Olivier is superb at conveying Dunkirk camaraderie and that professional regard which Henry and Montjoy find for each other as performers, we lose whatever would complicate that view of a comradely king—including the calculating entrapment of Cambridge, Scroop, and Grey, or the order to execute Bardolph, and Henry's reference to "None else of name." Olivier is no less implacably opposed than are the exponents of the ESC's "alternative narrative" to any effortful, adult thinking: he will trust neither the play nor the audience, so that the gulf between Shakespeare's dramatic thinking and this predigested pap is as wide as that between the Gettysburg address and the political babyfood prepared by any modern president's anonymous speechwriters; perhaps our endgame is a choice of paps.

Yet it is still possible to see how (although the phrase is forbidden) *the play itself* never relinquishes its critical perspectives on Henry. Consider how its final scene builds on the sly point of what the New Arden editor loftily dismissed as a pointless departure from the chronicles— when Bardolph is executed for stealing a "Pax of little price" from a

French church.[15] Both Hall and Holinshed had reported the execution of a common soldier for stealing a "pyx," usually a more valuable ecclesiastical item. Unlike most modern readers Shakespeare knows the difference between pyxes and paxes. In ecclesiastical Latin the word *pax* refers both to the object, a little tablet which is passed between communicants to be kissed, and, by association, to the "kiss of peace." Bardolph is executed for petty looting, while the final scene shows Henry looting on a truly regal scale as he steals a "Pax" of great price, insisting on every article of the forcefully imposed peace. Ransacking the princess and stealing the kiss is part of that price: before the so-called wooing we hear (though Olivier cut it out) Henry's blunt insistence that the princess is "our capitall Demand, compris'd / Within the fore-rank of our Articles," and all the other "articles" of the doomed Henrician *pax* are being forcefully thrashed out offstage, on his instructions, even as he goes unto Katherine's breach. The play's imagery repeatedly associates war with rape,[16] and this final scene provides the culminating examples (which the vigilant Olivier also removed). Indeed the first part of this scene in the Folio attributes the King's speeches to *Eng.* or *England,* until he is left alone with Katherine; that seems both Shakespearean and revealing, although tidy-minded modern editors remove it, like the Folio's laconic references to Lady Macduff as *Wife.* Obviously, Katherine can no more offer resistance to "*Eng.*" than those cities which her father describes as "all gyrdled with Maiden Walls, that Warre hath entred"—at which point the Folio once again starts designating Henry as *England!* And now, having just finished his rather leery exchange with Burgundy by vowing to "catch the Flye, your Cousin, in the latter end," Henry gleefully elaborates the French king's analogy by insisting that the survival of these cities depends on the surrender of the princess's maidenhead: "I am content, so the Maiden Cities you talke of, may wait on her: so the Maid that stood in the way for my Wish, shall shew me the way to my Will." In this so-called wooing scene Olivier does keep faith with that high-spirited exuberance which anti-Henry readings so often suppress; but since he has also carefully removed whatever makes it more difficult to sustain or indulge a simply admiring view of "Harry England," there is no Shakespearean gestalt.

This kind of gestalt, with its flaring of complicating, contradictory energies, is not merely local: it depends on a more sustained organization. For another example, we might consider the disconcerting lead-up to Henry's soliloquy before Agincourt. Everybody likes Court, Bates, and Williams; significantly, they are the first thoroughly decent soldiers we've encountered in the ranks rather than the officer class; and there is much that should disturb Henry in Williams's quietly unassuming but morally somber comments on the responsibility the king must bear if he is waging an unjust war. Henry may be theologically correct in his confident reply to Williams that he is not responsible for the state of dead soldiers' *souls;* but, if the war is unjust, or something he has pursued to busy giddy minds with foreign quarrels, as his father advised, he most certainly bears a responsibility for those lives that are lost or wrecked in his service. And then, as Williams also reminds the King, there are the widows and children: although the soliloquy's indignant reference to "our carefull Wives" and "our Children" (4.1.231–32) show that he has been listening, Henry prefers not to talk about them with Williams. He opts for theology, and we see his predicament: he must reply for, but cannot reply as, the King. But then, far from revealing a more inwardly reflective and scrupulous private self, the soliloquy's self-pitying, self-justifying cast of thought shows how, although Henry has found the experience of being challenged by a serf intensely disagreeable, he continues to deflect the most substantial and specific moral items in that challenge. Nor does he recall any of those earlier, expedient decisions where we might have hoped that he felt, even if he could not reveal, some inner qualm—in the brutalities of the Harfleur speech, for example, or in giving the order for Bardolph's execution. Instead, the soliloquy suggests that Henry himself is incapable of seeing any connection between Bardolph's looting and his own dynastic ambitions, or between his wounded charge that Scroop, Grey, and Cambridge had betrayed his friendship and his own treatment of Falstaff (whose final illness is reported immediately before the scene at Southampton, and whose death is then reported immediately after Henry has the conspirators executed).[17] The soliloquy's heartfelt protest against having to be

> Subject to the breath
> Of every foole, whose sence no more can feele,
> But his owne wringing
>
> (4.1.234–36)

falls over itself, if we notice how Henry is far too preoccupied with *his* own "wringing" to be aware of Williams as anything other, and more, than a "foole," a "Pesant" and "wretched Slave" whose "grosse braine little wots, / What watch the King keepes, to maintaine the peace" (268–70).

There is that gulf which Williams mentioned, angering the king by demanding to know what "a poore and a private displeasure can doe against a Monarch" (197–99). As for Henry's idea that Williams and the other soldiers can sleep soundly, it is grotesquely at odds with what we have just seen of their restless anxiety in the early, noisily preparatory hours before the battle; but that only adds to the unsettling effect of our realizing that we have heard something very like this before, in the previous play—when Henry IV asks the "dull god" sleep, "why lyest thou with the vilde / In loathsome Beds, and leav'st the Kingly Couch?" (*2 Henry IV*, 3.1.15–16). That earlier royal soliloquy was also subverted in advance, by Falstaff's insistence on the burdens of the great: "You see (my good Wenches) how men of Merit are sought after: the undeserver may sleepe, when the man of Action is call'd on" (*2H4*: 2.4.374–77). Such rhyming juxtapositions and ironic splicings are like joints that articulate Shakespeare's poetic-dramatic thinking: in this case our seeing how adroitly Falstaff avoids settling his accounts is richly amusing in itself, but the joke then casts a longer, dark, and crooked shadow over the royal soliloquy that follows. Now we hear a regal virtuoso deflecting and reshaping recalcitrant realities, not least by displacing his guilt over seizing the throne into the less troubling idea that, if he cannot sleep, it is because he must constantly care for the realm.[18] Like a well-oiled machine, this contrivance delivers the slick, envious but self-protecting contrast with the "happy low" and the vile who can sleep well—the mystifying idea that Akira Kurosawa so sardonically inverts, along with much of *Hamlet*, in his magnificent, bitter film *The Bad Sleep Well*.[19] To hear that long-range echo on the eve of Agincourt is peculiarly disconcerting: like father like son, indeed. Yet both soliloquies are also heartfelt: all those perspectival ironies which prompt or support a diagnostic, "demystifying" view are complicated by Shakespeare's powerful and characteristic internalization, which challenges us to feel with these kings and to recognize the irreducibly different way in which they see and feel their situation. Their verse carries the swell of intense feeling, and to regard them as *hypocrites* would deflect that poetic-dramatic challenge: their sense of burdened loneliness is as genuine as their absolute conviction that their own wishes and interests must coincide with the needs of the common weal.

If Harry England's attitude to Williams does trouble us, as I think it should, we won't have forgotten that disquiet a hundred lines later when he launches into the Crispin's Day speech. Earlier, in "Once more unto the Breach" Henry had addressed his flagging army as his "deare friends" (3.1.1), appealing to their noble "breeding" and likening them to leashed greyhounds—moments before the play's other Welshman drives the frightened stragglers on in very different tones: "Up to the breach, you Dogges; avaunt you Cullions." That dramatic irony was clearly organized, although it could be taken in different ways. Now, before the battle of Agincourt, all distinctions of rank and birth once again seem as nothing in a dark hour of need, and the happy low are elevated: "we few, we happy few, we band of brothers" (4.3.60). But as soon as the battle has been won, the "happy few" hear their now victorious but markedly less fraternal and egalitarian monarch express his delight that the English losses include only the four well-born men he mentions and "None else of name: and of all other men, / But five and twentie" (4.8.100–101). That inspiring conception of a precious band of brothers suddenly counts for less, and of course it *did* count for less: the speech is firmly based on the chronicles, and Shakespeare had to invent names for common soldiers like Bates and Williams. To be sure, Henry does not go so provokingly far as Clarendon in *The History of the Great Rebellion*, with its notorious reference to "dirty people of no name"; but then, regardless of his inspiring rhetoric in an earlier hour of need, the victorious Henry is clearly moving in that, rather than in the other, direction.

Again, responses will vary, and such interrogative ironies would have nothing to interrogate if the magnificent, inspiring rhetoric isn't first allowed to tell, as it certainly does in Olivier's thrilling delivery. But then the play keeps catching us up (or out) in a complicated experiential process, which gives dramatic force to the fundamental historiographical question: *Whose* history, and told from what point of view? The structural dynamics of *Henry V* assimilate that question and make it no less pressing for a modern than for an Elizabethan audience. To take the most obvious example, which comes five times like Lear's "Never": each act begins with the Chorus's "official," take-me-to-your-leader way of doing history, but as soon as the Chorus leaves the stage, there is an eruption of subversive, complicating energy.

If the Chorus's view of history were to prevail, the audience might respond like that monolithic audience of which historicists dream— Greenblatt's "collectivity." But what happens whenever the Chorus vacates the stage is more in keeping with the effect Brecht sought when he urged his company to "*divide* their audience" by "addressing themselves" to its divided and competing interests. We see what the Chorus would prefer to edit, reshape or suppress, although this is not to say, nor should the Brechtian analogy suggest, that the Chorus is always reassuringly wrong. To think so is like supposing that the soliloquizing kings must be hypocrites if their way of seeing things is not the only way of seeing things: it defeats the challenge to think, and to think about history. But then the dramatic rhythm I am describing, with its movement from the unifying into the divisive, from an approved view into a proliferation of interpretative possibilities, can also be seen as a highly organized and critically reflective representation of what happens in reading the chronicles, and especially Holinshed. As G. K. Hunter observes in a brilliant essay:

Modern scholars usually tell us that the Chronicles (particularly Edward Hall's) are marked by an overall design that controls their presentation of detail. But to read continuously in the Chronicles is to discover that they exemplify less the grand historical design than the complexity, dispersal, randomness, even incomprehensibility of actual happenings. We are regularly told about the genealogical tree on the title-page to Hall's Chronicle as a kind of aerial map of the dynastic conflict that "explains" the history of this period. But when we turn over the page and actually begin to read in Hall (or better still in Holinshed) word by word and page by page, then we must descend from the hot-air balloon of theory that floats *above* history and see events from the level of the human eye, share in the bemusement and mistakenness that characterizes the 'truth' of historical experience as here retailed. . . .

The chroniclers' annalistic method of year-by-year accounting further reinforces the general effect of one-thing-after-another randomness. In this mode the idea of an individual's purposive career is difficult to sustain. . . . What is entirely and continuously obvious is that life in feudal England is most adequately represented as a series of individual raids on the inarticulable: a castle is besieged here or there and then retired from when a larger army appears on the horizon; the Scots do their annual thing, try to burn Carlisle or Berwick, drive away cattle, then give up when the weather gets too bad (or too good); the price of wheat rises and falls, a high wind destroys houses, people try to avoid taxes and get hanged, drawn, quartered, beheaded, burned, massacred—random events suffered by individuals continually trying to derandomize them, including Holinshed himself, who offers us the guidance of "some say," "others allege," "it is reported that," but makes little or no sustained effort to assess accuracy or probability. And when the absence of explanatory connection is particularly blatant he throws up his hands in a gesture that might be despair or might be piety, as when he says of the usurpation of Bolingbroke that he cannot make sense of it: "But . . . the providence of God is to be respected and his secret will to be wondered at. . . . For as in His hands standeth the donation of kingdoms, so likewise the disposing of them consisteth in His pleasure." . . . In such cases a providential pattern emerges, but not as an overall explanation, only as a justification for the humanly inexplicable.

A dramatist who makes his way through such actual chronicles—and we should remember that Shakespeare could not lay his hands on a copy of *Shakespeare's Holinshed*—has to achieve his design by means of rigorous exclusion and reshaping.[20]

But reshaping to what end? For a fascinating and very powerfully sustained example of the historiographical challenge in the play's structural dynamics, let us consider what the first act makes of one familiar kind of historical problem which, in his own far from artless fashion, Holinshed himself could not resolve but would not conceal.

The Historiographical Challenge

Critics have argued at length about Henry's motives for going to war with France, and whether he is right or wrong to do so. Such arguments usually polarize into pro-Henry and anti-Henry readings, in which the critical assumption that we need to establish what view the play "really" takes produces incompatible readings; old and new historicist interventions often depend on assumptions about what view (not views) the Elizabethan audience would have taken. But then history never tells us what Henry's motives were, because it can't; in this simple but important sense a history play that pretended to make Henry's motives clear would be historically irresponsible.

Holinshed does indeed tell us, in a very interesting passage with no parallel in Hall, that when Henry was dying he was especially anxious to have it understood that his motives were of the best:

> And herewith he protested unto them, that neither the ambitious desire to inlarge his dominions, neither to purchase vain renowme and worldlie fame, nor anie other consideration had moved him to take the warres in hand; but onlie that in prosecuting his just title, he might in the end atteine to a perfect peace, and come to enjoy those peeces of his inheritance, which to him of right belonged: and that before the beginning of the same warres, he was fullie persuaded by men both wise and of great holinesse of life, that upon such intent he might and ought both begin the same warres, and follow them, till he had brought them to an end iustlie and rightlie, and that without all danger of Gods displeasure or perill of soul.[21]

But of course what this *also* tells us is that other, less favorable accounts of Henry's motives were circulating, so that he found it necessary to "protest." It evidently told Shakespeare as much, since his play is historically responsible, both in its ultimate reticences and in its habitual way of exposing the Chorus's hagiographic account of "the Mirror of all Christian Kings" to other, competing interpretative possibilities. Whether Henry was right or wrong to go to war with France is a question that depends not only on whether the "title" was "iust" but on whether one is taking what Edward Powell's book on Henry V calls a "king's-eye view" or, say, the view of the French king, or of a dead conscript's widow, or of Shakespeare's Michael Williams, or of Archbishop Chicheley. In other words, the historiographical challenge involves what Shakespeare's King of France calls seeing "perspectively," and the challenge corresponds with the poetic-dramatic framing of opposed or discrepant perspectives.

Any argument that the play presses us toward one single, inclusive judgment deflects the historiographical challenge and (what is really the same thing) smothers the play's interrogative, skeptical, and exploratory energies. To suppose that the play "addresses its audience as a collectivity" short-circuits its dramatic thinking, in which the challenge is that of seeing "perspectively." The Chorus does indeed keep calling for some such collective or communal response in accord with his own "king's-eye view," which in turn steadily and sturdily assumes that the interests of a nation continually and happily coincide with those of its ruler or ruling class. Even in the first Prologue, which is often taken as an engagingly modest and indirect authorial appeal, the Chorus is richly characterized and anxious in interesting ways. To address the mixed audience as "Gentles all" is strategic precisely because they are not all "Gentles." It flatters, and appeals to, the audience in the very same way that Henry will appeal to his straggling army:

> let us sweare,
> That you are worth your breeding: which I doubt not:
> For there is none of you so meane and base,
> That hath not Noble luster in your eyes.
>
> (2.1.27–30)

The Chorus is *right* to fear that neither the play nor the audience can be relied upon to become "Cyphers" to the "great Accompt" (line 18). "Into a thousand parts divide one Man," he appeals, even as he seeks to bond the audience and make them as one. He withdraws, asking us "Gently to heare, kindly to judge," but without in any way preparing us for the play's first jolting, ungentle probing of competing interests—when we find ourselves eavesdropping on a necessarily private conversation between the Archbishop of Canterbury and the Bishop of Ely. This descent is moral as well as stylistic; doubt and division thrive.

As the bishops consider the danger posed by the Crown's claim on the Church's "temporall lands"—that is, those properties not used for strictly religious purposes, which make up "the better halfe of our Possession" (1.1.8)—they are not concerned to consider whether anything might justify or give credence to the Crown's claim. In Canterbury's indignant summary, almshouses and the needs of the lepers and indigent take their place alongside Henry's wish to provide for fifteen earls, fifteen hundred knights, over six thousand esquires, and the King's own "Coffers":

> *Cant.* And to reliefe of Lazars, and weake age
> Of indigent faint Soules, past corporall toyle,
> A hundred Almes-houses, right well supply'd:

> And to the coffers of the King beside
> A thousand pounds by th' yeere. Thus runs the bill.
> *Ely.*   This would drink deepe.
> *Cant.*   'Twould drink the cup and all.
> *Ely.*   But what prevention?
> *Cant.*   The King is full of grace and fair regard.
> *Ely.*   And a true lover of the holy Church.
>
>   (1.1.15–23)

That break in the meter, when Ely puts his practical question, orchestrates a small but significant adjustment[22]: now Canterbury reminds Ely that to resolve the practical problem, which is already in hand, will require a very different style of public performance. The guileless bluntness of Ely's question is no more spiritually becoming than Canterbury's near-blasphemous joke about drinking the cup; the worldlywise must know when and how to seem unworldly. Ely responds at once, like a *commedia dell'arte* player recognizing his cue to improvise; to lean on the phrase a little, these men are not bishops for nothing. So we have that sudden, *seemingly* inconsequential duet on the King's miraculous virtues: the man who wants to "strip" the Church to fill his "Coffers" is now praised as "a true lover of the holy Church." The subtext to this hymn of praise is that the miraculous reformation is unbelievable: "Miracles are ceast," after all—"And therefore we must needes admit the meanes, / How things are perfected" (lines 67–69). We have entered a world where role-playing is crucial, and a world of which the Chorus knows nothing. He *believes* that Henry is "the Mirror of all Christian Kings," whereas these bishops know when to *say* such things—so that the printer's abbreviation of "Canterbury" to Cant seems, in its fortuitous way, singularly happy. In his unholy worldliness, Canterbury resembles Pandulph in *King John:* he is not the man to represent "right and conscience," so that when Henry deferentially speaks as though he is, it is hard to know who is using whom, or whether the two are functioning as accomplices in a more or less cynical public routine. Since Canterbury also reveals that he has had a private meeting with Henry which was interrupted by the ambassador's arrival, it is worth asking why Shakespeare chose not to stage it so. The most plausible answer, I suggest, is that this first scene is busily working to promote—not resolve—uncertainty about Henry's motives for going to war with France.

To hear Canterbury argue why Henry should go to war is still more unsettling and divisive. Here it's worth emphasizing that there is no reason to doubt that individual members of an Elizabethan audience would have responded in very different ways. Some would have seen how the argument is contrived, both as a tactical diversion to ensure that the bishops retain "our possession" and in its substantive claims: as the New Arden editor observes, Pharamond was the "legendary king of the Salian Franks," and the "Salic Law was actually a collection of folk laws and customs and had nothing to do with the right of succession" (15). Some would have seen how the biblical text that Canterbury cites to establish the right of succession on the female side ("When the man dyes, let the Inheritance / Descend unto the Daughter") is certainly to the point but produces a potentially catastrophic difficulty: accepting this argument would destroy Henry's claim to the *English* throne, so that he, like King John, would be no more than a de facto king.[23] For others, who are only thinking about the claim to the French throne, Canterbury's argument might seem good enough on its own quasi-legal terms. But then these terms are also being exposed to scrutiny, and here the argument's remoteness figures as an important part of its dramatic effect. Even as the speech ponderously tracks back through centuries to revive and give weight to the seventy-year-old dynastic claim entered by Henry's great-grandfather Edward III, it summons a sense of France's historical, geographical, and cultural *separateness.* This is also why it matters in this play that the French frequently speak French, and make their own appeals to "God"; as Alexander Leggatt remarks, in "*Henry VI* and *King John* the French, like all sensible people, speak English," but in *Henry V* they have a curious habit of breaking into French, "especially when alarmed or excited."[24] And when Canterbury goes on to recall the thrilling "Tragedie" played out "on the French ground" when Edward III "Stood smiling, to behold his Lyons Whelpe / Forrage in blood of French Nobilitie," his jubilantly bloody-minded celebration of what our boys once did and might still do to "the full pride of France" emphasizes the traditional enmity between these countries and cultures. (Here Canterbury's lines on the Black Prince are so close to those of the King of France (2.4.53–62) as to suggest what could be, and perhaps was, gained by giving both parts to the same actor, who would then deliver the two passages with a wholly different emotional emphasis.) It is clear enough that the historically remote and self-aggrandizing dynastic claim makes war not love, as Henry's brutal joke in the final scene also reminds us: "I love France so well, that I will not part with a Village of it: I will have it all mine." This war is obviously not being undertaken for France's good—but then whom, among the English, could it benefit? The dynastic ambitions and interests of a particular royal family are utterly remote from the concerns and interests of the Williamses of this world. "Unckle Exeter," "brother Lancaster," "brother Clarence," and the others who eagerly join with Canterbury in urging the King to press his claim can at least hope, like the King, to fill their Lancastrian "coffers." To say that the burden of deciding whether to go to war falls on the king is only another, more "mystifying" way of saying that *he* can choose not to—whereas in Henry's reign, as in Elizabeth's, a conscripted common soldier had no choice, little prospect of profit and none of ransom, and would be lucky to survive. So, Henry very solemnly reminds Canterbury that he must, "in the Name of God, take heed," since

> never two such Kingdomes did contend
> Without much fall of blood, whose guiltlesse drops
> Are every one, a Woe, a sore Complaint,
> 'Gainst him, whose wrongs gives edge unto the swords
> That makes such waste in brief mortalitie.
>
> (1.2.24–28)

Here Henry himself is exposing that moral can of worms which Williams's speech will open. The crucial difference is that Henry always takes for granted the coincidence between his family and caste interests and those of the common weal, whereas Williams needs more convincing.

So will members of the audience who notice what the dramatic sequence tells us about Henry's way of pressing his claim. *Henry IV* had finished with Prince John's prediction of war:

> I will lay oddes, that ere this yeere expire,
> We beare our Civill Swords, and Native fire
> As farre as France. I heare a Bird so sing,
> Whose Musicke, to my thinking, pleas'd the King.

In *Henry V* we then hear Canterbury regretting that, since his preliminary private meeting with the King was interrupted,

> there was not time enough to heare,
> As I perceiv'd his Grace would faine have done,
> The severalls and unhidden passages
> Of his true Titles to some certaine Dukedomes,
> And generally, to the Crowne and Seat of France.
>
> (1.1.83–88)

However, there evidently was time (first things first) to float the financial deal:

> As touching France, to give a greater Summe,
> Then ever at one time the Clergie yet
> Did to his Predecessors part withall.
>
> (1.1.79–81)

The more alert will wonder how this could have found "good acceptance of his Majestie" *before* any discussion of the justice of the claim. The next scene picks up and develops that quietly suggestive irony. As soon as we see the King, we hear him piously emphasizing his need to "be resolv'd" (1.2.4) before he sees the French ambassadors. Apparently, no decision will be taken before the Archbishop's judgment of what "Or should or should not barre us in our Clayme":

> And God forbid, my deare and faithfull Lord,
> That you should fashion, wrest, or bow your reading ...
> For God doth know, how many now in health,
> Shall drop their blood, in approbation
> Of what your reverence shall incite us to.
> Therefore take heed how you impawne our Person,
> How you awake our sleeping Sword of Warre.
>
> (1.2.13–14, 18–22)

Only after being "well resolv'd" that he can indeed "with right and conscience make this claim" will Henry call in the French ambassadors—or so it seems. But then we learn from the ambassador's speech that Henry has already claimed "some certaine Dukedomes" (the phrase is repeated) as one of his first actions on becoming king:

> Your Highnesse lately sending into France,
> Did claime some certaine Dukedomes, in the right

Of your great Predecessor, King *Edward* the third.
In answer of which claime, the Prince our Master
Sayes, that you savour too much of your youth.
(lines 246–50)

This dramatic revelation becomes the pivot for the whole stunningly structured scene, and for that very reason it's worth emphasizing how there is nothing like this in the chronicles. True, Holinshed's report of the Archbishop's oration is preceded—characteristically, without comment—by an account of the clergy's anxiety about the threat to its properties. But then his narrative becomes very diffuse, spanning large distances and periods of time. We learn that "during" the same parliament, "there came to the king ambassadors, as well as from the French king that was then in the hands of the Orlientiall faction, as also from the duke of Burgognie, for aid against that faction," and that Henry then sent Exeter, Grey, and others to the French king who "receiued them verie honorablie, and banketted them right sumtuouslie" (*Chronicles*, 67). In time, Henry's ambassadors tell the French king that if he will "without warre and effusion of christian bloud, render to the king their maister his verie right and lawfull inheritance, that he would be content to take in marriage the ladie Katharine, daughter to the French king, and to indow hir with all the duchies and countries before rehearsed"; the French ask for time to consider, promising to "send ambassadors into England, whereupon Henry—evidently dissatisfied with that stalling—determines to make war and set forth. The Chorus in Shakespeare's play would be happy with a versified dramatic version of this and, if he noticed how the account raises questions, would certainly not want to see them pressed.

Shakespeare presses them and shows how the whole court scene is being staged by Henry himself. If we understand the significance of the ambassador's revelation, it affects our sense of everything that happens in this richly equivocal, and richly dramatic, scene. We now see that the claim was entered before Canterbury's ponderously prepared speech "inciting" the King to war and taking "The sinne upon my head"; but now Canterbury can see that too, and a good production might let us see him seeing that—as any doubt about which man was using the other is resolved. We now see that Henry had already made his claim when he declared his need to be "resolv'd" and spoke so solemnly of the horrors of war; but the court can now see that too, and it is neither critical of the King nor any less determined to go to war. Once we know that this claim is what provoked the Dauphin's insult, the moment—a few lines earlier—when Henry declared himself "well prepar'd to know the pleasure / Of our faire Cosin Dolphin" seems wonderfully or appallingly insouciant; having heard him add, with regal casualness, "we heare, / Your greeting is from him, not from the King," we might reflect that nobody seems concerned to wait for the King of France's reply. We can also now see why the discreet ambassador offered to deliver the Dauphin's message to the King "sparingly," and why it was politically shrewd of the King to prefer to be insulted before his court. First he can affirm, stirringly, "We are no Tyrant, but a Christian King." Then, once the insult has been received, it—rather than the Archbishop's superfluous *nihil obstat*—can be treated as the incitement to war:

> tell the pleasant Prince, this Mocke of his
> Hath turn'd his balles to Gun-stones, and his soule
> Shall stand sore charged, for the wastefull vengeance
> That shall flye with them: for many a thousand widows
> Shall this his Mocke, mocke out of their deer husbands;
> Mocke mothers from their sonnes, mock Castles down:
> And some are yet ungotten and unborne,
> That shal have cause to curse the *Dolphins* scorne.
> But this lyes all within the will of God,
> To whom I do appeale, and in whose name
> Tel you the *Dolphin*, I am comming on,
> To venge me as I may, and to put forth
> My rightfull hand in a wel-hallow'd cause.
> So get you hence in peace: And tell the *Dolphin*,
> His Jest will savour but of shallow wit,
> When thousands weepe more then did laugh at it.
>
> (lines 281–96)

Henry's adroitness in providing himself with retrospective justifications for what he has already determined to do is characteristic; we will see it again when Henry makes the slaughter of the boys a justification for the order he has already given, to cut the French prisoners' throats. The speech to the ambassadors is another powerful imaginative summons to consider how the horrors of war will devastate the lives of so many, including those who "are yet ungotten and unborne"; but as soon as the ambassadors leave with that "merry Message," the merry Harry England can urge his loyal lords to "omit no happy howre" in preparing for "this faire Action."

Henry and his army will already be at Harfleur when we learn, in the Chorus's prologue to Act 3, that

> th'Embassador from the French comes back,
> Tells *Harry,* That the King doth offer him,
> *Katherine* his Daughter, and with her to Dowrie,
> Some petty and unprofitable Dukedomes.
> The offer likes not: and the nimble Gunner
> With Lynstock now the divellish Cannon touches,
>   *Alarum, and Chambers goe off.*
> And down goes all before them. Still be kind.
> (lines 29–34)

And here, once again, the dramatic sequence exposes troubling questions that the Chorus's official hagiography doesn't acknowledge, let alone consider. Those critics (like Leonard Tennenhouse) who suppose that the marriage to Katherine is the crucial "article" in the English attempt to dominate France all too often fail to notice how Henry could have achieved that merely by accepting the King of France's offer—without risking his soldiers' lives and the nation's safety, and without making "such waste in briefe mortalitie." Characteristically, the play includes the evidence for this damaging line of argument, but without ever suggesting that Henry himself ever considers that rushing to war might have been imprudent or wrong; Shakespeare's Henry seems no less convinced than Holinshed's that he is "prosecuting his iust title," "without all danger of Gods displeasure or perill of soul." No less characteristically, the dramatic sequence is exposing the Chorus's loyally royal version of history to scrutiny: just as we see how the Chorus's rousing "down goes all before them" is followed by a scene showing the English army in retreat, we see what is unthinking in the Chorus's simple, too automatic assumption that this mirror of Christian kings is right to dismiss the French king's attempt to prevent war.

Of course, to say "we see" begs a question: not everybody does see, or would have seen, what is there to be seen. Yet we can be perfectly sure that the play's (various) subversive implications were not lost on some members of the original audience—precisely because the Elizabethan audience wasn't a monolithic entity, as old historicists liked to suppose.[25] The representational complexities in this first act suggest a sure knowledge of how mixed that audience's responses would be: the play plays to—sifts, and explores—such differences, and it is a measure of the power of that extraordinary second scene that the responses of individual spectators are also likely to be mixed or divided. To take one instance: once we are at last in a position to see how the King has been several steps ahead of Canterbury, do we approve or disapprove? Given the detonating force of the ambassador's revelation on our sense of all that we have seen so far, it is perfectly possible that we will be more engaged by other issues. It is also possible that we will be both relieved that the king—or, shifting the emphasis, the theatrical protagonist—is too clever to be used, and uneasy that Henry as prince and king is so adept at using others and exploiting any occasion. Much depends on whether the actor playing Canterbury is more or less formidable; on whatever we are bringing to the show, in our own attitude to the (Catholic) church and ecclesiastical politicians, or to the horrors of war, or to the French; and on our intellectual adequacy to issues raised by Canterbury's speech on the Salic law. The challenge to think is directly related to the play's refusal to tell us what to think.

As for the original audiences, we can be sure that they included some who agreed with Michael Williams, along with others who did not; those whose approval or disapproval of Henry's French expeditions reflected their attitude to the contemporary French, Spanish, and Irish expeditions; those who admired the way in which Henry forbids looting, and those who glumly observed the workings of a double code that allows only the well-born their pickings; those who knew from their reading of the chronicles what really happened after the surrender of Harfleur,[26] and others who hadn't read the chronicles or couldn't read; those severe "morallers" who thought the king right to make no exception for Bardolph and Nym, and those who were disgusted by such glacial firmness; those who were as patriotic as the Chorus, and those who were terrified of being conscripted and forcefully wrenched from their families and livelihoods; those who were profiting from the contemporary wars—from monopolies, patents, and other court perks—and those who were being crushed by the ever-increasing burden of taxation during the last years of Eliza-

beth's reign (when, to take one example, the Irish establishment cost
nearly two million pounds); those groundlings who felt a bit lost and
fidgety while Canterbury is insisting that "the Art and Practique part
of Life, / Must be the Mistresse to this Theorique," elders who nodded
sagely, and clever irreverent young men from the Inns of Court who
reflected that, far from showing how praxis is the mistress to theory,
Canterbury's own actions, words and motives show how theoretical
principle is a willing whore to practical self-interest.

Here it is worth noticing that the Chorus's dramatic function is
sometimes to remind the audience of pressing perplexities and provokingly contemporary issues that the Chorus would prefer to deny
or ignore. So, although the play might seem to be prudently silent on
the dangerously topical matter of conscription, the loyally flagrant lie
in the second Chorus is also a dramatically devious reminder that
both Henrician and Elizabethan actualities were very, very different:

> Now all the Youth of England are on fire,
> And silken Dalliance in the Wardrobe lyes:
> Now thrive the Armorers, and Honors thought
> Reignes solely in the breast of every man.
> (Prol. 2, lines 1–4)

As a stirring fantasy this is superb; the Chorus similarly asks, in Prologue 3 who "will not follow / These cull'd and choyse-drawne Cavaliers to France." Yet Edward Powell's study of criminal justice in
Henry's reign gives a somewhat different picture, for instance when
Powell remarks that "the muster-roll of the earl of Arundel's retinue
at the siege of Harfleur . . . reads like a catalogue of those indicted
in king's bench."[27] The historical Henry V followed Edward I's practice of giving criminals, including rapists and murderers, pardons
(and military training) in return for military service. Of course
Shakespeare's Henry leads a very different kind of army—if we are
to judge from "Once more unto the breach" or the Crispin's Day
speech; but then Henry's speech before Harfleur summons a much
more familiar and terrifying vision of the "blind and bloody Souldier"
whose "licentious Wickednesse" can only with difficulty be restrained
from "Murther, Spoyle, and Villany." As for culled and choice-drawn
cavaliers, Elizabethans were likely to know what the studies by C. G.
Cruikshank and Lindsay Boynton amply confirm: although an Eliza-

bethan army would usually include a few "gentlemen volunteers" (not all of them on fire with honor's thought) and a few ordinary volunteers who joined up as privates, by far the largest part of the army consisted of conscripts of two kinds—honest men taken away from steady employment (which was not often waiting for them when and if they returned), and "the unemployed, rogues, and vagabonds."[28] Cruikshank's study concluded with this somber account of those years in which the second tetralogy was written and staged:

> The nation became more and more war-weary. . . . The evasion of military service by one device or another became more frequent. Burghley sadly exclaimed that the country was weary of the ceaseless expenditure of money and life in foreign service. The Privy Council became apprehensive at the hostile attitude of the people. By the end of the century it was well-nigh impossible to raise money for troops. (283)

Peter Clark's magnificently detailed study of English provincial society presents an even more somber picture of social and economic crisis.[29] After the returns on land had been driven down in the early 1590s by unusually bountiful harvests, a run of ever more disastrous harvests produced a crisis in the food supply; increases in recruitment, taxation, and indirect levies like patents and purveyance all contributed to the severe economic recession. There was a great increase in crime, vagrancy, poverty, and disease, and severe outbreaks of bubonic plague drove the mortality levels still higher. The government could neither resolve nor delegate all the problems posed by the destitute families of dead soldiers and by the returning soldiers who were maimed, diseased, and unable or unwilling to find employment. Clark's account of town suburbs that were infested with emaciated soldiers raiding houses and terrifying the inhabitants reminds us that, whatever his medieval credentials, Pistol was a thoroughly contemporary figure and not so bad as some. Yet in all this misery a voice was heard: "Now all the Youth of England are on fire, / And silken Dalliance in the Wardrobe lyes."

This is to say that the Chorus has his work cut out, in relation to both audience and play—and, up to a point, knows it. His conviction that everybody *should* respond as he does to the inspiring "Story" about "the Mirror of all Christian Kings" if only the play can do justice to the "great Accompt" is, on a sympathetic view, naive but decent. On a less sympathetic view it resembles the conviction of so many politicians that opposition to their policies cannot be opposition to their policies but must be attributable to some reparable break-down in public relations or "presentation." Having real horses is not the answer, although those who admire Branagh's jejune travesty are unlikely to see that joke. But then the Chorus also betrays intuitive anxieties that, as often happens, are more obviously justified than his passionate convictions: he is quite right to fear that the dramatic representation won't be adequate to his view of history, and right to fear that the mixed audience's "imaginary forces" may not function in a docile, unremittingly obedient fashion as mere "Cyphers to this great Accompt." When the Chorus worries that the play's make-be-lieve won't be adequate to the glorious history, the play's eruptive, complicating energies break in and expose the element of make-be-lieve (or make-them-believe) in the Chorus's own attempts to collectiv-ize and control the audience's responses, as well as the inadequacy of the Chorus's approach to the problems of "doing" history. What the Chorus would unite the play divides: so, after each eloquent choric attempt to bond the audience in a single, stirringly eloquent vision, the play uncovers those divisions and conflicts of principle, interest, or sympathy which the Chorus would prefer to edit or suppress and which speak to and explore the differences and divisions within the audience itself. So far as the audience is concerned, the Chorus thinks like Greenblatt while the play behaves like Brecht.

In Prologue 2 the Chorus's troubles begin even before he has fin-ished. His dream of England ("O England!") as a "little Body with a mightie Heart," in which "Honors thought / Reignes solely in the breast of every man" collides with the facts (some values are more fact-laden), while the hasty explanation that the "Traitors" were se-duced by "the gilt of France" is later contradicted by Cambridge's own dark claim that "for me, the Gold of France did not seduce" but was merely another "motive, / The sooner to effect what I in-tended"—that is, the Yorkist attempt to make Edmund Mortimer king (2.2.155–57). Before that, we see Pistol and Nym resolving to go to France not from thoughts of "honour" but from the hope that "profits will accrue" (2.1.107)—just as the Chorus's wistfully rhetorical ques-tion in Prologue 3, "who is he, whose Chin is but enrich't / With one appearing Hayre, that will not follow / These cull'd and choyse-drawn Cavaliers?", is no less wistfully answered by the Boy's feelings about the war in which he will soon be slaughtered: "Would I were in an Ale-house in London, I would give all my fame for a Pot of Ale, and safety" (3.2.10). Such effects douse the Chorus's noble dream with cold splashes of reality.

But then, although the relation between whatever the Chorus says and what the play shows or suggests is so challengingly interrogative, this doesn't mean that the Chorus's thoroughly pro-Henry views only make an anti-Henry view more compelling. The "Henriad" nowhere suggests that any of the rebel leaders and factions are less inclined than the monarchs to identify their own interests with those of the common weal.[30] This might prompt bleak thoughts about power and history, or a more positively pragmatic sense of Henry's relative merits, but it doesn't make an anti-Henry view more compelling; if anything, it suggests why indulging a narrowly characterological judgment is simplistic and reductive, a form of social unrealism that (like Joyce's Mrs. Mooney in *Dubliners*) deals "with moral problems as a cleaver deals with meat."

The final act brings another, more perplexing but climactic collision between the Chorus and the play. The Chorus is historically correct when he reminds "those that have not read the Story" that Henry and his army returned to London after Agincourt, and that five years passed between the battle of Agincourt and the Treaty of Troyes, which is represented in the play's final scene. To the extent that this protest against "abridgement" seems in place, in a straightforwardly historical sense, it might appear to be an unequivocal example of the way in which—as Herbert Lindenberger assumes—"Shakespeare awkwardly excuses himself" through the Chorus, recognizing that "the modest theatrical piece he has created can at best supply a few hints about the glory it purports to depict."[31] For A. P. Rossiter, who wrote so superbly about "ambivalence" in the history plays, *Henry V* is an exception, a "propaganda-play on National Unity"—the sort of play the Chorus would certainly prefer; Sigurd Burckhardt similarly supposes that in this play Shakespeare "knowingly chooses a partial and partisan clarity" so that we hear his "epic," rather than his "dramatic," voice—which, once again, is just what the Chorus would wish, although he certainly wouldn't agree with Burckhardt that this amounts to taking "a rest."[32] Yet when the Chorus asks "such as have read" the "Story" to

> admit th'excuse
> Of time, of numbers, and due course of things,
> Which cannot in their huge and proper life,
> Be here presented.
>
> (Prol. 5, lines 3–6)

something more complicated, and deviously intricate, is happening, which should—if we ourselves are not taking a rest—render far more suspect the idea of a self-deprecatory Shakespeare apologizing through the Chorus.

First, we might notice how the Chorus's use of the word "Story" unleashes ironies he certainly does not intend. As a late Elizabethan who prides himself on his knowledge of history, he takes for granted that his own "king's-eye" version of the "Story" is the truth. This precludes any concern with the way in which a historical narrative is constructed and shaped, like any fictional story, by the narrator's sense of how best to make sense of events and lives. Just as the Chorus is entirely untroubled by historiographical doubts, he is entirely innocent of any *positive* conception of dramatic and narrative form, and complains about what the play cannot do without ever registering what it does do. Pistol would have no place in his "great Accompt," but then, far from considering what the "low" characters and episodes are doing in the play's version of the "Story," the Chorus never even acknowledges their existence: he always speaks about the play he so nervously inhabits as though they weren't there, and as though he himself weren't a part of it either. Here, as ever, he places himself between the play and its audience and apart from both, while worrying whether either will measure up to his "Story." Clearly he is apart from the dramatic action, which spans the period from April 30, 1414 to May 20, 1420; Fluellen is the amateur historian within the play's action, and still another fervently loyal, take-me-to-your-leader historian. So, as Anthony Brennan nicely observes, Fluellen provides "a comic parody within the plot of the homage to tradition that the Chorus presents outside it."[33] But to reflect on the relation between the Chorus and Fluellen as amateur historians is to respond to the play's very different way of presenting the "Story" and to see how, although the Chorus is apart from the play's action, he is very much a part of its dramatic thinking. Seeing himself as a judiciously detached and wholly authoritative commentator who can appraise, correct, and (in his own account of the king's triumphal return) supplement the play, he cannot see how he is assimilated into it, or how the play's irony enfolds his own nonironic use of the word "Story." When he apologizes for the play's inability to present things in their "huge and proper life" the play eats him, smiles expansively, and suggests why his own ideal version of the "Story" is so *small* and proper.

His version is more like Branagh's, not just in having real horses and more than four or five vile and ragged foils, but in altogether suppressing scenes like 5.1—which, as Branagh himself explains, isn't even very funny.[34] The Chorus wants a linear, annalistic account of what the high and mighty did from one year to the next, which keeps closer to the chronicles while carefully excluding anything like Holinshed's "some say" or "others allege," since such things let on that the "Story" hasn't been universally received as the Truth. Although seemingly unstructured, this ideal version would be forcefully structured or "abridged" by its automatic omissions and "proper" suppressions, and by the Chorus's unwavering assumption that the truth about how it really was—Ranke's *wie es eigentlich gewesen*—can and must be "presented" in a unified and uniformly "high" or "epic" fashion. In the Chorus's terms 5.1 is doubly offensive: the already displeasing, historically inaccurate "abridgement" makes room for another "low" and irrelevant comic scene or side-show thrown in for those groundlings who are incapable of responding to the "Story" like true "Gentles." But in that case what *is* 5.1 doing in Shakespeare's play?

Far from being apologetic, Shakespeare builds in another teasing, wittily defiant provocation. For as soon as the Chorus leaves the stage, 5.1 gives the contrary impression that the army has never left France, that barely any time has passed between 4.8 and 5.1, and that the victorious Henry proceeds directly from the battlefield to the French court. True, the King's final words in Act 4 referred to the return to Calais, then England; but that token gesture toward getting the "Story" right, in the Chorus's sense, has little dramatic weight if set against the impression of continuity. Act 5 abruptly opens in "*France. The English camp,*" and in the course of a further conversation between Fluellen and Gower, which we pick up as the latter remarks, "Nay, that's right: but why weare you youre Leeke to day? / S. *Davies* day is past." Fluellen replies, "There is occasions and causes why and wherefore in all things," and explains that he is looking for "that rascally, scauld, beggerly, lowsie, pragging Knave *Pistoll,* which you and your selfe, and all the World, know to be no petter then a fellow, looke you now, of no merits" (5.1–5.8). It is at once clear that this is unfinished business. In 4.1 Pistol had assured the disguised king that he would "knock" Fluellen's "Leeke about his Pate upon S. *Davies* day," and now the angry Fluellen reports the insult he received "yesterday," when Pistol "prings me pread and sault yesterday, looke you, and bids me eate my Leeke: it was in a place where I could not breed no contention with him; but I will be so bold as to weare it in my Cap till I see him once againe, and then I will tell him a little piece of my desires" (lines 9–13). We have just heard the Chorus telling us of the *years* that passed between 4.8 and 5.1, but, as we readjust to the play's quite different way of telling the "Story," who counts the number of times St. Davy's day must have passed?

Here, instead of supposing that Shakespeare is "awkwardly excusing himself" by ventriloquizing through the Chorus, we should notice how he is engineering this exuberant collision between the Chorus and the play's different ways of "doing" history. So far as the "abridgement" of time is concerned the Chorus is right, and 5.1 is wholly irrelevant to the kind of play or dramatic "chronicle" this play makes its Chorus want and expect. Why conclude the play and the second tetralogy in such a fashion? Dr. Johnson was famously dismissive, commenting that "the poet's matter failed him in the fifth act, and he was glad to fill it up with whatever he could get."[35] Yet an alternative possibility, to which that climactic, finely engineered collision points, is to consider the fifth act as a highly organized design or poetic-dramatic conceit, in which the two final scenes make up an ironic diptych of "low" and "high" conclusions framed by the Chorus's protesting prologue and still more discontented epilogue. Act 5.1 may not be very funny in Branagh's sense, but it is a remarkably witty and disconcerting example of Shakespeare's dramatic rhyming.

Dramatic "Rhyming"

Dramatic "rhyming" is very important in Shakespeare's dramatic thinking: it shows how he works to integrate and "musicalize" his

poetic-dramatic material. Usually the rhyme is "off" in some dramatically pointed or provoking way: there is enough of a resemblance to
set us thinking about differences, which may be far more important.
So, for example, it is by now a critical commonplace to observe that
Hamlet presents the differing responses of three sons and a daughter
to the loss of their fathers, so that our reactions to Fortinbras, Laertes,
and Ophelia figure in our thinking about Hamlet; or to observe that
Banquo resists the temptation in the witches' prophecy whereas Macbeth does not; or that the generational conflict in *King Lear* involves
Lear in one kind of blindness, Gloster in another. These examples are
enough to suggest why the familiar and related concept of "double
plotting" is awkwardly restricting: the analogical relationships in question don't always come in pairs, and the relationship may be less sustained than the word "plotting" suggests.

It is often hard to tell whether an unexpected but provoking, quizzing rhyme is merely local and sportive, or has a more sustained
significance. In *The Tempest* it is clear enough that there is a structural,
contrapuntal relationship between the "low" conspiracy of Caliban,
Stephano, and Trinculo to overthrow Prospero and the "high" conspiracy of Anthonio and Sebastian to kill Alonso; and, if we listen to
poetic drama, it should also be clear that the rhyming of these "low"
and "high" conspiracies is complicated in poetic-dramatic terms by
the fact that Caliban doesn't speak low prose, like Stephano and Trinculo. Moreover, his verse differs significantly from that of other characters, notably Prospero: Caliban's tactile, earthy, sensuously concrete
or violent verse shows how he does indeed know, love, and relish every
fertile inch of that island, which Prospero will leave without regret
once it has served his imperious purpose. But then what should we
make of the quite unexpected rhyming between Miranda's and Caliban's adoration of the first strangers they have seen?

In 2.2 we see the drunken Caliban kneeling to his "brave God,"
while defying Prospero's authority by determining to bear him "no
more Stickes"; "Ile kisse thy foot. Ile swear my selfe thy Subject," he
adoringly affirms, prompting the disregarded Trinculo to comment,
"A most rediculous Monster, to make a wonder of a poore drunkard."
Then in the next scene, where the onstage blocking could also emphasize the unexpected dramatic rhyming, we hear Miranda "pray" Ferdinand to let her "beare youre Logges the while," while she defies

Prospero's authority by begging Ferdinand to marry her; "Ile be your servant / Whether you will or no," she adoringly affirms.

Early in 3.1, when Miranda's defiance of her father's wishes was still limited to making this "visitation" and wanting to bear logs, the concealed Prospero's comment was scoffing and apparently angry: "Poor worme thou art infected" (3.1.31). That remark underlined the dramatic rhyme, for it was no less applicable to the "infected" Caliban, who had been offering Stephano the devotion and service he had once given to Prospero. But when Miranda carries her rebellion two stages further, breaking her father's "hest" by revealing her name and defying his "precepts" by "too wildly" confessing her love, Prospero's next comment is ecstatic rather than angry, and now underlines the *difference* between the "rare" Miranda's situation and Caliban's:

> Faire encounter
> Of two most rare affections: heavens raine grace
> On that which breeds betweene 'em.
> (3.1.74–76)

Murderous rebellion is what was *breeding* at the end of the preceding scene, which finished with Caliban singing "'Ban ban' Cacalyban / Has a new Master, get a new Man" and exulting in the "freedome" he thinks this new service brings. Miranda's own defiance of her father's authority culminates in another kind of freedom as she sets aside "cunning" in favor of "plaine and holy innocence" (not her father's forte) and boldly proposes to Ferdinand—while also vowing that if he refuses to have her as "wife" she will "die your maid," and that if he will not have her as "fellow" she will be "your servant / Whether you will or no." She too wants to have a new master, even if she cannot have the man; but this culminating rebellion prompts Prospero's pregnant, ecstatically approving comment that although he cannot be so "glad of this" as those to whom it is a surprise, his "rejoycing / At nothing can be more" (92–95). This looks forward to his grim response to Miranda's wonder at a "brave new world"—"'Tis new to thee" (5.1.184)—just as it looks back to his earlier excitement and relief when the lovers were first drawn to each other: "It goes on, I see, / As my soul prompts it. Spirit, fine spirit, I'll free thee" (1.2.420–21).

In 3.1 there is far too much evidence of a design—Shakespeare's as well as Prospero's—for us to suppose that the Caliban-Miranda rhyme is merely sportive; and, since so much of the play's thinking goes on in and through such analogical relationships and progressions, not noticing them is like listening to a sonata for its tunes without any interest in what the tunes have to do with one another. But in this instance we might speak of counterpointed rhymes, since the dramatic rhyming of Caliban and Miranda's situations is developed in relation to another rhyming contrast between Ferdinand and Caliban as willing and unwilling log-bearers. The intertwining of the two rhymes produces a teasingly intricate and suggestive knot of contrasts between willing and forced "service," or self-commitment and enslavement. Yet to call this suggestive is very much easier than saying just what it suggests, and polemical pro-Prospero and anti-Prospero readings, like those I mentioned in my prologue, won't unravel this knot, although they try to cut through it.

For example, Ferdinand is willing to "endure" the "sore injunction" of removing and piling up "Some thousands of these Logs" *because* this "wooden slaverie" will be temporary and will win him his "sweet Mistris": as he tells her, "for your sake / Am I this patient Loggeman." But here the log-bearing rhyme also suggests why it is brutally unreasonable to think the worse of Caliban because *he* cannot see and say, as the "noble" Ferdinand can, that "Some kindes of baseness / Are nobly undergon" or that "poore matters / Point to rich ends." Caliban has no hope of having Miranda, unless by forcing her submission, nor has he, like Ariel, as well as Ferdinand, been given any grounds for thinking that there will be some limit on, or rich end to, his own forced submission. Because Prospero and Miranda could not survive on the island without him, Caliban can only expect a lifetime of "wooden slaverie" and celibacy (having to lug that log too) for as long as Prospero is alive; his violent fantasy of "paunching" Prospero with a "stake" gives a comically sinister twist to the log-bearing conceit, but in a (murderously) logical way. But then this also suggests how the interest of the poetic-dramatic situation has much to do with its apparent *intractability:* Prospero can no more be expected to restore the island to Caliban, acquiescing to his own death and his daughter's rape, than Caliban can be expected to submit willingly to his own enslavement. Neither can "prosper," unless the other is enslaved or put down.

The knot of dramatic rhymes is far too intricate and unsettling to support any polemical, anti-Prospero account of the play's "colonial discourse" or the polemical readings that admire Shakespeare for presenting Caliban as a "natural" slave or as a fuzzy-wuzzy "bound by his nature to service." Caliban's longing to serve Stephano—his capacity for devotion—is a disquietingly ironic replay of his earlier submission to the man who gave him water with berries in it but took the island. And a comparison with Lear suggests how difficult it is to disentangle politics and erotics: if one difference is that Prospero rejoices when his daughter so completely surrenders herself to the man she loves, another difference is that Prospero's willing surrender of his own daughter is also a means of regaining his kingdom. Instead of working in some single direction to deliver some simple, reducible point, the intricately complex rhyming in these scenes brings out what is—absorbingly, excitingly—intractable in the dramatic situation. But then, to see that is to see more than any of the play's characters, including Prospero: in refusing to see how his usurpation of Caliban's island rhymes with the usurpation of his own kingdom, and in refusing to countenance any idea that Caliban has a case, Prospero is regarding one term of the intractable problem as the solution to the problem.

Let us now compare the way—or ways!—in which the first "low" scene in *Henry V* rhymes with the preceding scene. That had finished with Henry in high spirits, telling his lords to "omit no happy howre" in preparing for the "faire Action" of war. Court and church unite behind their king, and now this happy mood spreads through and unites the whole nation—or so the Chorus tells us, offering his late sixteenth-century appraisal of the mood of early fifteenth-century England with the confidence that is the reward of his diligently uncritical study of the chronicles: "Now all the Youth of England are on fire," and "Honors thought / Reignes solely in the breast of every man." Eager to get on with his "Story," the Chorus concludes, "Unto Southampton do we shift our Scene". But instead the scene is now transported, ungently, to London, where *Corporall* Nym and *Lieutenant* Bardolph are discussing Nym's quarrel with Pistol; and now, in the play's very different way of telling the "Story," there is a sharp descent from the grand quarrel about vast amounts of money and who should possess France to a sordid quarrel about petty cash and who should possess Mistress Quickly (and the Boar's Head tavern).

In another and elaborately disconcerting rhyme, Pistol's first extended explosion not only parodies the *conjuratio* in the service of exorcism but also sounds suspiciously reminiscent of Henry's retort to the Dauphin:

> Solus, egregious dog? O Viper vile;
> The solus in thy most mervailous face,
> The solus in thy teeth, and in thy throate,
> And in thy hatefull Lungs, yea in thy Maw perdy;
> And which is worse, within thy nastie mouth.
> I do retort the solus in thy bowels,
> For I can take, and *Pistols* cocke is up,
> And flashing fire will follow.
>
> (2.1.45–53)

The Folio prints this as prose, and Alexander Pope was the first editor to show that Pistol's fustian is always verse, if not poetry—until 5.1, when Fluellen not only breaks his head but beats the verse out of him too. Here, as in *The Tempest*, the presence of a verse-speaker complicates the "low" scenes, and all the more when Pistol is trying to do what the King does so much better. We might also notice that this speech contains the only one of the scene's several references to throats that isn't also a reference to throat-cutting; in such talk the Pinteresque Nym is in a class of his own, but if his warning that "men may sleepe, and they may have their throats about them at that time, and some say, knives have edges" is most charged with Mack-the-Knife menace, Pistol's "Couple a gorge" is the most obviously prophetic. Eventually this low quarrel is patched up, like that in the preceding scene, when a financial deal is agreed upon and giddy minds are busied with foreign quarrels: the "three sworne brothers"—whom the Boy later describes as "sworne Brothers in filching" (3.2.44)—prepare to leave for France, in the hope that "profits will accrue." That expectation isn't at all what the Chorus had in mind when he said "now sits Expectation in the Ayre"; but then, although nobody describes Henry and his Lancastrian lords as "sworne Brothers in filching," this is one perspective on dynastic claims that these dramatic rhymes open up.

But only one, since these dramatic rhymes—like those in *The Tempest*—don't only work in one direction and can be heard in different ways. They are not heard at all by those who think the "low" scenes provide comic relief, or a side-show with no bearing on the main action. The rhymes are at least being heard, but in a partial or selec-

tive way, by those who would assimilate them to the polemical alternatives of the "either/or" debate. But here (my thesis in this book) the
play can help us to listen to one another and to ourselves, when we
compare notes and make out connections between what we hadn't
heard and what we want to hear. What do we hear in Pistol? In Phillip
Mallett's polemical anti-Henry reading, which is acute within those
limits, "Pistol's 'O braggart vile and damned furious wight' (2.1.60)
provides an appropriate gloss on Henry's threats to the Dauphin."[36]
But Anthony Brennan hears the rhyme differently when he suggests
that "by providing this parody of heroism Shakespeare induces us to
believe the more in the genuine heroism of Henry," and observes that
"there are many scenes which carry on a ribald commentary on the
glorious action, but Shakespeare carefully dissociates the king from
all of them, despite his former proclivities, until late in the play."[37]
Indeed, Brennan is hearing a different rhyme, since he argues that
Pistol is rhymed against the Chorus, as the other "extreme of the
spectrum of ideas on patriotism," where the "king holds the balance"
and "cannot be the embodiment of patriotic zeal because he is faced
with the human responses which separate men from their ideals"
(179). Nonetheless, in Brennan's reading as in more polemical pro-
Henry readings, the "parody" works to expose the difference between
Pistol's bogus heroism and the royal real thing; in anti-Henry readings Pistol exposes Henry. Yet both kinds of polemical reading work
from the premise that there is only one right response to Henry;
then, when they attend to the dramatic rhymes, they find them confirming the rightness of that undivided response in a gratifying way.
That is, the rhymes tell us what to think of Henry if we already know
what we think of Henry. But if our first responses to Henry in 1.2
are already divided, neither simply approving nor simply disapproving, we are more likely to hear how the dramatic rhymes in the
play's first "low" scene work in unsettlingly complicated ways, like
those in *The Tempest*, carry the play's dramatic thinking forward and
startle us into new or different ways of seeing, instead of providing
merely confirmatory variations on an unchanging pro-Henry or anti-
Henry theme. The exploratory interest, in this play's dramatic rhymes
and analogical progressions as in those of *The Tempest*, isn't restricted
to whatever we might think about Henry or Prospero in preparing
the moralistic equivalent of a school report or testimonial. In this first
"low" scene, as in the last, the "rhyming" is interrogative, rather than

coercive, so that we can recognize some overlap between dynastic claims and the hope that "profits will accrue" without having to suppose that Henry has no more concern with "right and conscience" than Pistol.

Indeed, that last remark does Pistol some injustice, if we notice how little *his* reason for quarreling with Fluellen has to do with what prompts Fluellen's quarrel with Pistol. Pistol first gives Fluellen the "figo" (or Renaissance equivalent of a "fuck you") in 3.6, when Fluellen flatly refuses to intervene on Bardolph's behalf. After this, the outraged Pistol takes every opportunity to insult Fluellen, but in this case at least there is nothing knavish or self-interested: Pistol is trying to save a friend, and is genuinely upset. His outrage is misdirected, in that Bardolph's fate is sealed not by Fluellen or by Exeter when he sentences him, but by Henry's order that looters must be executed; but here the brilliant integration of "high" and "low" material delivers a pregnant contrast—between Pistol, the unlovely bully who is so recklessly angered and upset by the fate of a friend, but continues to regard Henry indulgently as a "lovely Bully" with "a Heart of Gold" (4.1.48,44), and Henry himself, who registers no response when Fluellen asks about "one *Bardolph,* if your Majestie knows the man" but impassively declares, "Wee would have all such offendors so cut off."

As for Fluellen's quarrel with Pistol, this too commences in 3.6, but for significantly different reasons. The scene begins with Fluellen's astonishing report of the part played by Pistol in the important action on the bridge: "There is an aunchient Lieutenant there at the Pridge, I thinke in my very conscience hee is as valiant a man as *Marke Anthony,* and hee is a man of no estimation in the World, but I did see him doe as gallant service" (3.6.12–16). If we recall Henry's all too automatic reference to "None else of name" and the chronicles' indifference to men "of no estimation in the World" (whose world?), we could welcome this corrective tribute to someone in the ranks—if only Fluellen were not so obviously mistaken about *this* "man of no estimation." But then, how is this obvious? The conventional view, which we soon hear from Gower, is that Fluellen *must* be mistaken, since Pistol is a conventional type or stereotype: the braggart soldier who (as the Boy puts it) "breaks words, and keeps whole weapons." Yet that doesn't explain Fluellen's mistake. Unlike Gower, Fluellen has just come from the bridge and is reporting what he "did see"; Pistol is not merely a conventional type, and even the greatest coward might show some mettle if cornered on a bridge by somebody intent on killing him. A likelier and far more suggestive explanation comes immediately after Pistol's furious departure; it is that Fluellen's idea of what he "did see" before him was based (like Le Fer's) on what he *heard.* When Gower recalls that Pistol is "an arrant counterfeit Rascal," Fluellen indignantly but revealingly protests, "Ile assure you, a utt'red as prave words at the Pridge, as you shall see in a Summers day"— happily reenacting that confusion between what is seen and heard. The unconvinced Gower responds with his long scornful account, or "character," of Pistol, and at one point makes Pistol sound all too like Fluellen: "such fellowes are perfit in the Great Commanders Names, and they will learn you by rote where Services were done." Gower's conclusion is witheringly condescending: "you must learne to know such slanders of the age, or else you may be marvellously mistooke."

Once Fluellen himself is convinced that his own judgement was deficient, he becomes furious not with himself, or Gower, but with Pistol: "I tell you what, Captain *Gower:* I doe perceive hee is not the man that he would gladly make shew to the World hee is: if I finde a hole in his Coat, I will tell him my minde: hearke you, the King is comming, and I must speake with him from the Pridge" (3.6.82–86). Fluellen is now determined to avenge himself on the man who had been the occasion for this humiliating warning about being "marvel-lously mistooke." And when the King asks Fluellen about the action on the bridge, our amateur historian pays eloquent tribute to the gallant Duke of Exeter but makes no mention of Pistol or any other common soldier—until he mentions the one man who was "lost," not in the splendid action but because he "is like to be executed for rob-bing a Church," and stealing a "pax." This rich joke about how history gets reported, or made, is nicely rounded off if we know that the historical duke of Exeter played no part in the action on the bridge.

The origins of this "low" quarrel matter because the third and fourth acts interweave three rhyming quarrels, and give Fluellen a significant role in all three. In Act 3 this "low" quarrel is set in counter-point with the "high" quarrel with France; this setting is further com-plicated in the fourth act by the "high"/"low" quarrel between the King and a common soldier; Act 5 then brings the first two quarrels to their seemingly separate conclusions—reasserting, in its final ironic diptych, that separation of "high" and "low" the play so vigorously interrogates. In 3.6 the interweaving of "high" and "low" is so astonishingly witty, resourceful, and unsettling that it is hard to keep up with the ways in which each variation, rhyme, or analogical progression bears on the others. For example, the irony of Bardolph's being the only casualty is a further progression in the unsettling exploration of the difference between hoping that "profits will accrue" and pressing dynastic claims, and of the contrast between the rewards of a short-lived royal triumph and what the surviving "low" gain from this war—that is, nothing, unless we think Michael Williams accepts the king's crowns while spurning Fluellen's shilling. The scene also develops that unsettling contrast between Pistol's and Henry's response to Bardolph's fate. A different contrast—between what provokes Pistol to quarrel with Fluellen and what provokes the amateur historian within the action to quarrel with Pistol—bears on the issue of why the "low" figure so largely in this play and scarcely at all in the kind of history the Chorus likes to read and wants to see staged in a more "proper" fashion.

The Chorus never doubts the difference between "high" and "low"; but then, in a richly ironic way, what provokes the private "high"/"low" quarrel between the King and Michael Williams is the way in which Williams insists on the absolute gulf between the King and "us." Throughout the play Henry has not spoken with a common soldier, until his accidental and unwanted encounters with Pistol and Williams in 4.1. At that point, he is not angered by Williams's calmly skeptical response to the report that the King said he would not be ransomed: "I, hee said so to make us fight chearefully: but when our throats are cut, hee may be ransom'd, and wee ne'er the wiser." What so angers the King is the nettled Williams's vigorous insistence that to prattle of whether one trusts a monarch's word is "foolish," when the subject has no way of making the King who breaks his word "pay": "You pay him then: that's a perillous shot out of an Elder Gunne, that a poore and a private displeasure can doe against a Monarch: you may as well goe about to turne the Sunne to ice, with fanning in his face with a Peacocks feather: You'le never trust his word after; come, 'tis a foolish saying" (4.1.197–202). Quite simply, the "low" have no recourse. Williams's realism cuts through the Chorus's loyal variation in Prologue 4, on the Harry myth—the King whose "liberall Eye" gives "Largesse universall, like the Sunne," to "mean and gentle" alike—and does so not by being less loyal, but by opposing sentimental fervor with uncomplaining sanity. But such realism is "too round" (or unceremonious) for the King who has just insisted, engagingly, that "the King is but a man"—"his Ceremonies layd by, in his Nakednesse he appeares but a man"—but never ceases to assume that "Every Subjects Dutie is the Kings." The loyal, unassumingly pious Williams takes that for granted too, but as a fact of life; he expects to die soon, in discharging that duty, but reserves the right not to be "foolish"—either by assuming that his King's "Cause" must be "just, and his Quarrel honorable," or by presuming that it makes any difference what any "low" subject or "Servant" (in the King's analogy) thinks.

Fluellen is "foolish" on both these counts, and in 4.7, when he is drawn into the third of this act's rhyming quarrels, we see how he has learned nothing from his first bitter experience of being "marvellously mistooke": the only consequence of that humiliation is his own quarrel with Pistol. So, in the first part of this craftily constructed scene we hear his ludicrous comparisons between Monmouth and Macedon: Henry is "Alexander the Pig" as Pistol was once a "Mark Anthony." Next Montjoy appears, humbly asking permission to "wander ore this bloody field"—and "sort our Nobles from our common men": those who think that concern to be peculiarly French think like Fluellen rather than Williams, and will make nothing of Henry's response to the roll of casualties: "None else of name" (4.8.105). Then we hear the King asking Fluellen whether he thinks it "fit" for Williams to "keep his oath"; he receives a characteristically prompt reply: "Hee is a Craven and a Villaine else, and't please your Majesty in my conscience." What if "his enemy is a Gentleman of great sort quite from the answer of his degree"? Again the reply is prompt: "Though he be as good a Jentleman as the divel is, as Lucifer and Belzebub himselfe, it is necessary (looke your Grace) that he keepe and his vow and his oath" (and more of the same). What follows is rather like that moment in the final scene of *Measure for Measure* when Escalus is eager to help rack a friar "joint by joint" for criticizing authority, whether or not the criticism is true; when the friar turns out to be the disguised Duke himself the case is different. Once it becomes clear that Michael Williams's "enemy" is not Lucifer or a gentleman but the King himself—albeit a king who *appears* "but a man" when "Ceremonies" are "layd by"—Fluellen's judgment and "conscience" bow low: "And please your Majestie, let his Neck answere for it, if there is any Marshall Law in the World" (4.8.43–44). Here the only thing to recall his eagerly delivered judgments in the preceding scene is that automatic phrase, "And please your Majestie." But then, as soon as it is clear that his Majesty is pleased to give Williams money, the play's amateur historian can approve the "mettell" of the "fellow," warn him against "quarrels and dissentions," and throw in his "twelve-pence"—which Williams refuses, thereby suggesting how far the "low" can surpass the "high."

All of this gives point to Anthony Brennan's succinct observation, in *Onstage and Offstage Worlds,* that Fluellen provides "a comic parody within the plot of the homage to tradition that the Chorus presents outside it"—perhaps more point than Brennan's own account allows. In the play's final "low" scene Fluellen reappears, wearing a leek rather than the King's glove in his cap, and looking to settle his own vendetta. Now, as this final act's ironic diptych seems to reassert the separation of "high" and "low" by showing how seemingly separate quarrels are seemingly settled, we see Fluellen breaking Pistol's crown with "an English cudgell" as he forces Pistol to swallow the last bit of leek, before we see how the play's other Welshman, "Harry England," forces the King of France to submit to the very last, shaming "article." Pistol, whose companions are now dead—killed by the English, not the French—and who lost his only hope of financial gain when he obediently cut Monsieur Le Fer's throat ("Couple a gorge") is now left with a "broken" and "ploodie" head and "cudgeld scarres" to come. A cudgel is a nasty thing, but although the severity of the beating is clearly indicated in the text this is usually glossed over when the scene is not altogether disregarded by critics or cut by directors who think it not very funny. "Doeth Fortune play the huswife with me now?" laments Pistol (while at least recovering his verse); "Fortune made his Sword," exults the vicariously triumphant Chorus, when the "Starre of England" has finished cudgeling France into submitting to the last article, while surrendering his daughter. As in the first "low" scene, anti-Henry readings can still insist that Pistol is exposing Henry, while the similarly reductive alternative reading insists that the bogus hero is exposed by the genuine hero—and by the amateur historian with a cudgel. The play's other amateur historian has hindsight rather than a cudgel, and does not even acknowledge the existence of a Pistol; but even as the Chorus pronounces "Thus farre," he is despondently recalling that "Fortune" soon played the hussy with Henry too, and "made his England bleed." But that is all the more reason for considering why the only blood shed on stage is Pistol's and, though this is debated, that of the unarmed French prisoners whose throats are cut.

Throughout this section, I have been trying to show how Shakespeare's dramatic "rhymes" integrate the action, even as the rhyming variations work in too many directions to be assimilable to polemical "either/or" readings. This musicalization of the poetic drama's internal relationships prompted glancing comparisons with the sonata form in music, where the developing relationship between different "subjects" *is* the "action." Talk of Shakespearean "subplots" easily becomes misleading, if it implies or assumes that the "subplot" is detached from the "main" plot or action, and develops independently. Our sense of the complex design is distorted by that assumption, and altogether destroyed if we suppose that the "low" scenes are merely there to provide comic relief and can be cut if they seem "unfunny": that is why Branagh's decision to cut 5.1 was uncomprehending vandalism. In *Henry V*, as in *The Tempest*, the developing, contrapuntal relationship between "high" and "low" scenes and perspectives *is* the action—and the *locus* for the play's "dramatic thinking."

Indeed, another musical analogy seems helpful. The typical classical sonata—though not, say, Beethoven's last piano sonata—produces a conventionally satisfying resolution. The ironically rhymed, and ironically framed, diptych that concludes *Henry V*, and brings the second tetralogy to an end, doesn't offer that kind of resolution. In comparing the complex rhymings in this play's first and final "low" scenes, we might well have a sense of the distance traveled in the play's perspectival underminings of any simple and confident contrast between "high" and "low," but that clash is not "resolved": what we have instead is a culminating instance, where the exploratory interest in what is ultimately intractable might be compared with that in *The Tempest*. Because the clashes between "high" and "low" cannot be resolved, the final act also gives climactic force to the historiographical challenge— Whose history? and from whose point of view?—and opposes the providential view of God as an Englishman actively involved in a chosen people's fate to a far more dispiriting view of "Fortune." Nor is the highly organized play of discrepant and opposed perspectives on Henry resolved; as we consider what "made his England bleed," we finish by looking backward, to Richard as a quite different kind of player king, and forward, to Henry VI and the horrors to come. The conditions for a *conventionally* satisfying resolution are not met. We may find the ending *profoundly* satisfying, but that would have to do with the sense of having reached what Kretzchmar in Thomas Mann's *Doctor Faustus* calls "an end without any return."

In his magnificent study of the genesis and structure of Beethoven's *Diabelli Variations* William Kinderman also quotes Kretzchmar, and for a similar reason—similar, that is, if we think that composition provides a more helpful musical analogy for the way in which Shakespeare's dramatic rhymes and variational development combine the urge to vary with a no less powerful urge to integrate, and so carry the work forward to a profoundly integrated conclusion that nonetheless seems "unresolved."[38] Beethoven saw Diabelli's trivial theme as a vast reservoir of unrealized possibilities; but then, even as he broke down and explored its different motifs, intervallic relationships, and constitutive sonorities in his own variational rhymes, he was also taking extraordinary pains to integrate his own work—over several years and through various notebooks.

As Kinderman observes, the *Diabelli Variations* and other works from Beethoven's last decade "can seem decidedly unclassical when measured against Haydn and Mozart or Beethoven's own earlier works" because, in their tendency to avoid symmetrical forms, literal restatements, and even cadential articulation, they depart so radically from the "classical aesthetic framework" based on "balance, symmetry, and proportion"; as earlier critics complained, they are indeed weak in form—if form is regarded as "an architectural framework imposed from without." But there is also a profound, and profoundly unconventional, "fidelity to classical principles" which appears in the way these works so "relentlessly exploit the procedures of thematic integration and unification forged by Haydn"; Kinderman's analyses triumphantly show—as I have been trying to show in the Shakespearean context—how the exploratory impulse to vary and transform combines with the urge to integrate. What is especially instructive, in the context of my own argument, is Kinderman's account of the sense in which these late works seem "unresolved":

The radical, titanic fugal Finale of the original version of the Quartet, Op. 130 with the *Grosse Fuge;* the end of the *Missa Solemnis,* with its ambiguous message underlined by threats to "inner and outer peace"; the open-ended vision at the conclusion of the Arietta in the Piano

Sonata, Op. 111—each of these is in a sense left "unresolved", for the evolution of the work itself leaves no room for a return to the conditions of its initial stages. In a real sense, none of these works is bound as a formal whole. Each embodies an ongoing process, and ends not in satisfying resolution, but in pointed pregnancy of effect. (66)

The structure, though demonstrably so powerfully integrated and progressive, evolves from within: to the extent that it is unconventional, unpredictable, and unrepeatable—not imposed from without—the conditions for a conventionally "satisfying resolution" are not present. Instead there is that sense of having reached "an end without return."

When an intelligent interviewer picked up Paul Ricoeur's remark that "narration preserves the meaning that is behind us so that we can have meaning before us" and asked, "What about the modernist texts of Joyce and Beckett, etc., where the narrative seems to disperse and dislocate meaning?" Ricoeur replied:

These texts break up the habitual paradigms of narrative order in order to leave the ordering task of creation to the reader himself. And ultimately it is true that the reader recomposes the text. All narrative, however, even Joyce's, is a certain call to order. Joyce does not invite us to embrace chaos but an infinitely more complex order. Narrative carries us beyond the oppressive order of our existence to a more liberating and refined order.[39]

So far, I have been wanting to attend to the complexity of Shakespeare's design as a "call to order" in Ricoeur's sense; polemical and narrowly characterological readings reject the Shakespearean "call" to recognize "an infinitely more complex order" (and Ricoeur's eschatological hope). In the next two sections of my argument I consider how the either/or debate has resurfaced in American new historicist and British cultural materialist readings, although it is now conducted in ideological rather than characterological terms. But the course of my argument will be clearer if, in concluding this part and approaching the next, I first enter my disagreement with the seminal account of a "radically ambiguous" *Henry V* in Norman Rabkin's *Shakespeare and the Problem of Meaning.*

Rabkin's attack on "either/or" readings is very powerful, and to the extent that my own argument replaces an "either/or" with a "both/

and," it is aligned with his; certainly I feel indebted, and grateful. Nonetheless, one very troubling effect of Rabkin's teasingly paradoxical argument that the play resembles the gestaltist's duck-rabbit is to dissociate the dramatic challenge from what I have called the historiographical challenge. After arguing, in two pointedly independent sections of his essay, that the play can be seen as a pro-Henry duck or as an anti-Henry rabbit, Rabkin himself actually rejects what seems to follow—namely, the conclusion that the play should not be regarded polemically:

> A third response has been suggested by some writers of late: *Henry V* is a subtle and complex study of a king who curiously combines strengths and weaknesses, virtues and vices. One is attracted to the possibility of regarding the play unpolemically. Shakespeare is not often polemical, after all, and a balanced view allows for the inclusion of both positive and negative features in an analysis of the protagonist and the action. But sensitive as such analysis can be, it is oddly unconvincing, for two strong reasons. First, the cycle has led us to expect stark answers to simple and urgent questions. Is a particular king good or bad for England? Can one be a successful public man and retain a healthy inner life? Has Hal lost or gained in the transformation through which he changes name and character? Does political action confer any genuine benefit on the polity? What is honor worth, and who has it? The mixed view of Henry characteristically appears in critical essays that seem to fudge such questions, to see complication and subtlety where Shakespeare's art forces us to demand commitment, resolution, answers. Second, no real compromise is possible between the extreme readings I have claimed the play provokes. Our experience of the play resembles the experience Gombrich claims for viewers of the trick drawing: "We can switch from one reading to another with increasing rapidity; we will also 'remember' the rabbit while we see the duck, but the more closely we watch ourselves, the more certainly we will discover that we cannot experience alternative readings at the same time."[40]

In these terms, seeing how the play is a duck-rabbit also entails that, as spectators or readers, we can never see it as a duck-rabbit; rather, we know that it must be a duck-rabbit because we "switch" from one reading to the other without ever being able to experience alternative readings at the same time.

Yet the logical pivot for this teasing paradox is an unsupported premise: why, and how, has the cycle "led us to expect stark answers to simple and urgent questions"? The questions Rabkin then puts are indeed questions that the cycle makes "urgent," but why should we think them susceptible to "stark answers"? In the first place, they are not: for example, there is no "stark" or compellingly (rather than uncompellingly) simple answer to that question about honor—either in life, or in plays like the first part of *Henry IV, Hamlet,* or *Julius Caesar.* But then, second, Rabkin is assuming that Shakespeare's cycle is exceptional in this respect: although "Shakespeare is not often po-lemical," his "art" in *Henry V* "forces us to demand commitment, resolution, answers," not "complication and subtlety." So, critical argu-ments that take a "mixed view" of Henry "seem to fudge"—even though Rabkin's own argument that the play is a duck-rabbit clearly presupposes that the play itself takes a thoroughly and alarmingly "mixed view of Henry."

In a very awkward sense this means that we cannot follow the play, since what the play is doing in its representation of Henry is precisely what we cannot do: "We are made to see a rabbit or a duck," whereas the "terrible fact about *Henry V* is that Shakespeare seems equally tempted by both its rival gestalts." A further consequence, which is logically as well as critically alarming, is that putting the "terrible fact" this way rules out any possibility of the kind of convergence I have suggested between the play's historiographical challenge and its wholly characteristic dramatic perspectivism. In his concluding para-graphs, Rabkin argues that "Shakespeare's habitual recognition of the irreducible complexity of things has led him, as it should lead his audience, to a point of crisis," but at the same time *denies* the basis for any serious and sustained historiographical challenge: "Suggest-ing the necessity of radically opposed responses to a historical figure about whom there would seem to have been little reason for anything but the simplest of views, Shakespeare leaves us at a loss" (61). On these terms, there can be no connection between "the irreducible complexity of things" and the problems of making or "doing" history: to take anything other than the "simplest of views" of the "historical" Henry is seen as some kind of unreasonable perversity, which then "points to a crisis in Shakespeare's spiritual life." After that, Rabkin can finish his essay with some finely suggestive remarks on what makes the play "most valuable for us" *without* relating what he values to a complex but intelligent and intelligible dramatic design. The play is "most valuable for us" because it "shows us" the "simultaneity of our hopes and fears about the world of political action," and "contrasts our hope that society can solve our problems with our knowledge that society has never done so": "The inscrutability of *Henry V* is the inscrutability of history" (62). Any of these concluding suggestions might have provided an excellent way into the play's complex but scrutable design—if Rabkin had not already ruled out the possibility of a gestalt-experience which admits, and makes that kind of sense of, "simultaneity." And here, if my musical analogies are convincing, they should show why Rabkin's visual analogies are misleading.

The usefulness of the duck-rabbit analogy is that it suggests how the play repeatedly challenges us with different or "rival" ways of "reading" what we see; but in another important sense the visual analogy is deeply misleading. We can't take a play in at a glance, like a visual image; it unfolds in time, like music, and our responses also unfold, in an experiential process that follows the dramatic process.

Rabkin's related metaphor of "switching"—of finding oneself seeing the same duck again, and then the same rabbit again—is no less misleading, since it implies a series of alternations between static images. The play does indeed engage us in an immensely varied series of interpretative choices, but they are not always the same choices, are not always reducible to a clear "either/or," and are almost always not assimilable to some narrowly characterological choice between a pro-Henry and an anti-Henry view. But then what should we make of those more recent and currently very influential materialist readings which reformulate the "either/or" in ideological rather than narrowly characterological terms?

Who Them? Where Us?

It's difficult to know what kind of staging would answer to new historicist readings of the "Henriad." This difficulty follows from the new historicist insistence that subversion is contained—not finally, but constantly and inexorably. The concept of "containment" applies not so much to anything the plays are demonstrably doing, at some specific moment, as to something that the new historicist does with his or her own sense of the plays and their effect on an imaginary and monolithic audience. So, one remarkable feature of the discussion of the "Henriad" in Stephen Greenblatt's "Invisible Bullets" is that, wherever his commentary is detailed and specific, it is directing us to instances of the "subversive doubts the play continually awakens"; but then the bleakly contrary theory of "containment" is brought down like a gigantic clamp: somehow, and "paradoxically," the "very doubts that Shakespeare raises serve not to rob the king of his charisma but to heighten it."[41] That's some catch, as Joseph Heller's Doc Daneeka might say. Yet the real catch is our not being shown who or what controls this "paradox," and does the containing. What is at issue— not only the argument or thesis, but the method of argument—matters very much: in relation to Shakespeare and to the question of whether and how the so-called new historicism differs from the old historicism or from British cultural materialism; and in relation to our general sense of what has been happening in English studies. In his 1986 presidential address to the Modern Languages Association, Hillis Miller found it necessary to insist on the continuing need for deconstructionist readings; Miller's defensiveness registered his own somewhat disconsolate sense that, within the United States at least, new historicism had now displaced deconstructionism as the dominant "ism."[42]

In the moving epilogue to *Renaissance Self-Fashioning*, the book that established new historicism only six years before Miller's reluctant tribute, Greenblatt didn't attempt to historicize that cultural and historical moment at which the new historicist approach came to seem so compelling and satisfying. Instead, he told an extraordinary anecdote, in order "to bear witness at the close to my overwhelming need to sustain the illusion that I am the principal maker of my own identity."[43] To be anecdotal myself, I remember how, after reading that last sentence, I thumbed through *Nostromo* until I found the strikingly similar passage in which Conrad writes of the need for "the sustaining illusion of an independent existence as against the whole scheme of things of which we form a helpless part".[44] This markedly Nietzschean concept of the "sustaining illusion" recurs throughout Conrad's work, and finds another significant contemporary parallel in Clifford Geertz's cultural anthropology, in which man is considered as "an animal suspended in webs of significance he himself has spun":[45] "thick description" becomes the means of engaging with what is culturally alien or historically removed—like Geertz's Islam, or Greenblatt's Renaissance. These interdisciplinary continuities and convergences suggest why there was nothing very surprising in Greenblatt's echo of Conrad; rather, the echo alerts us to the relation between Geertzian cultural anthropology and Greenblatt's "cultural poetics"—the term he prefers to "new historicism." Both are intensely concerned to genealogize in Nietzsche's sense: to trace what Geertz calls "the social history of the moral imagination" and to uncover the structures of the imaginative life by exploring what is culturally and historically bound in different ways of seeing and interpreting the world as text. But here, if we are to understand why Greenblatt's and other new historicist accounts of Shakespeare's "Henriad" turn on the concept of "containment," my heraldlike roll call must include the name of another self-proclaimed Nietzschean: Michel Foucault. Indeed, I want to suggest that the magnificent imaginative urgency of Greenblatt's criticism corresponds with its Geertzian aspect, while what prompts deep misgivings corresponds with its Foucauldian aspect.

Although it will seem a backhanded compliment, the concept of "containment" can be illustrated by applying new historicist terms and procedures to new historicism itself. Its "subversive" energies are both "produced" and "contained" within institutional "discourses" that have grown in self-importance in direct proportion to their social and cultural marginalization. If we are seeing "from inside," in Geertz's sense,[46] the triumph of new historicism seems momentous. When seen "from outside," however, the triumph is wholly contained within the institutions and by whatever "official strategies" determine the "allocation of resources." So, in seeing how new historicism itself is "historically and ideologically situated" we see what, in *Shakespearean Negotiations,* Greenblatt sees in the "Henriad": "the subversiveness that is genuine and radical . . . is at the same time contained by the power it would appear to threaten" (30). In historiographical terms the old ruler-centered way of doing history has been replaced by the search for "institutional strategies" and a culture's master fictions. But when this approach is applied to Shakespeare—the directing intelligence at work within fictions which are in some sense his, like those "subversive doubts"—we need to know who or what does the containing; or indeed "plotting," since Greenblatt's argument also invokes, and turns on, that "carefully plotted official strategy whereby subversive perceptions are at once produced and contained" (56). Who, if not the dramatist, plots "the play"? In new historicist and

Foucauldian terms that question is naive, since the "who" should be a "what." The careful plotting isn't being attributed to some individual official strategist: what is in question is Foucault's vision of systems in force, which no subversion can subvert.[47] Yet trying to rephrase the question in terms of the desired answer doesn't help much: asking "what" replots Shakespeare's "Henriad" sounds odd, and too like voodoo.

It is more helpful to examine the shape of Greenblatt's argument, since this shows how its internal connections actually depend on a prior commitment to the thesis about containment which is then "instantiated" in a number of very different and more or less "complex" texts. The essay begins in the distinctive new historicist fashion, by using a somewhat marginal text to raise a very important historical question about Renaissance atheism. Yet what will link this to the later discussion of Shakespeare is not atheism, but the "interpretive model" suggested by Harriot's *Brief and True Report,* in which atheism figures as a preliminary instance of subversive thought that is produced and contained by "institutional" and "official strategies." Consider this nice distinction, which comes soon after the comment that the atheistical "stance that seemed to come naturally to me as a green college freshman in mid-twentieth-century America seems to have been almost unthinkable to the most daring philosophical minds of late sixteenth-century England": "I am arguing not that atheism was literally unthinkable in the late sixteenth century but rather that it was almost always thinkable only as the thought of another."[48] Since the very niceness of that distinction has much to do with its elusiveness, we need to see what it draws away from, and what it points toward. It is clearly preparing us to think in certain ways about "institutional" or "official strategies" that in this case used atheism "as a smear": "hence," Greenblatt next observes, "the ease with which Catholics can call Protestant martyrs atheists and Protestants routinely make similar charges against the Pope." Here words like "ease" and "routinely" and "smear" quietly but busily fend off any idea that some Protestants believed, strenuously and passionately, that the Pope *was* the Anti-Christ; in some parts of what is called the United Kingdom they still do. At the same time, the distinction and the argument pull away from some problems that concern historians and, indeed, British cultural materialists. There is no attempt to establish, historically, whether atheism was or was not "unthinkable"—or whether, given the increasing vigilance of the Tudor and Stuart censors, it was not so much "unthinkable" as unprintable. Yet any modern historian or critic who forgets about the censors becomes their accomplice, some four centuries too late to receive his pieces of silver. It is sobering to remember that nearly half a century has passed since Don Cameron Allen observed, in that devastating review of Tillyard, that in any presentation of a world picture "we must also learn to read the unprinted works of the suppressed majorities"; Allen went on to add that, although he knew of no published Renaissance defences of atheism, "the multitude of treatises against atheism are an evidence of its reality." We might think that some kinds of indirect evidence could slip past the censor—dramatic evidence, like the remarkably unremarkable, man-in-the-street atheism that underlies Claudio's terrified vision of death in *Measure for Measure,* or the glimpses of unreformed village life in spiritual autobiographies like Bunyan's *Grace Abounding;* yet Greenblatt's distinction excludes such things, since they involve the ascription of atheism to others.[49] Since science offered no alternative account of creation in this period, and since there were also obvious and compelling reasons why nobody would be eager to acknowledge atheism directly,[50] we might conclude in a helplessly inconclusive fashion that the claim about the "unthinkability" of atheism is fascinating but undeterminable, while the claim that "institutional" and "official" strategies" used atheism "as a smear" is true but unsurprising; yet the function of these earlier claims is to float the thesis about containment before pressing more startling critical claims—including the claim that, although *Henry V* "deftly registers every nuance of royal hypocrisy, ruthlessness and bad faith," those "very doubts that Shakespeare raises serve not to rob the king of his charisma but to heighten it."

That reference to "royal hypocrisy" seems to me particularly worrying—and revealing. I have already argued that to regard the soliloquies of Henry IV or Henry V as hypocritical short-circuits the unsettlingly interrogative and exploratory processes of Shakespeare's dramatic thinking; here we can also notice how one effect of the emphasis on "hypocrisy" is to prevent any Geertzian attempt to "see from inside." Greenblatt's reference to "royal hypocrisy" is twentieth-century American, in being so strongly inclusive: it posits the hypocrisy of these kings and of kingship. So, Henry IV's soliloquy is said to be both "testing and confirming an extremely dark and disturbing hypothesis about the nature of monarchical power in England: that its moral authority rests upon a hypocrisy so deep that the hypocrites themselves believe it" (*Shakespearean Negotiations*, 55). The first, fundamental objection to this is logical: if they believe it they are *not* "hypocrites." Another objection depends on our sense of one of the most important conventions of Shakespearean poetic drama: in a soliloquy a character may, like Macbeth, deceive himself or fail to keep his thought in the intended trajectory, but never consciously lies or deliberately misrepresents his thoughts and feelings.[51] Most disappointingly, Greenblatt invokes the question of "moral authority" only to exclude any consideration of what moral authority (of an un-twentieth-century, un-American kind) Henry IV or Henry V takes to sanction his behavior. Instead, because the critic is himself so convinced by that "extremely dark and disturbing hypothesis about the nature of monarchical power in England," Henry must be a "hypocrite." But then, having argued that the play confirms this dark thesis, and is subversive to a degree Tillyard would have found hair-raising, Greenblatt bangs down the lid of containment. All those "subversive doubts which the play continually awakens" are produced and contained by "power"—that is, by a half-mystical, half-nightmarish and wholly Foucauldian vision of "power" as a faceless text.

To argue in this fashion that "power" produces and contains the Shakespearean subversion is to argue that the "historical and ideological situation" produces and *governs* the literary text; in other words, old historicism with a Foucauldian facelift. This is all the more disappointing because Greenblatt's fascinating and fertile concern with "cultural transactions" and "negotiations" most naturally and properly implies various kinds of two-way processes in which text and context, the work of art and its "historical and ideological situation," are (as Edward Pechter puts it) "mutually generative."[52] I certainly don't believe that the literary text transcends history, or that selfhood is entirely unconstrained by social system; nor do I know anybody who does believe that, although I keep reading that such people exist. Nor, at the other extreme, can I believe, or think Greenblatt really believes, that works of art and individuals are the secondary and determined products of their "historical and ideological situation." And yet, whatever he means to mean, that is the force of his argument that the "ideological strategies that fashion Shakespeare's plays" and "help in turn to fashion the conflicting readings of the play's politics" are "no more Shakespeare's invention than the historical narratives on which he based his plots": when the "interpretive model" derived from the rich analysis of Harriot's *Brief and True Report* is applied to "the far more complex problem posed by Shakespeare's history plays," they also show how "in the discourse of authority a powerful logic governs the relation between orthodoxy and subversion" (*Shakespearean Negotiations*, 23).

How this "logic" governs the plays' dramatic thinking is anything but clear, since the reading will not tell us whether the directing intelligence at work within the work is implicated in or helpless before that "logic which governs the relation between orthodoxy and subversion" and those "ideological strategies" which "fashion" plays that are in some sense his. But it is evident how the "logic" in question governs the reading itself: "subversion" is *already* "contained" by that "interpretive model" which the critic reads into each play, and then, not surprisingly, reads out of it. Indeed this outcome becomes all the more inevitable because the model determines which parts of the "Henriad" are to be discussed. New historicist criticism—and here Greenblatt's approach is wholly representative—never provides anything like the traditional, or old-fashioned, act-by-act analyses, since it is concerned to situate the literary text in relation to other cultural texts and practices. But if this is often liberating, opening up and transforming our sense of Renaissance culture, the readings it produces can also seem to function like a closed system that in a more damaging sense depends upon an approach so selective as to be inevitably self-confirming—not least because there is little or no attempt to follow that dramatic process of unfolding on which Shakespeare's dramatic thinking depends.

To ask *why* Greenblatt should impose this nightmarish vision of systems in force, which no subversion can subvert, when he is so keenly responsive to Shakespeare's subversive energies, is to initiate that Nietzschean process of "backward inference" which prompted my earlier remarks on how we might historicize the new historicism. The vision does answer, very well, to the desperation of an intelligentsia that feels itself to be marginalized and contained—well rewarded institutionally yet nationally impotent—in the America of Ronald Reagan and George Bush; the concern with "institutional" and "official strategies" answers to what was powerfully conveyed in Greenblatt's devastating discussion of Reagan in the (Australian) *Southern Review*[53]—the frightened sense of invisible powers that govern the rather too visible president. If this suggests why Greenblatt twice varies Kafka's gloomy remark about "hope" by observing that "there is subversion, no end of subversion, but not for us," it also suggests why the new historicist concept of the "subversive" is itself too coercive and limiting. It is always already contained, since the constant concern with the antithetical relations between domination and subversion, authority and transgression, ensures that the concept of the "subversive" is only allowed to function as one term within a duality that already privileges state and institutional authority. The very idea that anything might be so radically subversive and liberating as to overturn this binary system becomes "unthinkable."

The sense of some unacknowledged compulsion at work grows stronger when we notice how this very subtle critic seems unconscious of the assumptions his own language reveals. So, for example, when Greenblatt observes in *Shakespearean Negotiations* that "the subversive doubts the play continually awakens originate paradoxically in an effort to intensify the power of the king and his war" (62–63), the "effort" in question must be Shakespeare's. An "effort" has to be made by somebody and Shakespeare is the only possible candidate. Moreover, this talk of an "effort" comes at that very point in Greenblatt's argument where he is suggesting ("may we suggest") the inadequacy of readings that take the play to be either anti-Henry or "radically ambiguous." In rejecting the anti-Henry readings of those "critics since Hazlitt" who think that the play's apparent glorification of the monarch is "bitterly ironic," Greenblatt argues that "even today, and in the wake of full-scale ironic readings and at a time when it no longer seems to matter very much, it is not at all clear that *Henry V* can be successfully performed as subversive." Nor is he convinced by those readings which, like Rabkin's, turn an "either/or" into a "both/and" by arguing, "more plausibly," that "Shakespeare's depiction of Henry V is radically ambiguous" (62). Here, "more plausibly" is the polite critical equivalent of the nice distinction logicians make when they find an argument good but not compelling. Yet this makes it all the more important to get some purchase on the "paradox" that Greenblatt's own reading is proposing ("in the light of Harriot's *Brief and True Report*") as the most plausible, or compelling, alternative. Despite that reference to a paradoxical origin that involves an "effort," and so presupposes an intention, it is evident that we are not being offered the kind of genetic account in which Shakespeare be-

gan by intending to write a "panegyric" but then found his hero
rather boring (Tillyard's view) or even disgusting (Hazlitt's view, already rejected). Since at this level of abstraction and generalization
so few alternatives remain, it is worth setting them out.

One, let us call it the first alternative, would be to suppose that
Shakespeare was a loyal fool or innocent, not unlike his Chorus, and
kept to his original intention of writing a "panegyric" without ever
realizing that he had "repeatedly demonstrated" the "illegitimacy of
legitimate authority." This need not detain us. Since the repeated
demonstrations would be unwitting rather than deft, the first alternative is not consonant with the arresting paradoxicality of the claim
that, although *Henry V* "deftly registers every nuance of royal hypocrisy, ruthlessness, and bad faith, . . . it does so in the context of a
celebration, a collective panegyric to 'this star of England'" (56).

The second alternative, which is more consonant with that claim,
is to suppose that Shakespeare was not a fool but a knave, whose
repeated demonstrations of the "illegitimacy of legitimate authority"
were *not* inadvertent, but were quite deliberately and craftily assimilated to his "effort to intensify the power of the king." This is to
suppose that Shakespeare himself intended, and was cynically controlling, that effect which Greenblatt describes in claiming that "the very
doubts that Shakespeare raises serve not to rob the king of his charisma but to heighten it." That many readers would be shocked and
disappointed to think Shakespeare was doing that wouldn't be a
proper objection to the second alternative, but merely one possible
consequence of having to accept it; as we shall see, Dollimore and
Sinfield's reading of *Henry V* does set out to administer that kind of
shock. Yet this second alternative still wouldn't answer to what seems
most alarmingly, painfully paradoxical in Greenblatt's general thesis
that "the subversiveness that is genuine and radical . . . is at the same
time contained by the power it would appear to threaten." Doubts
that Shakespeare himself was deliberately "awakening" only in order
to ensure that they are "contained" could hardly be described as
"genuine" or "radical"; rather, Shakespeare's own "effort" would be
wholly in accord with the "carefully plotted official strategy." Since
such collusion would make the mysterious "official strategy" redundant, accepting the second alternative would *dissolve* that very "paradox" which Greenblatt is emphasizing.

So, if the second alternative were in place, it would have been both more logical and less pusillanimous to say, unequivocally, that "the subversive doubts Shakespeare continually awakens are not paradoxical, but are *intended* to intensify the power of the king and heighten his charisma." We would then also know how we were expected to fill in the gap I have marked with a bracketed question mark in this passage: "What remains is the law of nature: the strong eats the weak. Yet this is not quite what Shakespeare invites the audience to affirm through its applause. Like Harman, Shakespeare refuses to endorse so cynical a conception of the social order; instead [?] actions that should have the effect of radically undermining authority turn out to be the props of authority" (53). Precisely because this passage volunteers an account of Shakespeare's dramatic intentions by telling us what he did *not* "invite" the audience to "affirm" and what he himself "refused" to "endorse," we naturally want to know whether Shakespeare *did* intend to prop up authority by seeming to undermine it. The account of the "effect" not only raises the question of intention, or of what is *meant;* it also assumes that "the audience" would not see and understand the "strategy." But then, at the crucial moment, the passage suddenly swivels away from intention and effect to considering effect but not intention.

This happens elsewhere, notably when Greenblatt calls attention to the "major structural principle" that stages "what we may term anticipatory, or proleptic, parody" (55). This concern to establish "structural principles," which accords with my own concern to characterize the play's structural dynamics, doesn't require speculation about the dramatist's prior intentions; rather, it involves trying to make out and make sense of whatever the play is more or less consistently doing. For example, I have emphasized the interrogative, complicating effect of that structural rhythm which recurs in each act of *Henry V* when the Chorus presents *his* way of doing history as *the* way, before the "play" sees things "perspectively." The "major structural principle" that Greenblatt describes is directly opposed to this, in its sequence as well as its effect: we are to suppose that throughout the cycle the subversive "parody" precedes, and then only helps to consolidate, "official truth." One of Greenblatt's examples has already been mentioned: the way in which, immediately before Henry IV's pronouncement "Then happy low, lie down: / Uneasy lies the head that wears the crown," Falstaff "parodies this ideology, or rather—and more significantly—presents it as humbug *before* it makes its appearance as official truth" (54). And yet, as we have seen, Greenblatt himself thinks that the King is hypocritical, and that the play is *actually* demonstrating the illegitimacy of legitimate authority: so who is convinced by the "official truth," and correspondingly incapable of seeing what the play repeatedly demonstrates? The Elizabethan audience, of course. That dramatically terse contrast between "humbug" and "official truth" shows how the "either/or" that provoked earlier pro-Henry and anti-Henry readings is still very much alive, although now it has been abstracted and refracted into ideological antitheses. On these terms any contemporary pro-Henry reading seems impossible; yet the anti-Henry readings of "critics since Hazlitt" have been rejected, while readings which discover "radical ambiguity"—converting the "either/or" into a "both/and": Rossiter's "two-eyedness"—are said to be implausible.

This leaves the third, or final, Alternative, which is predicated on the idea of an estranging gulf between the modern and Elizabethan audiences. Here it's important to see how this idea functions as a premise. So, for example, readings like Rabkin's must seem unacceptable because thinking the play ambiguous would allow for division and diversity in the responses of Elizabethan as well as modern audiences, and so for some *continuity* between their mixed responses and our mixed responses. But that is incompatible with the Foucauldian thesis about containment; the final alternative insists instead on *discontinuity*—and on an absolute, epistemic rift between Them and Us. Old historicists also liked to do that, of course, and an old historicist version of the final alternative would be to claim that Elizabethan audiences could not but take a pro-Henry view, since They all thought like that, while moderns who think they know better and talk of irony or ambiguity merely betray their ignorance of the Elizabethan Mind. Greenblatt's new historicist version of the final alternative is more subtle and more chilling. Once again we are to suppose that the Elizabethan audiences could not but take a pro-Henry view, since Their subversive doubts were always contained. The exciting twist comes with the idea that We are able to see and admire the "subversive doubts" not because we know better, but only because the doubts are no longer subversive or threatening to our own version of "official truth" and "reality," which is also historically and culturally bound.

Here we may turn to the final paragraph of "Invisible Bullets," which, in the revised, and presumably final, version printed in *Shake-*

spearean Negotiations, has become more elaborately paradoxical. The paragraph begins with another variation on the paradox of containment: we are to suppose that "Shakespeare's drama, written for a theater subject to state censorship, can be so relentlessly subversive" because "the form itself, as a primary expression of Renaissance power, helps to contain the radical doubts it continually provokes" (65). This is followed by a curiously arbitrary comparison with *King Lear.* In showing how "subversion contained" can "be for the theater a mode of containment subverted," *Lear* shows how there are "moments in Shakespeare's career" when "the process of containment is strained to the breaking point," whereas "the histories consistently pull back from such extreme pressure." But here the paradox Greenblatt wants to elaborate conceals another, unintended or at any rate unexamined, paradox: the pithy and beguiling contrast between "subversion contained" and "contained subverted" shows the materialist critic spinning out an idealist fiction. The contrast between the plays and the degree to which they contain subversion must depend on their effect—but on whom, and when? Are we to suppose that all members of the original audience saw, or, in some more obscure way, felt and understood that although Lear occasionally shows "containment subverted," the "histories" constantly show "subversion contained"?

It is, after all, historically the case that people haven't always thought that subversion is contained in the second tetralogy. This was clearly not the view taken by those Elizabethans who commissioned the special performance of *Richard II* on the eve of the Essex rising, or by the official who ensured that its deposition scene didn't appear in the three quartos of *Richard II* published in the queen's lifetime; nor is it the view of all those moderns who think—like Hazlitt, or Harold Goddard and Phillip Mallett, or the directors of the English Shakespeare Company—that *Henry V* is ironic, and exposes the mirror of Christian kings as an unprincipled Machiavellian.[54] Of course we may argue that Goddard and Mallett, and the ESC directors, Bogdanov and Pennington, misunderstand *Henry V* and fail to see how (as Sherman Hawkins maintains) the "main thrust of the play is toward the heroic, the ideal and the exemplary"; we might even think it a pity that the queen, who angrily exclaimed "Know ye not? I am Richard II," couldn't have calmed herself by reading Greenblatt or Tillyard.[55] But what we can't do, or shouldn't do, is slither between a very strong-minded and prescriptive critical argument about what effect these plays should have, and a historical account of the variety of ways in which they were understood or misunderstood. Because Greenblatt's contrast between "subversion contained" and "containment subverted" swivels between an ideal *is* and a material *was* it offers the critical equivalent of a Penrose tribar, or "impossible object" in four-dimensional space.[56] His reading is powerfully original, because nobody has perceived the relation between *King Lear* and the history plays in quite this way; but in being critically original the argument explodes itself historically, because nobody has perceived the relation between *King Lear* and the history plays in quite this way. In this tribar-like way the argument fascinates: it is critically fascinating, historically untrue, and logically impossible.

Nonetheless, the paragraph's final sentences reduce the ramifications of this paradoxical and ahistorical "process" of containment to another elegant theorem: "Like Harriot in the New World, the Henry plays confirm the Machiavellian hypothesis that princely power originates in force and fraud even as they draw their audience toward an acceptance of that power. And we are free to locate and pay homage to the play's doubts only because they no longer threaten us. There is subversion, no end of subversion, but not for us" (*Shakespearean Negotiations*, 65). Here the repetition of that elegantly resigned variation on Kafka's remark to Max Brod recalls the earlier, no less elegantly paradoxical argument that "the term *subversive* for us designates those elements in Renaissance culture that contemporary audiences tried to contain or, when containment seemed impossible, to destroy and that now conform to our own sense of truth and reality":

> That is, we find "subversive" in the past precisely those things that are *not* subversive to ourselves, that pose no threat to the order by which we live and allocate resources. . . . Conversely, we identify as principles of order and authority in Renaissance texts what we would, if we took them seriously, find subversive for ourselves: religious and political absolutism, aristocracy of birth, demonology, humoral psychology, and the like. That we do not find such notions subversive, that we complacently identify them as principles of aesthetic or political order, replicates the process of containment that licensed the elements we call subversive in Renaissance

texts: that is, our own values are sufficiently strong for us to contain alien forces almost effortlessly. (39)

This seems admirable as a challenge to "complacency", and to that conception of "relevance" which, since the late 1960s, has been ever less shameless in its demand that literature must confirm and conform with, and never make us revise or relativize, our own preconceptions of what is Just So. Rather, we are being urged to recognize the need for a Foucauldian genealogy of the present. But then religious and political absolutism isn't unknown in the twentieth century; aristocracy of birth still counts in queer countries like England (in university admissions, in the House of Lords); even demonology has had a varied and colorful afterlife (gynocriticism, Reagan's foreign policy); and the "dynamic" models provided by humoral psychology have been positively revalued by such bioanthropologists as Melvin Konner.[57] Sadly, the striking challenge to complacency itself relies on a late twentieth-century American academic conception of who "we" are.

This is what we also saw working behind Greenblatt's references to "royal hypocrisy" and "the nature of monarchical power in England." It appeared, more poignantly, in his earlier remarks about how atheism seemed "to come naturally" to an American freshman; that measures the isolation of those who figure in Greenblatt's "we"—the precious, happy few, the beleaguered band of brothers—from the overwhelming majority of Americans, who are, in their own view and to a degree probably unparalleled in any Western society "religious" and "Christian."[58] Indeed, it is worth remarking how often the undeniable appeal of all those vignettes and anecdotes which typically launch new historicist essays is that they invite—or play to, instead of challenging—predictable responses to what is culturally or historically alien. Greenblatt's superb essay on Marlowe in *Renaissance Self-Fashioning* begins with an English merchant's account of the systematic destruction of a village in Sierra Leone in 1586; this is offered "as a reminder of what until recently was called one of the glorious achievements of Renaissance civilization" (193). Yet the confidence of that deftly ironic comment engages more than our sense of Renaissance brutality, of "the acquisitive energies of English merchants, entrepreneurs, and adventurers." It *expects* its reader to respond to the "moral blankness" of John Sarracoll's account with a moral horror Sarracoll plainly didn't expect; but it can do this because what is in question is

also, in another way, horribly familiar—say, from the testimonies received in the trials of Lieutenant Calley and Captain Medina after
the My Lai massacre. Renaissance entrepreneurs had no monopoly
on "moral blankness," and the chief difference between Sarracoll and
the My Lai witnesses may well be that, regardless of rank, most of the
My Lai testimonies were linguistically, as well as morally, subliterate.
Mary McCarthy was astonished and appalled by the misuse of words
like "conscience," and by the way in which, when Calley told a journalist, "I may be old-fashioned, but I don't approve of rape on the battlefield," he was "apologizing to the journalist for *drawing a line*
somewhere, that is, for still having a standard of two."[59] Greenblatt's
criticism is addressed to those who would be appalled by Sarracoll's
and Medina's "moral blankness"; it isn't addressed to, and barely acknowledges the existence of, all those Americans who enjoyed Medina's subsequent appearance as a celebrity on the David Frost show,
or more recently rallied to the support of Oliver North.

Another example of this invitation to thrill in a predictably "modern" way over the horrors of the English past—rather as Olive Chan-
cellor and Verena thrill over the history of feminine anguish, in
Henry James's *The Bostonians*—is provided when Greenblatt quite
properly scoffs at C. S. Lewis's way of talking about Wyatt's court
poetry as "material for social occasions." "The whole scene comes
before us," Lewis writes: "We are having a little music after supper.
In that atmosphere all the confessional or autobiographical tone of
the songs falls away." There is indeed a sense in which Lewis's post-
prandial fantasy deserves Greenblatt's devastating response: "But is
this really what it meant to write from within the court? Entertainment in the court of Henry VIII must have been like small talk with
Stalin."[60] Yet it ought to be possible to question Lewis's fantasy (which
Wyatt might have found grimly amusing) without confusing Henry
VIII's notions of entertainment with Stalin's.

These disagreeable reflections seem in place because the difference
between an old historicist version of the final alternative and
Greenblatt's subtle, chilling version appears at the modern, rather
than at the Elizabethan, end of his estranging contrast between Them
and Us—between what They received as "official truth" and what We
see as "humbug." This conception of Us and "our own values" is
not merely twentieth-century American, but also reveals the gulf that
separates his Us from the vast majority of twentieth-century Ameri-

cans. Yet the final alternative insists on—or invents—that other, absolute rift between the Renaissance Them and the Modern Us. We are
to suppose that They—the original audiences, and perhaps (though
here the essay is suddenly reticent) Shakespeare too—would all have
been taken in by what We all know (though we mustn't be complacent)
to be "mystifying" falsehood, "fraud," or "humbug." What is consistent in this rift is the determination to *estrange* the Renaissance and
Shakespeare, and a marked fear of being *taken in*. This anxiety isn't
so much Kafkaesque as Pynchonesque, a view from Vineland after
the Big Chill; if a Central European analogy were needed, for a touch
of classy angst, the somber final chapter of Stanislaw Lem's *Eden*
would be nearer the mark.

One consequence is that, although Greenblatt's way of writing about
Shakespeare is far more lovingly perceptive than, say, Leonard Tennenhouse's in *Power on Display,* the difference isn't at all important in
terms of the controlling thesis about "containment." True, there is
nothing so depressingly bald, unequivocal, and unperturbed as Tennenhouse's flatly stated assumption that Shakespeare is attempting
"to idealize political authority" and that the "hagiographical theme of
this play understands power as the inevitable unfolding of order"
(82); and that Shakespearean "stagecraft collaborates with statecraft"
(15). As I observed earlier, Tennenhouse's readings follow all too predictably from his candidly stated but critically incapacitating prem-
ises: since "the audience was always implicitly the queen, . . . we *have
to* consider the drama as a forum for staging symbolic shows of state
power and as a vehicle for disseminating court ideology," and we "*have
to* assume these had to be presented without challenging her policies
or demeaning her person" (39, my italics). So, Tennenhouse *has to*
assume, and of course does assume, that the point of the "comedic
ending" to *Henry V* is to leave "no possibility of conflict between the
French and English forms of patriarchy": "The English line should
dominate the French just as the husband should dominate the wife
and the sovereign should rule over the subject. It is clear that Katherine embodies all these forms of otherness—France, wife, and subject—which the ending of the play inscribes within the hierarchy of
English patrilineage as if by a natural process," (71). But another
assumption is at work here: if this is what They believed, it is clearly
not what the critic believes or expects Us to believe. We are to see how
"these chronicle history plays demonstrate . . . that authority goes to

the contender who can seize hold of the symbols and signs legitimizing authority and wrest them from his rivals to make them serve his
own interests," and that "power is an inversion of legitimate authority
which gains possession, as such, of the means of self-authorization";
but They were all taken in by that "idealizing process that proves so
crucial in legitimizing power" (83)—and Shakespeare wrote for
Them, or for "the queen." But, for all their differences as critics,
Greenblatt's reading converges with Tennenhouse's: the rift between
Them and Us which underlies Greenblatt's own contrast between
"humbug" and "official truth" is no less absolute, and no less arbitrary.
Its effect is not merely to emphasize cultural and historical difference,
but also to insist—in a Foucauldian rather than Geertzian manner—
on an absolute discontinuity: like Chaucer before him, Shakespeare
is safely locked away in the cultural dungeon which is the historicist
version of Duke Bluebeard's Castle.

This habit of generalizing about the responses, or rather, the response, of "the" audience persists even in new historicist criticism that
offers a contrary account of the situating conditions and effect of
Shakespearean poetic drama. So, for example, in Steven Mullaney's
Place of the Stage we are told that "when Shakespeare's audience heard
. . . Ulysses' notorious speech on degree, they heard what Tillyard
refused to hear. Not a commonplace verbal portrait of the Elizabethan world picture, but an ironically framed parody of such por-
traits,"[61] although Mullaney's account of Hal's early effect on "the
audience" barely allows for the possibility of divided responses:

> Hal's initial appearance on stage . . . would have met with immediate
> and self-gratified recognition from the audience. Immediate, yet point-
> edly short-lived: [here Mullaney quotes Hal's first soliloquy]. Hal alien-
> ates himself from the audience in an unexpected sense, falsifying *their*
> hopes . . . Henry continues to see a prodigal son, but for the audience
> Hal's participation in the taverns represents a prodigality of a different
> order—the sign not of errant youth but of power (81).

Yet such passages sit rather curiously in Mullaney's absorbing study.
The shape of each chapter's argument is distinctively new historicist
in moving from historical and cultural texts to some Shakespearean
instantiation; but although the passages generalize about, and collec-
tivize, the original audience's response, Mullaney does not insist—

wants not to insist—on that absolute rift between Them and Us which the thesis about containment requires. On the contrary Mullaney argues that, in "watching its values and pretensions enacted at a critical distance, Elizabethan London would have understood our formulations of the ideological power of literature quite well" (56). The following passage is particularly interesting and, in relation to my own argument, encouraging:

> Like *Macbeth*, Shakespeare's second tetralogy and *Measure for Measure* could be called "royal plays," chronicles of rule composed with reigning ideologies well in mind. All were performed before royalty, and from the viewpoint of their respective monarchs they readily take the shape of dramatic compliments. In each case, however, compliment is accompanied by a more complex design, radical in its comprehensiveness. These are critical histories of the contemporaneous moment, anamorphic genealogies of power: they need to be viewed from more than one perspective, and cannot be fully comprehended from any single vantage point, no matter how privileged or dominant. Viewed from a marginal perspective—a perspective aligned with the cultural situation of the popular stage itself, receptive to lines of affiliation drawn between that stage and other eccentric or liminal phenomena—such plays take on the contours of amphibologies writ large. Shakespeare rehearses Tudor and Jacobean ideologies with a fullness, a "two-eyedness" (in A. P. Rossiter's phrase) that opens up a critical perspective on his own day and age— on the cultural pretexts and practices that were sharpening the larger dramaturgies of Elizabethan and Jacobean society. The effect, to quote Louis Althusser once again, is to "make us 'perceive' . . . from the *inside*, by an *internal distance*, the very ideology" in which such plays and such a stage were held (129–30).

In its refusal to theologize the issues, the passage keeps open the possibility of critical dialogue. While content to describe his work as new historicist, Mullaney clearly doesn't think Shakespeare's audience was "always implicitly the queen" or king, nor does he suppose that it was monolithically incapable of understanding ideological "strategies."

In his introduction Mullaney sets out some of the differences between American new historicism and British cultural materialism and explains where he has been drawn to the latter.[62] Other details in the passage show him working out a kind of independent, transatlantic compromise between different materialist approaches that can also draw, without embarrassment, on the insights of so-called humanist criticism. Doubtless Rossiter would have been startled to see his seminal argument about ambiguity in the history plays associated with Althusser, who carries more extra baggage than this passage suggests, but it's more important to notice why that admiring reference to Rossiter is so welcome. On the one hand there is no trace of that insistent anti-humanist emphasis of so much British cultural materialist criticism. On the other hand, it quietly opposes that "powerful logic" of the thesis about containment, which, as we have seen, *requires* that Greenblatt reject readings of *Henry V* which turn on some notion of "radical ambiguity." In sharp contrast, Mullaney directly appeals to Rossiter's concept of "two-eyedness" (Rossiter's most memorably Joycean metaphor for truly radical ambiguity) while arguing that Shakespeare's "complex design" is "radical in its comprehensiveness." Mullaney's eclecticism—his "appetite to digest," in Jonson's phrase— allows for an admirably flexible conception of the relation between the "effect," its historical and social contexts, and a directing intelligence which fashions that "complex design." In comparison, Dollimore and Sinfield's essay on *Henry V* is a theological treatise, which shows how much of the play is blocked out when it is viewed through their thick and inflexible ideological grid.

Systems in Force

I have argued that Greenblatt's use of the term "subversive" is itself too coercively loaded, so that the "powerful logic" which for Greenblatt "governs the relation between orthodoxy and subversion" in the "Henriad" as well in Harriot's *Brief and True Report* is actually a "powerful logic" produced by that theory of containment which governs the new historicist reading. The "logic" and the interpretive model" it provides had considerable appeal after "*les événements de* 1968." This, I take it, is why my own remarks on how we might historicize the new historicism were, in effect, anticipated by Frederick Crews in *Skeptical Engagements,* when Crews discusses the change in Foucault's preoccupations and procedures after 1968: "Not coincidentally, it was immediately after 1968 that Foucault switched from his quasi-structuralist 'archaeologies' of Western 'epistemes' to more drastic Nietzschean 'genealogies' reducing all truth claims to exercises of power. The attractive new ingredient in Foucault's thought was Sixties paranoia toward the hidden, all-powerful oppressors whom he never attempted to identify."[63] Here we have the origin, and birthday, of Greenblatt's "carefully plotted official strategy," in which power breeds, feeds and fattens on "subversion."

The term "interrogative" might seem and indeed can be less coercively loaded, but this is not why it is so frequently used by British cultural materialist critics. Rather, their own concept of the "interrogative" is not radical enough: the concept is ideologically stipulative and terminal, since it is always other ideologies—and above all, the ideological errors and fallacies of "essentialist humanism"—that are to be "interrogated" or "exposed." The first half of Dollimore and Sinfield's essay on *Henry V* consists of an assault on "liberal-humanist" ideology and its errors, which comes to a head in their claim that such strikingly different critics as E. M. W. Tillyard, Jan Kott, and Wilbur Sanders all make the same "fundamental error." We shall see how this determines their own reading of Shakespeare's play, but first it is worth noticing why, once again, 1968 is a crucial date, if we are to "situate" this insistent anti-humanism and see what job it is doing.

Luc Ferry and Alain Renault address this issue in an admirably thorough and trenchant fashion, in showing how anti-humanism connects various "thinkers of 68" who are in other important respects very different, most notably Foucault, Derrida, and Lacan. For Ferry and Arnaut, the "originality" and appeal of these French writers derives, problematically, from the ways in which they naturalize and "radicalise" earlier German philosophers by assimilating them to the attack on "humanism" conceived as an ideology: "At least one tenacious misrepresentation has to be refuted. Far from being a purely indigenous product, '68 philosophy is in fact the use of themes and theses borrowed, in more or less complex combinations, from German philosophers, for example, Marx, Nietzsche, Freud, and Heidegger, to mention the fundamental ones. . . . French philosophy seems to take up the themes it borrows from German philosophy in order to radicalize them, and it is this radicalization that is the source of its antihumanism, the thing peculiar to it."[64] Hence the paradox that becomes so pressing in British cultural materialist criticism: the characterization of "essentialist humanism" as a monolithic ideology is inescapably essentialist. Dollimore's *Radical Tragedy* shows how this ideological fiction is also a necessary fiction. The "materialist perspective" is constantly defined in opposition to—and in this sense depends upon—the allegedly humanist "idea that 'man' possesses some given, unalterable essence which is what makes 'him' human, which is the source and essential determinant of 'his' culture and its priority over conditions of existence" (250): If so-called humanists don't advocate or subscribe to this "idea," the claim to be advancing Beyond Essentialist Humanism dissolves. But then, as Stephen L. Collins wearily but succinctly protests, it is just not the case that every humanist or "nonmaterialist interpretation posits an *a priori* essence to 'man' which makes him what he is absolutely. . . . Not every non-Marxist is a Husserl."[65]

Once we consider what their respective "interpretive models" block out or accentuate in Shakespeare's play, we can isolate important differences between the British and American critics, along with those resemblances which have encouraged all those conflating references to "the 'New Historicism' of cultural materialism." The British critics are no less concerned than the Americans with ideological "strategies." For Dollimore and Sinfield, as for Greenblatt, ideology is "not just a set of ideas, it is material practice, woven into the fabric of everyday life"; *Henry V* shows how "power works" by being seen to contain whatever threatens it, and the "principal strategy of ideology is to legitimate inequality and exploitation by representing the social order which perpetuates these things as immutable and unalterable."[66] But then, like Tennenhouse and unlike Greenblatt or Mullaney, they aren't particularly interested in—responsive to, or distracted by—the Shakespearean play as a work of art; the final sentence of their essay coolly proposes that "the ideology which saturates his texts, and their location in history, are the most important things about them" (227). Moreover, where Greenblatt's chilling account of "containment" is, in political terms, paralyzing rather than mobilizing, and perhaps reflects the absence in the United States of any parallel to the British Labour party, Dollimore and Sinfield's anti-humanist reading is militantly oppositional. Indeed, one might caricature this difference by observing that the American critics write as though the English Civil Wars couldn't ever have started, while the British critics write as though they never ended.

Not that I want to caricature: rather, I am trying to characterize what I take to be the most important difference between these critics.

This appears when we see why the concluding paragraph of Greenblatt's "Invisible Bullets" is so incompatible with—so instructively at odds with—the assumptive basis for the first half of Dollimore and Sinfield's essay in which they undertake to explain the "fundamental error" committed by critics like Tillyard, Jan Kott, and Wilbur Sanders. And here, as a way in, we might notice why Sanders receives a double whipping for "veering" between Tillyard's more authoritarian version of "liberal humanism" and Jan Kott's "tragic scepticism."

Dollimore and Sinfield first praise Tillyard. The overt point of this self-consciously delicious irony is that, although Tillyard is ideologically beyond the pale, he at least doesn't pretend, like some other humanists, that "Shakespeare was wonderfully impartial on the question of politics." Kott is then brought in, but swiftly dismissed again for doing "little more than invert the Elizabethan World Picture: the terms of the debate are not changed. As Derrida insists, a metaphysic of order is not radically undermined by invoking disorder; the two terms are necessary to each other, within the one problematic" (208). Dollimore and Sinfield suppose that Kott's Theater of the Absurd "takes its whole structure from the absence of God", and therefore "cannot but affirm the importance and desirability of God." Sanders then receives his *two* whippings. The first is for assuming, like Kott and unlike Tillyard, that "Shakespeare saw through the Tudor Myth" and saw "the futility of politics." The second is for this humanist degenerate's "next move," which is "not into the absurd, but into a countervailing ideal order of individual integrity": for Sanders "the issue is how far any character 'has been able to find a mature, responsible, fully human way of preserving his integrity in face of the threatening realities of political life'" (209). And for Dollimore and Sinfield this characteristic humanist move is not only "selfish and inconsequential" but fundamentally erroneous—since, like Tillyard and like Kott, Sanders's "emphasis on moral or subjective integrity" implies an essentialist notion of "subjective autonomy." They state, "Perhaps the most fundamental error in all these accounts of the role of ideology is falsely to unify history and/or the individual human subject": to talk of "individual integrity" presupposes, even at the level of "etymology," an "ideal unity: the undivided, the integral," a presupposition that is a "fundamental" mistake, since one can only "understand history and the human subject in terms of social and political process. . . .

Crucial for such an understanding is a materialist account of ideology" (210).

In reading this, we might wonder how cultural materialism escapes the nutcracker logic used on Kott: if materialism takes *its* structure from the denial of "idealist," "essentialist" humanism, is it affirming the importance and desirability of that contrary ideology? We should notice how these critics simply rule out the possibility that Sanders might be correct in supposing that Shakespeare did see through the Tudor myth. As for Sanders's own concern with "individual integrity," if what is so wrong, "selfish and inconsequential" about his concern is its allegedly necessary dependence upon an "ideal" notion of the "integral," does the denial of the "integral" similarly entail a denial that we should even be concerned with "individual integrity"? This issue is historically important, since those who achieve political power but, like Marx, habitually mock or "demystify" any concern with "integrity," or with principles that regulate behavior, have no *language* of morality.

Another crucial issue appears when we notice how confidently these critics appeal to Derrida while asserting that history and the human subject are only understood in the terms of "a materialist account of ideology." They see themselves as providing a materialist *account of* ideology that is in some curiously privileged and unexplained way not itself ideological, and not fundamentally metaphysical. But Derrida is rigorous and unequivocal in his insistence that any such assumption is incompatible with the "radicality of deconstruction": "I have of course had occasion to take a specific political stand in certain codable situations, for example, in relation to the French university institution. But the available codes for taking such a political stance are not at all adequate to the radicality of deconstruction. . . . all of our political codes and terminologies still remain fundamentally metaphysical, regardless of whether they originate from the right or the left."[67] Dollimore and Sinfield's use of Derrida is opportunistic and evasive, and this in turn distinguishes their stance from that of the best new historicist critics. The radical challenge to consider what is "fundamentally metaphysical" is being confronted, not evaded, in Greenblatt's or Mullaney's attempts to develop a Foucauldian genealogy of the present that would historicize our notions of truth and reality. But Dollimore and Sinfield assume that their own ideologically committed notions of "truth" and "reality" are not historically and culturally bounded, but are transhistorically and transculturally true.

So, the first half of their essay on *Henry V* is entirely given over to the assault on "liberal humanism" and its various deviant positions; the end of any "interrogative" exposure must always be in line with the materialist Truth. When critical differences are theologized in this depressingly representative way, one lamentable consequence is that it then becomes difficult or impossible to protest without sounding similarly oppositional. Another, more curious, and by now very tiresome, consequence has been the resurrection of Tillyard as an oppositional caricature, a development that diverts attention from the more worrying revival of the Tillyardian method, as I argue in the prologue. In terms of the depressing analogy with the British two-party system, this also means that those who are equally unconvinced by the Tillyardians on the Right and the anti-Tillyardian neo-Tillyardians on the Left find that they are critically, as well as politically, disenfranchised. Only in these farcical terms is it true that those who oppose Tillyard's High Tory authoritarianism must support the authoritarianism of the unthinking Left; in critical terms both alternatives are reactionary. But then the ideological point of the unhistorical assault on "essentialist humanism" is to equate the politically "reactionary" with the critically reactionary, as Graham Holderness does in contrasting the "reactionary or liberal-humanist appropriation of a text" with the "progressive and materialist reading," and as Dollimore and Sinfield do when they claim that one must be a materialist to oppose what all liberal humanist criticism actively supports or passively condones—a "social order which exploits people on grounds of race, gender and class."[68]

So are we to suppose that Shakespeare is evilly in favor of such exploitation in *Henry V*? Dollimore and Sinfield's answer is clearly yes, even though they won't concern themselves directly with Shakespeare's dramatic intentions. The orthodox cultural materialist position is that outlined by Catherine Belsey when she rejects the search for "imaginary coherence" and the misleading notion that texts are produced by "autonomous individuals": cultural materialist criticism's claim to be "scientific" (and to represent what Belsey modestly describes as a new Copernican Revolution) depends on its resolute concern with "ideology itself in all its inconsistency," and with "the play of contradictions which in reality constitutes the literary text."[69] That position chimes exactly with Dollimore and Sinfield's conclusion that *Henry V* reveals "not only the strategies of power but also the anxieties informing both them and their ideological representation," and that "the ideology which saturates" Shakespeare's "texts, and their location in history, are the most interesting things about them" (227). And it corresponds with the queer passage in *Shakespeare: The Play of History* where Holderness explains why "we have not . . . the personal qualities of William Shakespeare our subject": "with no disrespect to the writer's talents or powers, it seems safer to locate the drama's play of ideological contradictions in the heterogeneous and pluralistic fields of discourse from which it emerged, rather than to infer superhuman potencies in an 'author' whose name may have been, for all we know, legion" (16). Certainly it won't do to attribute everything in a work of art to "personal qualities" and "talents or powers"; but neither will it do to deny human agency, put "author" in scare-quotes, and write as though great works of art somehow just emerge from "fields of discourse." Works of art are worked.

Nonetheless, what happens in practice is that these critics do repeatedly imply or assume a dramatic intention, and often of an ugly sort. So, for example, when Dollimore and Sinfield write that *Henry V* reveals the strategies and anxieties of power, they are not paying tribute to the play's exploratory and analytical intelligence; they are assuming that Shakespeare did not mean to reveal these things, and in a more ominous sense meant not to. When they write that "nothing is allowed to compete with the authority of the King," and that "the point where the issue might have presented itself—the plot of Cambridge, Scroop and Grey—is hardly allowed its actual historical significance," they clearly imply that Shakespeare has decided what to allow or not to allow, and that he chose to make the conspirators seem "motivated by greed and incomprehensible evil" because he wanted to conceal or paste over "the structural fault in the state" (220). Yet, as we have seen, Shakespeare's complex design actually challenges us with the contradiction between the Chorus's claim that the conspirators were "corrupted" by "the Gilt of France (O guilt indeed)" and Cambridge's insistence that

> the Gold of France did not seduce,
> Although I did admit it as a motive,
> The sooner to effect what I intended.
>
> (2.2.155–57)

It is the *critics* who make that interpretative choice not to "allow" any dramatic weight to Cambridge's "oblique reference" to the Yorkist claim, and to assume instead that the play is trying to conceal "the actual historical significance" of the "eventually successful" Yorkist claim—which they are careful to explain by referring to Holinshed, rather than to the many relevant passages from Shakespeare's tetralogies. In this way they claim to reveal what the play is trying but failing to conceal.

The structure of Dollimore and Sinfield's essay presents an iron-clad, critical example of what, in another, more human context, Ted Hughes calls the "carapace of foreclosure."[70] Once we attend to this essay's logic and language we see how the demonizing construction of the essentialist humanist Other in the essay's first half quite properly comes first: it dictates, instead of being prompted by, the reading that follows. The second half then begins by exhibiting its own assumptive straitjacket:

> It is easy for us to assume, reading *Henry V*, that foreign war was a straightforward ground upon which to establish and celebrate national unity. In one sense this is so and it is the basic concern of the play. But in practice foreign war was the site of competing interests, material and ideological, and the assumption that the nation must unite against a common foe was shot through with conflict and contradiction. This was equally true for the hegemonic class fraction, though it was they who needed, urgently, to deny divisions and insist that everyone's purpose was the same. (215)

Why should we make any such "easy" assumption, and why "assume" that *Henry V*—the play itself, to use that forbidden phrase again—doesn't reveal and explore those "competing interests, material and ideological"? Why should we assume that the play is trying—as its Chorus certainly tries—to "deny divisions" and further the interests and need of a "hegemonic class fraction"? The answer to these questions has less to do with Shakespeare's play than with the assumptive basis and confrontational purpose of Dollimore and Sinfield's essay—as we see when we consider a few more of their local readings.

After assuming that the author of the first tetralogy had somehow forgotten, or wanted his audience to forget, about the Yorkist claim, Dollimore and Sinfield argue, more reasonably, that "the Archbishop's readiness to use the claim to France to protect the Church's interests tends to discredit him and the Church." But of course they can't sup-

pose that this is a case where Shakespeare is exploring "competing interests" in a purposive and intelligent fashion: who, him? Instead, they suppose that the beastly Bard's purpose—or rather, since they repudiate a concern with dramatic intentions, the play's "main effect"—is to concentrate "power, now spiritual as well as secular, upon the King," in whom "contradictions are resolved or transcended" (221). So, we discover, "the high point of Henry's priestly function" comes when he "gives spiritual counsel" to Williams, and this is also "the point at which the legitimation that religion could afford to the state is most fully incorporated into a single ideological effect" (221–22). But why assume that the "effect" is "single"? It is clearly isn't, in one important respect, since Dollimore and Sinfield go on to spell out what is incoherent and unsatisfactory in Henry's responses to Williams. In their terms the "high point" is a pretty low point; but here, once again, their unexamined assumption is that Shakespeare wasn't intending that complicating "effect," but was intending to concentrate spiritual power upon the King so that he "seems to transcend all worldly authority."

Similarly, we are told that the "scene of the four captains (3.3) seems to effect an effortless incorporation," in which the humanists' brutal Bard approves of the "English domination of Wales, Scotland and Ireland," which "over the centuries" may have caused even "more suffering and injustice than the subjection of the lower classes" (224). "Seems" is nifty, but why doesn't it also *seem* worth mentioning that the same scene shows the captains exploding into a furious, potentially bloody argument over nationalist issues? Once again we see critics bringing forward "evidence" from the play to show how Shakespeare is "implicated in" an attempt to legitimize the illegitimate, without ever asking whether the "evidence" might be so conveniently there, *in* the play, because the play is "actually" more intelligently "radical" and more genuinely "interrogative" than their own prematurely politicized, frenetically oppositional reading.

The ugliest instance is saved for the end of the essay, where we learn how "*Henry V* represents the fantasy of a successful Irish campaign" (225). After coolly explaining that the "assumption that the Irish were a barbarous and inferior people was so ingrained in Elizabethan England that it seemed only a natural duty to subdue them and destroy their culture," Dollimore and Sinfield affirm that "like Philip Edwards, we see the attempt to conquer France and the union

in peace at the end of the play as a re-presentation of the attempt to conquer Ireland and the hoped-for unity of Britain."[71] Within the play, the rather cautious comparison between Henry in France and Essex in Ireland occurs in Prologue 5, but Dollimore and Sinfield present no argument to explain why the Chorus's views should be identified with those of "the play" or Shakespeare on this or any other occasion; here is another fine flower of the Tillyardian method. Nor are they content with assuming that "the play" (which here means the "implicated" Shakespeare) is offering "a displaced, imaginary resolution of one of the state's most intractable problems": they go on to make the extraordinary suggestion that the play's "fantasy of a successful Irish campaign also offers, from the very perspective of that project, a disquietingly excessive evocation of suffering and violence" (225) in Henry's speech before Harfleur, which they quote as a kind of lurid grand finale to show what genocidal horrors the humanists' precious Bard is prepared to countenance or encourage.

For Dollimore and Sinfield the Enemy is very much with us; that is another instance of the difference between the British cultural materialist and American new historicist versions of Them and Us. With that difference in mind, it is worth comparing Dollimore and Sinfield's genocidal "fantasy" with the estranging effect Tennenhouse's and Greenblatt's remarks about the play's "comedic" and "conventional" conclusion. These readings also prompt unpleasant conclusions about what Shakespeare was doing, and they too depend on blocking out much that the play is doing whenever this won't fit the historicists' "interpretive model." So, when Tennenhouse observes, in *Power on Display*, that Shakespeare "chose to dramatize the conquest of France as Henry's wooing of Katherine" (69), he doesn't add that Shakespeare also chose to dramatize Henry's so-called wooing as the final part of the temporary conquest, or rape, of France. That omission then helps in driving home the new historicist wedge between Them and Us, between what benighted Elizabethans could not find delightful and what we children of light cannot but find alien and repugnant: "The English line should dominate the French just as the husband should dominate the wife and the sovereign should rule over the subject." Greenblatt's account in *Shakespearean Negotiations* is much more subtly nuanced—but because that's the way he writes, not because he thinks Shakespeare's conclusion more subtle or more nuanced: "By the play's close, with a self-conscious gesture towards the conventional ending of a comedy, the sexualized violence of the invasion is transfigured and tamed in Hal's wooing of Princess Katherine" (59). So are we to suppose that the grimmer force of those rape metaphors, and of the various uncomic, unconventional final reminders that France was soon lost again, after all the expense of lives and money, has somehow *drifted* into the play, and has nothing to do with its dramatic thinking? If not, the British critics' attempt to see the short-lived, illusory triumph in France as a "fantasy" analogue for the final solution of the Irish problem and the American critics' attempt to see the final scene as soothingly, smoothly comic and conventional, both look decidedly more problematic. Is the problem that Shakespeare is so alarmingly simple, or that all these critics simplify what Shakespeare has made problematic?

The answer seems clear, especially when we consider how dissonant the "comedy" is. That the Chorus should think of Essex, "Generall of our gracious Empresse," is thoroughly in character: his attitudes are indeed representative, but not simply authorial or authoritative. I have already suggested how, far from endorsing the Chorus, the play's final act presents an ironic dyptich of "low" and "high" conclusions that quizzes the Chorus's very different sense of how the "Story" should be staged: "Fortune" plays the hussy with Pistol "now," while placing Henry and "his England" on hold. The various proleptic ironies play bleakly on the audience's knowledge that France would soon be lost, and England made to "bleed." So, hindsight complicates our response to Henry's stirring fancy that he and Katherine can "compound" a warrior son, and to his jubilant assumption that he can keep France through a marital alliance. We know, as we hear Queen Isabel's final speech, that God *didn't* speak that "Amen"; and this makes it more difficult to accept Henry's claim that God's hand, rather than Fortune's, was at work in Agincourt. The Epilogue twists the knife: "Thus farre," says the Chorus, recalling what the blood drip of history would make of the achievements of "mightie men," even as he remembers to apologize for the way in which "our bending Author" has also been "Mangling by starts the full course of their glory." If there is comedy here, it is of the harshly discordant and unsettling kind Shakespeare was soon to provide in the third act of *Troilus and Cressida*.

In music a discord may be a merely local event, where the chord can be analyzed as a kind of startling tune that is vertical not hori-

zontal; but what is "discordant" in the divergent responses *Henry V*
keeps provoking might rather be compared with the way in which a
discord in Bach, Mozart, Wagner, or Schoenberg usually issues as the
suddenly dramatic result of a continuously unfolding counterpoint
between different voices that proceed independently but then, like
members of a family, keep encountering each other in different and
sometimes startling ways. To return to a tiny but instructive instance,
Henry's fantasy about how Katherine must "needs prove a good sol-
dier-breeder" engages our sense of what is past, present, and to come:
of whatever mixed feelings we have already had about Henry's invasion of France; of whatever we are making, now, of this strange wooing, which in performance will depend on many things, including the
princess's response to the stirring paternal fantasy—a response which
may be more or less encouraging, fascinated, interested, doubtful,
hostile, or uncomprehending; and of what we know from history or
the earlier history plays about Henry VI, his father's early death, the
loss of France, and the English Civil Wars. All of these different,
competing possibilities make sense, even as they diverge; they intersect
in intelligible, intelligent ways, even though the resulting discord
admits no simple, harmonious resolution and cannot unite or "bond"
the audience in any reassuringly single or simple, collective response.
It is perfectly possible, and even likely, that the individual spectator's
responses will be both divided and unstable. If the sense of Henry's
imperious male energy is what registers most strongly, this still admits
divergent responses: the male energy may be exhilarating; its imperi-
ousness may buttress an anti-Henry view. If the bleakly proleptic
irony seems to overpower other responses—those various inner
"voices" that are clamoring to be heard at this point—it too might
register in a variety of ways. The irony can be assimilated to an unsympathetic or hostile view of Henry, if this further reminder of the
futility of his familial and dynastic ambitions increases our horror
over the devastation and misery "this faire Action" brings about; but it
can also be assimilated to a sympathetic sense of Henry as a tragically
defeated victim of history, or of the nation itself as tragic victim. To
accept the Chorus's loyally authoritarian view in the Epilogue that the
later catastrophes followed when England's state was "managed" by
"many," and not by one all-powerful monarch, may go against the
modern grain; but it is not more difficult than to believe with Tennenhouse, that "our bending Author" makes Cordelia die to ensure the

male succession and preserve the "patriarchal principle" (*Power on Display*, 142).

Moreover, all these competing ways of "making" sense, in dramatic and experiential terms, of that one momentary dissonance also carry a historiographical challenge: to recognize that only historians "make" history, and that they "make sense" of it in correspondingly different ways. These organized discords and perspectival collisions are true to the kind of argument about Henry V in which historians like Powell and Clanchy are still engaged.[72] They suggest how, as Wentersdorf concludes, Shakespeare had become "increasingly aware of the difficulty of arriving at an objective view of major historical events, and of the ease with which the truth can be misrepresented" ("Conspiracies of Silence," 286). We are not bound to find them unintelligible and incoherent, and we may think them altogether consistent with the whole play's structural dynamics—or with what, in terms of the musical analogy, is so richly and recalcitrantly contrapuntal.

Indeed, that musical analogy provides another way of characterizing what these materialist critics are doing. Old editions of Bach fugues often mark each voice's initial entry with a capital T for "Theme," encouraging the unmusical practice of emphasizing every entry, as though what each voice says as it enters is more interesting and dramatic than what it goes on to say, or sing. Dollimore and Sinfield can only claim that Shakespeare is gratifying his audiences with a violent "fantasy" solution to the Irish problem because they listen vigilantly for any appearance of the big T or Imperial Theme and then, whenever they think they hear it (and no matter whose voice they hear), regard all the other voices as mere accompaniment. That wouldn't matter so much if Henry V consisted largely of Big Tunes and solo arias, like a Puccini opera or a John Osborne play; but reading it that way blocks out too much, like playing a Bach fugue as though it were an aria. Here the way in which a reading (as a mental or actual staging) resembles a musical performance suggests that Belsey's insistence that reading "produces" meaning confuses creation with re-creation: when we play a Bach fugue we are not creating it; Bach's score itself shows why a performance in which some voices could not be heard would be a bad performance of Bach's work even if it seemed "effective" in its own terms. As for Greenblatt and Tennenhouse's assumption that the final scene is comic and conventional—in ways that would satisfy and convince Them, if not Us—

this is too prescriptive about the main effect, and too ready to block out or subordinate the uncomic, unconventional "voices" in this scene's "broken Musick" (5.2.243): we are asked to suppose that Elizabethans obediently responded to the stately tune, while Moderns, who dance to different drummers, find the tune less interesting than its harmonically complicated accompaniment.

As these readings contradict each other they also show how, in each case, what is overdetermined and simplistic follows from the "interpretive model," or theory, that provides an assumptive basis the play is not allowed to test. Greenblatt is far too subtle and intelligent to believe that materialism offers a nonideological "account of ideology," but the Foucauldian thesis about containment altogether governs and determines his reading of the "Henriad." That thesis *requires* the absolute rift between Them and Us, and the correspondingly determined stress on cultural and historical discontinuity. This leaves the reader to discover whether the thesis about containment could ever correspond with theatrical experience, or with any more patient, less purposeful tracing of the unfolding dramatic sequence.

As for Dollimore and Sinfield's essay, the demonizing view of humanism as a monolithic ideology altogether controls their own reading by determining what they oppose and block out. I suggested earlier that the play interrogates Henry's unquestioning assumption that his personal and dynastic interests must coincide with those of the commonweal; but then, as I also suggested, the "Henriad" never presents rebels who seek power for more disinterested reasons. Predictably, Dollimore and Sinfield make that first point through their frequent and resentful references to the "hegemonic class fraction"; but they shy away from the second point, which would be incompatible with their politicized reworking of an either/or debate into a confrontation between Them (selfish Tory establishment humanists) and Us (compassionate Sussex Marxists). Although this seems a little simplistic in Shakespeare's terms, it is a necessary consequence, not only of their determination to align themselves with those who are marginalized, but also of their curious disposition to believe that the "marginal" perception of political, class, and sexual issues is always superior. Because they are concerned only with what they take to be the "most interesting things about" Shakespeare's "texts"—namely, the ideological strategies, anxieties, and inconsistencies that "saturate" them—and because they are convinced that the concern with structural coherence is just another repressive humanist strategy, they cannot consider whether the play's challenging ironies and perspectival clashes might be intelligibly consistent and structurally coherent. So, even as they refuse to engage directly with the directing intelligence at work within the work, their own persistent and unexamined assumptions about what Shakespeare "offers" or "will not allow" make their "Shakespeare" only a little more intelligent and no less repellent than Tennenhouse's court toady.

As for Shakespeare, the chief criticism to be brought against all these readings is that his drama is demonstrably more genuinely "interrogative," more "radical" and, above all, far more intelligent than they allow. I want to finish by suggesting how, as it engages in a more comprehensive sense of human potentialities, the "Henriad" also furnishes a perspective on what these materialist critics find altogether "unthinkable": the littleness of power.

Being Oneself

I have argued that we should be trying to address *Henry V* in ways that better acknowledge its power to read us. The representation of Hal as prince and king frames perspectival conflicts that are developed and sustained throughout three plays and never finally resolved. I want to isolate two such developing conflicts that, in their very tense relation to each other, also illuminate what is so peculiar and challenging in the structural dynamics of *Henry V:* Henry is constantly before us as king, yet he also seems to be constantly receding from us, and perhaps from himself.

My first instance involves Greenblatt's subtle and fertile concept of "self-fashioning." Immediately after Hal's first soliloquy, when we have heard him calculating how to show himself "more goodly," to "attract more eyes," and be "more wondred at," we hear his father's ominous resolution:

> be sure,
> I will from henceforth rather be my Selfe,
> Mighty, and to be fear'd, then my condition.
> (*1H4*:1.3.4–6)

I argue in Chapter 2 that Shakespeare thinks of the "self" as something more like a family of possible selves or a matrix of everything we have it in us to become. Here, it is clear that "being oneself" doesn't mean being one's self in some simple or simplistic sense, but rather subordinating any contrary personal inclinations to the exigencies of staging oneself—one self—as king; later we will hear Hal promising his father, "I shall hereafter, my thrice gracious Lord, / Be more my selfe" (3.2.92–93). In *Shakespearean Negotiations* Greenblatt directs attention to the crucial contrast between different ways of being oneself, but his commentary shows how he isn't concerned with what makes this contrast so timely and telling at this moment in the unfolding drama: "To be oneself" here means to perform one's part in the scheme of power rather than to manifest one's natural disposition, or what we would normally designate as the very core of the self. Indeed it is by no means clear that such a thing as a natural disposition exists in the play except as a theatrical fiction" (46). The play's first scene had shown—only minutes before—how the King is personally (or even naturally) inclined to like Hotspur, and wishes that Hotspur were his own son, rather than the other Harry. But now, when Henry IV so determinedly sets political exigencies above personal inclinations, to give any hint of those feelings which made him envy Northumberland "so blest a Sonne" would be at odds with his declared sense of what the successful exercise of power requires.

But politics is about people as well as power, and the immediate result of Henry's mighty and fearful self-staging is that, within a few more minutes, he has thoroughly alienated Hotspur and turned the champion of the royal cause into a rebel. In other words, Henry's decision about what is politically wise or expedient involves a massive and catastrophic *political* miscalculation. Unlike the King and the Prince, Hotspur would sooner "ease my heart, / Although it be with hazard of my head" (1.3.127–28); his response to Henry's self-staging is disgust—with the "vile Politician," and with the "base and rotten Policy" of a "King of Smiles" who has used his supporters but offered only "half-fac'd Fellowship." But then, in a consummate example of Shakespeare's poetic-dramatic thinking, Hotspur's disgust also reflects back on the purposefully half-faced fellowship of that *prince* of smiles whom we have just heard planning to use Falstaff and the others in staging his dazzling reformation. So, immediately after Hal's soliloquy in the second scene, the unfolding drama provides terms in which to go on thinking about it—through the third scene's contrasts between being ruled by the "head" or by the "heart," and through that no less pregnant contrast between different ways of being oneself. We shall see how these contrasts are still at work in the final scene of *Henry V.*

But that is no less true of my second instance, which involves the unfolding of discrepant or opposed perspectives on Hal's stylistic virtuosity. Pro-Henry readings always assimilate this virtuosity to the familiar, more or less authoritarian theme of the "education of the prince," whose knowledge of his subjects is manifest in his Hamlet-like ability to adapt his language to any hearer or subject. In the first part of *Henry IV* we hear an exuberant Hal congratulating himself for being able to become "sworn brother to a leash of Drawers," and able to "drinke with any Tinker in his owne Language" (2.4.6–7). In the second part of *Henry IV* Warwick assures the doubtful King that "The Prince but studies his Companions, / Like a strange Tongue, wherein, to gaine the Language"—while also insisting, in an unconscious echo of Hal's first soliloquy, that the Prince will "Cast off his followers . . . like grosse termes" (4.4.68–69). In the first scene of *Henry V* the bishops warily testify not only to the miraculous "Reformation" as a stunning spectacle (again recalling Hal's plan to stage himself) but to the new king's ability to "reason in Divinitie," to "debate of Common-wealth Affaires," to "discourse of Warre," and to deliver "sweet and honeyed sentences." In contrast with the other Harry—the Hotspur whose uncle calls him "harebrained Hotspur, governed by a spleen" and whose own wife describes him as "altogether governed by humors"—Hal is the prince "of all humors," able to govern himself and others.

But another series of metaphors opposes this view of "temperate" self-control. Just as Henry IV alienates the hot-blooded Hotspur not because his "blood" has been, but because it always is, "too cold and temperate," Falstaff dislikes the "sober-blooded" Prince John and worries about Prince Hal's Lancastrian blood:

> the cold blood hee did naturally inherite of his Father, hee hath, like leane, stirrill and bare Land, manured, husbanded, and tyll'd, with excellent endeavour of drinking good, and good store of fertile Sherris, that hee is become very hot, and valiant. (2H4:4.3.117–22)

In seeing the measured self-control of the "prince of humours" as a

Lancastrian disability or blight that leaves the country sterile and bare (politicians as polluticians), such passages anticipate a quite different verdict on the emergent sun-king: "The King has killed his heart."

From that opposed perspective Hal's stylistic virtuosity is associated with heartless calculation; but here we need to be careful, in isolating and talking about "opposed" perspectives. What is in question is a range of discrepant perspectives and richly diverse potentialities of meaning; the divergence can become, but isn't always and constantly, so extreme that we feel pressed to make some kind of choice between "opposed," utterly divergent views of Hal. Polemical readings misrepresent that richness and diversity, while readings that insist on "radical ambiguity" too easily imply or assume that there are always two, and only two, sharply opposed possibilities. This is why Rabkin's duck-rabbit analogy is less appropriate to Shakespeare's representation of Hal/Henry than it would be to, say, T. S. Eliot's *The Hollow Men*, in which a constant, and necessarily contrived, ambiguity admits two incompatible readings. Shakespeare's richly complex representation of Hal isn't like that; if we wanted a modernist analogy for what it is like, we might rather think of Joyce's Stephen Dedalus.

In the first part of *Henry IV* the young prince, who is so preoccupied with how to "shew more goodly, and attract more eyes" (*1H4*,1.2.214), never considers whether his self-staging reformation might actually repel, not dazzle, beholders; when he does finally reject Falstaff, the only character who says how much he likes "this fair proceeding of the King's" is—Prince John. However, there are glimpses of a more troubled inner development, particularly when his father is dying and Hal feels an intense need to open his "heart" to Poins. He is at first touchingly diffident, in confessing how "humble considerations make me out of love with my Greatnesse," and how "my hart bleeds inwardly, that my Father is so sicke" (*2H4*,2.2.11–12,48). Yet his sense of isolation is not relieved but confirmed: to the finally direct, jumpy question, "What would'st thou think of me, if I shold weep?" Poins replies, "I would thinke thee a most Princely hypocrite." Hal is suffering here, but to describe this suffering Hal as a tragic figure would be both too vague and too contentious; rather, the play is framing different possibilities. The tragic possibility is that Hal will go on feeling utterly lonely, and discover that his inner life is contracting or shriveling even as his power increases; but here our aroused sense of Hal as a *potentially* tragic figure depends, for confirmation, on our having some continuing access to Hal's sense of his own situation. For another (but not the only other) possibility is that Hal may become a smaller man by unconsciously adapting to the exigencies of being an absolute king, and never see or feel what is happening to him: he would then be a "tragic" figure only in a correspondingly diminished sense. This is why it matters so much when, as Part Two finishes, it also establishes what will make the structural dynamics of *Henry V* so peculiarly tense: although we see and hear what effect the rejection has on Falstaff and others, we cannot see what it costs Hal and cannot know whether he continues to feel that frightened, burdened loneliness which he had labored to admit ("but Oh, to no end!") to Poins. Once he is king he must labor in his vocation, and we spectators in ours: we repeatedly see Henry's virtuoso performances as he stages a royal "self," but are not allowed to see—and consequently want all the more to know—whether there is still a human face behind the royal mask. It is as Machiavelli instructs his prince: "Everyone sees how you appear, few touch what you really are."[73]

The theatrical richness of this carefully managed recession appears when we notice how, although Hal's stylistic virtuosity is Hamlet-like, his situation is almost antithetical. Once "Hal" becomes "Henry" he is constantly performing, and his private self is, as Gary Taylor observes, "visible only through the starts and fissures of his public one."[74] Since any good actor will respond to this challenge, it is not surprising that so many fondly remembered details in performance, like Richard Burton's reaction when Fluellen names Bardolph, involve moments when the actor projects an inner disturbance that the performing king cannot afford to show or reveal. There is also a danger here, of course, which I suspect figured in Shakespeare's reasons for not including battle scenes, and not having Bardolph (or Nym) executed onstage: the extraordinary dramatic tension and interest which this theatrical recession creates, by making us so concerned to know what is going on *inside* this consummate player king as he performs, may actually be dissipated by ill-judged actor's business.[75] For that tension depends on our *not* being sure how to take the measure of whatever difference exists between the "self" that is staged—being oneself as king, in Henry IV's sense—and a private, "inner" self that must be subordinate to the demands of the regal performance. The play sustains this tension into Act 4, when Henry borrows Erpingham's cloak and there is at last the promise of some clarifying self-revelation: "I and my Bosome must debate a while." But the meetings intervene, turning the screw still further as we see Henry once again constrained to speak for, if not as, the king. We also see how the virtuoso who had congratulated himself on his ability to master the languages of his subjects cannot convince Williams, and cannot even listen well enough to understand why Williams is more than a gross-brained peasant. When we do at last hear Henry giving vent to private feelings, these suggest that he cannot afford now—or, perhaps, ever again—to engage in any drastic questioning of the public "self." That he should echo his father's earlier soliloquy, which in turn recalls Richard II's speech on the hollow crown while giving another twist to the idea of the actor king, is striking evidence of the continuities within the "Henriad"; but a far more unexpected echo is to come. For if we ask why Shakespeare changed the name of Hotspur's wife to "Kate" in the first part of *Henry IV,* the only answer that makes any kind of sense is that he was already thinking ahead to the second tetralogy's final scene, and to the culminating masterstroke in his exploration of the contrast between the two Harrys.

Dr. Johnson certainly heard the echo in question, but without considering the possibility of a deliberate and telling irony, when he remarked that Henry's amorous register is startlingly reminiscent of Hotspur.[76] And so it is, for example, when we hear how the manner of the *other* Harry—teasing (and delighting in) his "Kate" for her deficiency in the courtly arts of Mortimer's wife, while mocking Glendower's courtliness and "these same Meeter Ballad-mongers"—is recalled by this prose from a suddenly bluff and "plaine" King:

Marry, if you would put me to Verses, or to Dance for your sake, *Kate,* why you undid me: for the one I have neither words nor measure; and for the other, I have no strength in measure, yet a reasonable measure in strength . . . deare *Kate,* take a fellow of plaine and uncoyned Constancie, for he perforce must do thee right, because he hath not the gift to wooe in other places: for these fellowes of infinit tongue, that can ryme themselves into Ladyes favors, they doe always reason themselves out againe. What? a speaker is but a prater, a Ryme is but a Ballad; a good Legge will fall . . . but a good Heart, *Kate,* is the Sunne and the Moone, or rather the Sunne, and not the Moone; for it shines bright, and never changes, but keepes his course truly. If thou would have such a one, take me? and take me; take a Souldier: take a Souldier; take a King. (5.2.132–33).

This is a magnetic and appealing speech, but the Henry who here insists on the virtue of "a good Heart" is borrowing his voice from the other Harry. The speech even recalls the earlier play's imagery, in which both Hotspur and Falstaff were repeatedly associated with the moon, while Hal associated himself with the sun—just as he does here, in quickly and smoothly adjusting his metaphor: "a good Heart, *Kate,* is the Sunne and the Moone, or rather the Sunne, and not the Moone." Hotspur could never mimic Henry, since he is so helplessly himself and cannot even govern his own "thick" speech: rather his speech speaks him, in being so governed by his humors, and by his "heart" not his "head." But Henry's wooing register is very much a choice, a decision to "speake to thee plaine Souldier," just as his disclaimer of "strength in measure" and his insistence that he has "no cunning in protestation" and cannot "gaspe out my eloquence" involve the familiar rhetorical posture of pretending to be plain. This recollects and reconcentrates many of those doubts and questions which were provoked by all the earlier contrasts between the two Harrys—including the opposed ways of responding to this stylistic versatility, and to the contrast between being ruled by the heart and being ruled by the head. Do we like or dislike this final exhibition of virtuosity, or the way in which even that winning insistence on the "good heart" is calculated, and depends on finding, or choosing, this voice?

Pistol called Henry a "lovely Bully"; one possibility—at one end of the relevant spectrum—is that Henry's performance as wooer will seem so unlovely as to be disgustingly consonant with this scene's other demonstrations of his stylistic virtuosity as the self-staging bully king, "mighty, and to be fear'd." Equally, we might—perhaps with some surprise, or even a kind of shamed perplexity—find Henry's exuberant performance fascinating and enthralling. This may sound like another "either/or," but again it is important to see how the play resists being reduced to any one single, abstractly inclusive set of alternatives. In responding to this scene few readers or spectators will be constantly rigid with resentment or limp with admiration. For example, it is possible to find the very theatricality of Henry's performance exhilarating even while thinking that it prompts a distinction like the one Stephen Booth draws in a superb essay on *Richard II*.[77] Booth is discussing cases in which our disapproval (or approval) of what is said or done by a dramatic character, considered as a person, is at odds with our approving (or disapproving) response to the theatrical character. So, we may enjoy a wicked character's theatricality, or resent even a virtuous action or speech that blocks what was theatrically promising—although this argument will not recommend itself to those who share what Jonas Barish calls the "anti-theatrical prejudice."[78]

I suggested earlier that Olivier's loyalty to his part kept faith with that high-spirited exuberance in the wooing scene which anti-Henry productions often suppress. However, since I was then objecting to cuts that make it easier to indulge a simply admiring view of Henry, and since most of my other comments on this scene have emphasized its discordant or disturbingly uncomic aspects, it is worth asking what could prompt an *un*indulgent admiration or sympathy at that moment when Henry—always the lord and owner of his face, and voices—chooses to sound like Hotspur. If it is important in general terms that the actor should be loyal to his part, what is there here that invites loyalty?

To answer, "the display of power," may seem shocking, but "power" has many senses. When Tennenhouse comments, in *Power on Display*, that Henry's "manner of wooing" only "displays his power of dissembling all the more forcefully" (70) he assumes, in the estranging new historicist fashion, that the play's original (monolithic) audience would admire what any modern (selectively monolithic, sensitized) audience is more likely to dislike. But his argument is also estranged from theatrical experience, in at least one important way. Within the play, this "display" of "power" is directed to Katherine, whose presence and responses are very important: Tennenhouse's indifference to her dramatic presence as something more than an embodiment of "forms of otherness" that assent to their own subjection is, in its own way, curiously patriarchal. Are we to suppose that Henry thinks that his "power of dissembling" could ever deceive *her* into believing that he is, after all, a "plain soldier," without "eloquence" or "cunning in protestation"? Hardly: she knows perfectly well that he is not, knows that she herself is this formidable enemy's "capitall Demand," and knows that, despite Henry's private show of eagerness for her "answer" ("and so clap hands, and a bargaine"), her father must answer the public and political question "Shall *Kate* be my wife?" and can give only one answer. Moreover, so long as we remember it, we may be sure that she could not have forgotten Henry's earlier, negative response to her father's attempt to prevent war by offering Henry his daughter and a dowry of dukedoms. The princess knows that this earlier rejection had nothing to do with Henry's feelings about her, and everything to do with the view (loyally endorsed by the Chorus) that a dowry of "petty and unprofitable dukedoms" wouldn't be nearly enough—even if they were those very dukedoms he had originally demanded, without waiting for an answer. Nor does Katherine need Henry to remind her of the only thing that is enough: "in loving me, you should love the friend of France: for I love France so well, that I will not part with a Village of it; I will have it all mine." None of this leaves much room for dissembling, or for any normal kind of wooing. Henry hasn't been visiting France, as Othello visits Brabantio, and then suddenly noticed his host's lovely daughter. We first see Katherine immediately after the surrender of Harfleur, when she is already surrendering to her own likeliest fate by starting to learn English.

All these considerations might figure in an anti-Henry reading, yet they also suggest how Henry might be regarded more sympathetically. That joke about loving France certainly has its brutal aspect, like the play on verb moods in "Nay, it will please him well, *Kate;* it shall please him, *Kate.*" But the power it displays to Kate herself is anything but a "power of dissembling": all these near-the-bone jokes acknowledge what Henry knows she knows. The complicated inner dynamics of another such joke—when Henry pleads to Katherine to "mocke me mercifully, the rather gentle Princesse, because I love thee cruelly"— ironically acknowledge that the princess has every reason to mock this belated attempt at wooing. His suggestion that she should be the more merciful *because* he has loved her "cruelly," and won her by "scambling," wrests a wittily paradoxical and provocative joke from what is so pointedly un-Petrarchan in their situation: she cannot but yield since, despite his rhetorical pretense to be her suitor and subject, she is entirely subject to his absolute power. And yet Henry's plea, and his mock-Petrarchan pose as suitor and subject, answers to another, quite different necessity: the power politics that deny Katherine any choice about when and whom she marries also constrain Henry himself—and once the human swag has been carried back to England, these two must live together. Seen in this way, those very jokes which acknowledge the brutal realities of a "power" that admits no "dissembling" figure in an appeal *to Katherine* to move *beyond* helpless acquiescence.

If that seems important, Hal's exuberantly witty assumption of a Hotspur-like register, and his performance as the bluff plain soldier, who is doubly at a loss in having to deal with a woman and with a courtly French princess, will not register as a merely insentient, macho display of power. Rather, it starts from the all too real sense in which Katherine *is* being claimed by a victorious soldier, who doesn't have to woo her or win her "answer"; but its appeal for us involves that appeal to her to recognize that their respective situations make it necessary—or impossible, unless she reciprocates—to create a space for the "good Heart" in a marriage wholly determined by political necessity. True, the appeal includes (or, to be more thin-lipped, isn't above) various reminders that Katherine can enjoy sharing power, as a queen and maker of manners; in this scene power is something Henry evidently enjoys having and exercizing. But the exuberant wittiness—for example, in those obviously self-refuting disclaimers—is directed first of all to Katherine, and not as something that could deceive her, but as something she too might enjoy and find liberating. We might even think of those numerous Donne poems in which the speaker not only enjoys his own consciously self-exploding illogicalities, but assumes that the woman will enjoy them too: although it is not among the poems moderns most admire, "The Flea" is a good example, and is one of the poems which most frequently appears in surviving commonplace books. Henry's performance similarly compliments Katherine by addressing her as a grown-up, even as it appeals to her to act like one.

Because this scene also releases, or sustains, other more damaging or depressing perspectives, it doesn't allow us to settle into some simply admiring view, where, as a *Time* reviewer might put it, we are happily blissed-out. Its richly diverse energies, and its ways of engaging and reconcentrating our various responses to the cycle it concludes, ensure that this is one of those Shakespearean scenes that always "plays" differently, in different performances and readings. Only an academic critic could feel compelled or think it right to look for some constant, fixed response. Indeed, the scene helps us to understand why one response to the experience of complexity and perplexity is to abstract and simplify, to try to make sense of the play by abstracting and reducing the "issues" to some inclusive "either/ or"—for example, by trying to determine whether Henry is an ideal monarch or a Machiavellian militarist. But it is more important to see how the play resists abstracting moves, and why an intelligent actor like Alan Howard is right to protest against critics who find the play "shallow or jingoistic": "Well, they haven't had to play it."[79] And, because the play's dramatic thinking so frequently plays on, and prompts us to think about, the very notion of *making* sense, or *making* history, it is not inappropriate or anachronistic to think of Nietzsche or of Joyce's *Ulysses*. In its own way *Henry V* carries the profoundly subversive Nietzschean insight: we interpret the world as we interpret the text. And its irreducibly complex representational strategies suggest, like *Ulysses*, that the difficulty of making sense of life, lives, and history follows from what is problematic both in all attempts to represent experience and in experience itself.

The wonder of it all, sighs Kenneth Branagh, is that Henry and Kate "do literally in one brief interview fall in love."[80] Branagh does add (without misgivings) that "almost the greatest challenge" was "to make credible that this was the same man whom we had seen throughout the play." Indeed, and the same man whose so-called wooing is inseparable from brutal power politics in this very scene: even in choosing his mate, Henry has no private life or wishes that are not entirely determined and engulfed by considerations of state. But then—we might think, as we struggle to collect our responses to this final gestalt—doesn't that suggest a basis for sympathy? Perhaps; but is it not also a devastating measure of Henry's diminished human potentialities that now, when he needs to find an attractive, manly voice, like that heard long ago in his own "holiday" prose with Falstaff, the man who had determined to *imitate* the sun can only borrow the voice of the other Harry? The tragic experience of an Othello, an Angelo, or a Macbeth, involves the terrible discovery of inner dimensions, of what they have it in them to become; Hal's tragedy, if we choose to call it that, is that he can become nothing other and nothing more than a King. "'Tis paltry to be Caesar."[81]

Although I have tried to give an account of those complexities that make prematurely politicized readings of *Henry V* seem simplistic, I doubt that my analysis furnishes any adequate reply to a reader who is sympathetic but critical, and protests: "Indeed it is a complex play and I quite see why you admire it so much; I admire it too, but I love the first part of *Henry IV,* and could never love *Henry V.*" This is because . . . but I cannot go on; that reader I imagined has now appeared, and is clamoring to be heard.

"Yes, I'm sorry about that, and just when you were attempting a stagily judicious summary. But I'm going to insist on having the last word, since I've kept quiet for so long, and I certainly won't let you speak for me now you've suddenly acknowledged my existence. Men! Try to understand. I do agree about the play's intellectual and analytical power, and its foxy way of quizzing each and every viewpoint; so far as all that's concerned, I can't imagine any more effective ending to the cycle. And I see that the play can't be collapsed into a polemical pro-Henry or anti-Henry reading, since—to use your own cherished terms—attempts to do that 'short-circuit' its 'poetic-dramatic thinking.' Instead of looking for what the play 'really' thinks, we should be seeing how it really *thinks*. Oh yes, I knew you'd like that! And yet, can't you see, it would be easier to love this play if it *did* present Henry as a mirror of Christian kings or even as a Machiavellian hypocrite, and if only that 'historiographical challenge' weren't so relentless.

"The result for me is *strain*. That 'interrogative rhythm' you so prize—moving from what 'bonds' an audience to what divides it, and so on—it's so unrelenting. So is that 'carefully managed theatrical recession': after being made to care so much about whatever rift may be opening between Henry's public and private selves, why shouldn't we know? Rabkin's quite right, I *want* some more direct answer to the question, 'Can one be a successful public man and retain a healthy inner life?'

"You don't allow—or allow enough—for what makes this play's 'structural dynamics' like those of *Troilus and Cressida*, another driven play that most people don't like as much as you do, and never will. Both plays are always several paces ahead of their interpreters, but that's because they never allow us to respond wholeheartedly, and unguardedly, to any speech, let alone a scene, without our being cabined, cribbed, and confined by some quizzing irony or 'perspectival' complication. This may be intellectually satisfying, even salutary; but it's inhibiting. Think back to those Eastcheap scenes with Hal and Falstaff, or the achingly Chekhovian scenes in Justice Shallow's garden: there are ironies and complexities in plenty, but they're rich, generous, capacious. They aren't so restless, so unnerving. Very few Shakespeare plays are: *Henry V* is peculiar.

"Notice, please, I'm not saying what a lot of readers will say—that all these unsparingly analytical complications are a feature of your own analysis, not of the play. But can't you see how, if the play does match your account of it, that might be a reason for valuing it less highly than you do? Interpretation isn't the only game in town. You write as though going round and round were the only good."

[Exit.]

Dramatic Intentions:

Two-Timing in Shakespeare's Venice

Jessica's Lie

Like Homer, Shakespeare nods. Sometimes, his lapses provide oblique but instructive glimpses of his workshop: to borrow a metaphor from Arnold Schoenberg, we see the artist responding to the evolutionary needs of an embryonic conception.[1] For some distinguished modern editors, the most spectacular example of Shakespeare's getting himself into and then out of a potentially "ruinous" difficulty is provided by the "double-time" scheme in *Othello*.[2] If we agree that the difficulty exists, getting into it took some trouble, since it isn't present in Giraldi Cinthio's Italian story and Shakespeare could have avoided it altogether by keeping closer to the original story: he chose not to. And since the difficulty in question results from his drastic compression of the loose and indeterminate time scheme in Cinthio's novella, it cannot profitably be discussed without a more fundamental and ranging consideration of the dramatic reasons for that compression. Something is wrong with any reading that "makes sense" of a Shakespeare play in ways that do not and cannot accord with a plausible account of what Shakespeare was working toward in evidently purposeful departures from his source materials.

For another example, we could recall that moment in *Measure for Measure*—another play that draws on, but transforms, a story in Cinthio's *Hecatommithi*—when Barnardine refuses to be executed. The troubled Duke concedes, even as he determinedly gives the order to bring Barnardine to the block, that "to transport him in the minde he is / Were damnable" (4.3.64–65). The Provost promptly reports the death, that very morning, of the pirate Ragozine, whose beard and head are just of Claudio's color—and the delighted Duke hails "an accident that heaven provides." But it is hard for us to share in this surrogate dramatist's pious delight, when it is so jarringly apparent that this "accident" is not provided by heaven but contrived by the real dramatist, who is at the same time calling attention to his own rapidly multiplied contrivances. These are demonstrably not some clumsy inheritance or opportunistic mechanism imposed by the "story": once again, Shakespeare deliberately chose to get into, or make, a difficulty more extreme and provocative than any in his source materials. His response to the inherited problem of needing a substitute head if Claudio's life is to be saved is to invent Barnardine and a new situation that can be "saved" only by finding a substitute for the substitute; and because that exposes, instead of underscoring, the Duke's immense and pious relief, it looks more like a deliberately signaled and ironically reflexive comment on contrivance.[3] If we don't like the reflexive reading we must find another, one that will explain why Shakespeare's contrivances are not only more provocative but purposeful, and *meant*.

Here it is helpful to recall Stanley Cavell's disagreement, in *Must We Mean What We Say?*, with Monroe Beardsley and other proponents of what A. D. Nuttall has called the "fallacy of the intentional fallacy."[4] Cavell observes that "a certain sense of the question 'Why this?' is essential to criticism, and that the 'certain sense' is characterized as one in which we are, or seem to be, asking about the artist's intention in the work":

> The philosopher, hearing such claims and descriptions, has his ancient choice: he can repudiate them, on the ground that they cannot be true (because of his philosophical theory—in this case of what poems are and what intentions are and what criticism is); or he can accept them as data for his philosophical investigation, learning from them what it is his philosophizing must account for. Beardsley's procedure is the former, mine the latter. According to Beardsley's, when a critic inquires about intention, seriousness, sincerity, etc., he is forced outside the work. My point is that he finds this true because of his idea of where an intention

is to be searched for, and because he has been reading unhelpful critics. For the *fact* is that the correct sense of the question 'Why?' directs you further *into* the work. In saying that this, if true, is a fact, I mean to be saying that it is no more than a fact; it is not an *account* of objects of art, and intention, and criticism, which shows the role of this fact in our dealings with art. (227)

Much of this chapter consists of a sequence of "Why this?" questions applied to critical readings and elisions as well as to plays. My assumption is that the critical value of considering Shakespeare's creatively purposeful departures from his source materials is like that of following an author's revision processes: it can concentrate attention on whatever is now being done to replace what had been done, which in turn can confirm our sense of when we need to ask "Why this?" or alert us in cases where we might not have thought, or wanted, to put that question. We see into the workshop.

Of course there are cases where the "Why this?" is so pressing as to make any other confirmation seem critically nugatory: nothing, we might say, could *stop* us asking why Cordelia dies or pondering the equivocal miracle of Hermione's survival. But then *King Lear* is a play in which (to echo Edmund) nothing, least of all the "catastrophe," comes "pat," while *The Winter's Tale* has Paulina reflecting, within her play's world, on how people would "hoot" if the happy ending she has contrived occurred in a play—such as that contrived by the real dramatist who invents Paulina as another surrogate dramatist, like Duke Vincentio or Prospero or Iago. In each case we are challenged, again, to think about what has been contrived, and what kinds of contrivance we accept or expect or find unacceptable. Learning that Cordelia survives and that Hermione dies in the relevant source materials confirms, and even adds to, our sense that what Shakespeare has done is very much *meant*. To quote Cavell again: "What counts is what is *there*, says the philosopher who distrusts appeals to intention. Yes, but everything that is there is something a man has *done* (236).

To claim that considering Shakespeare's departures from his sources can show where we need to ask "Why this?" is not to claim that we will then know how to answer that question, since any such answer depends for its cogency on what happens in the play. But that first, more modest claim still has consequences, not least in relation to the new historicist habit of sampling a text in a very partial way to corroborate a cherished thesis. So, to anticipate, the prominent references to sheets in *Othello* take their significance from Shakespeare's decision to make his lovers newlyweds whose marriage is still unconsummated when they arrive in Cyprus. Greenblatt's own immensely influential reading usefully asks why the sheets matter so much to Othello, but never asks why they matter no less to Desdemona, and what I take to be the best or only coherent answer to that question explodes Greenblatt's reading. As for the "double-time" theory, the alleged "evidence" consists of a series of answers to "Why this?" questions; yet the theory collapses when we see what other answers are possible, and see how the theory both introduces further, unexamined difficulties and fails to address the crucial question why Shakespeare so drastically compresses the Italian story's indeterminate but extended time scheme. However, I want to approach this controversial issue—and *Othello*—by way of Shakespeare's other Venetian play, in which a comparable problem seems to have escaped notice.

In the first part of *The Merchant of Venice* Shakespeare also compresses the characteristically relaxed time scale of an Italian novella; but then, in response to other pressing dramatic necessities, he needs to reestablish a looser "romance" time, like that in Ser Giovanni's prose story.[5] Although this shift is brilliantly managed in dramatic terms, it throws out one curious lapse which, so far as I have been able to tell, hasn't troubled anybody. Yet one reason for noticing this lapse and discussing it is that it escapes notice, even though it's one of those things which, once seen, can't be unseen. Another reason is that it bears on the important general issue raised in A. J. A. Waldock's *Sophocles the Dramatist,* when Waldock says subtle and rewarding things about what he terms the "documentary fallacy."[6] Yet another reason is that it can remind us of the extent to which the energies of Shakespearean drama depend upon the "framing" of questions that we must register as questions, or dramatic potentialities, before we can know whether any answer is available.

In the first two acts of *The Merchant of Venice,* the "realistic" handling of time allows a very deft counterpointing of events in Venice and Belmont, and is most clearly established through numerous references to supper. The importance of the "dinner-time" engagement is twice emphasized in the first scene: "at dinner-time / I pray you have in mind where we must meet," says Lorenzo, and a few moments later the departing Gratiano and Lorenzo take their leave, each stressing again the importance of the forthcoming dinner. In the fourth scene Shylock declines Bassanio's invitation to this same dinner, and leaves to "purse the ducats straite." We then move to Belmont, where we hear Portia denying the Prince of Morocco's request to make his choice of caskets at once (people are in a hurry in these two acts): "First forward to the temple, after dinner / Your hazard shall be made" (2.1.43–44). In the next scene we're back in Venice with the same clock ticking: Bassanio enters, giving instructions that supper should be "readie at the farthest by five of the clocke," and this scene ends with Gratiano's promise to rejoin Bassanio at "supper time." In the next scene (2.3) Jessica gives Launcelot a letter for the lover whom "soone at supper shalt thou see." In 2.4 Lorenzo is planning to "slinke away in supper time," and we learn that the masquers have only "two houres" in which to get their act together since it is "now but foure of clock." In the next scene—while the last was taking place— Launcelot has made his way back to Shylock's house, as directed, to renew the supper invitation, which Shylock now accepts. After being summoned several times, the elusive Jessica is told of this—and never sees her father again. In 2.6 she elopes; we learn that since it is "nine a clocke," supper is over and the masque must be abandoned. The next scene returns to Belmont, where by now Portia and Morocco have also finished dining, and Morocco braces himself to make the choice that was postponed in 2.1. That leisurely postponement of a "venture" that will make or mar his life had of course heightened the dramatic tension; and so does the contrasting rapidity of the Venetian action, as various characters rush from one place to another between their last exit and their next appearance. In short, Shakespeare has taken obvious pains to synchronize events in Venice and Belmont and to compress events into a realistic, tautly dramatic time scale.

But then a looser "romance" time must be established instead, if this dramatic tension is to be preserved. Obviously: the period of the loan must pass. Moreover, Shakespeare needs to create a definite but not too definite impression that all of Antonio's ships have been destroyed—including those which, as it later turns out, were not destroyed. This temporal shift is managed in a subtle, unobtrusive way. The first rumor of a shipping disaster comes in 2.8, and Act 3 begins with the rumor of another remote catastrophe. In the next scene, news of the ruinous extent of Antonio's losses reaches Belmont, while, in this same indeterminate period of time, Shylock has been appalled by the reports of his daughter's travels and extravagant escapades. That these different reports come in at the same time matters dramatically. In 3.1 we see and hear the Christians mocking Shylock's grief; we also hear Shylock gloating that Antonio "dare scarce shewe his head on the Rialto," and instructing Tubal to "fee" an officer and "bespeake him a fortnight before." Some critics, like Harold Goddard and A. D. Moody, see this temporal coincidence as a causal connection—arguing that the cruel mockery of Shylock's grief provokes him into demanding the pound of flesh.[7] This is an important interpretative issue, and I shall return to it, but my immediate point concerns the way in which, as the city buzzes with vicious or sympathetic gossip, we scarcely notice how the spans of time are lengthening. Where before we had a realistic sense of how long it took Shylock or Launcelot to rush, between scenes, from one Venetian suburb to another, we now have a *needfully* vague sense of the time it will take Portia to journey across the "Continent."

The puzzling lapse occurs in 3.2—that is, when the play is shifting from "realistic" to "romance" time. Now in Belmont, Jessica speaks of a conversation she has overheard between her father and his "countrymen":

> When I was with him, I have heard him sweare
> To *Tuball* and to *Chus,* his Countri-men,
> That he would rather have *Anthonio's* flesh
> Then twenty times the value of the summe
> That he did owe him: and I know my Lord,
> If law, authoritie and power denie not,
> It will goe hard with poore *Anthonio.*
>
> (3.2.286–92)

As with the more familiar "double-time" problem in *Othello,* the oddity here is a consequence of a generally masterly, and explicably purposeful, handling of time. For although Jessica's testimony comes after or during the needful shift into "romance" time (so that "When I was with him" sounds loose rather than very specific), and although it may also come after an interval, it concerns that period in which time was handled in a strict and tautly "realistic" fashion. In the period between the signing of the bond and her own elopement, Jessica had neither the time nor the opportunity to overhear any conversation between her father and his cronies. If we have attended to the time scale Shakespeare took such pains to establish, Jessica must be lying.

I should say at once, and very firmly, that although this conclusion would not be inconsistent with the unattractive aspects of Jessica's character, I don't like it. It feels quite wrong—too clever by half, too much the armchair deduction. And the smell of that kind of argument is, to borrow Thomas Mann's phrase, bad nineteenth century. It is all too like the kind of argument one might have encountered in *Blackwood's Magazine,* in which John Wilson (writing as "Christopher North") first propounded the theory of the "double-time" scheme in *Othello.* But it doesn't seem more helpful when critics take Jessica's report as a clinching piece of "evidence" that shows why sympathy for Shylock is misplaced.

So, for example, John Palmer has suggested that the speech shows Shakespeare going "out of his way to inform us expressly that Shylock has made up his mind to kill Antonio long before Jessica's flight with Lorenzo," and that the dramatist here "slips in an explicit repudiation" of any "romantic" idea that Shylock was "moved to extremity by paternal anguish."[8] Similarly, in *Shakespeare and His Comedies* John Russell Brown remarks that Shakespeare has here "gone out of his way to inform us" that Shylock's intentions were vengeful and murderous "before Jessica eloped and before he had news of Antonio's losses."[9] This view is very much at odds with, and is offered as a refutation of, any suggestion that in 3.1 Shylock is provoked into demanding the pound of flesh by the Christians' cruel mockery of his grief. Since neither Goddard nor Moody provides an alternative account of the significance of Jessica's report, the Palmer-Brown explanation of its significance might seem all the more compelling; yet their explanation also seems awkward, and in two quite different ways.

In the first place, we should notice how both Palmer and Brown speak of Shakespeare going "out of his way"—as though they were registering, without quite bringing to the surface, some impression that Jessica's speech is out of keeping with the play we had hitherto been watching. Yet that very doubt about Shylock and his motives, which they think this speech settles, had seemed enriching, rather than distracting—the kind of doubt from which much of the play's dramatic and moral interest derives. When Moody remarks that Shylock's lamentations are both elegiac and grotesque, in that the "passionate cry of outraged humanity" is "inseparable" from Shylock's "equal and undiscriminating concern for his lost precious stones," he very well catches the way in which this play repeatedly catches and involves us, by setting our sympathetic or empathetic *apprehension* of a character's feelings against a diagnostically detached *comprehension* of his or her situation.[10] In this case, we (like Solanio) can see what is "undiscriminating" in Shylock's "passion," but we (unlike Solanio) can also feel how that passion hurts. But, for Palmer and Brown, Jessica's speech provides clinching, quasi-legal evidence that Shylock is, *tout court,* the black-hearted villain of a less absorbingly intelligent and interesting comedy than the play we thought we were watching or reading.

If we don't want to lose that play, Palmer's speculative suggestion that Shakespeare gave Jessica this speech because he feared that he had gone too far in arousing sympathy for Shylock might easily be countered by a quite different (though no less speculative) suggestion of a "genetic" kind. For there is clearly one sense in which Shakespeare began with a conception of Shylock as a racist stereotype and black-hearted comic villain: that is what "the Jew" is in Ser Giovanni's *Il Pecorone,* which provided the story of the bond and the ring imbroglio, though not the story of the caskets. It is no less clear that—to *some* degree, and it can only be the degree, rather than the tendency, which is in dispute—Shakespeare became more concerned to show, through a characteristic exercise of imaginative inwardness, how Shylock apprehends his own situation. Taken together, these two obvious points establish a major contrast between the Shakespearean drama and the Italian novella; indeed, I argue in *Shakespeare's Scepticism* that other similarly polarized critical debates—about Bertram, Isabella, and Othello, as well as Shylock—may also be traced to the contrast between Shakespeare's compulsive habit of creative interiorization and the almost total absence, in the Italian novelle that furnished "stories" for *The Merchant of Venice, All's Well That Ends Well, Measure for Measure,* and *Othello,* of any corresponding concern with psychological motivation and the inner dynamics of character and feeling. If we are going to speculate as Palmer does, we might rather wonder whether Jessica's problematic speech derives from an earlier Shakespearean scenario that was drafted *before* Ser Giovanni's monstrous "Jew" had evolved into the Shakespearean Shylock.

Moreover, by speculating in the way he does, Palmer should remind us of something important, which both he and, uncharacteristically,

John Russell Brown forget. Literary and textual "evidence" does not have the same status or effect as legal evidence. In a court of law, accepting Jessica's testimony would indeed mean rejecting and altogether discounting contrary testimony; but in a play or work of art the sequence of our responses is never to be discounted. Indeed, this is even true of the activity in which a single Shakespearean line or sentence may engage us: as Stephen Booth's brilliantly provocative edition of the *Sonnets* repeatedly demonstrates, differentiating that sense which an ambiguous word may eventually take—in time, as the sentence unfolds—does not always "dispose of" the effect of momentarily entertaining a "wrong" sense.[11] What we learn in 3.2 may or may not suggest some need to revise an impression formed in 3.1; but Jessica's report cannot show that Moody was wrong to respond to 3.1 as he did. That is, it cannot show that the earlier scene does not or should not produce a complicating sympathy for Shylock.

The second objection to the Palmer-Brown reading appears once we start weighing the implausible alternative—that Jessica is lying. For both readings are open to the same objection, insofar as they offer to stabilize and simplify what had been shifting, tellingly and interestingly complex responses. If Jessica is telling the truth, Shylock is a vengeful, bloodthirsty monster; if she is lying, in order to curry favor and/or expose a hated father to the "law, authoritie, and power," then she is monstrous. In either case, Shakespeare has evidently nodded. If he wants us to believe Jessica, then making that impossible within the play's carefully constructed time scheme is a lapse; if he wants us to suppose that Jessica is lying, he has not made this sufficiently clear in dramatic terms—since audiences certainly don't receive that impression. Although it seems messy, like many natural things, I suspect that audiences commonly respond to Jessica's suggestion that something must be done, and urgently, but that they respond without thinking the speech as significant, and clinching, as Palmer and Brown suppose. It is characteristic of critics, when they are caught up in an interpretative dispute, to *lean on* a particular speech or passage. In my own case, my worries about this speech began when I was trying to make sense of the polarized debate about Shylock—that is, when I was reading critics, not the play—and felt an inner tremor of dissent at the very idea that this speech could bear as much weight as these critics want it to carry. But then what grounds could we have for supposing that Jessica is not lying, if the text itself furnishes "evidence" that she is?

It is not sufficient, I take it, to dismiss that question as an example of "neo-Bradleyan literalism." Indeed, and here Waldock's warnings about the "documentary fallacy" come into range, deciding which questions should not be asked seems to me very much more difficult than is usually allowed by those critics who berate Bradley.

A striking instance of the hazards of literal-mindedness is provided by a difference between Stephen Greenblatt and Harry Berger, Jr., over how to explain the references to milk in *Macbeth*.[12] For Greenblatt, the manly anarchy of Malcolm's Macbeth-like threat to pour the sweet milk of concord into hell involves an onanistic avoidance of woman and her generative power; Berger also assumes that the "milk" is seminal, but directs attention to Lady Macbeth's attempt to rob her husband of his potency by draining him of his "milk of human kindness." Certainly, I don't care to think of Malcolm as an onanist or of Macbeth as the drained victim of a dairymaid *dentata*. But then neither do I think that the literal-minded question these critics address is, in itself, objectionable or improper. *Why milk?* We cannot begin to think about the play's unexpected associations of "milk" with sweetness, nature, concord, and human kindness—associations more insistently, challengingly present in this play than they are in *King Lear,* when Goneril scoffs at her husband's "milky kindness"—unless we first ask that question.

As a hostage to fortune, I offer my own literal-minded explanation. Although semen is not usually "sweet," *colostrum*—the first breast milk, which Elizabethans called "green milk"—certainly is. And, although it leads us straight into another well-signposted minefield, giving suck to a child matters in *Macbeth*. Far from being mysterious or incongruous, it is moving, and revealing, that Lady Macbeth first associates that "human kindness" which she fears in her husband's "Nature" with the first milk and kindness a newborn babe imbibes, and then, even as she so fiercely repudiates her own "kind" and natural instincts, recalls giving suck to her own child. Like Donne's reference to "Kinde pitty" in *Satyre III*, her speech calls into play that richer sense which the word *kind* took, in this period, from its closer association with *kin* and *kindred*. Similarly, when the soliloquizing Macbeth of 1.7 associates "Pitty" with a "naked New-born-Babe," it is moving and revealing that he—like his wife, and like many men and women, not only Christians—associates his deepest sense of what natural and heavenly concord means with the image of a newborn babe, with the idea of a nursing mother somewhere in the background. Some thirty lines later we hear Lady Macbeth reminding him that "I have given suck, and know / How tender 'tis to love the babe that milks me." But the grounding imagery of concord and natural process also connects with nightmarish variants and perverting inversions, as some other process works to deliver Scotland and its heroic deliverer into horror:

> Why doe I yeeld to that suggestion,
> Whose horrid Image doth unfixe my Heire,
> And make my seated Heart knock at my Ribbes,
> Against the use of Nature?
>
> (1.3.134–37)

Whatever fathers or mothers it, the unmanning image that possesses Macbeth's mind in Act 1 can be exorcized only through action, when it is delivered or released into the world like a birth. The horrors, but not the Macbeths, breed and multiply as the very firstlings of the heart become the firstling of the hand—until these deformations of natural process are answered and avenged by that husband and father who abandons his own kin to deliver his country, and whose own Caesarean delivery, or untimely ripping, so eerily rhymes with Macbeth's seemingly timely unseaming of the rebel Macdonwald from nave to chops.[13]

Nothing can or should stop an attentive reader from wondering why Lady Macbeth's bairn is in the text but not, as it turns out, in the play. Her child does indeed matter in Holinshed, because the historical Makbeth's claim to the throne actually depended upon his relation to his wife and her child by her first marriage, and because the Duncan of the *Chronicles* did all that "in him lay to defraud him of all maner of title and claim" to the Scottish throne.[14] Here too Shakespeare adjusted his sources in various ways, and it seems likely that in writing Lady Macbeth's speech he simply failed to notice the leakage from source material he was choosing not to use elsewhere. Such things happen, even in the greatest works: in the third act of Wagner's *Tristan und Isolde* Tristan's desperate anxiety about the color of the sails is yet another example of this kind of leakage, which only becomes intelligible when we examine the dramatist's sources. Some-

body who asks troubled questions about Wagner's sails or Lady
Macbeth's child is not being idle, or falling into Waldock's "documentary fallacy": that person is *attending*. Here we may note that Bradley
himself never asked, "How many children had Lady Macbeth?" (The
caricaturing title of L. C. Knights's famous and pugnacious essay was
not taken from one of Bradley's more distracted appendixes; it was
proposed, as a good though very malicious joke, by F. R. Leavis.) To
ask how many *children* Lady Macbeth had would indeed be idle, since
there is no point in the play where we are pressed to ask that question.
Yet it is hard to know what "attending" to a play could possibly mean,
if we simply do not care to notice that Lady Macbeth is saying in an
intense and unforgettable speech that she has had a child, or if we
do not remember that speech later, when it matters so much that the
Macbeths are childless.

True, the child is not mentioned, and so in that sense does not
matter, in the rest of Shakespeare's play; but we cannot know that, in
the play's fifth and seventh scenes. A play unfolds in time; in responding to it, as it unfolds, we are constantly registering more or
less provisional impressions, and lodging interrogative impressions of
what may or may not "turn out" to "matter."

By now it should be clear that the quarrel I'm entering here is not
with Waldock's own subtle and helpful account of the "documentary
fallacy," but rather with its illegitimate progeny—those crudely mechanical dogmas which treat a play as a static text without regard
for the dynamic process of unfolding, and which also obstruct our
understanding of the ways in which a dramatist's embryonic conception evolves. Such dogmas are rife in the New Arden *Hamlet,* where,
for example, we find the editor skidding from Waldock's sensible observation that we should not treat a work of fiction as a record of fact
to the queer assertion that we should not ask questions that the "play"
does not answer.[15] This assertion implies that an attentive spectator
can know in advance, like an editor who has devoted years of his life
to the play as text, which questions the play *will* answer. The New
Arden editor offers an example that actually explodes his argument:
since the whole purpose of Hamlet's "Mousetrap" is to provoke some
reaction from Claudius, it will not do to argue, like the New Arden
editor, that we should not be concerned to know how Claudius reacts
to the dumb show because the "play" does not tell us.[16] A printed text
is at best an imperfect record of a dramatist's conception; although

the text of Hamlet does not tell us how Claudius reacts, we may be perfectly sure that the original stagings of the play did. The New Arden editor advises the actor playing Claudius to do nothing, since Shakespeare's play doesn't tell him—or, more to the point, the New Arden edition of the text cannot tell him—what to do. But, as Wittgenstein's parable of the policeman[17] nicely reminds us, to do nothing is to do something, and this is a case where to show no reaction is very definitely a reaction: after all, we have heard Hamlet planning the "Mousetrap" at the end of Act 2 precisely so that he can observe the King's reaction, and then later telling Horatio why he too must watch no less closely:

> Observe my Uncle, if his occulted guilt
> Do not it selfe unkennil in one speech,
> It is a damned ghost that we have seene,
> And my imaginations are as foule
> As *Vulcans* stithy; give him heedfull note,
> For I mine eyes will rivet to his face,
> And after we will both our judgements joyne
> In censure of his seeming.
>
> (3.2.80–87)

Hamlet's last words anticipate the conclusion he expects; yet, to his credit, he does recognize how much he wants to believe in Claudius's "guilt" and the Ghost's unhellish provenance, and is scrupulously determined to distinguish the truth from wishful thinking. This is why Claudius's reactions matter so much—and why it matters so much, later, when the text seems as equivocal as Horatio.[18] The problem the New Arden editor wants to dismiss is so vexing because it is there *in* the text—like Lady Macbeth's bairn, and like the questionable but disconcerting "evidence" that Jessica is lying.

Characters do lie in Shakespearean drama, of course, and it is not always clear who is lying: the dramatic significance may depend on a skilfully implanted doubt. We miss something important in *Richard II* if we do not register the dark, necessarily oblique hints that Richard himself was implicated in the death of Woodstock; but the play never establishes whether the charge was true or false. In the third scene of *1 Henry IV,* Hotspur and the King violently disagree about whether Mortimer fought with Glendower; both men cannot be telling the truth, and both have reasons or motives for suppressing the truth.

We are not attending if we don't wonder which man is lying, but the play never answers that question. Jessica's speech is more vexing, if we do start leaning on it, because it threatens to diminish the play we have hitherto been watching. Palmer and Brown want to believe her, as Hamlet wants to believe the Ghost. But at least Hamlet knows what he is disposed to believe, and worries that his "imaginations" *may* be "foule"—whereas Jessica's speech seems so clinching to Palmer and Brown only because they are *already* opposed to what they think of, and discount, as "romantic" or sentimentally indulgent views of Shylock, and because they don't ever worry that their responses to the play's Christians might be correspondingly indulgent—prejudiced and clannish, if not racist.

This appears to be a case where asking "Why this?" sends us further into the text, but the text drives us back again. It is natural to assume that Shakespeare had some reason for giving Jessica those lines: in undertaking to "make sense of" her speech or the play we assume that it made some sense to the writer when he wrote it. Yet the peremptorily logical assumption that Jessica must either be lying or telling the truth involves us in larger difficulties if we think that each of these alternatives would be demonstrably at odds with the evolution of the Shakespearean conception. Where do we go?

My suggestion is that we try to follow Shakespeare—that is, to see in what direction he was going when he so deliberately departed from his sources, as his own play took imaginative shape. That development was essentially complicating, a matter of seeing various characters— Shylock and Jessica, and also Antonio, Portia, Bassanio—in ways that are both sympathetic and diagnostic, and at odds with the clannish perspectives taken within the play by the Jews and the Christians. So, if we are giving weight to that development, the very idea that Jessica's speech should settle anything seems retrograde. It remains true that no explanation can be other than speculative; if we lean on this speech we fall over. The explanation that seems to me most likely is that Shakespeare had forgotten, in 3.2, how much stage time had passed since Jessica's elopement in 2.5: after watching 3.1, we can imagine Shylock having conversations of the kind Jessica describes in the scene that follows, but it is another matter to suppose that Jessica could have heard them. True, this explanation will not remove the textual difficulty, but nothing seems likely to remove that, and Palmer and Brown don't notice it.

As we have seen, they both suggest that Shakespeare felt he had gone too far in allowing that sympathetic view of Shylock which their own readings oppose, so that Jessica's speech represents Shakespeare's belated attempt to rescue the situation and reassert a simpler, less complicated, and markedly unsympathetic view of Shylock which corresponds with their own. Despite their uncompromising conclusion—that Shylock is monstrous and that to think otherwise is to sentimentalize—they are allowing that the play *had* been developing in other, complicated, and complicating ways, and had been prompting a measure of sympathy for Shylock which (for whatever reason) Palmer and Brown were disposed to resist even before they could claim to find a retrospective "justification" for this conclusion in Jessica's speech. But that resistance—like their strikingly coincidental references to Shakespeare "going out of his way"—exposes and clarifies the critical issue, which is whether we admire the complicating development in the first half of the play, or, like Palmer and Brown, find it more satisfying to suppose that Shakespeare was trying—belatedly—to *settle* the question of what we are to think of Shylock.

Complex Designs

I have argued that the chief objection to the idea that Jessica's speech settles that question is not that any such attempt on Shakespeare's part to put his thumb in the pan is belated, but that it is retrograde in dramatic and moral terms: it represents a retreat from a challengingly complex mode of dramatic thinking about characters and issues into something more conventional and less absorbing. This objection can be reformulated as a more general claim about what went on in the Shakespearean workshop. Put baldly, this claim is that Shakespeare's departures from his source materials constantly show him working to complicate and integrate what critical readings all too often attempt to simplify and fragment.

One kind of complication follows from the creative concern, or compulsion, to imagine how a character sees and feels his or her situation. As I observed earlier, this challenge to our own imaginative sympathies then produces all those heated "either/or" debates about Shylock, Angelo, Caliban, Henry V, and Othello—in which critical attempts to settle such debates both testify to and, paradoxically, try to deny or suppress those energies which make the play work. But then, Shakespeare's no less characteristic concern to *integrate* his dramatic material produces another kind of perspectival complication, one that invites or challenges us to see how one part of the play bears on another.

In *The Merchant of Venice* Shakespeare is alive to that excitingly problematic element in the story of the bond that had earlier interested Anthony Munday,[19] but he then complicates matters further by interweaving—or ensnarling—Ser Giovanni's story of the bond (and the rings) with the wholly independent story of the caskets. A kind of structural, poetic-dramatic conceit is in question, which then challenges us to reflect, as the play's characters never do, on whether and how these stories bear on each other. It is apparent, for example, that Portia's immediate attraction to the glistering Bassanio, and her corresponding distaste for all of Morocco's "complexion," is ironically at odds with the ostensible moral of the caskets story, with its conventional warning against judging by appearances; it is then also apparent that we should be asking how that irony bears on the story of the bond, on the clannish behavior of both the Christians and the Jews in this play, and on the trial scene.

Here it is instructive to see how John Russell Brown's influential reading resists both kinds of complication, when he protests against "sentimental" responses to Shylock's most famous lines. Brown is perfectly right to observe that the passage in which Shylock insists on the Jew's humanity occurs in the middle of a speech that attempts to justify the most appalling revenge; but Brown doesn't go on to remark that the speech occurs in the middle of a play that disconcertingly confirms Shylock's view that the Jew who wrongs a Christian must expect "revenge." Yet the Shakespearean complications matter: first, that complicating challenge to our imaginative sympathy, which in this case involves seeing how a Jew sees and feels his situation, and the further complication that appears when we ask whether and how Shakespeare has integrated his dramatic material, in choosing to combine the story of the bond with the story of the caskets.

Shylock's speech comes in 3.1; in *Measure for Measure* a comparable challenge to avoid a compelling but simplistic judgment also comes in 3.1, when we first learn of Angelo's earlier relationship with Mariana. For many critics this revelation confirms a hostile view of Angelo as man and governor, and an admiring view of the Duke's legal and moral authority; yet these views simplify what Shakespeare has worked to complicate. *Measure for Measure* explores, even more profoundly than *The Merchant of Venice,* the collisions between intractably different conceptions of legal, moral, and (through Isabella's appeal to the Sermon on the Mount) divine justice. In this play Shakespeare has chosen to yoke Giraldi Cinthio's story of the corrupt governor—which George Whetstone had already drawn on in his 1578 play *Promos and Cassandra*—to the quite different story involving Mariana and a bed trick. Indeed, the play assembles *three* "rhyming" legal cases: two (Claudio's and Angelo's) involve dowries, and two (Claudio's and Lucio's) involve illegitimate children. That they are invented is important. They are there because Shakespeare has put them there; they bear on each other in ways that the Duke altogether fails to perceive, let alone consider.

Claudio's case involves both a dowry and an illegitimate child, but only after Shakespeare has made a crucial change to the earlier versions of the story. In his play Claudio is *not* sentenced to death for fornication—which is a necessary but not a sufficient condition for the crime in question—but "for getting Madam *Julietta* with child" (1.2.72–73). Claudio's relationship with Julietta is the only mutually loving relationship in the play: they have postponed their marriage because they hope to secure a dowry—but then, since Julietta is pregnant, Claudio falls foul of that "strict statute" which Angelo has been instructed to revive and enforce. The statute is "strict" in the precise legal sense: it treats Claudio's offense as a matter of strict liability admitting no plea of mitigation. Whatever the extenuating circumstances, they have no *legal* relevance; strict liability sentencing is always opposed to the requirements of *moral* justice. The justifying argument in its favor, or defense, is usually that the likelihood of (moral) injustice in individual cases is outweighed by considerations of public good, and that is the argument we hear the Duke advancing in 1.3, when he tells the Friar that the state of Vienna (after fourteen years of his rule or misrule) requires that the strict statutes be revived and enforced—although he also wants somebody else to enforce them, and has murkier reasons for delegating that unpopular task to Angelo. Here, in implicating the Duke and raising doubts about his motives and competence, Shakespeare also departs from his sources in a creatively purposeful way.

The discrepancy between the claims of legal and moral justice, which this first case starkly isolates, is not what troubles Escalus and Isabella; neither denies that the law is "needful," or argues that it is bad law. In her first meeting with Angelo, Isabella begins by approving of the law because it treats as a crime what she regards as a sin; that doubtful reasoning is characteristic, and consistent with the shocked Isabella's shocking indifference to the fate of her pregnant childhood friend, the "groaning" Julietta. Later, when she appeals to the Sermon on the Mount ("Judge not, that ye be not judged"), she has no answer to Angelo's lucid argument that a judge must judge and shows most "pittie" in showing "Justice": to release a criminal (like Barnardine) shows no pity for those prospective victims whom the law should protect; once Isabella herself becomes a victim we hear her loud demands for "Justice, Justice, Justice, Justice" (5.1.25). As for Escalus, he too wants the law to be bent, not changed, since Claudio is a "gentleman" who had "a most noble father" (2.1.9–10); Angelo properly dismisses this appeal in a speech which shows how his own commitment to enforcing the law is moral, as well as legal—and also inhuman, since he is incapable of recognizing any moral concern or obligation which isn't also legal. Nothing in Claudio's case disturbs him.

That indifference of course gives point to the sudden revelation in 3.1, when we learn how Angelo abandoned the helpless woman to whom he was betrothed, and who still loves him. His offense seems far worse than Claudio's in moral terms, but he is also innocent of any legal crime: since there had been no premarital consummation of their betrothal there was no legal—as opposed to moral—obligation. By tricking Angelo into sleeping with Mariana, the Duke wants to create just such a legal obligation, so that Angelo can be forced to marry a woman he plainly does not love. Although this trick is acceptable to Mariana and Isabella, it is morally questionable (like Portia's legal trick) and would certainly have seemed questionable in Elizabethan law, under which anybody who was tricked in this fashion could plead *error personae*. There is of course no excuse for supposing that Angelo has committed the same offense as Claudio.

But Lucio has. The next carefully timed revelation, as Shakespeare assembles his three "rhyming" cases, is that Lucio had appeared before the Duke three years earlier "for getting a wench with child" (4.3.169) and had escaped by perjuring himself and denying his relationship with Kate Keepdown. Here there are no extenuating circumstances: Lucio has committed the legal crime for which Claudio was sentenced to death, and his offense, like Angelo's, is far worse in moral terms. His relationship with Kate was entirely unloving and mercenary, and he has been brutally indifferent to the fate of his bastard son; worse still, he malignantly arranges the arrest of the woman whose kindness, in caring for his bastard infant, Lucio resents. If the Duke believes that the strict statutes are "needfull" he could find no fitter victim—but he does not even notice. In the final scene, where the Duke is so intent on staging his fantasy conception of himself as ideal governor, he has forgotten the crisis that allegedly required such draconian measures. Lucio is forced to marry Kate, but when he protests that marrying a punk is a fate worse than death, the Duke's reply could hardly be more revealing: "slandering a prince deserves it." That, in the Duke's view, is Lucio's worst transgression; but this view, like the stagy release of the unrepentant Barnardine, suggests how the contrast between the inhuman Angelo and the all too human Duke as *governors* might best be considered as a contrast between unbenevolent principle and unprincipled benevolence. Those who accept the self-regarding Duke's view of himself as ideal governor fail, like the Duke, to recognize and confront the legal and moral issues that Shakespeare has made all the more pressing by inventing those three "rhyming" cases.

In *Measure for Measure,* as in *The Merchant of Venice,* we are challenged to see further than any of the characters, by seeing how the different parts of the play they inhabit bear on one another. Portia comes closest to saying—but *not* seeing—how the stories of the bond and the caskets bear on each other, when her first extended speech reflects on the gulf between principles and practice; but this is a proleptic dramatic irony, since she knows nothing of the bond. It is left to us to recognize how that speech and Shylock's speech on the discrepancies between Christian principle and Christian practice bear on the trial scene. The Italian stories by Ser Giovanni and Giraldi Cinthio are combined with other stories or invented material, which produces something like a conceit in Dr. Johnson's sense—a yoking together of seemingly heterogeneous elements. If we do attend to their complex design, we can see how both plays work to complicate what critics then want to simplify.

Shylock is not the main character, or protagonist, of *The Merchant of Venice:* he appears in only five scenes. Portia is far more important in structural terms since she links the two actions or stories and in this sense—as Verdi said of Mistress Ford in *Falstaff*—stirs the porridge. Similarly, Caliban is not the main character, or protagonist, in *The Tempest:* he also appears in only five scenes, with 177 lines compared with Prospero's 653; in the percentages that Marvin Spevack's *Complete and Systematic Concordance* so usefully provides, Prospero speaks 29.309 percent of the text's words, as compared with Caliban's 8.393 percent, Ariel's 7.888 percent, Gonzalo's 7.221 percent, and Miranda's 6.242 percent.[20] Of course such calculations don't determine relative importance: Stephano, with 8.137 percent, has the third-largest part in the play, not because he is more important than Ariel or Miranda, but because he is (like Gonzalo) more garrulous. But if those percentages can be misleading, they are also instructive, since they help to show why it is both natural and critically disquieting that so much recent criticism of *The Merchant of Venice* and *The Tempest* concentrates on Shylock and Caliban. This focus is natural because these characters are at the center—or rather, at the epicenter—of their respective plays. But the failure to engage with Shakespeare's complex design (as in all those discussions of Shylock which say nothing of the Belmont caskets) produces partisan or authoritarian readings, in which the conflicts these plays explore are treated as problems with a solution. Indeed from this point of view the term "problem plays" is in a peculiarly exact sense misleading. The term became current in Shakespearean criticism at the time of Ibsen and Shaw, when classicists like Wilamowitz also began considering *Antigone* as though it were a classical *Hedda Gabler.* But the objection to the term is not merely that it might with equal justice be applied to plays like *Julius Caesar* or *Antony and Cleopatra* (as Ernst Schanzer noted years ago),[21] but that it is blurring to use the same term for resolvable problems as for genuinely intractable dilemmas—like that conflict between legal and moral and religious concepts of justice in *Measure for Measure.*

Even when a character dominates a play, his or her dramatic significance is still determined not by the size of the part but by its contributory significance within the complex Shakespearean design. Duke Vincentio's part is one of the largest in Shakespeare, and all the more remarkably large since he doesn't begin to dominate the play until 3.1—when that scene slides into prose as the Duke steps forward with the first of his many stagy, hastily improvised "solutions." But the Duke makes that very mistake which then reappears in critical commentaries: he regards an intractable conflict as a "problem" that admits a "solution." The conclusion that the play explores dilemmas that the Duke cannot even recognize as dilemmas seems all the more inescapable once we attend to the play's complex design and to the numerous telling complications Shakespeare has introduced: he invents those three "cases," Julietta's baby, Lucio's infant, and Barnardine and Abhorson; he makes Isabella a religious novice; and he implicates his Duke by making him responsible for those fourteen years of lax misgovernment which, in the Duke's own view, have produced a crisis in Vienna. The Duke's unshaken belief in his legal and moral authority and his benevolent but unprincipled attempts to "resolve" problems and dilemmas he cannot even understand ensure that he dominates the play; yet his absolute trust in his own legal and moral judgment is exposed, not endorsed, by the play. But then, in all these plays characters with relatively small but "epicentral" roles like Caliban and Shylock, as well as those characters who are in some sense dominant or dominating, are presented within a complex, highly organized, and integrated design; hence that perspectival challenge to see more, and farther, than any of the characters in the plays.

When I referred to Arnold Schoenberg at the beginning of this chapter I was recalling the passages in *Style and Idea* and *Fundamentals of Musical Composition* in which Schoenberg describes the compositional process:

> A real composer does not compose merely one or more themes, but a whole piece. In an apple tree's blossoms, even in the bud, the whole future apple is present in all its details—they have only to mature, to grow, to become the apple, the apple tree, and its power of reproduction. Similarly, a real composer's musical conception, like the physical, is one single act, comprising the totality of the product. The form in its outline, characteristics of tempo, dynamics, moods of the main and subordinate ideas, their relation, derivation, their contrasts and deviations—all these are there at once, though in embryonic state. The ultimate formulations of the melodies, themes, rhythms and many details will subsequently develop through the generating power of the germs. (*Style and Idea*, 65)

Similarly, although Schoenberg allows that the "beginner" will not be "capable of envisaging a composition in its entirety" and must instead "start by building musical blocks and connecting them intelligently," he emphasizes that the real composer "does not, of course, add bit by bit, as a child does in building with wooden blocks," but "conceives an entire composition":

> Used in the aesthetic sense, form means that a piece is *organized;* i.e. that it consists of elements functioning like those of a living *organism.*
>
> Without organization music would be an amorphous mass, as unintelligible as an essay without punctuation, or as disconnected as a conversation which leaps purposelessly from one subject to another.
>
> The chief requirements for the creation of a comprehensible form are *logic* and *coherence.* The presentation, development and interconnexion of ideas must be based on relationship. (*Fundamentals of Musical Composition,* 1–2)

Schoenberg's organic and embryonic metaphors are not very fashionable in the language of current literary theory. However, they bear on my own argument in two ways.

In the first place, Schoenberg's own concern with variation—"development" and "interconnexion"—as a means of integration provides a helpful analogy, if we are concerned with the ways in which Shakespeare works to integrate his dramatic material. Here, for example, the contrast between *Promos and Cassandra* and *Measure for Measure* resembles that between *The Famous Victories* and *Henry V.* Neither of the earlier non-Shakespearean plays succeeds in integrating the "lowlife" scenes with the main action, although *The Famous Victories* makes some attempt to relate them. But, as we have seen, the second act of *Henry V* sets up an ironic, quizzing relationship between the "high" and "low"; in the third and fourth acts the interweaving of "high" and "low" quarrels becomes so elaborate as to undermine the distinction itself—which is nonetheless reasserted, still more quizzingly, in the last act's ironic diptych. In *Measure for Measure* the practical problem of linking the "high" and "low" social worlds is most obviously resolved by having Lucio move freely between them; yet the more profound dramatic integration is achieved by ensuring that the different parts of the action bear on each other in unexpected and usually disconcerting ways. If we are following that process, the endings of both *Measure for Measure* and *The Merchant of Venice* are all the more disconcerting, because the characters on stage behave as though all problems have been resolved, although they haven't.

Second, Schoenberg's emphasis on "germs" and embryonic evolutions can usefully remind us of what, in contemporary terms, is odd about the activities in the Shakespearean workshop. Schoenberg writes, all too romantically, of the way in which the real composer "conceives an entire composition as a spontaneous vision," and then "proceeds, like Michelangelo who chiseled his *Moses* out of the marble without sketches, complete in every detail, thus directly *forming* his material." The prefaces Henry James provided for the New York edition of his works are no less concerned than Schoenberg with "germs"—stray remarks, dinner-party anecdotes, and the like—and with the ways in which, as the sense of the "subject" gradually declared itself, there was an answering sense of the appropriate "form" and methods of "notation." But Shakespeare repeatedly found his "germs" and raw material in other writers' *finished* works, which he then took apart and recombined with other material in fashioning his own poetic drama.

Although I have been emphasizing the importance of "dramatic rhyming," and although the three counterpointed cases in *Measure for Measure* can be seen to "rhyme" like the counterpointed quarrels in *Henry V*, it seems too contrived to speak of the "rhyming" of the stories of the bond and the caskets, or (to anticipate) to speak of the three "rhyming" couples in *Othello*. But what matters, in all these cases, is the way (or variety of ways) in which different parts of the play bear on each other—even when, or expecially when, the characters in the play don't see this happening. Moreover, since these are all examples of variational development, we need to be correspondingly alive to the internal relationships within a complex design. Keats observed that we hate works that have a palpable design on us; but, without quarreling with the spirit of that famous insight, we can notice that other important sense in which any great work of art *is* a palpable design. So, although we cannot but be concerned with "dramatic intentions" if we are engaging with a palpably complex Shakespearean design, our model of intention should not resemble that of Palmer and Brown, or indeed of the critics they oppose. Rather, Shakespeare's variational developments and perspectival complications repeatedly show the difficulty of trying to sustain any one, or one-eyed, view; they are exploratory and liberating, nor coercive or "morally instructive" in Dr. Johnson's inferior sense, and in this way pass their own comment on the all-too-human and authoritarian impulse to extract some simpler, preemptive or prescriptive judgment.

This liberating complexity is magnificently, and painfully, present in *Othello*, and in that play, as in *Measure for Measure*, the transformation of the original Italian story could hardly be more radical. I want to consider this transformation more closely, and to begin by returning to that "Why this?" question I broached earlier: why should Shakespeare have taken such pains to get into a potentially ruinous difficulty that never existed in Cinthio's story and that, we are told, only the "trick" of "double time" could resolve?

Obeying the Time

Although it is factitious and distracting, the theory or myth of "double time" is still respectfully trundled out in every modern scholarly edition of Othello, even the most recent.[22] It has been as long lived as Nahum Tate's adaptation of *King Lear*, which held the stage for a century and a half, and, like that adaptation, it deserves to be firmly laid to rest. It betrays its bad nineteenth-century provenance in three different (though related) ways. First, it expects Shakespearean poetic drama to repay an approach that (as C. P. Sanger's examination of the handling of the time scheme in *Wuthering Heights* memorably showed) is more appropriate to mid-nineteenth-century novels; this, as Jane Adamson crisply put it, leads "our attention away from Othello's obsession, towards the kind of details that might obsess an Inspector from Scotland Yard."[23] Second, it is bardolatrous, and offends against what Richard Levin has called the "undiscussed principle of Knowing When to Give Up."[24] For the theory describes and depends on what is unashamedly called a trick, a device usually seen as an occasion for bardolatrous rejoicing, except by a few scrupulous critics like Bradley and Emrys Jones. Finally, the theory cannot be separated from that nineteenth-century tendency which found its glorious apotheosis in Verdi's *Othello*. Othello is the "Noble" Moor, Desdemona is beatified, Iago is demonized—and, in the opera, even sings a satanic "Credo." There is then no need for a drastically compressed time scheme, and indeed Verdi's lovers, like Cinthio's in the Italian source story, have been married for some time: here Arrigo Boito, Verdi's brilliant librettist and collaborator in *Otello* and *Falstaff*, might just as well have claimed of *Otello* what he claimed of *Falstaff*—that he had returned the Shakespearean play to its native Italian source.[25] *Otello* is a work of genius, and the "double-time scheme a product of misguided bardolatrous ingenuity; but neither makes sense of (more bluntly, the nineteenth century couldn't make sense of) the dramatic and psychological effect of Shakespeare's purposefully drastic compression of the loose, indefinite "romance" time in the Italian novella.

As Emrys Jones emphasizes in *Scenic Form in Shakespeare*,[26] it is important not to confuse "double time" with accelerated time, which is theatrically indispensable, commonplace, and usually untroubling. So, for example, nearly five hours of "stage" time and less than a minute of "real" time pass between that moment in 2.2 when we hear the Herald proclaim "full libertie of Feasting from this present houre of five," and our hearing Iago observe in 2.3 that "'tis not yet ten o'th'clock." What follows in 2.3 is more remarkable, since the first night in Cyprus passes during this scene; Jones pertinently compares this with *Richard III*, 5.3, which takes us through the night before the battle of Bosworth. So, by the time the scene ends, the triumphant Iago can tell Roderigo that

> Thou know'st we worke by Wit, and not by Witchcraft
> And Wit depends on dilatory time,

and exclaim, with self-congratulatory cheerfulness:

> Introth 'tis Morning;
> Pleasure, and Action, make the houres seeme short.
> (2.3.362–63, 368–69)

Indeed this is exuberantly and unnervingly witty: the surrogate dramatist who has produced chaos in this scene, and whose reference to "Witchcraft" gleefully recalls his earlier triumph over Brabantio, seems here to be sharing a professional joke with the real dramatist, whose own skill in managing this scene's accelerated time has helped to "make the houres seeme short."

The third act follows in similarly precipitate fashion. When Iago encounters Cassio again in 3.1 he asks, "You have not bin a-bed then?" and Cassio reminds him that "the day had broke before we parted"; Emilia then enters, telling Cassio (and us) that the "Generall and his wife are talking" of Cassio's disgrace—not *were*, but "are," talking of it, now. Although Emilia has heard enough of this conversation to be able to assure Cassio that Desdemona "speakes for you stoutly," while Othello "protests" that he "needs no other Suitor, but his likings" to reinstate Cassio after a prudent interval, Cassio determines to stay for "some breefe Discourse" with Desdemona "alone." The brief glimpse of Othello in 3.2 shows him already busy with the day's work: the letters for the Senate have already been written, and he sets off to inspect the "Fortification." By now the play is half over, without its being at all obvious that this is a play—the play—about "adultery" and "jealousy."

Throughout this first half of the play the only indeterminate period of time is that taken up by the voyage to Cyprus, when (it is emphasized) Othello and Desdemona are in different ships. This carefully managed compression of the Italian story's time scheme maximizes tension and the continuity between the scenes is a theatrically impressive way, but it also ensures—takes pains to ensure—that the newly married lovers have so little time together. When Othello leads Desdemona off to bed some hours after their arrival in Cyprus (and immediately after telling Cassio to report the next morning at his "earliest" convenience) he confirms that the marriage still has not been consummated:

> Come my deere Love,
> The purchase made, the fruites are to ensue,
> That profit's yet to come 'tweene me, and you.
> (2.3.10–12)

The stage direction for Iago's entrance follows these lines, leaving open the possibility that he arrives on stage just in time to hear Othello's words and perhaps register some malignantly interested response. Be that as it may, his next words show that Iago is well aware that the marriage still hasn't been consummated, and he immediately insinuates, in his busy, tirelessly malicious way, that Othello is neglecting his official duties:

'tis not yet ten o'th'clocke. Our Generall cast us thus earely for the love of his *Desdemona:* Who, let us not therefore blame; he hath not yet made wanton the night with her. (2.3.13–16)

Learning that the marriage still hasn't been consummated is, for the audience, a confirmation rather than a surprise—precisely because Shakespeare's handling of time has been both careful and suggestive, constantly bringing home how little time these lovers are allowed together. In the second scene they were interrupted by Iago's warning that Brabantio's posse is on its way. Then, after Desdemona's bold affirmation, in the Senate scene, that she would not be "bereft" of the "Rites," it was determined that the newlyweds would leave that night, in different ships; as Othello tells Desdemona, he has

> but an houre
> Of Love, of worldly matter, and direction
> To spend with thee. We must obey the time.
> (1.3.329–31)

And of course in 2.3 they are disturbed once again, by the riot that Iago engineers; after quelling the riot Othello goes off to dress Montano's wounds, while Desdemona goes back to bed. Indeed, the accelerated time in 2.3 makes it impossible to know how much time the lovers have together before they are disturbed; although critics assume that the marriage is consummated, it is not clear whether the consummation happens before or after the riot, or not at all.

I return to this point later, but advocates of the "double-time" theory are more concerned that Desdemona hasn't had time to sleep with Cassio. So, the "difficulty" that—as the New Arden editor puts it—threatens to make "nonsense" of the "dramatic action" is that, within the play's "short time," there is no time in which "adultery" could have occurred. Nobody doubts that (as Frank Kermode assures us in the Riverside edition) Shakespeare "is clearly aware" of this difficulty.[27] But we are to suppose that, having taken such pains to get into it, Shakespeare "resolved" it not by a real extension, or loosening, of the stage time, like that in the second half of *The Merchant of Venice*, but by what the New Arden editor, M. R. Ridley, describes as a craftily engineered "trick": "What Shakespeare is doing is to present, before our eyes, an unbroken series of events happening in 'short time', but to present them against a background, of events not presented but implied, which gives the needed impression of 'long time'" (lxx). Instead of feeling uneasy about a play that must resort to a trick "to make the whole progress of the plot credible" (lxix), the excited Ridley affirms that this "throws light on Shakespeare's astonishing skill and judgment as a practical craftsman. . . . He knew to a fraction of an inch how far he could go in playing a trick upon his audience, and the measure of his success is precisely the unawareness of the audience in the theatre that any trick is being played" (lxx). Dover Wilson similarly invites us to discover and marvel over "yet another piece of dramatic legerdemain, the most audacious in the whole canon, which has come to be known as Double Time."[28]

One strange feature of this argument appears in that question-begging emphasis on a needful "impression": since "short time" is also, and no less, an "impression" or dramatic illusion, it is hard to see what could prevent the one "impression" jarring against the other. Moreover, although having an "impression" of "long time" is thought to be wonderfully helpful where Desdemona's (alleged) relationship with Cassio is concerned, it wouldn't be at all helpful to any spectator who then began wondering about Desdemona's (actual) relationship with her husband. What would they be talking about? Where would Othello sleep for however many nights are in question? I hasten to add that I don't for one moment think we do ask such questions, in reading or watching Shakespeare's play. But then *Othello* is constantly making us think, whereas the presumed point of creating the "impression" of "long time" is to prevent thought.

Another general difficulty is that the "trick" can work only if we first notice, but then don't *think* about, the various alleged "instances" and "indications" of an "illusory" period of "long time."[29] Here the argument becomes alarmingly circular, and also depends on an elaborate but confidently predictive set of assumptions about what our old, dim friend—the Audience as Monolithic Entity: that fabulous beast with many bodies but a single, unimpressive mind—can be relied upon to notice or not to notice. Evidently, we *don't* reflect, when reading or watching *Othello,* that there has been no time for Desdemona to commit adultery. But then, it's assumed, we *would* notice this, or would have noticed it, were it not for all those craftily planted "indications" of an illusory period of "long time." This in turn assumes that we *will* notice, and be tricked by, the "indications" of "long time." Finally, this magic circle closes with the futher assurance, or assumption, that we *won't* also notice and reflect on the discrepancy between the "short time" of the stage action and the illusory "impression" of "long time." Noticing this discrepancy would of course expose the very "difficulty" that the "trick" is to prevent us noticing—along with other new difficulties that, we shall see, the "trick" introduces. But later, as a kind of reward, we are also being invited to notice, and marvel at, this "legerdemain" as a supreme instance of Shakespearean art. Part of the theory's appeal is that of our feeling superior—of our being initiated into a bardolatrous inner circle that knows how the trick works and is (as Catherine Earnshaw might say, but all this is very nineteenth century) incomparably above and beyond that dumb uncomprehending block, the Audience.

Something is evidently wrong, but how much is wrong in Shakespeare's play? To take one of the "instances," it is apparent—on reflection, if not in the theater—that Lodovico's arrival in Cyprus in Act 4 is implausibly rapid, and involves the sort of discrepancy which diligent editors are quite properly expected to spot, and try to account for. As the very diligent New Arden editor observes, "the government of Venice can hardly be supposed to recall Othello till there has been time for the report of the Turkish disaster to reach them and for them to send the order for recall" (lxx). Here is a case where we might readily agree that Shakespeare has nodded. Perhaps he failed to notice the lapse; perhaps he noticed it but saw that nothing was to be done, since he could hardly postpone the play's climax for however many days would suffice to forestall such a literal-minded objection. We cannot know either way; more to the point, we have little reason to care. As long as we do regard it as an instance of nodding—of Shakespeare failing to notice what few members of his audience would notice—it is not difficult to account for as a loose end or unwanted consequence of Shakespeare's drastic compression of the Italian story's indeterminate but extended time scheme. However, it is a quite different matter to suppose that this is, as the New Arden editor tells us, a "very clear instance" of the conscious, deliberate, and wonderfully crafty way in which the Bard tricks us by including various "indications" of an illusory period of "long time." Nor could we suppose that the trick works in this "very clear instance" unless we believe what seems inherently unlikely: that the dim but sturdily reliable Audience (which, if we gave it a shape and form, might resemble Orwell's Boxer) could be counted upon to take in the "indication," though without thinking any more about it.

Let us try another, instructively different "instance." Beady-eyed sleuths have assumed that Bianca's complaint about Cassio's week-long absence (3.4.173) must refer to a period of time spent in Cyprus.

Bianca.   'Save you (Friend *Cassio*).
Cassio.   What make you from home?
   How is't with you, my most faire *Bianca?*
   Indeed (sweet Love) I was comming to your house.
Bianca.   And I was going to your Lodging, *Cassio.*
   What? keepe a weeke away? Seven dayes, and Nights?
   Eight score eight houres? And Lovers absent houres
   More tedious then the Diall, eight score times?
   Oh weary reck'ning.
Cassio.   Pardon me, *Bianca:*
   I have this while with leaden thoughts beene prest,
   But I shall in a more continuate time
   Strike off this score of absence.

(3.4.168–79)

I have quoted so much of this dreadfully undistinguished exchange because I don't want to be accused of special pleading: Cassio must live in army lodgings and Bianca clearly can't, but it's easy to see how the references to her "house" and his "Lodging" made "double-time" sleuths pounce—supposing that the week in question has passed in Cyprus, and that Cassio's fumbled excuse for his week-long absence refers back to his catastrophe on the first night in Cyprus. Nonetheless, this must be wrong. If we do take Bianca's reference to a week-long absence as another "indication" of "long time," then a moment's reflection is enough to suggest that the long time in question must be real, not "illusory," while the period of time spent in Cyprus must then be considerably longer than a week—since it is also being assumed that the liaison between Cassio and Bianca has run its whole course in Cyprus. We see the New Arden editor assuming this (without reflecting further) when he observes that, although there is "no doubt" that Iago's reference to Bianca as a "Huswife, that by selling her desires / Buyes her selfe Bread, and Cloath" (4.1.94–95) gives "Huswife" its bawdy sense, meaning that Bianca is a courtesan, "there is also little doubt that Bianca is also a housewife in the normal sense, a citizen of Cyprus, with her own house, and not a mere camp-follower" (141). Norman Sanders hedges on this point in the New Cambridge edition, saying that "there is no clear evidence in the play for or against the idea that Cassio knew Bianca before he landed in Cyprus" (189). But again a moment's reflection suggests what more is "clear," for if the relationship was going on before the journey to

Cyprus, there is no need to take Bianca's reference to a week-long absence as an "indication" of "long time". Moreover, the alternative—supposing that they have been in Cyprus for more than a week—produces a quite horrendous difficulty, since the business with the handkerchief in 4.1 is so important within the main action. Nobody can suppose that 4.1 is taking place on the second day in Cyprus and more than a week after the arrival in Cyprus. Iago acquires the handkerchief in 3.3, and that scene clearly takes place on the first morning in Cyprus. In the latter part of 3.4 Cassio enters (with Iago) and gives Bianca the handkerchief he has just found in his "lodging"; in scene 4.1, she angrily returns it, having examined it and found it impossible to "take out." Time passes between and during these successive scenes, but how much time? Pressing Ridley's argument to its logical conclusion would mean having to suppose that in the handkerchief scene we have that impression of "short time" which the stage action establishes, and a cunningly contrived "impression" of an illusory period of "long time," and a logically inescapable impression of nonillusory "long time."

The "double-time" theory cannot resolve this difficulty, since the theory is what has produced it. Nor can I believe that any spectator or reader who was not already distracted by the theory, and peering excitedly round every textual corner for "evidence" to support it, could suppose that Bianca's complaint shows that a week has passed in Cyprus without also feeling some disturbance and dissatisfaction. Yet the difficulty dissolves if we forget the theory and stay with the "short time." If the meetings between Cassio and Bianca in Acts 3 and 4 take place later, on the second day in Cyprus, Bianca's complaint about a week-long absence then confirms that she was already Cassio's mistress in Venice—where he was already avoiding her, since he likes sleeping with her but has no intention of marrying her. The doting, determined Bianca has followed him to Cyprus, provoking Cassio's complacent complaint to Iago that she "haunts me in every place" (4.1.132): she is a camp-follower in this literal sense, while he, like Mann's Felix Krull, understands that since he is irresistible he should try to make some allowances.

It is not easy to believe that in inventing the Cassio-Bianca liaison Shakespeare never considered when and where it starts. If we suppose that it starts in Cyprus, this produces far more problems than the only alternative, which is to stay with the "short time." But then that also helps with two textual cruces that have led editors who are loyal to the nonsense about "double time" to pronounce Shakespeare "careless" in his handling of Cassio. They are another part of the mess the myth of "double time" has made.

We know from Othello's first speech to the Senators that he has spent the last nine months in Venice and found this first experience of civilian life enervating:

> since these Armes of mine, had seven yeares pith,
> Till now, some nine Moones wasted, they have us'd
> Their deerest action, in the Tented Field.
>
> (1.3.83–85)

We also know that during this period Cassio has been with Othello, who *prefers* him to Iago not only as his chosen lieutenant, but also as the close, trusted friend who frequently accompanied him in his secret wooing and knew of Othello's love "from first to last" (3.3.97). The obvious need for discretion in that case explains Cassio's circumspection in the play's second scene when he pretends not even to know whom Othello might have married, and asks Iago, "To who?" (1.2.53). Similarly, keeping to the "short time" yields a consistent explanation of that other much debated "crux" which is so often said to show that Shakespeare is careless or that the text needs emendation: Iago's apparently knowing but mysterious joke about Cassio being "A Fellow almost damn'd in a faire Wife" (1.1.18) seems mysterious and *is* knowing because Iago already knows what we cannot yet know.[30] Cassio is "almost damn'd in a faire Wife" because, although he wants nothing more than a sexually convenient liaison with the "very faire Bianca," she is determined to marry him—and because, for Iago, to be almost married is to be almost damned.

Iago clearly knows about the Cassio-Bianca relationship and its difficulties in 4.1, when we hear him planning to make use of that knowledge:

> Now will I question *Cassio* of *Bianca*,
> A Huswife, that by selling her desires
> Buyes her selfe Bread, and Cloath. It is a Creature
> That dotes on *Cassio*, (as 'tis the Strumpets plague
> To be-guile many, and be be-guil'd by one)

He, when he heares of her, cannot restraine
From the excesse of Laughter.

(4.1.93–97)

Unless we have been distracted by the "double-time" theory, it is also clear that whatever Iago knows about this liaison in 4.1, on the second day in Cyprus, must also have been known to him in the play's first scene, which takes place only hours before Iago and Cassio set off (again in different ships) for Cyprus. But the New Arden and New Cambridge editors have been distracted by the theory. Ridley explains in his long note on "A Fellow almost damn'd in a faire Wife" that this cannot allude to Cassio's liaison with Bianca, since at this "moment he has not met her" (4); similarly Barbara Everett refers to Iago's cynical joke and supposes that it cannot refer to "Cassio's future affair with the whore, Bianca" (209). And in the New Cambridge edition Norman Sanders recycles the idea that both Iago's remark and the way in which Cassio "appears to be completely ignorant of Othello's interest in Desdemona" in 1.2 are "inconsistencies" that make the character of Cassio "something of a puzzle" (189, 16).

I think this wrong but had better confront the objection that the kind of explanation I offer is embarrassingly like the argument for "double time," which hangs on an elaborate and implausible tapestry of assumptions about what an audience would or would not notice in performance. I think there is an important difference.

Certainly, no spectator watching the play for the first time could know that Cassio has reason to be discreet when he asks, "To who?". Edwin Booth's recommendation[31] that the actor playing Cassio should signal circumspection—letting on that there is something Cassio isn't letting on—is fussy and dramatically unhelpful: even if we noticed and stored the signal, we couldn't make sense of it until the revelations in 3.3, and any such signaling would threaten to make Cassio seem the kind of friend who couldn't be trusted to keep a confidence. Similarly, nobody watching the play for the first time and hearing Iago describe Cassio as "almost damn'd in a faire Wife" could know about the liaison with Bianca and its difficulties. Shakespeare is giving Iago and Cassio lines that are consistent with their characters and situation, but the first-time spectator or reader is in no position to see how.

In other words, this kind of explanation is peculiar because it addresses a peculiar kind of "problem": the problem is just as remote as its solution from theatrical experience. No spectator would see the "inconsistency" in Cassio's question or start trembling before a "crux." As for Iago's joke, since it is ambiguously phrased, a spectator might feel uncertain how to take it, or might just mistake it, supposing that Cassio must be married and, for some reason, badly matched. The play has only just begun, Cassio has only just been mentioned, and we know nothing about Bianca. We are only beginning to put things together and make sense of what is before us: in a significant sense we expect to understand, and have no reason to suspect that our information may be contradictory. In both cases the "problem" or "crux" appears only when we are studying the text closely and, as it were, reading and thinking forward and backward—or when we are reading the text in a modern scholarly edition and letting our eye be dragged down to the ballast of notes beneath the precious ribbon of Shakespearean matter. As that ribbon thins, we know that scrupulous editors have discovered a difficulty that we had better attend to, now, if we want to be sure we won't forget its existence; but unfortunately, because editors are usually more concerned with the play as text than with the text as play, they rarely point out (or notice) when a difficulty that the text throws out and that has exercised generations of editors isn't apparent in performance. The "problem" is there in the text but, like its explanation, cannot be a part of our initial dramatic experience.

This peculiar kind of problem is best considered as a question about dramatic intention. Shakespeare clearly was in a unique situation to be thinking backward and forward, and wouldn't have given Cassio his question or Iago that joke unless he thought the lines meant something when he wrote them. Shakespeare wrote quickly, and on the whole rather well, but he could write badly, as in that slovenly verse exchange between Cassio and Bianca; he could fail to notice some problems that are there in the text and there in the play, like Lady Macbeth's giving suck or Jessica's account of conversations between Shylock and Tubal which could only have taken place after her elopement; he could be negligent about minor matters and characters, like Lodovico's implausibly rapid arrival in Cyprus. But such things aren't as surprising as it would be if, after taking pains to compress his time scheme and keep Othello and Desdemona apart, Shakespeare had carelessly given them an extra week or two in Cyprus without considering what they might do there, or talk about. As for Cassio and Bianca, Shakespeare is perfunctory about filling in the background of their relationship. Ibsen once remarked that he liked to work everything out "down to the last button" before beginning to write; Shakespeare doesn't attend to buttons so closely, but there is an important difference between not working things out and not making them clear. That an explanation is available within the play's "short time" suggests that in this case—as indeed with Iago's joke—the perfunctoriness is that of a dramatist who is writing rapidly and with a very sure sense of his characters and their situations, but hasn't paused to consider whether what is clear to him might seem less than clear to an audience. Once we comb through the text, putting together scattered references and weighing alternative possibilities, the text shows why the Cassio-Bianca relationship must have been going on during the same nine-month period as Othello's secret wooing. To say this is not to suppose that Othello's specific reference to "nine Moones" would be noticed and remembered by every attentive spectator: the theater is not a court or classroom, and we might well pay more attention to the information that this was his first experience of civilian life than to his specification of the precise period of time in question. The point is rather that we would expect, and can confirm, that Shakespeare thought carefully about what important matters need to have taken place before his play starts.

But now we can observe what is most strange about that basic assumption on which the "double-time" theory rests. It is always taken for granted that there is a "difficulty" that, as Dover Wilson proudly observes, "might well have seemed insuperable to any ordinary dramatist": "For, if Othello and Desdemona consummated their marriage during the first night in Cyprus, when could she have committed the adultery that Iago charges her with?" (Preface, New Shakespeare *Othello*, xxxii). This is true only if we are using the word "adultery" in a strict, legalistic sense, but what warrant does the play provide for supposing that Othello is concerned only with what might have happened *after* his marriage? The answer is, none.

Early in 3.3, the ever-vigilant Iago hears Desdemona protest to Othello that she should not have "so much to do" in pleading on behalf of that very friend who

came a wooing with you? and so many a time
(When I have spoke of you dispraisingly)
Hath tane your part.

(3.3.71–73)

This is news to Iago, and once he is alone with Othello he can launch his first direct assault by concentrating on that very question to which Desdemona has just provided the answer:

Iago.   Did *Michael Cassio*
          When you woo'd my Lady, know of your love?
Othello. He did, from first to last: Why dost thou aske?
Iago.   But for a satisfaction of my Thought,
             No further harme.
Othello.   What of thy thought, *Iago?*
Iago.   I did not thinke he had bin acquainted with hir.
Othello. O yes, and went betweene us very oft.
Iago.   Indeed?
Othello. Indeed? I indeed. Discern'st thou aught in that?
             Is he not honest?
Iago.   Honest, my Lord?
Othello. Honest? I, Honest.
Iago.   My Lord, for ought I know.
Othello.   What do'st thou thinke?
Iago.   Thinke, my Lord?
Othello. Thinke, my Lord? Alas, thou ecchos't me;
             As if there were some Monster in thy thought
             Too hideous to be shewne.

(3.3.94–108)

In exploiting what Desdemona revealed, Iago must tread very carefully: if the marriage was consummated hours before, Othello is likely to know whether his wife was a virgin. Throughout this first stage of the assault, what is in question is *not* the absurd suggestion that Desdemona has committed adultery with Cassio since her wedding, in what would indeed be "stolen hours"; Iago's insinuation, as he feels his way forward, is that something took place *before* the wedding, something that can be expected to continue and that would explain Desdemona's passionate concern to have Cassio reinstated—and we see the "Monster" emerging in Othello's own mind as he begins to discern what is in question. Similarly, when Iago later promises

Othello that he will persuade Cassio to "tell the Tale anew; / Where, how, how oft, how long ago, and when / He hath, and is againe to cope your wife" (4.1.85–86), this is not another "indication" of "long time," as editors tell us: Iago is once again conjuring up that nightmare of a promiscuous liaison which began when Cassio was the trusted friend who "very oft" went between the lovers. Part of this nightmare of betrayal is familiar; the situation in the *Sonnets* is not as irrelevant as Dover Wilson supposes.[32]

In other words there is no "difficulty" that requires a "needful impression" of "long time." Not only does the theory of "double time" not work, or work to ruinous effect; it is redundant. At this point, and with these various objections to the theory in mind, it is worth quickly running through those other alleged "indications" of "long time" which are conveniently (and confidently) set out in the New Arden introduction and notes. The first two "instances," involving references to the handkerchief, are perhaps the most troubling, but suggest negligence rather than the carefully laid foundation for the edifice of double time. The others are no more compelling than the "very clear instance" of Lodovico's premature arrival (really an instance of Shakespeare nodding) or of Cassio's week-long absence from Bianca (which makes good sense in the play's "short time," and produces nightmarish complications if taken as evidence of "long time"):

(1) 3.3.296 [Iago's asking Emilia to steal the handkerchief's "a hundred times"]. There is no reason to suppose that Iago had not often seen it, in Othello's possession or in Desdemona's when, in her girlish way, she kisses and talks to it (3.3.295).

(2) 3.3.313 ["so often did you bid me steale"]. Ditto; and, as Ridley himself observes, this "might have been on voyage."

(3) 3.3.344–48 [Othello on "stolne houres of Lust" which "harm'd not me"]. Othello's speech is rapid and excited, but makes better sense in relation to the lengthy period before the marriage. His reference to "the next night" need not refer to the first night in Cyprus, unless we refuse to suppose that Othello could have kissed Desdemona before marriage.

(4) 3.3.419 ["I lay with Cassio lately"]. That is, in Venice, where (as Iago now knows) Cassio was "very oft" alone with Desdemona; the "foregone

conclusion" Othello tormentedly imagines would have preceded the marriage.

(5) 3.4.97 ["I nev'r saw this before"]. Desdemona (who has been pursued by other suitors) is simply saying that she has never before seen any sign that Othello is prone to jealousy.

(6) 4.1.50–51 [the "second Fit" of "Epilepsie"]. This is the first such fit; Iago is lying when he says it is the second, in order to get rid of Cassio. Any direct confrontation between Othello and Cassio could be catastrophic, so he improvises cleverly, assuring the concerned Cassio that this has happened before and that he knows what to do.

(7) 4.1.85–86 [Iago's promise to make Cassio "tell the Tale anew"]. Iago is speaking of the whole period from the wooing to the present—and into the future.

(8) 4.1.132 ["I was the other day talking on the Sea-banke with certaine Venetians"]. The conversation took place in Venice; ironically, Ridley finds in "Sea-banke" a "suggestion of something raised above sea-level"— which might in turn have suggested Venice if Ridley were not so sure that Bianca is a Cypriot.

(9) 4.1.274 [Iago's "what I have seene and knowne"]. It is quite arbitrary to take this as an indication of "long time."

(10) 4.2.23 ["she'le kneele, and pray: I have seene her do't"]. Othello's remark makes perfectly good sense if he has only seen her kneel and pray once, on their first night in Cyprus.

(11) 4.2.1–10 [dialogue between Emilia and Othello]. This is compatible with "short time"; Emilia was with Desdemona and Cassio, at the beginning of 3.3.

(12) 5.2.213 ["a thousand times committed"]. Othello is speaking wildly, not attempting a sober calculation of what sexual feats a young hot-blooded Florentine might manage; still, the exaggeration is less grotesque if the period in question includes the months (up to nine) of the wooing.

To dismiss this horribly long-lived idea that the play depends upon a trick to make its action credible is a critical relief, but it is historically disquieting—unless we can also see why the theory has had so long a life. Here, rather than simply dismiss it as groundless, we should notice how it is grounded on that willingness to generalize about the audience as a monolithic entity which has now resurfaced in the "new" historicism and on a corresponding *interpretative* assumption about Jacobean attitudes which emerges very clearly in Dover Wilson's New Shakespeare edition: "An accusation of premarital incontinence would not have served either [Iago's] purpose or Shakespeare's, since adultery was required to make Othello a cuckold, and it is the dishonourable stigma of cuckoldry that maddens Othello once his confidence has gone and, we may add, greatly increased the excitement for a Jacobean audience" (xxxii). This of course raises fundamental questions about what Shakespeare's play is "about," but Dover Wilson tells us: in "its simplest terms, . . . the tragedy of *Othello* represents the destruction of a sublime love between two noble spirits through the intrigues of a villain devilish in his cunning and unscrupulousness" (xxx). These terms are indeed "simple," not least because they preserve the Coleridgean assumption that murdering Desdemona would have been all right, or at least compatible with being very noble, if only she had committed adultery.

"We must obey the time," Othello tells his bride: the "rites" she so eagerly awaits must wait. But here, too, critics who are obedient to the myth of "double time" get into further difficulties. As I observed earlier, there is nothing in 2.3 to tell us—and the accelerated time makes it more than ever difficult to guess—whether the marriage is consummated before the riot, or after it, or not at all. The established assumption is that it is consummated, and some readings—like Stephen Greenblatt's in his immensely influential *Renaissance Self-Fashioning*—fall apart if we think that it isn't.

Here it seems worth recording how my own experience ran counter to what critics and editors assume we "naturally" assume. Having seen the play twice as a schoolboy before I ever read it, having then read it several times before I "studied" it and consulted critics, I had always supposed that the marriage wasn't consummated. I still thought that in a 1979 article in which I referred to the murder as this marriage's "poetic consummation," giving that word "poetic" the unfairly cruel sense it has in talk of "poetic justice."[33] That was unguarded—my assuming what is by no means an inevitable reading—and I found myself prompted to a more systematic consideration in 1983, when

T. G. A. Nelson and Charles Haines published an article titled
"Othello's Unconsummated Marriage."[34] The authors carefully explored the question of whether the marriage is consummated, and
concluded that it isn't. Since they were also arguing that Othello's
behavior is the result of unbearable sexual frustration, their reading
was diametrically opposed to Greenblatt's, though similarly reductive.
Setting that aside, their textual arguments for thinking that the marriage is not consummated were unprecedentedly thorough, but open
to three objections.

The first may well seem the most important to readers who assume
that consummation takes place in 2.3. Nelson and Haines are confusing "stage" time with "real" time when they say that "Othello and
Desdemona have hardly gone to bed when a brawl begins (4), and
that when Othello does, "in the end, get back to bed" (after going off
with the seriously injured Montano to tend his wounds), "there is,
indeed, nothing left of the night" (5). Later, Desdemona's touchingly
innocent assumption that the "pain" on Othello's forehead is caused
by "watching" (3.3.289) confirms that Othello has spent much of the
night looking after Montano, but doesn't tell us how much. In other
words, Nelson and Haines don't reckon with the complications caused
by accelerated time, which is not to be confused with double time.
The second objection is prompted by what these critics say of the
scene between the clown and the musicians at the start of Act 3. Most
critics ignore this scene; Nelson and Haines argue, picking up some
suggestions of Lawrence Ross and Linda Boose,[35] that its dramatic
"point" is to signal that the serenade is "ill-timed, for the event it is
intended to celebrate has not yet taken place" (6). Unfortunately, the
persuasive argument that the incompetently executed serenade becomes a badly timed, inadvertently mocking charivari is shackled to
a far from persuasive argument about Othello's "impotence" and
"temporary failure of virility" (17). The third objection, which seems
to me the most important, also shows how the textual argument is
weakened by the critics' interpretative assumptions. Like Leavis and
Greenblatt, Nelson and Haines offer a psychologically reductive account of Othello as a "case." Because they are so sure *how* the failure
to consummate the marriage matters, they aren't sufficiently concerned to specify *when* it most clearly matters, as the play unfolds,
and don't see why the references to sheets are even more significant
than they suppose.

The wedding sheets evidently matter very much to Desdemona in 4.2—either because she has already lost her virginity on them or because she still hasn't and still wants to. "Prythee," she carefully instructs Emilia, "Lay on my bed my wedding sheetes, remember" (4.2.105). And when Emilia returns in the next scene to assure Desdemona that she has "laid those Sheetes you bad me on the bed," she receives this unnerving reply:

> All's one: good Father, how foolish are our minds?
> If I do die before, prythee shrow'd me
> In one of these same Sheetes.
>
> (4.3.23–25)

And in the penultimate scene the idea of bloodied sheets is inflaming Othello's mind, as he determines, "Thy Bed, lust-stain'd, shall with Lusts blood bee spotted" (5.1.36). But is he thinking of the *wedding* sheets?

Here, if anywhere, is a "difficulty" that threatens to make "nonsense" of the "dramatic action"—or, since an interpretative choice is in question, of all those readings which depend upon the assumption that the marriage is consummated. To take the most extreme but influential case, Greenblatt's reading altogether depends upon his assumption that on the first night in Cyprus—which was "perhaps" Othello's only experience of "marital sexuality"—Othello "took" Desdemona's "virginity," "shed her blood," and then not only noticed but became violently obsessed by the condition of the wedding sheets.[36] Greenblatt doesn't notice the difficulty in this reading, because his sampling of the text is so partial, and because in offering his curious explanation of why the sheets matter so much to Othello he never explains, or asks, why they also matter so much to Desdemona. Part of the difficulty, put bluntly and indelicately, is that of understanding why, if Desdemona is no longer a virgin, she should want lust-stained sheets relaid. (Doubtless there is someone, somewhere, who believes that she wants to confront her husband with ocular proof of her chastity, so that it is a great pity when Othello decides to put out the light.) The other part of the difficulty is that of understanding what kind of mental defective could first take his wife's virginity and then, the morning after, become convinced of her continued infidelity. Here Greenblatt's reading seems to need—or, if it is not to become

risible, depend upon—the "double-time" theory, a need that his "perhaps" discreetly acknowledges. Yet that theory cannot help here, since
3.3 clearly takes place the morning after the first night in Cyprus,
and not even the most convinced advocates of "long time" suppose
that Othello and Desdemona make love between 3.3 and the murder.
In other words, if the marriage isn't consummated on that first night
in Cyprus, it isn't consummated at all; here the "double-time" theory
merely blurs the textual and dramatic issues.

Were it not for those dramatically prominent references to the
sheets, the question whether this marriage has been consummated—
whether Othello and Desdemona had slept together once, like Romeo
and Juliet, or not at all—wouldn't matter in the same way. It might
still occur to us to wonder how Othello could entertain the idea of
Desdemona's infidelity if, as Greenblatt supposes, he so recently took
her virginity and "shed her blood"; but such a worry would still be,
as it were, dispersed through the latter half of the play. The references
to the sheets—not to mention a strawberry-spotted handkerchief—
are what make this worry immediately pressing and alarmingly definite. Another difficulty appears, as soon as we ask what on earth
Shakespeare is up to. For it seems inconceivable that, in so drastically
compressing the Italian novella's time scheme, making Othello and
Desdemona newly married lovers, and then taking such pains to keep
them physically apart, Shakespeare never considered whether this
marriage was consummated. If we are to think that it is, Shakespeare
should have been no less anxious than Iago that Othello shouldn't
consider (and that the audience shouldn't notice Othello failing to
consider) any physical evidence of Desdemona's virginity—especially
in an age when it was not uncommon, after nuptials, to display the
bloodied wedding sheets or a blood-spotted napkin.[37]

By now we might feel relieved that the textual evidence of whether
the marriage is or is not consummated in 2.3 is so uncertain. For if
we think the received idea that it is consummated throws out too
many problems, we are free to prefer the alternative reading. Desdemona wants the sheets to be relaid because she is still a virgin, and
still poignantly longs for "such observancie / As fits the Bridall"
(3.4.147–48). When Othello determines that "Thy Bed lust-stain'd,
shall with Lusts blood bee spotted" he is tormenting himself with the
deluded thought of what somebody else has done: as Montaigne
might say, another bed, other sheets. Virginity, like a life, can only be

taken once: in Othello's diseased, self-tormenting imagination all that remains for him to do—the only way in which *he* can "shed her blood"—is bloody murder.

That tragicomic irony is horrible enough, but the final scene then gives it a still more dreadful visit. Just as Desdemona could not bring herself to say the word "whore" in 4.2, Othello tells the "chaste Starres" that he cannot "name" the "Cause," but will not—after all—"shed her blood" (5.2.2–3): "Yet Ile not shed her blood. . . . Yet she must dye." That tangle of yets shows that what he is talking about—what he has not changed his mind about—is not whether to kill her, but how; it also shows how this latest resolution is still insanely ensnarled with his obsessive sense of what he has never done and thinks he can never do—and what his still-virginal bride still hopes he will do, as she lies waiting for him on those relaid, unspotted wedding sheets. The murder is indeed this marriage's only consummation, and the ghastly tragicomic parody of an erotic "death."

> *Desdemona.* And yet I feare you: for you're fatall then
>   When your eyes rowle so. Why I should feare, I know not,
>   Since guiltinesse I know not: But yet I feele I feare.
> *Othello.* Thinke on thy sinnes.
> *Desdemona.*   They are Loves I beare to you.
> *Othello.* I, and for that thou dy'st.
> *Desdemona.* That death's unnaturall, that kils for loving.
>   Alas, why gnaw you so your nether-lip?
>   Some bloody passion shakes your very Frame.
>
> (5.2.36–44)

The "Light" is finally "put out"; in that way, but only in that way, Desdemona's "Rose" is "pluck'd." I find myself wanting to ask not only Greenblatt but every critic who thinks Othello took Desdemona's virginity not long before, on this bed and these relaid sheets, how they understood Othello's wrenching words when he realizes what he has done and bends over what is now a corpse:

> Cold, cold, my Girle?
> Even like thy Chastity.

Indeed he has never "shed her blood": that final sniffing and snuffing has indeed been his only "possession of this Heavenly sight." And that culminating tragicomic irony, perhaps the most horrible in drama, is indeed as "grim as hell."

Fashioning *Othello*

A work of art is worked, or fashioned; it isn't "out there" in the way the solar system and seas are, since it didn't precede human activity. What is absorbingly suggestive about Shakespeare's departures from Cinthio's story is that they show how he works to complicate our responses to Othello, and even Desdemona. Indeed that is the general effect and tendency of Shakespeare's dramatic perspectivism, but *Othello* is also a special case. There is no other play that so depends on rival interpretations and the destructive power of misconstructions and strong misreadings: they torment Othello in the play's second half, but they disturb the reader or spectator long before; nor does it seem implausible to suppose that they issued from or answered to some moral and imaginative disturbance in the dramatist—some compellingly creative tension between skepticism and magnanimity.

I want first to examine a series of departures from the Italian story which tend to prompt or be compatible with a magnanimous view of Othello, like that of Coleridge or Bradley; and then to examine another series of changes that tend to prompt, or be compatible with, some more unsparingly diagnostic view. The word *series* seems justified, since in each case the changes in question are intricately connected.

In the Italian story the Cassio-figure is married, while the Iago-figure is the father of a three-year-old infant. For us, it's not easy to imagine Iago as a daddy, but then Shakespeare's imagination had to work in the reverse direction, turning that daddy into his Iago while seeing why his Cassio should be a bachelor and ladies' man. In each case the critical decision about what not to do was inseparable from the creative decision about what to do instead. Doubtless, to speak of decisions is too summary as a way of representing a process of creative solicitation and divination; but the decisions that were made are our best, and usually our only, means of access to that gestatory process. I have already taken issue with the familiar charge that Shakespeare was "careless" with Cassio; it would be surprising if he hadn't thought carefully about Cassio, since he makes Cassio so much more important than his counterpart in the Italian story. In the first half of the play—up to 3.3, and using the New Cambridge edition's lineation—Cassio has 155 lines to Desdemona's 58, and is on stage for 791 lines against her 298.

Of course such tallies are a crude indication of relative importance: in 2.1, the scene at the harbor, Desdemona has 29 lines and is on stage for 123, while Cassio has 51 lines and is on stage for 163, but these ratios don't mean that she makes a weaker dramatic impression. But then Cassio is dramatically, and structurally, prominent. In this first half of the play we follow his fortunes from his new appointment to his disgrace, which prefigures Othello's devastating collapse while also providing a cautionary comparison, since Cassio is not a black outsider but a handsome young Florentine—*da noi*, or, as a Shakespearean Marlow might say, "one of us." This does not save him from Iago or the shaming, Circe-like transformation—"To be now a sensible man, by and by a Foole, and presently a Beast" (2.3.305–106). The engineering of Cassio's downfall—within minutes of our seeing him at his most attractive—tests Iago's malign skills more than manipulating Brabantio and Roderigo does, and it is also an essential preparation for the coming assault on Othello: as we watch Cassio with Desdemona at the harbor we also see Iago watching, registering the possibilities of a strong misreading, and immediately testing his "interpretation" on Roderigo in an impromptu rehearsal. Nonetheless, that most critics deal with Cassio very perfunctorily suggests a want of proportion either in the play or in critical accounts of the play. Since the distribution of interest in a Shakespearean drama is not usually so strange, this might seem one aspect of a larger problem: if Othello is to be regarded as a play about love and jealousy it would seem to follow that—as H. A. Mason argues in *Shakespeare's Tragedies of Love*[38]—it lacks effective *données*. But this is a case where considering what Shakespeare decided not to do helps us to understand why he chose to do something else.

One result of the decision to unmarry Cassio and unfather Iago—making the one a bachelor who has no intention of marrying, and the other a married cynic who thinks that to be almost married is to be almost damned—is to emphasize the fear or distrust of domesticity that is so often heard in this play. We hear it even in Othello's references to housewives and skillets and the *wasting* effects of nine months of civilian life. It is qualified though not eliminated by an important "but," when he confides to Iago,

> But that I love the gentle *Desdemona,*
> I would not my unhoused free condition
> Put into Circumscription, and Confine,
> For the Seas worth.
>
> (1.2.25–28)

This play's dramatic world is a markedly military, not to say macho, world in which (to put the matter as nicely as Purcell's sailors) soldiers regularly take a boozy short leave of their nymphs on the shore, and are (as Iago knows) ready to believe that a married general's wife may be the general's general. Even in 2.3 when the soldiers are celebrating and productions sometimes bring in townswomen, girls, and camp followers (including Bianca), the stage directions do not mention women: this appears to be a male booze-up. And this male, military world has been Othello's whole world, until his nine months in Venice.

Here another effect of the Shakespearean changes is to emphasize the isolation (and consequent vulnerability) of his own very differently conceived lovers: Othello and Desdemona are the *only* couple in this play's dramatic world who attempt any kind of enduring love relationship. Dover Wilson's reference to "a sublime love between two noble spirits" might remind us that nobody in the play thinks about Othello and Desdemona or love and marriage in these terms. In this important respect Emilia's attitudes resemble—or are, in Kenneth Burke's sense, "consubstantial" with[39]—her husband's. To be sure, there is a crucial difference between the husband who pronounces "not I for love and dutie" and the wife who knowingly risks and loses her life, impelled by nothing other than "love and dutie." But Emilia never thinks of Desdemona as "sublime," and regrets that she "forsooke so many Noble Matches" (4.2.124)—always seeing her as a lovably innocent, inexperienced girl whose pitiful ignorance of men and marriage led her into a grotesque and disastrous union. She regards Othello with dislike, considering him a man like other men, just as her own husband regards Desdemona as a woman like other women. Cassio *does* idealize "the divine *Desdemona*" and loves his friend and general, but in ways that never impinge on what he expects from, and brings to, a sexual relationship. Even the Duke's benign comment in the Senate scene, that Othello's tale would have won his own daughter's heart, implies a worldly view of the world and young women without suggesting that he sees this union as ideal, or as "a sublime love between two noble spirits." Within this play's dramatic world it is not Iago but the lovers who are set apart, by their own idealistic and self-committed aspirations.

Such things suggest how, for Shakespeare, thinking about what to do with Cassio, Iago, or Emilia and inventing Brabantio and Bianca was part of his thinking about Othello and Desdemona and their respective places in this "world," or poetic-dramatic ensemble, of contrasted human potentialities. Unmarrying Cassio and providing him with a mistress then allows further examples of dramatic "rhyming." Othello's secret wooing takes place in the same period as Cassio's fairly public liaison, and is apparently the more questionable in Venetian terms. Like Desdemona, Bianca loves her man enough to follow him to Cyprus, and has occasion to insist that she is "no Strumpet, but of life as honest / As you that thus abuse me" (5.1.122–23). It is a fine, thought-provoking touch that Bianca's final, furious claim to respectability must be asserted against Emilia and her very different view of men and marriage, and is heard just before "It is the Cause, it is the Cause (my Soule)." Something like Bianca's outburst is what we want to hear from Desdemona; its truth is far more questionable in Bianca's case, but is also asserted with far more vigor than Desdemona can command—as is Emilia's powerful crypto-feminist denunciation of the sexual and marital double code:

> But I do thinke it is their Husbands faults
> If Wives do fall: (Say that they slacke their duties,
> And powre our Treasures into forraigne laps;
> Or else breake out in peevish Jealousies,
> Throwing restraint upon us: Or say they strike us,
> Or scant our former having in despight)
> Why we have galles: and though we have some Grace,
> Yet have we some Revenge. Let Husbands know,
> Their wives have sense like them; They see, and smell,
> And have their Palats both for sweet, and sowre,
> As Husbands have. What is it that they do,
> When they change us for others? Is it Sport?
> I thinke it is: and doth Affection breed it?
> I thinke it doth. Is't frailty that thus erres?

It is so too? And have not we Affections?
Desires for Sport? and Frailty, as men have?
Then let them use us well: else let them know,
The illes we do, their illes instruct us so.

(4.3.86–103)

That speech alone might have given pause to all those male cham-
pions of the "Noble" Moor who write as though murdering Desdemona would have been compatible with nobility if only she had
committed adultery. But then Emilia's speech, like that most famous
speech of Shylock's which it recalls, is likely to provoke a more mixed,
disturbed response if we also value Desdemona's idealistic self-commitment and don't want to see her come round, and down, to Emilia's
embittered view of the marriage hearse. Moreover, the ensemble of
characters is a means of exploring representative attitudes to sex, the
other sex, and marriage, and if we are responding to the contrasts
between three *couples,* we are more likely to see Emilia's hostility to
men as the counterpart of her husband's misogyny. In this perspective, her attitude to "Affections" and "Desires" seems as limited as her
husband's, so that the contrast between the couples is likely to increase
our sympathy for Othello and Desdemona's vulnerably isolated attempt at a more enduring, mutually loving relationship. However,
in the Shakespearean nexus of contrasts the three couples are also
presented as two male-and-female *trios,* so that Desdemona, Emilia,
and Bianca make up a triad of women who all suffer from their men
and from a disquietingly representative range of male attitudes; in
this perspective, we are more likely to warm to Emilia's speech as a
perceptive crypto-feminist denunciation of a double code.

This kind of dramatic structuring is light years away from Cinthio's
story. Because it requires that Cassio (the lyric tenor in operatic terms)
should be attractive but somewhat loose—decent but not rigorously
principled in *anständig,* in Wittgenstein's exacting sense—it calls for
fine, not "careless," tuning. Cassio must now be somebody whom
Othello and Desdemona could like so much, while also being the
Florentine finger-kisser whose "smiles, gestures, and light behaviours"
(4.1.102) might—just—make him capable of doing what Iago says he
has done. We see the man Othello "loves" (3.1.48) in 2.3, when Cassio
innocently deflects Iago's leerily prosaic[40] nudges and worldly winks,
about Desdemona:

Iago.	She is sport for *Jove.*
Cassio.	She's a most exquisite Lady.
Iago.	And Ile warrant her, full of Game.
Cassio.	Indeed shes a most fresh and delicate creature.
Iago.	What an eye she has? Methinks it sounds a parley to provocation.
Cassio.	An inviting eye: and yet me thinkes right modest.
Iago.	And when she speakes, is it not an Alarum to Love?
Cassio.	She is indeed perfection.
Iago.	Well: happinesse to their Sheetes.

(2.3.17–29)

The moral comedy in that exchange is all the more welcome and enjoyable because it momentarily defeats the vulgarly reductive Iago—but only for a while; in 4.1, when Bianca rather than Desdemona is the subject of the conversation between Iago and Cassio, we see the sniggering, vain, and ruttish young buck, whom Iago can easily lead by the nose.

Emilia's speech in 3.1 provides a convenient checklist of several important departures from the Italian story, and not only where Cassio is concerned. Although it rarely figures in critical accounts of the play—which needs some explanation—it would be difficult to exaggerate this speech's dramatic importance:

> Goodmorrow (good Lieutenant) I am sorrie
> For your displeasure: but all will sure [Q:soon] be well.
> The Generall and his wife are talking of it,
> And she speakes for you stoutly. The Moore replies,
> That he you hurt is of great Fame in Cyprus,
> And great Affinitie: and that in wholsome Wisedome
> He might not but refuse you. But he protests he loves you
> And needs no other Suitor, but his likings
> [Q: To take the safest occasion by the front]
> To bring you in againe

(3.1.41–50)

In the Italian story the Captain draws on and wounds a soldier, but the soldier is not the ex-governor of Cyprus, there is no war, and the Captain is not drunk; his offense is far less grave, so that there is more excuse for Disdemona's plea that it is minor, *un picciolo fallo.* Shakespeare's Cyprus is a garrisoned city, under martial law, and when Shakespeare's Moor asks his new lieutenant to stand in for him as commander he even gives Cassio—his closest friend, the one man he trusted in his secret wooing—a tactful warning not to "out-sport discretion." Nonetheless Cassio get drunk and starts a riot, while the man he seriously wounds and almost kills—for trying to keep the peace—is that very ex-governor whose services to the state were commended in the Senate scene. Cassio betrays a personal as well as a professional trust, and for the first time in the play we see Othello having to *fight* to keep his own self-control, or "government":

> Now by Heaven,
> My blood begins my safer Guides to rule,
> And passion (having my best judgement collied)
> Assaies to lead the way.
>
> (2.3.204–7)

Moreover, it's important to see how Cassio yields to Iago twice: first, in committing the offense, but then—after his paroxysm of self-blame proves too painful to sustain—in allowing Iago to persuade him that he is "too severe a Moraller" and should persuade Desdemona to intervene on his behalf. That decision involves another betrayal and gives Emilia's speech a pivotal significance: if Cassio were a more intelligently loyal friend to Othello, he would abandon his (or Iago's) plan of involving Desdemona as soon as he heard Emilia's report— and the play, or the play Iago is now staging, would stop.

As it is, Othello has every reason to emphasize to Desdemona that Cassio's offense is far more serious than she appears to realize, and to explain why "in wholsome Wisdome / He might not but refuse" to reinstate him. Indeed, Emilia's report suggests that Othello was gently, and with a tact like that shown in his earlier warning to Cassio, reminding Desdemona that she is out of her depth. But here another change has momentous consequences. In Cinthio's story Disdemona's appeals really do provide the Captain with his only hope, but in Shakespeare's play the effect of Emilia's report is to make Desdemona's subsequent appeals in 3.3 redundant, and even offensive: her husband has just told her that he "loves" Cassio, has already determined to reinstate him, and "needs no other Suitor, but his likings." Although Shakespeare has made his Moor a Christian convert much concerned with his "Soule," "government," and the need for the "safer Guides to rule," this avowal reveals the Moor as a man ready to trust his own generous impulses and disregard "wholsome Wisdome" where those he "loves" are concerned. "Noble" is a word to use very cautiously in discussing the play, but Othello's decision is noble, and provides another example of finely calibrated characterization: we see both the experienced general and the man whose "free and open Nature" appeals to the impulsively generous Desdemona.

So, another effect of Emilia's speech is to suggest how, at this crucial moment, Othello is to be the victim not only of his ensign's brilliantly malignant improvisations but also of the two people he most "loves" and trusts. Not only Cassio but Desdemona herself, who has evidently not been listening to her husband—or rather listening but not thinking. Her own report to Cassio echoes Othello's remarks about what "wholsome Wisdome" requires, but with a troubling difference:

> Do not doubt *Cassio*
> But I will have my Lord, and you againe
> As friendly as you were . . .
> . . . be you well assur'd
> He shall in strangenesse stand no farther off
> Then in a politique distance.
>
> (3.3.5–7,11–13)

Instead of pondering Othello's insistence that her own role as "Suitor" is both inappropriate and redundant, Desdemona actually encourages Cassio to believe that she is the general's general and that Cassio's reinstatement really does depend on overcoming Othello's resistance with her own eager and relentless suit:

> before *Æmilia* here,
> I give thee warrant of thy place. Assure thee,
> If I do vow a friendship, Ile performe it
> To the last Article. My Lord shall never rest,
> Ile watch him tame, and talke him out of patience;
> His Bed shall seeme a Schoole, his Boord a Shrift;
> Ile intermingle every thing he do's
> With *Cassio's* suit. Therefore be merry, *Cassio*,
> For thy Solicitor shall rather dye,
> Then give thy cause away.
>
> (3.3.19–28)

Most astonishing, she even invites Cassio to "stay, and heare me speake." He at least knows better than that, but we soon hear her explaining to her astonished husband why he was quite mistaken about the seriousness of Cassio's offense:

> In faith hee's penitent:
> And yet his Trespasse, in our common reason
> (Save that they say the warres must make example)
> Out of her best, is not almost a fault
> T' encurre a private checke. When shall he come?
>
> (3.3.63–67)

That tripping appeal to what "they say" is all too characteristic of her behavior in the first part of this scene.

Worse, by speaking like this in front of Iago, Desdemona provides him with the two weapons he needs. Now he learns for the first time what Cassio had carefully not revealed—that Cassio accompanied Othello on his secret wooing. Secondly, Iago can see how Desdemona's behavior is so extraordinary as to *need* some explanation; *mammering* is not characteristic of Othello, but he has every reason to be astonished by this persistence, when he has already assured her that he will reinstate Cassio after a prudent interval. The first part of this scene charts his increasing astonishment and confusion, as he makes each concession:

(1)   *Desdemona.* Good Love, call him backe.
      Othello.   Not now (sweet *Desdemon*) some other time.
      Desdemona. But shall't be shortly?
      Othello.   The sooner (Sweet) for you.
                                      (3.3.54–57)

(2)   *Desdemona.*   Trust me, I could do much.
      Othello.   Prythee no more: Let him come when he will:
                      I will deny thee nothing.
                                      (3.3.74–76)

(3)   *Othello.*   I will deny thee nothing.
                      Whereon, I do beseech thee, grant me this,
                      To leave me but a little to my selfe.
                                      (3.3.83–85)

(4)   *Othello.*   Excellent wretch: Perdition catch my Soule
                       But I do love thee: and when I love thee not,
                       Chaos is come againe.

                                        (3.3.90–92)

Othello's bewilderment is entirely natural, and explained by the intricately connected series of changes Shakespeare has made in departing from the Italian story. What seems harder to explain is that way in which critics tend to disregard Emilia's speech and its bearing on what follows. There is, after all, something peculiar about discussing whether or not Othello is too "easily jealous" in 3.3—the issue which Coleridge saw as central, and which virtually every critic does discuss—without considering why Othello is so vulnerable to Iago's obscene way of accounting for Desdemona's passionately importunate interventions on Cassio's behalf. Is the critical elision a consequence of that nineteenth-century tendency to beatify Desdemona, instead of seeing her as a brave and generous but very green girl? In putting that question I certainly do not want to press for some moralistic (or Rymeresque) judgment of Desdemona: a severe "moraller" might insist that she behaves *badly*,[41] but I am more inclined to say that she behaves thoughtlessly and that her want of judgment is closely related to those very qualities which make her loveable. Desdemona is virtually (or virtuously) incapable of being a severe "moraller" herself, of judging those she loves—Cassio in this instance, Othello later. The worst doubt her behavior with Cassio might prompt is whether she knows herself well enough to have chosen her husband wisely. That question must be put sooner or later—if only when we are looking at her corpse and having to listen to the murderer she exonerates claiming to be what she so much more obviously is, or was: "one that loved not wisely, but too well." Charles Lamb raised that question in his characteristically mild, ironic way, but Bradley's reponse was quite uncharacteristically acerbic;[42] that fervently protective reaction suggests (like the resistance to Freud's almost contemporary theories of infantile sexuality) some peculiarly intense emotional investment or need.

That, at least, is one way of accounting for the otherwise puzzling critical elision of Emilia's speech—a speech that seems all the more significant because it was invented, and figures in an intricately connected series of creatively purposeful departures from the Italian story. Shakespeare's radical replotting places Othello in a situation quite unlike that of Cinthio's Moor, and the changes in question work to increase, rather than diminish, sympathy for his own Moor; they make it easier, not more difficult, to see the play as a tragedy of idealism. Significantly, the speech of Othello's that best answers to this view—"Had it pleas'd Heaven," in 4.2—is not even mentioned by Leavis or Greenblatt; yet there is nothing in it to suggest Greenblatt's deluded Christian, and the speech itself suggests what is inadequate in Leavis's view of Othello as a deluded, self-dramatizing egotist. In the preceding scene Othello was quite incapable of speaking like this, so that the verse itself measures a recovery—perhaps partial, and precarious, but remarkable after those earlier, catastophic collapses:

> Had it pleas'd Heaven,
> To try me with Affliction, had they rain'd
> All kinds of Sores, and Shames on my bare-head:
> Steep'd me in povertie to the very lippes,
> Given to Captivitie, me, and my utmost hopes,
> I should have found in some place of my Soule
> A drop of patience. But alas, to make me
> A fixed Figure for the time of Scorne,
> To point his slow, and moving [Q: unmoving] finger at.
>
> (4.2.47–55)

True, those who take Leavis's condemnatory view of Othello's "self-dramatization" can find it in this first half of the speech: the comparison with Job's afflictions, the hint of paranoia in "they," and the self-pitying reference to his exposed, enduring "bare-head," all powerfully convey Othello's sense of himself as a noble, much-tried victim. He asserts that he could still have found a "drop of patience," but the sense of himself as a "Figure" for "Scorne" to point at is harder to bear; here too is that concern with his own (shrunken) stature that might seem to support Leavis's unsparingly hostile view of Othello as a deluded egotist—were it not that Othello immediately goes on to say that he could "beare that too." These things are not what is unendurable.

Although the speech is a great swell of pain, it is also purposive and exploratory, discounting this and then that as it moves on to locate the source of the deepest, unendurable agony. Its syntax is remarkably controlled and sustained ("Had it pleas'd Heaven . . . But alas . . . Yet . . . But there") until the idea of rejection—"To be dis-

carded thence"—brings an annihilating sense that the basis of his
moral existence has been shattered:

> Yet could I beare that too, well, very well:
> But there where I have garnerd up my heart,
> Where either I must live, or beare no life,
> The Fountaine from the which my current runnes,
> Or else dries up: to be discarded thence,
> Or keepe it as a Cesterne, for foule Toades
> To knot and gender in. Turne thy complexion there:
> Patience, thou young and Rose-lip'd Cherubin,
> I heere looke grim as hell.
>
> (4.2.56–64)

As he confronts what he cannot "beare" his mind, syntax, and sense
all break down, but not, as before, into prose. His mind now floods
with an image of obscene, purposeless creation and Iago-like bestial-
ity, and *flooded* seems the right word when we notice how the imagery
pursues its own dreadful inner logic: the other liquid agonies *(raining,
steeping)* could all be endured (resisted by the *drop* of patience) if only
his *current* still *ran* from that *fountain,* but with the idea of being
"discarded" the images smash against *dries up,* and reform into the
wrenchingly gross, unhinging image of "it"—"it"!—as a foul *cistern.*
"Or keepe it" is the point where the thought in this hitherto remarkably controlled speech cannot keep to its trajectory: everything breaks
down, so that it isn't clear whether "I" means "I" or "Ay," or what
"there" is doing in relation to "heere," or whether "Patience" addresses Desdemona or a personified virtue, or where the "Cherubin"
comes from. The one thing that does seem clear in these last lines is
that they register a terrifying complete collapse, and are not (as the
New Arden notes suggest) "a most tiresome crux, coming at a moment when any clog on apprehension is particularly vexatious."

Since this is one of the most remarkable moments poetic drama
affords, it's worth reflecting on what poetic drama does and doesn't
do. Imagine a father discovering his dead daughter: what does he
say? Quite probably nothing—he just moans or howls. Perhaps he
might manage a sentence, or some broken phrases. What he certainly
won't do is speak in blank verse like Lear, or sing an aria like Rigoletto.
That kind of appeal to "realism"—to what in real life we would expect

to see or hear—underlies Tolstoy's complaints about Shakespeare and his reductive parody of operatic conventions in *War and Peace,* when Natasha goes to the opera: people just don't speak like that or behave like that, so why prize any art in which they do? One answer—the kind of answer we might offer if we were reading *War and Peace* with *Ulysses* fresh in our minds—is that "realism" is subject to representational conventions. A representation of mental and emotional processes is never transparent, unmediated presentation; it is always something more, or less. But then how can it be, positively, more? Here it seems helpful to consider Lear's blank verse or Rigoletto's music as a species of metaphor: it doesn't merely intensify the feeling in question because poetry and music can be intense; it allows us to *see,* as well as feel, what the character is feeling. A kind of metaphorical and exploratory charting is in question, since the drama in each case is being articulated through its verse or music. We see, for example, why Othello's agony in this crucial speech is so unlike that of Leontes, so that applying the term "jealous" to both men brings out what is insentient and vague in that Gladstone-bag notion. In real life nobody subject to these feelings would speak of "garnering" and "fountains"; and Dr. Johnson objected to the mixed metaphor. Yet no transcript or video of what somebody might really say could show so much. As I suggested in *Shakespeare's Scepticism,* that "mixed" metaphor *shows* how the "idealistic Othello first endows, or invests, Desdemona with unique significance, garnering up his heart by making her his storehouse of value; and then he sees her as the fountain or source, from which his life *derives* significance and value" (4). In this sense the metaphor charts that process of disjunction through which, once someone or something has been endowed with value, the value *appears* to be inherent in the valued and detached from the valuer. There is that "tragedy of idealism."

On the other hand, those departures from the Italian story I have so far considered are, in a sense, "plotty," or situational. They make Othello more than ever vulnerable at the beginning of 3.3, but such changes don't in themselves suggest how or why he has it *in* him to become what he becomes, and do what he does do. That question isn't ever an issue for Iago, because he takes such a reductive view of Othello, and human potentialities. The question is pressing to the extent that we take, or want to take, a less reductive and Iago-like view of Othello's nature, and human nature. If, after seeing what

Othello has it in him to become, we still ask, "How *could* he?" we create, in a painful way, our own problem. Iago's insouciant answer is in his last speech—"what you know, you know"—while that intricately connected series of changes I have so far been considering stops short of suggesting any more inward answer. It is all the more striking that Shakespeare makes another series of intricately connected changes that prompt, or seem to support, a more detached and even unsparingly diagnostic view of the Noble Moor: here we see how Shakespeare works, from the first, to produce what in our century has become "the Othello debate."

As has often been remarked, the first half of *Othello* owes very little to Cinthio's story in the *Hecatommithi*. Shakespeare seems more concerned to establish how and why his lovers are profoundly unlike Cinthio's. So, in the Italian story the lovers have been married long enough for Disdemona to wonder in all seriousness whether her husband's changed behavior is the result of his having grown tired of her *after using her so much*. The Italian is as blunt as that, and, in this area, so is Cinthio's Disdemona. Shakespeare's Desdemona isn't, and couldn't be; in the not very plausible reading of Nelson and Haines she should wonder whether (or simply fail to see how) her violently frustrated husband's changed behavior is the result of never having "used" her at all. But then it is important that Cinthio's Moor is physically demonstrative, assured, and direct in his expressions of passion, and in the Italian story it is the Moor who finds the prospect of a long absence unendurable, and says so: "having to leave you behind," he affirms (in Spenser's Penguin translation), "would make me intolerable to myself; for parting from you would be like parting from my very life." Shakespeare notes that speech, but then his Moor expresses no such regrets, even though he is now a bridegroom whose marriage has not yet been consummated. Instead, it is Desdemona who pleads to accompany her husband, boldly insisting—even as she acknowledges her "downright violence"—that she did love the Moor to live with him, and would not be "bereft" of "the Rites for why I love him." Why should Shakespeare make that change—in effect, a transposition—and why should he so deliberately make his lovers a newly married, idealistic couple, whose marriage is still not consummated when they arrive in Cyprus?

They are not merely newlyweds, they have eloped, and this major departure from the Italian story is the result of another, since Shakespeare decided to make so much more of the differences in age, race, culture and color. Yet another effect of—or reason for—the drastic compression of Cinthio's indeterminate "romance" time is to ensure that both the Shakespearean lovers are, unlike Cinthio's, inexperienced idealists who are idealistic in ominously different ways. They are magnificently committed to each other without knowing each other—that is, without being allowed any *time* in which to live together and establish, through the continuing, reciprocal intimacies of marriage (think of the Macbeths, or Brutus and Portia) any basis for that kind of domestic familiarity and trust which is wholly unlike Grand Passion and shows itself (blessedly, dangerously) in the habit of taking the other for granted.

As for the other differences between the lovers, which make it necessary for them to woo in secret and then elope, they matter so much to Brabantio that he eventually dies of a broken heart; nor would Shakespeare have included that information in a busy final act unless he wanted spectators to think about it. Here it's worth noticing, if Shakespeare's Othello had looked as magnificent as Lawrence Olivier's Caribbean Othello, or as fine as that "negro Pullman conductor" whom the New Arden editor excitedly recalls (li), any modern father with eyes to see would have been looking to his daughter. But for Brabantio (Shakespeare's invention) the differences in age, culture, color, and race had made the danger of an alliance inconceivable. His imagination reels at the very idea that his own daughter was able,

> in spight of Nature,
> Of Yeares, of Country, Credite, every thing,
> To fall in Love, with what she fear'd to look on.
>   (1.3.96–98)

Othello's color clearly matters more in Shakespeare's play than it did in Cinthio's story; just as clearly, it is not all that matters. Brabantio's list is comprehensive, while the violence of his syntactically contorted insistence that

> For Nature, so preposterously to erre,
> (Being not deficient, blind, or lame of sense,)
> Sans with-craft could not.
>   (1.3.62–64)

measures his conviction that "every thing" made this alliance unthinkable.

Here both the liberal reminders that black is beautiful and the more or less illiberal, anxious fretting about the degree of Othello's blackness can be equally distracting. Like Brabantio and like that lady from Maryland whose conviction that Othello *must* be white is preserved in the Variorum, Coleridge also thought it "monstrous" to suppose that Desdemona could love a "veritable negro." More recently Barbara Everett has argued for a tawny, "Spanish" Moor, warning that "if we visualize Othello as black, we see him as essentially standing out from the white faces around him."[43] But Othello *should* stand out; he is *the* Moor of Venice and, although our modern responses to color and miscegenation are shaped by our concerned sense that these are familiar and troubling "issues," Brabantio has seen no "thing" like Othello. Writing from a more confidently enlightened modern standpoint, Karen Newman has argued that "in *Othello,* the black Moor and the fair Desdemona are united in a marriage which all the other characters view as unthinkable" and that "for the white male characters of the play, the black man's power resides in his sexual difference from a white male norm."[44] Yet this is simply and demonstrably untrue: Cassio doesn't think like that, any more than Montano, or Lodovico. For Brabantio, and indeed Desdemona, Othello's exotic uniqueness has been part of the appeal that had hitherto made him a welcome guest. Newman discovers a "cultural aporia" involving "the play's other marginality, femininity," but aporias are a last resort, and the fear of miscegenation that Newman presents as a discovery rather works within a more inclusive, overt, and socially intelligible nexus of attitudes which make it "unthinkable" to the senator that his young daughter could be deeply attracted to this unique and impressive man as a mate.

So, although the difference in "Yeares" rarely figures in critical accounts and doesn't matter to Desdemona, it is another thing that appalls Brabantio. Iago insists that "she must change for youth" (1.3.350), and age figures in Iago's own no less comprehensive list of "all" the things "the Moor is defective in"—including "loveliness in favor, sympathy in years, manner, and beauties" (2.1.229)—while Othello anxiously weighs this difference: "I am declin'd / Into the vale of years (yet that's not much)" (3.3.265–66). As for Desdemona, although we are not told how old she is, it seems a mistake to have her played by any actress (or boy) who couldn't play Juliet: her girlishness appears in her habit of kissing and talking to the handkerchief, in her credulous, wide-eyed responses to Othello's account in 3.4 of its magical properties ("Is't possible? . . . Indeed? Is't true? . . . Bless us"), in her naively uncomprehending insistence that Cassio's "Trespasse" is trifling, and in all her conversations with the sexually experienced and formidable Emilia (one cannot imagine Cintio's Disdemona responding in those ways). In commenting on the harbor scene Harley Granville-Barker observed that Othello's "if it were not to die" speech "gives us the already aging, disillusioned man" while "Desdemona, in her youthfulness, is confident for happiness"; the critical resistance that observation provoked has less to do with what the text tells us than with the habit of idealizing Desdemona and having the part performed by established actresses who are no longer girls.[45] The young, virginal Desdemona is also brave and generous, like her husband, but her life stretches before her, whereas Othello characteristically—and revealingly—thinks of his as a long "pilgrimage" that has found its goal (1.3.153).

My point here is not that these changes to Cinthio's story diminish our sympathy for the lovers or Othello, but that they are what sympathy must work against. Some visual and imaginative shock is essential, both as a measure of Desdemona's youthfully idealistic high-mindedness and to produce a kind of shaming struggle in our own responses. So, any production that wants to keep faith with the problem Shakespeare is setting his audience needs to take aim at its audience. If the play were being produced in Johannesburg, or in those cities in the American South where people tooted carhorns and danced in the streets after the assassination of Martin Luther King, the "sooty bosom" would be enough; but in more hygienic zones where that isn't enough, the play's dynamics require that he should be formidably ugly, or a disturbingly old mate for this idealistic girl who sees "Othello's visage in his mind."

Let us return to that interesting "transposition"—at that moment in the Senate scene when Desdemona, who has already taken the initiative in the wooing, now both shows and acknowledges her "downright violence" by affirming that she loved the Moor to live with him, and would not be "bereft" of the amorous "rites." Before this arrestingly bold, frankly passionate speech, Shakespeare's Moor has taken for granted—and, unlike Cinthio's Moor, simply accepted—that they

must be parted for some time. After directing attention to his own
remarkable qualities in a suitably lofty but somewhat stilted fashion—
"agnising" the natural and prompt alacrity he finds in "hardness,"
which wouldn't be "natural" to most men, let alone newly married
husbands—he asks merely that "my wife" should have "such accom-
modation and besort / As levels with her breeding." It then falls to
Desdemona to show her own quite different kind of natural and
prompt alacrity:

> That I [Q: did] love the Moore, to live with him,
> My downe-right violence, and storme of Fortunes,
> May trumpet to the world. My heart's subdu'd
> Even to the very quality of my Lord;
> I saw *Othello's* visage in his mind,
> And to his Honours and his valiant parts,
> Did I my soule and Fortunes consecrate.
> So that (deere Lords) if I be left behind
> A Moth of Peace, and he go to the Warre,
> The Rites for why I love him, are bereft me:
> And I a heavie interim shall support
> By his deere absence. Let me go with him.
> (1.3.248–59)

Othello at once supports this request, but does so by insisting in a
curiously awkward, unconsciously disparaging way that *he* begs it not

> To please the pallate of my Appetite:
> Nor to comply with heat the yong affects
> In my defunct, and proper satisfaction
> (1.3.262–64)

that is, by insisting that *he* is not subject to those youthfully intense
"affects" or affections which, as we or the senators might reflect, have
led the more impulsive Desdemona to the downright violence of an
elopement.

"Defunct" is a shocking word here and, although it appears both
in the Folio and in the 1622 Quarto, most editors habitually adopt
Theobald's emendation; but the "emendation" cannot remove that
more general shock which is established through another quietly purposeful departure from Cinthio's story. The youthful, passionately

idealistic Desdemona declares, "I saw *Othello's* visage in his mind," while also insisting that she desires those "Rites"; but Othello's no less idealistic insistence that his wish is "to be free, and bounteous to her minde" is associated with a series of *nots* and disparaging references to the palate of appetite, sexual heat, young "affects," corrupting disports, and wanton dullness—as well as to housewives and skillets. We understand, of course, that he is drawing a contrast between maturity and youthful passion, to emphasize that he will not neglect or "scant" the Senate's "serious and great business"; yet his speech so far exceeds that brief as to suggest how he is disposed to think of those amorous "Rites"—which Desdemona desires so frankly, and with such chastely passionate eagerness—as "light wing'd Toyes / Of feather'd Cupid." (Later, when Othello is leading Desdemona off to bed in 2.3, his mercantile imagery of *purchasing* prompts in us a similar unease: she would never talk like that.) In a deeply moving way, her mind is entirely concentrated on what she feels for the unique and particular man she loves and desires: "my Lord," to whom "My heart's subdu'd." He, in a more unwelcome attempt at mature knowingness, is thinking and speaking of sex and what it is and does to other people. After Othello's long speech, the Duke, who had responded in a warmly appreciative way to the account of a wooing in which Desdemona also took the initiative, now responds with something almost like curtness: "Be it as you shall privately determine, / Either for her stay, or going."

I am trying to give an account of some qualm, some tremor of misgiving that I think Othello's speech produces in us. Since the criticism I've read doesn't suggest that many others feel this unease, it's a relief to be able to connect it to things that Shakespeare has rejected, changed, or transposed in the Italian story—while seeing how it also bears on what is to follow. Here, when the Duke goes on to say "You must hence tonight," it is Desdemona who (in the Quarto) asks in dismay, "Tonight, my lord?" and Othello who affirms, with an enthusiasm that displays the loyal soldier rather than the lover, "With all my heart." Later, when the lovers are eventually reunited at Cyprus, Othello exclaims,

> If it were now to dye,
> 'Twere now to be most happy. For I feare,
> My Soule hath her content so absolute,

> That not another comfort like to this,
> Succeedes in unknowne Fate.
>
> (2.1.189–93)

These lines express a feeling both rare and familiar (I imagine many or most of us have felt something like this at some time, but not often), and so touchingly, magnificently ardent that it seems almost gross to reflect that this marriage has still not been consummated. Yet the earlier part of this scene has emphasized Desdemona's sexuality in various ways; here, when Othello marvels at his private and "absolute" ecstasy, it is Desdemona who pulls him back to earth and her. In a more ordinarily human but undiminishing and shareable way, her reply looks forward to *their* living and loving together:

> The Heavens forbid
> But that our Loves and Comforts should encrease
> Even as our dayes do grow.
>
> (2.1.193–95)

As in the Senate scene, her idealistic love for her lover's "mind" is entirely consonant with her eager anticipation of the amorous "Rites"; we might even notice how her eagerness here seems less close to her husband's feeling than to the generously vicarious pleasure with which Cassio had anticipated the lovers' reunion and consummation:

> Great Jove, *Othello* guard,
> And swell his Saile with thine owne powrefull breath,
> That he may bless this Bay with his tall Ship,
> Make loves quicke pants in *Desdemonaes* Armes,
> Give renew'd fire to our extincted Spirits.
> [Q: And bring all Cypresse comfort]
>
> (2.1.77–82)

But then that frank and forward, happily human quality in Desdemona, to which fair young Cassio is so responsive, is something that Othello seems both above and below. Again the question that might be stirring in our minds seems coarse: what is the relation between Othello's ardently soulful intensity and those earlier, disquietingly generalized references to the palate of appetite and "Disports" which will not "corrupt, and taint my businesse"? Earlier he was speaking of sex as something remote from the "Soule"; here he is overwhelmed by a love so much of the "Soule" that he has no thought of that sexual "content" which still lies ahead. There seems to be some kind of rift, or disjunction, which again has to do with the ways in which Shakespeare has made his Moor and this marriage so unlike Cinthio's.

I assume that in the first half of this play we probably don't *want* to ask this kind of question, even when we are registering some more or less inchoate sense of difference between these idealistic lovers: we resist it, rather as Cassio resists Iago's smuttier suggestions about Desdemona being "full of Game" in 2.3. But in that case what we suppress or put down earlier resurfaces later. If we had registered something momentarily disquieting or at least unwelcome in Othello's imaginative dwelling on the "pallate" of "Appetite," wouldn't our alarm at these later lines include some shock of recognition?

> I had been happy, if the generall Campe,
> Pyoners and all, had tasted her sweet Body,
> So I had nothing knowne.
>
> (3.3.345–47)

That dirty Iago-like way of thinking of Desdemona as a "sweet" body to be "tasted" confirms and goes far beyond the very worst misgiving Othello's earlier reference to the palate of appetite might have prompted, while the dirtiness is all the more shocking if we remember not ony that pioneers were the lowest rank of soldier but that other Shakespearean references associate them with the work of mining and countermining: Desdemona's reified body is being gang-mined as well as "tasted."[46]

Now there is an appalling sense of filth surfacing in Othello's mind. It was rising to the surface moments before, when Othello spoke of keeping "a corner in the thing I love / For others uses" (3.3.274–75); and his first reference to a "Toad" in that speech looks forward to the later filthiness, when the "corner" becomes a *cistern* for "foule Toades / To knot and gender in" (4.2.60–61). When the play's final scene begins we again see Othello thinking of Desdemona's body as an object and gourmet dish for the palate of appetite—contemplating and appraising that "whiter skin," which is "smooth as Monumentall Alablaster," and even bending down to "smell" her defenseless body on the relaid wedding sheets. And in that same speech the Moor,

whom Shakespeare had made into a Christian convert (another significant departure from Cinthio) and who is, throughout the play,
much given to making references to his "Soule," addresses his soul
again—but now in a monstrously deranged way, seeing the murder
itself as some heavenly mission or cause to save mankind or, rather,
men: "It is the Cause, it is the Cause (my Soule) . . . else shee'l betray
more men." Here is the dreadful culmination of that disjunction
which could be glimpsed in the first acts, but which, if we thought
about it then, we probably wanted to discount or dismiss as an "uncleanly Apprehension."

So far, I have directed attention to two intricately organized series
of changes to the Italian story, which appear to move in different
directions—on the one hand to increase, on the other to check or
complicate, our sympathetic engagement with Shakespeare's Moor.
Readings that insist that the Moor is "too easily jealous" make little
or nothing of the first series of changes, with its radical replotting of
Othello's situation; to withhold sympathy, or deny Othello's nobility,
is to be drawn toward that diminished and diminishing view of human
motives and relationships which Iago represents in its most virulently
reductive form. But the second series of changes makes it more than
ever difficult to displace the responsibility for Othello's "monstrous
Acte" onto a demonized Iago, and to sustain a view of Othello as the
"Noble Moor"—not least by showing how exactly that view corresponds with Othello's view of himself in the final scene. At first
Othello insists that even though "this acte shewes most horrible and
grim," that is only how it "shewes," or seems: he "did proceed upon
just grounds / To this extremity," since the extremity was justified by
Desdemona's own "Act of shame, a thousand times committed." Then,
when Emilia's revelations explode this argument, Othello's response
is to try to sever the *monstrous act* from the noble *agent,* by insisting
that his "Soule and Body" were "ensnar'd" by "that demy-Divell" and
that he was "one that lov'd not wisely, but too well." Hearing Othello
describe himself in that way—or as "an honourable Murderer, if you
will," who did nothing "in hate, but all in Honour"—should make it
all the more difficult for us to take that view. It is almost a relief, or
compensation, to hear the disgusted Emilia reviling him as a
"murd'rous Coxcombe" and insisting on Desdemona's better claim to
be considered as one that loved not wisely, but too well—or, as Emilia
blisteringly puts it, one "too fond of her most filthy Bargaine." Earlier,

Othello's gloating, morally bestial response to the screams of the permanently crippled and, as Othello thinks and hopes, dying Cassio similarly measured the degradation of the "Noble," even as Othello used that word:

> 'Tis he: O brave *Iago*, honest, and just,
> That hast such Noble sense of thy Friends wrong,
> Thou teachest me. Minion, youre deare lyes dead,
> And your unblest Fate highes: Strumpet I come.
>
> (5.1.31–34)

Nothing "in hate, but all in Honour"?

What I have called the second series of departures from the Italian story does allow a more inward view of Othello—and an answer, or range of answers, to the question of how Othello has it in him to become what he becomes, and do what he does. But the effect of these departures is to expose and chart those disturbing features in the Shakespearean Moor which have prompted various sharply diagnostic accounts of Othello as a "case": as Leavis's deluded egotist, Greenblatt's deluded Christian, Edward Snow's deranged victim of "sexual anxiety and the male order of things,"[47] and Karen Newman's "instrument of punishment" who "enacts the moral Rymer and Cinthio point, both confirming cultural prejudice by his monstrous murder of Desdemona and punishing her desire which transgresses the norms of the Elizabethan sex/race system" ("Wash the Ethiop White," 153). Although these diagnostically knowing accounts differ in their explanatory emphases—that is, in the relative importance attached to moral, psychological or historical considerations—their effect is always estranging: they are *directionally* opposed to that investment of imaginative sympathy which characterizes the accounts of Othello offered by Coleridge, Bradley, and Dover Wilson. Here Iago enters by another route, as we see if we compare Leavis's reading with Greenblatt's and notice how neither account of Othello is an account of *Othello.*[48]

A Choice of Delusions

Considering how Greenblatt's account of Othello resembles Leavis's is instructive if we are concerned with how the play itself—Shakespeare's play, not the simpler play Iago is staging—frames different perspectives on its main character. Although both critics take a sharply diagnostic and reductive view of Othello and represent him as being, in the limiting sense, a "case," it might seem strange to consider Greenblatt's reading as an "anti-Othello" intervention in a familiar twentieth-century debate. First, Greenblatt shows no interest in that earlier debate, and his essay is one of his more conspicuously all-American pieces: the copious references take in the work of Altman, Martz, Spivack, Snow, Kirsch, Mack, Hyman, Bersani, Fiedler, Burke, Bloom, Barber, Cavell, Stone, and Rabkin, among others, and of a few British historians and scholars like Yates, Strong, and Thomas, but there is no suggestion that British literary critics have contributed anything to twentieth-century critical thinking about *Othello*.[49] Second, although Leavis had criticized Bradley for being preoccupied with character, his own essay is more narrowly characterological than Bradley's; here the contrast of Leavis's essay with the magnificent scope and *élan* of Greenblatt's *Renaissance Self-Fashioning* might seem decisive—until we notice how its sampling of Shakespeare's play is no less partial than Leavis's, and how neither critic attempts to integrate what he sees in Othello into any account of what the play is doing. Greenblatt's essay does indeed present an "anti-Othello" reading, but in the way his account of the "Henriad" is "anti-Henry": the old-fashioned, narrowly characterological analysis is recast in gleamingly contemporary ideological terms, so that it is something of a shock to realize that the reading still centers on a diagnostic analysis of Othello's character and what this gives Iago to "play upon."

Hence the paradoxical relation between the critics' perceptions of Othello and those of Iago, who is "nothing, if not Criticall" and provides the most savagely reductive view of Othello within the play. So, for example, that "Othello music" to which Wilson Knight warily thrilled and which prompted Bradley to consider Othello as a "poet" is for Leavis related to Othello's self-regard, while for Greenblatt "Othello's rhetorical extremism" is one of the "habitual and self-limiting forms of discourse" to which Iago is so "demonically sensitive" (*Renaissance Self-Fashioning*, 235). Whether we choose to speak (like Leavis) of self-regard, or (like Greenblatt) of self-fashioning and self-limiting, or (like Martin Elliott) of "self-publication,"[50] it is clear that all these terms refer us to something in Othello which the play *makes* problematic and which has no counterpart in the Italian story. Early in the first scene we hear Iago refer, scathingly, to what Othello "evades" with "bumbast Circumstance" (or bombastic, circumlocutory padding) and "horribly stufft" epithets. Iago's view is critical and reductive: this is how an uppity Moor talks, "in loving his owne pride, and purposes." But then, to the extent that Leavis and Greenblatt see an obvious truth in Iago's diagnostic way of relating Othello's eloquence to "pride, and purposes"—to what Leavis sees as egotistical self-regard, and Greenblatt as narrative self-fashioning—they are less inclined to consider that perception as an expression of Iago's way of seeing and mode of being. Precisely because Leavis's own view of Othello resembles Iago's he can, with no sense of contradiction, demote Iago's significance within the play, and protest against a critical tradition that would salvage Othello's nobility by having him brought down by a manipulator of such satanic power. Greenblatt doesn't demote Iago, and indeed provides an exceptionally powerful, inward account of Iago's "demonic sensitivity"; but, like Leavis, he also emphasizes the extent to which Iago is a catalyst who can "play upon" and release what is already in Othello.

Obvious differences shouldn't obscure this important resemblance. Where Leavis sees Othello as a deluded egotist Greenblatt sees him as a deluded Christian convert; but both concentrate on unpacking a disabling and finally murderous delusion. Leavis's account of Othello's egotism comes perilously close to repudiating any morally and imaginatively constructive aspiration to live up to a "better self"; Greenblatt attaches more importance to Othello's Christianity than any other critic, while at the same time emptying it of any positive religious or spiritual significance. In other words, both critics assume—like Iago—that understanding Othello means seeing *through* him in a reductively diagnostic fashion. For Leavis, this is a largely moral and critical matter; in the terms of his analysis, historical considerations and cultural contexts are largely or entirely irrelevant—whereas they are crucial to Greenblatt's argument that "Christianity is the alienating yet constitutive force in Othello's identity" (245). We are to believe that the "orthodox doctrine which governs Othello's sexual attitudes" (246) is the "traditional" Christian idea that (in Calvin's reformulation) "the man who shows no modesty or comeliness in conjugal intercourse is committing adultery with his wife" (248). As a Christian convert Othello cannot protect himself from the neurotic-making, finally murderous dynamics of "orthodox" Christian teaching on sexuality, since "he cannot allow himself the moderately flexible adherence that most ordinary men have towards their formal beliefs" (245). So, the play's "symbolic center" is Othello's "tormenting identification" between "taking excessive pleasure in the marriage bed" and "adultery," and the "dark essence of Iago's whole enterprise" is to "play upon Othello's buried perception of his own sexual relations with Desdemona as adulterous" (233). This is an unexpected reading and I must say more about it, but my immediate point has to do with the way in which Greenblatt, like Leavis, diagnoses Othello as a "case."

Moreover, in developing their very different diagnoses neither critic speaks to the play by considering whether the play prompts a diagnosis in these terms, or whether there is some significant difficulty in aligning the modern critic's analytical vocabulary with that of the play: the significance of any such difficulty is usually moral and historical. But then neither Leavis nor Greenblatt is concerned to ask whether the play calls for a diagnostic account of Othello in an intelligently purposive or merely inadvertent way. Here, once again, the issue of dramatic intention enters to the degree that it is excluded. Leavis writes as though Othello were an inadequately prepared examination candidate whose failure could be contemplated with something like satisfaction: "In this testing, Othello's inner timbers begin to part at once, the stuff of which he is made begins at once to deteriorate and show itself unfit." His tone is representative, morally ugly, and rather surprising from the critic who had observed that "if we don't see ourselves in Angelo, we have taken the play very imperfectly."[51] But then Leavis never confronts the question his own analysis makes so pressing: if the main effect of *Othello* is to provoke such extraordinary animus, wouldn't the play itself be less satisfactory than he supposes? Greenblatt's reading presents an equivalent difficulty because of the way it figures in an impressively ranging and often enthralling discussion of Renaissance *mentalité*. Presenting a reductively diagnostic view of Othello is neither the essay's main aim nor an incidental effect: rather, it is a *condition* of the way *Othello* is thought to fit into that ranging argument. Yet this makes the critical difficulty: Greenblatt is providing a *cultural* context, but not a *dramatic* context, for those parts of the Shakespearean text which he discusses. Once again a play is being used to instantiate, without being allowed to test, the controlling thesis, and a thesis that is characteristically new historicist in its insistence on what *estranges* us from the Renaissance and Shakespeare: in this case seeing through Othello turns *Othello* into a period piece.

For this very reason it matters whether Shakespeare could have recognized his play in Greenblatt's conspicuously contemporary—anti-Christian and Lacanian—account of its "symbolic center." If the play can be understood in different, less estranging terms, we need to know, and so does Greenblatt. If the play itself is exploring and diagnosing the malign, neurotic-making dynamics of that "orthodox doctrine that governs Othello's sexual attitudes," it would be a revolutionary document, rather than a museum exhibit. If, on the other hand, it merely illustrates or (worse) endorses that warped, warping doctrine, then Greenblatt's diagnosis of Othello extends to the play itself—and we would then know how to unravel, or cut through, Greenblatt's elaborately poised, suavely inconclusive conclusion:

> Shakespeare approaches his culture not, like Marlowe, as rebel and blasphemer, but rather as a dutiful servant, content to improvise a part of his own within its orthodoxy. And if after centuries, that improvisation has been revealed to us as embodying an almost boundless challenge to the culture's every tenet, a devastation of every source, the author of Othello would have understood that such a revelation scarcely matters. (253)

As Geoffrey Strickland observes in *Structuralism or Criticism?*, "We cannot possibly understand what is written or said unless we understand its interest and importance for the writer or speaker; which affects inevitably its interest and importance for us. Evaluation, in this sense, and interpretation are the same."[52] That is why the student of literature is and must be a student of history, learning to see with what Michael Baxandall calls the "period eye."[53] But at this point Greenblatt's own avowedly Lacanian, psychoanalytical account of the "symbolic center" presents a peculiar difficulty: it keeps telling us that the "symbolic center" is "concealed," but not by whom, or from whom.

To take one little cluster of examples from one page of Greenblatt's essay, even when we are being told that "Othello comes close to revealing his tormenting identification of marital sexuality—limited perhaps to the night he took Desdemona's virginity—and adultery" (251), *revealing* means something so close to betraying as to imply further *concealing.* When Greenblatt goes on to observe, of Iago, who so successfully improvises "on the religious sexual doctrine in which Othello believes," that "beneath his cynical modernity and professed self-love Iago reproduces in himself the same psychic structure," the same difficulty is revealed, or betrayed, or concealed: apparently, what "assures" Iago's "access to Othello" is not in any straightforward sense apparent to Iago himself. Greenblatt then observes that the "improvisational process we have been discussing depends for its success upon the concealment of its symbolic center, but as the end approaches this center becomes increasingly visible"—not before time, since the play is nearly over, yet the interpretation still will not tell us whether what becomes increasingly visible is being *made* increasingly visible by Shakespeare or by this mode of psychoanalytical analysis, which half creates what it half perceives. (Though peculiar, this difficulty is familiar in psychoanalytical interpretations; an Iago-like cynic might associate it with the practical difficulty confronting those psychiatrists who are well paid by the healthy and wealthy to represent inner vacuity as inner life.) Disquietingly, what is said to become "increasingly visible" apparently remained invisible for nearly four centuries, and certainly wasn't visible to earlier, Christian critics like Johnson and Coleridge, writing in centuries when "orthodox" Christian doctrine didn't have to be expounded by literary critics. In all these instances the analysis equivocates by not considering whether the play is diagnosing the perverting dynamics of the "orthodox doctrine that governs Othello's sexual attitudes," or whether the play itself is "governed" by the "doctrine." This difficulty corresponds with that in Greenblatt's discussion of the "logic which governs the relation between orthodoxy and subversion" in the "Henriad," and provokes the same objection: it is the critic's own thesis—Lacanian in this case, Foucauldian in that—which actually "governs" his reading, determining when he dips into the Shakespearean text, and determining what the partial sampling of the text is to instantiate.

The most spectacular instance of the peculiar difficulty posed by this Lacanian interpretative model is also the most important for Greenblatt's thesis, since it involves that speech of Iago's which is said to show how the play's "symbolic center" if both revealed and concealed:

> *Cassio's* a proper man: Let me see now,
> To get his Place, and to plume up my will

In double Knavery. How? How? Let's see.
After some time, to abuse *Othello's* eares,
That he is too familiar with his wife:
He hath a person, and a smooth dispose
To be suspected; fram'd to make women false.
The Moore is of a free, and open Nature,
That thinkes men honest, that but seeme to be so,
And will as tenderly be lead by'th'Nose—as Asses are:
I have't: it is engendred: Hell, and Night,
Must bring this monstrous Birth, to the worlds light.
                                        (1.3.392–404)

Greenblatt discusses this passage twice. First, he directs attention to
the "felicitous" way in which "the ambiguity of the third-person pro-
noun" delivers the suggestion that Othello himself is "too familiar
with his wife": he adds that "though scarcely visible at this point, it is
the dark essence of Iago's whole enterprise which is, as we shall see,
to play upon Othello's buried perception of his own sexual relations
with Desdemona as adulterous (233). Later, Greenblatt returns to this
supposedly "felicitous" and more than merely "syntactic" ambiguity,
to explain "how Iago manages to persuade Othello that Desdemona
has committed adultery" (247). The two ways of understanding "he
is too familiar with his wife" allegedly correspond with two aspects of
"the centuries-old Christian doctrine": the "rigorist" condemnation
of (real) adultery as "one of the most horrible of mortal sins, more
detestable, in the words of the *Eruditorium penitentiale*, 'than homicide
or plunder'"; and that "still darker aspect of orthodox Christian doctrine" which compares taking pleasure in "conjugal intercourse"
with "adultery."

Greenblatt's exposition of this "darker" doctrine runs the course
from Jerome's dictum—"An adulterer is he who is too ardent a lover
of his wife"—and Augustine, to Calvin and sundry "orthodox" warnings like that in the *King's Book*, "attributed to Henry VIII," that says
a man can break the Seventh Commandment and "live unchaste with
his own wife, if he do unmeasurably or inordinately serve his or her
fleshly appetite or lust." In other words, Greenblatt assembles an old
historicist *cento* of quotations which briskly cuts through complicated
historical and theological issues and is most obviously selective where
it matters most—at the Renaissance end. There is no doubt that the
desert fathers took up the Pauline exaltation of celibacy with an anti-

sexual vengeance, or that—despite occasional dissidents, like the fifth-century Synesius of Cyrene—this dominated "orthodox" doctrine for the millennium from the fourth to the fourteenth centuries.[54] Nor can we soften the force of Jerome's enthusiastic recyclings of the stoic Xystus's leathery little maxim that "He who loves his own wife too ardently is an adulterer" *(omnis ardentior amator propriae uxoris adulter est)* by supposing that Jerome means that pleasure in marital sex should be ardent but not too ardent: in Jerome's majestic view any sexual pleasure is excessive and sinful. But this was not quite the view taken by Aquinas and Peter Lombard when they discussed Jerome's two reworkings of the maxim from Xystus, as appears in this modern theologian's explication: "The man thus denounced is not, apparently, he who entertains too warm an affection for his wife, but he whose *amor* (that is, his desire for venereal pleasure—the word here does not mean 'love,' as we understand it) is so vehement that it impels him to abandon the restraint which pays careful regard to the *bona matrimonii,* and incites him to treat her as if she were merely, like any other woman, a means of lustful gratification."[55] On this view sex is not sinful per se, even though it cannot be pursued for its own sake without sin—"a venial sin when sought within marriage, and a mortal sin when sought outside it." Greenblatt doesn't make room for Peter Lombard and Aquinas, and he quotes Calvin's warning that "the man who shows no modesty or comeliness in conjugal intercourse is committing adultery with his wife" as though Calvin thought on this matter like Jerome; yet Calvin specifically and very sternly repudiated Jerome's argument that "if it is good not to touch a woman, it is bad to touch one"—affirming that sexual intercourse is a pure institution of God and that the idea that "we are polluted by intercourse with our wives" emanates from Satan, not Paul.[56] Greenblatt quotes from the "influential" Raymond and Jacobus Ungarelli, but not from Luther, or Thomas Becon's *Book of Matrimony,* or Erasmus's colloquies on marriage—where there is a direct link, not only with the "marriage group" of Sonnets but with the witty sexual frankness of women in Shakespeare's romantic comedies.[57] After quoting Nicholas of Ausimo's warning that the conjugal act may be without sin, but only if "in the performance of this act there is no enjoyment of pleasure," Greenblatt solemnly concludes that "few *summas* and no marriage manuals take so extreme a position, but virtually all are in agreement that the active pursuit of pleasure in sexuality is damnable" (*Renais-*

sance Self-Fashioning, 249). But are we then to conclude that Shakespeare's audiences would have thought that Desdemona's forthright declaration in the Senate of what Greenblatt himself describes as a "frankly, though by no means exclusively sexual" passion was "damnable"? And if not, why not?

As for Iago's speech, Greenblatt's extraordinary reading is altogether severed from any dramatic context, and leaves the conscious and the unconscious to play peekaboo. Iago's speech occurs in the third scene, when the marriage has not even been consummated: far from being "too familiar with his wife" by taking "excessive pleasure" in the marriage bed, Othello hasn't taken any. Moreover, at this point in the drama, neither Iago nor the audience knows anything of Cassio's part in the secret wooing: he and we only learn in 3.3 that Cassio and Desdemona were "very oft" alone together. When Iago says "after some time" he is assuming, sensibly enough, he will have to wait before trying to convince Othello that Cassio is his wife's lover: how does one convince somebody who has just taken his wife's virginity that she is adulterous? Moreover, just as Iago cannot think that the attraction between Othello and Desdemona is anything but grossly physical and perverted, he is actually incapable of thinking that Othello is seriously committed to his Christian faith. In his soliloquy after the riot in Act 2, he sneers that Othello is so "enfetter'd" by his love for Desdemona that she could persuade him "to renownce his Baptisme, / All Seales, and Simbols of redeemed sin" (2.3.334–35). Consequently, one objection to the thesis that the "dark essence of Iago's whole enterprise" is "to play upon Othello's buried perception of his own sexual relations with Desdemona as adulterous" is that Iago doesn't and couldn't see what he is said to be doing and playing upon.

As the thesis becomes ever more ramified, we are invited to suppose that Othello unleashes upon Cassio "the fear of pollution, defilement, brutish violence that is bound up with his own experience of sexual pleasure" (250); finally, it is "as if Othello has found in a necrophilic fantasy the secret solution to the intolerable demands of the rigorist sexual ethic, and the revelation that Cassio has not slept with Desdemona leads only to a doubling of this solution, for the adulterous sexual pleasure that Othello had projected upon his lieutenant now rebounds upon himself" (252). Yet the crucial issue, on which Greenblatt's whole reading depends, is whether the newly married Othello does tormentedly identify his own sexual pleasure with sin.

In fact, Greenblatt is surprisingly specific about what he thinks happens on that first night in Cyprus. Yet this assurance involves a very curious assumption that what (allegedly) happens onstage during the lovers' "passionate reunion" at the harbor anticipates, and explains, what will (allegedly) happen offstage during the next scene. For Greenblatt, this reunion has a "rich and disturbing pathos" that derives from the lovers' very different attitudes toward sexuality. Othello's words are said to convey both "an ecstatic acceptance of sexuality, an absolute content," and "the longing for a final release from desire"—since "for him sexuality is a menacing voyage . . . one of the dangers to be passed," and a "tempest" that threatens "self-dissolution." As for Desdemona, her "response is in an entirely different key" and, although "spoken to allay Othello's fear," is far more likely to "augment it," since her own "erotic submission" threatens and "subverts her husband's carefully fashioned identity" (242–44). Yet the "ecstatic acceptance of sexuality" is Greenblatt's invention, or fantasy. When Othello speaks of that absolute content which his "Soule" already has, and which he fears can never be equaled in the future, he isn't even thinking of future sexual "content":

> If it were now to dye,
> 'Twere now to be most happy. For I feare,
> My Soule hath her content so absolute,
> That not another comfort like to this,
> Succeeds in unknowne Fate.
>
> (2.1.189–93)

It is Desdemona who then reminds Othello, in a lovingly corrective way, of the "Loves and Comforts" yet to come, which "should encrease," not diminish, his and their "content." But here Greenblatt's account of Desdemona's "erotic submissiveness" is no less curious, and disquietingly consistent with his argument that although Bianca and Emilia both have "moments of disobedience to the men who possess and abuse them," Desdemona "performs no such acts of defiance" (244). What of her "downe-right violence," her deception and defiance of her own father, her readiness to "trumpet to the world" that "I did love the Moore, to live with him," or her fatal refusal to stop pressing Cassio's case? Greenblatt's Desdemona is more tame, since he gives little or no weight to all those creatively purposeful changes through which Shakespeare made his Desdemona so unlike Cinthio's Disdemona. Nonetheless, this part of Greenblatt's analysis is very important to his reading, since he sees Othello's speech at the harbor as a tragically accurate "premonition" of "a rent, a moving ambivalence, in his experience of the ecstatic moment itself" (243): that is, when he "took Desdemona's virginity," "shed her blood," and not only noticed but became imaginatively obsessed by the condition of their own lust-stained wedding sheets.

This explanation of what allegedly happens on the first night in Cyprus is wholly untenable if, as I argue, weighing the textual and dramatic evidence suggests that the marriage is never consummated; but I do not assume that all readers will accept my own argument about that. The objection to Greenblatt's reading is more basic, and is that when he provides local analysis and commentary he is unable to establish the basic premise—that Othello himself tormentedly identifies his own sexual pleasure with sin and "adultery." The reading is willful because it is so partial, and because it disregards whatever conflicts with the forceful thesis. As we have seen, Greenblatt's explanation of why Othello is obsessed with sheets won't explain why they also matter to Desdemona, just as Othello's speech at the harbor doesn't show any "ecstatic acceptance of sexuality," and just as the extraordinarily tenuous reading of Iago's soliloquy at the end of Act 1 never asks why Iago should say, "After some time." Iago is thinking about the dramatic situation, but Greenblatt isn't. The dramatic situation makes it impossible that Iago could be determining to "play upon Othello's buried perception of his own sexual relations with Desdemona as adulterous." The fact that nobody before Greenblatt ever had interpreted Iago's speech in that way suggests how the Shakespearean chapter in *Renaissance Self-Fashioning* presents yet another critical tribar. As in his "Invisible Bullets" essay, the critic keeps slithering between an ideal *is* (a strongly prescriptive and "original" critical account of how the play should be understood) and a material *was*, where what makes the reading seem "original" is also what explodes it—precisely because no earlier critic, including Christian critics like Johnson and Coleridge, had ever understood the play in this way. The result, once again, is that the reading becomes an impossible object in four-dimensional (non-historical) space.

Although I agree with Greenblatt and Snow that there are disparities between Othello's and Desdemona's attitudes toward sexuality (to put the matter narrowly), their readings also show how such disparities can be described in very different ways. In "Sexual Anxiety and the Male Order of Things," Snow himself protests against Greenblatt's "scapegoating" of Christianity, while discussing forms of sexual anxiety that are not inconceivable today; for that very reason Snow's own psychoanalytical reading wouldn't be so attractive to the new historicist: it isn't so *estranging*. The appeal of Greenblatt's argument, in new historicist terms, is that it once again posits that gulf between Them and Us: the play becomes another period piece that can then only be "understood" in alienating or estranging terms—in this case by invoking that "orthodox" Christian "doctrine" which is said to "govern" Othello's attitude to sexuality, but really governs Greenblatt's thesis.

Some other explanation is needed for Shakespeare's decision to turn Cinthio's Moor into a Christian convert much given to making references to his "Soule." Nor should we suppose that if there is some disparity between Othello's and Desdemona's attitudes toward sexuality, it forces us to withhold sympathy from Othello and to regard him merely as a "case"; rather, I need to modify my own earlier argument that Shakespeare's departures from Cinthio's story show him moving in what appear to be opposite directions. It is indeed worth noticing how Shakespeare worked from the first, to complicate his material, and how these complications produced the twentieth-century debate about Othello in which each party to the debate disregards or plays down that "evidence" which most impresses the other. Yet the metaphor of departing in different directions is still potentially misleading, since all of Shakespeare's departures from the Italian story are directed to one end, which is to fashion—and integrate—his own work. Moreover, that work is a poetic drama, not another prose story or novella. A "novel," according to Dr. Johnson's *Dictionary*, is "a small tale, generally of love"; Cinthio's story is that, but *Othello* is not. The greatest difference between Cinthio's Moor and Shakespeare's has to do with those modes of metaphorical representation which transform the Italian story into a powerfully sustained poetic-dramatic conceit: Othello, his potentialities, and the dramatic world he inhabits are conceived and characterized in poetic-dramatic terms.

"A Horrible Conceite"

Even if we take a less dismissive view than Kenneth Muir of Cinthio's "sordid and melodramatic" tale,[58] scarcely anything of the original story is unchanged in Shakespeare's poetic drama; this suggests that the creative stimulus it provided was altogether, and limitingly, that of seeing what else might be done *with* it. One striking instance challenges modern pieties as well as the nearest thing we get to a moral piety in Cinthio's story, and helps us to see how that story is being turned into a moral torture chamber full of "uncleanly Apprehensions": although the Moor's blackness figures in the Italian story, what Shakespeare makes of that in poetic-dramatic terms has far more in common with the *Sonnets* and *Measure for Measure*—works in which racism isn't an issue.

At least some of the *Sonnets* were written before *Othello,* whereas the 1609 Quarto that also included *A Lover's Complaint* appeared five years after the play was performed. And since the *Sonnets, Othello* and, later, *The Winter's Tale* all present different permutations of an anguished triangular situation in which a man supposes that the male friend he most loves has betrayed him with the woman he loves, it might also seem tempting to suppose that Cinthio's story answered to that interest—but it doesn't. There is no corresponding close attachment between Cinthio's Moor and his Captain: although the Captain is a friend who has also served the Moor well, the Ensign is no less "dear to the Moor," and both friendships are very perfunctorily sketched in. The story can easily accommodate, but doesn't already show and repay, Shakespeare's interest in that agonizing triangle. Here it is more helpful to see how, in the Dark Lady sonnets as in *Othello,* the situational overlap combines with the "fair/black" antithesis or metaphor—and produces an alarming interpretative uncertainty about how to read that crucial metaphor.

What is repeatedly in doubt for the Poet in the Dark Lady sonnets is the relationship between the external and internal senses of "black" and "fair." Just as the beautiful young man may be externally fair but corrupted—a fair devil, which is what Othello calls Desdemona—the Dark Lady, who is "not counted faire" in the external or conventional sense, may or may not be *black* or *foul* in the internal or ethical sense. It is one thing to love a brunette while recognizing, in a playful or bantering fashion, that gentlemen prefer blondes, or royal redheads; it is quite another thing to be helplessly drawn to a faithless woman in whose bay all men, including the most loved male friend, can ride. In these sonnets the Poet's moral and imaginative disturbance concentrates in his fear that his own "judgement" is deranged:

Thou blinde foole love, what doost thou to mine eyes,
That they behold and see not what they see:
They know what beautie is, see where it lyes,
Yet what the best is, take the worst to be.

(Sonnet 137)

In faith I doe not love thee with mine eyes,
For they in thee a thousand errors note,
But 'tis my heart that loves what they dispise,
Who in dispight of view is pleasd to dote.

(Sonnet 141)

My thoughts and my discourse as mad mens are,
At random from the truth vainely exprest.
   For I have sworne thee faire, and thought thee bright,
   Who art as black as hell, as dark as night.

(Sonnet 147)

O me! what eyes hath love put in my head
Which have no correspondence with true sight,
Or if they have, where is my judgment fled,
That censures falsely what they see aright?
If that be faire whereon my false eyes dote,
What meanes the world to say it is not so?
If it be not, then love doth well denote,
Loves eye is not so true as all mens: no,
How can it? O how can loves eye be true,
That is so vext with watching and with teares.

(Sonnet 148)

It is not difficult to imagine that last passage occurring in any of the comedies where the idea that love adds a precious seeing to the eye—as Berowne affirms in *Love's Labour's Lost* (4.3.330) after declaring that Rosaline was born to make black fair—is opposed to something more like Theseus's skeptical view of the "seething braines" of "Lovers and mad men" whose "shaping phantasies" apprehend "More then coole reason ever comprehends" (*Midsummer Night's Dream*, 5.1.2–6). Similarly, "Thy blacke is fairest in my judgements place" is a line from Sonnet 131 that might have been spoken by Tamora, or by Berowne, or by Desdemona—though *not* by the Portia who comments, when the Prince of Morocco arrives, that "if he have the condition of a

Saint, and the complexion of a divell, I had rather he should shrive me then wive me" (1.2.116–18). We might even imagine the line being spoken, long before *The Tempest* begins, by Caliban's Algerian mother; that is fanciful, but considering Caliban as Shakespeare's last Moor is not more fanciful than thinking of him as Shakespeare's first American, or supposing that a ship traveling from Tunis to Naples is wrecked somewhere between the Bermudas and Nantucket. The "fair/black" antithesis, which so problematically slides into the "fair/foul" antithesis, is an immense Shakespearean force-field, or generative matrix—an associational crucible that connects the tragedies, comedies and the poems.

In the *Sonnets* these endemic tonal ambiguities also generate an interpretative uncertainty in the reader which is all too close to that of the Poet. Our own sense of the tone or pitch or (to recall Keats's wish for a poetical thermometer) temperature of a line like "Thy blacke is fairest in my judgements place" depends upon our sense of the context: like the Poet, we need to know whether the blackness involves external appearances or an internal and ethical foulness. The next line in Sonnet 131—"In nothing art thou blacke save in thy deeds"—might seem to make this distinction cuttingly clear; in his edition of the sonnets, Stephen Booth memorably refers to this sonnet's final couplet as a "single graceful razor stroke" (457). Yet the poem shows how, even as the Poet delivers that seemingly firm, final judgment, he still has no eyes to see what holds fast in his own "judgments place":

> Thou art as tiranous, so as thou art,
> As those whose beauties proudly makes them cruell:
> For well thou know'st to my deare doting hart
> Thou art the fairest and most precious Iewell.
> Yet in good faith some say that thee behold,
> Thy face hath not the power to make love grone;
> To say they erre, I dare not be so bold,
> Although I sweare it to my selfe alone.
> And to be sure that is not false I sweare
> A thousand grones but thinking on thy face,
> One on anothers necke do witnesse beare
> Thy blacke is fairest in my judgments place.

In nothing art thou blacke save in thy deeds,
And thence this slaunder as I thinke proceeds.

(Sonnet 131)

The first two lines compare the Dark Lady's tyranny with the cruelly proud behavior of genuine beauties, but they don't tell us what that conventional sonneteering word *tyrannous* refers to; for all we know, she might be refusing her sexual favors, like the cruelly proud beauties who get their comeuppance in Monteverdi's *Ballo dell' Ingrate*. The contrast with real "beauties" seems clearer: whether or not the mistress knows it, or needs to be told, she is apparently not beautiful or fair in the external and conventional sense. Yet the next two lines equivocally deny this, in implying that she only treats the Poet so tyrannously (whatever that means) because she knows that she is the *fairest* to his *doting* heart; so is he merely doting, or is she beautiful after all? Some who behold her *face* say, "in good faith," that she isn't; although the Poet won't "say they erre" he privately thinks so, and swears as much "to be sure"—which of course suggests that he isn't sure—"that is not false." Though the three quatrains are tortuous, they aren't obviously tortured or anguished, and all seem concerned with whether the Dark Lady looks good, not with whether she is good, or inwardly fair. Even in the final couplet the idea of a *slander* is witty because it's so slippery: it is not clear that those who say ("in good faith"!) that the mistress's *face* is not fair were thinking about, or even know about, her black deeds.

If we ask whether the Poet is or should be razor-slashing the Dark Lady in the final couplet, or whether that last "as I thinke" is despairing or playfully rueful, everything depends on what we read into the reference to the black "deeds." Very ugly possibilities press in from without and from within as "uncleanly Apprehensions," but it is never certain what these black "deeds" are, or how they connect with being "tiranous." If we then try to resolve this interpretative uncertainty about what is ambiguous within the poem by taking bearings from our sense of the implied narrative situation within a sequence, we quickly and repeatedly find ourselves involved in circularities. We don't know what happened between the bracingly positive ironies of Sonnet 130 ("My Mistres eyes are nothing like the Sunne") and Sonnet 131—or indeed between the apparently explosive and tormented, but perhaps more conventional, Sonnet 129 ("Th' expense of spirit in a waste of shame") and Sonnet 130.[59] The implied or postulated situation is too unspecific, in narrative terms, for us to know whether or how Sonnet 129 leads into Sonnet 130, or how Sonnet 130 leads into Sonnet 131, in the way any scene in *Othello* leads into the following scene.

Although *Othello* is more specific in that sense, the play delivers a comparable interpretative uncertainty, by framing its own alarmingly different ways of apprehending that "fair/black" metaphor. The relationship between the external and internal senses of *black* and *fair* seems clear to the Duke who describes Othello as "farre more Faire then Blacke," or to the Desdemona who "saw *Othello's* visage in his mind": the metaphor carries the familiar contrast between deceptive, merely external appearances—what one senator calls the "false gaze," when determining what the Turks are really up to (1.3.27)—and the inner qualities or virtues. For Emilia, this metaphorical relationship involves correspondence, not a contrast, when she sees Othello's mind in his visage and reviles his external and internal foulness: "Oh the more Angell she, and you the blacker Divell." Giving the metaphor that contradictory point is obviously disturbing, but another and less obvious disturbance arises from the resemblance between these very different applications of the metaphor. Emilia, the Duke, and Desdemona are all thinking of Othello's inner qualities or inner self as something fixed or stable, and decipherable: they think they can "read" what he really or essentially *is*. But the poetic drama is exposing and exploring those terrifying inner potentialities and inner processes which can transform an Othello—or an Angelo in *Measure for Measure*, or less stern architects of self like Brabantio and Cassio.

The Italian story holds no moral terrors of this kind. But, perhaps because Giraldi Cinthio is so worldly and knowing in the limiting sense, there is an almost casually unknowing discrepancy—which evidently interested Shakespeare—between the unidealistic worldliness of his story and that idealistic moral piety which is enunciated by Fabio in the dialogue that precedes the story proper:

There is no beauty, Flamminio, where there is no virtue, and where there is no virtue, there cannot be love, for love is born only among good things. Hence he who wishes to form a true judgement of beauty must admire not only the body, but rather the minds and habits of those who present themselves to his view.[60]

In its smooth unthinking way, this statement introduces the gruesome story of what happened to one "virtuous Lady" who believed in, and committed her life to, the truth of Fabio's idealistic commonplace:

> It happened that a virtuous Lady of wondrous beauty called Disdemona, impelled not by female appetite but by the Moor's good qualities, fell in love with him, and he, vanquished by the Lady's beauty and noble mind, likewise was enamoured of her.

These two passages, taken together, might suggest that the story has an interrogative or cautionary relation to the moral piety; but there is no interaction of that kind.

Instead, Fabio's moral piety figures merely as a Renaissance stock notion or familiar idealistic commonplace—something to be nodded through, not questioned, and not received as the kind of radical idea which (like the ideas in the Sermon on the Mount) requires that you change your life. Who would deny the relation between "love" and "virtue," or maintain that "love" could be merely love of the body and not the mind? Well, the unvirtuous Iago for a start ("not I for love and dutie"); but the question seems rhetorical because it turns on a stipulative definition: whatever you feel for somebody who seems intensely desirable but is not virtuous—say, the Dark Lady of the *Sonnets*, where the Poet is no Fabio—is not to be called "love," since "love is born only among good things." But who believes that "where there is no virtue, there cannot be love," and that we are only drawn to love the beauty of those who are virtuous? Not the self-abasing Poet of the *Sonnets*. Pressing harder on the smooth surface of Fabio's "not only . . . but rather," who could desire, and delight in, a lover who is inwardly virtuous but externally shocking or even repellent? One answer to both these disagreeable questions is Shakespeare's Desdemona—but why shouldn't we also answer, Cinthio's Disdemona?

For the young girl who insists,

> I saw *Othello's* visage in his mind,
> And to his Honours and his valiant parts,
> Did I my soule and Fortunes consecrate,
>   (1.3.252–54)

Fabio's idealistic commonplace is apprehended as an overwhelming truth to which she commits her whole life—and "soule." In the case of Cinthio's Disdemona the equivalent commitment is no more than a premise or plot mechanism to explain how she came to marry the Moor. Being "virtuous," she was "impelled" by the Moor's inner "qualities" and not repelled by his external appearance—in particular, that blackness which makes the marriage as unthinkable to Disdemona's parents as it would be (in Fabio's view) to less virtuous women with a more ordinary "female appetite." This is all background material, since the couple have lived together happily for "years" when the story begins; when it ends Disdemona is dead and her parents have had the Moor murdered, yet the story never sets the conventional unthinkability of marrying a black Moor against the conventionally approved moral piety in any imaginatively and morally challenging way.

Shakespeare, however, is so powerfully interested by this clash between the conventionally unthinkable and the conventionally unthinking that he immediately increases the stakes, placing far more emphasis on the Moor's blackness, while also emphasizing (or inventing) all those other features—"Of Yeares, of Country, Credite, every thing"—which make it inconceivable to Brabantio that his daughter could "fall in Love, with what she fear'd to looke on." But one exception to this process of making Othello shocking is really the condition of the moral and imaginative challenge: his Moor must be a Christian convert much concerned with his "Soule," if his inner "virtue" is to be set against everything that makes this match conventionally unthinkable.

One consequence is that vigorous battle of "Sentences," or moral *sententiae,* in the Senate scene, which turns on the difference between speaking what we feel and paying lip service to what we ought to say. This battle begins when, in trying to console the inconsolable Brabantio, the Duke recalls, in a gentle but pointed way, his old friend's fondness for moral maxims: "Let me speake like your selfe: And lay a Sentence." He then lays several, until Brabantio angrily deflects this ducal bombardment by entering his own pithily sententious but deeply felt protest against what is merely said:

> So let the Turke of Cyprus us beguile,
> We loose it not so long as we can smile:

He beares the Sentence well, that nothing beares,
But the free comfort which from thence he heares.
But he beares both the Sentence, and the sorrow,
That to pay griefe, must of poore Patience borrow.
These Sentences, to Sugar, or to Gall,
Being strong on both sides, are Equivocall.
But words are words, I never yet did heare:
That the bruized heart was pierc'd through the eare.
I humbly beseech you proceed to th' Affaires of State.
(1.3.210–20)

The Duke does just that, switching to business-like prose as he speaks
with Othello. But then he makes his final sententious appeal to the
broken Brabantio—offering a confidently lapidary but far more incisive reformulation of Fabio's vapidly conventional claim that there is
no beauty where there is no virtue:

If Vertue no delighted Beautie lacke,
Your Son-in-law is farre more Faire then Blacke.
(1.3.289–90)

That large and significant "If" is not at all "Equivocall," and is altogether too much for Brabantio. It exposes Brabantio's racism, but
here we had better pause to ask whether it also exposes the Duke's.
There is indeed a sense in which any suggestion that the Moor is
black *but* fair is problematic, and potentially racist. In a corresponding
sense Shakespeare's poetic drama isn't working if the audience feels
no more disturbance on first seeing the black, old, ugly Moor with
the senator's young white daughter than it feels on seeing the fair
Desdemona with the fair Cassio in the harbor scene. But then, as we
struggle to collect our own responses in the Senate scene, the Duke's
affirmation that the Moor is "farre more Faire than Blacke" is far
more incisive and challengingly to the point than are those contemporary readings which assume, explicitly or implicitly, that the Duke is
betraying his own racism. I have already remarked on what seems
odd and demonstrably untrue in Karen Newman's claim that "the
black Moor and the fair Desdemona are united in a marriage which
all the other characters views as unthinkable": characters like the
Duke, Cassio, and Lodovico don't take that racist view. Unless we think
Newman's reading almost unbelievably careless, it seems likely that

she is taking for granted what a critic like John Salway explicitly argues when considering "the complexity of racism as a cultural force."[61] For Salway, the Duke's "throwaway" couplet—and even Desdemona's own "apparently innocent remark" that she saw "Othello's visage in his mind"—show how "we should see 'colour prejudice' as not just a question of the conscious, overtly racist utterances of an Iago who, were he alive today, would quite possibly join the National Front; but far more as a matter of those unconscious utterances, unrecognized symptoms of an underlying culture of racism which propagates extreme racist attitudes and behaviour" (116). Newman similarly argues that the "Elizabethan sex/race system" produced all those "linked oppositions, especially of black and white and their cultural associations," which "characterize the play's discourse" ("Wash the Ethiop White," 144). Yet, even as they appear to resemble each other, these two essays provide another illustration of the difference between British cultural materialist and American new historicist concepts of Them and Us: Salway's account is confrontational, while Newman's is estranging.

Salway goes on to claim that the "fact that traditional literary analysis of the play has avoided" this issue of cultural racism "and pursued such absurd irrelevances as whether or not Othello is truly noble or merely self-dramatizing is itself a sign that the culture of racism has been at work in the very heart of liberal humanism" (116–17). That saber-rattling recalls Sinfield's smearing claim that "the" liberal humanist response to *The Merchant of Venice* is anti-Semitic: for Salway, "liberal humanism" and "traditional literary analysis" are covertly racist, and they work to perpetuate what Dollimore and Sinfield describe as a "social order that exploits people on grounds of race, gender, sexuality and class" (*Political Shakespeare,* viii). This Enemy is very much with us—not surprisingly, if even Desdemona fails to measure up. But for a "cultural materialism" that "registers its commitment to the transformation" of that "social order" the task of opposing and rooting out this Enemy can be a professional pleasure as well as a duty—for example, when one serves on academic committees discussing appointments, tenure, promotions, or research grants. In comparison, Newman's estranging new historicist account of that "Elizabethan sex/race system" is an improvement, in that critical dialogue is still possible, even with liberal humanists; but there aren't many things to talk about, since the shopping list of concerns is ideologically impeccable but somewhat brief: race and gender are in, of course, but poetry is a no-no, and it is never clear whether Newman sees Shakespeare's play as a product or as a criticism of that remote "Elizabethan sex/race system."[62] So, after claiming that "all the other characters view" the marriage of a "white" woman to a "black Moor" as "unthinkable," Newman goes on to explain to her modern readers that "in the Renaissance no other colours so clearly implied opposition or were so frequently used to denote polarization," and cites Winthrop Jordan's *White over Black* to clarify these "linked oppositions" and malign "cultural associations."

> As Winthrop Jordan points out in his monumental study, *White over Black*, the meaning of black even before the sixteenth century, according to the *OED*, included "deeply stained with dirt, soiled, dirty, foul. . . . Having dark or deadly purposes, malignant; pertaining to or involving death, deadly, baneful, disastrous . . . iniquitous, atrocious, horrible, wicked . . . indicating disgrace, censure, liability to punishment, etc." ("Wash the Ethiop White," 145)

Even as—or because—Newman's indignant "even" hints at some foul cultural conspiracy corresponding with Salway's "culture of racism," that citation obscures what it might have clarified.

As can be confirmed from the *OED* and almost any historical dictionary of proverbs, the metaphorical association between the black and the foul or dirty is not only deeply rooted in our own culture, as in others, but also preceded any direct cultural contact with "black" peoples.[63] In other words, although the metaphorical association has obvious and dangerous racist *applications*, it is manifestly not racist in origin; it is presumably rooted in the everyday experience of cleaning what is sooty or begrimed, and in the no less universal experience of nightfall. To assume otherwise, however protestingly, is in itself a paradoxical form of racism in which any reference to the black works like a thrown switch. And of course the metaphorical association is still very much alive, for example when Greenblatt refers to a "darker aspect" of "orthodox Christian doctrine" or when Empson describes the Christian torture-god as the "blackest invention of the black heart of man." On the other hand, precisely because the metaphorical association between *black* and *foul* is so deeply rooted and transcultural, it may *dispose* us to make that racist application, by being something at work in our minds, our language, and our culture that we need to recognize and resist. Doing that involves going through a consciously critical process exactly like that represented in the Duke's lapidary couplet. Far from being racist, the Duke recognizes and repudiates what is logically and morally vicious in supposing that fair is to black, in the merely external sense, as fair is to black or foul in an internal or ethical sense. Here, I suggest, the Duke is more intelligent and incisive than Salway or Newman about what is at issue in moral and dramatic terms, and in cultural, historical, and psychological terms.

The Duke's appeal to Brabantio to show more judgment is also a powerfully articulated challenge that Brabantio cannot dismiss or deflect by suggesting that it is "Equivocall," or yet another "Sentence" people are fond of repeating but don't really believe. Brabantio attempts no direct reply and in some productions, like Janet Suzman's powerful Johannesburg production, the Duke leaves after presenting his final couplet as an authoritative parting shot. Yet the Folio and Quarto stage directions show that the Duke and the other senators are still present to hear Brabantio's bitter warning to the man for whom he feels no concern, but loathes for stealing his daughter:

> Looke to her (Moore) if thou hast eies to see;
> She ha's deceiv'd her Father, and may thee.
>
> (1.3.292–93)

Though indirect, this is a telling—and, since Iago is listening, fateful—reply to the Duke's assurance that the Moor is externally "Blacke" but internally fair, with its implication that, if Brabantio cannot see this, his judgment is deficient. Brabantio's shocking response is to say that he had no eyes to see that his own fair daughter was foully deceptive: in effect, "farre more Faire then Blacke" is countered by "farre more Blacke, then Faire"—and by the doubt about who ever has "eyes to see." In their different ways both of these authoritative elders are echoing the grieving Duncan's remark, in *Macbeth*, that "There's no Art, / To finde the Mindes construction in the Face" (1.4.11–12). But the Duke confidently does so, while firmly closing the door on any doubt about *how* we have eyes to see when (as the witches in *Macbeth* proclaim) "Faire is foule, and foule is faire"; Brabantio opens that door.

It is as though that alarmingly ambiguous "fair/black" antithesis in the *Sonnets* were now being staged, but "seen" or interpreted in contradictory—reassuringly fair and unnervingly foul—ways. The contradictory interpretative possibilities that appear in that clash between the Duke's final couplet and Brabantio's reappear in the first of the Dark Lady sonnets, "In the ould age blacke was not counted faire" (Sonnet 127): the idea that there are "such who not borne faire no beauty lack" is very close to the Duke's couplet,

> If vertue no delighted Beautie lacke,
> Your Son-in-law is farre more Faire then Blacke,
> (1.3.289–90)

but is set against the Brabantio-like fear that one may have no "eyes to see" when the externally fair are "Fairing the foule with Arts faulse borrow'd face." When the Duke describes Othello as "farre more Faire then Blacke" while warning against the deceptiveness of external appearances, he is sure that he can "see" or judge what is within. This then provides a (deceptively) firm framework for "reading" the scene on stage as some kind of animated emblem, or masque-like moral allegory about Virtue and Blackness: just as the Moor is externally black but internally fair, Iago is externally fair or "honest" but internally foul, and of course Desdemona is externally and internally fair. And on this view, as in the terms of Fabio's moral piety, it is a *proof* of Desdemona's "virtue" that she could see Othello's "visage in his mind." But Brabantio's couplet carries a more terrifying doubt about how anyone—including Desdemona, Othello, the Duke, and Brabantio himself—*has eyes to see* the "mind." Whatever Desdemona thought she was looking at when she "saw *Othello's* visage in his mind," she didn't see the mind of her murderer.

We resist an interpretation by reinterpreting. So, in the play's first scene Iago's description of the Moor and his filthy suggestions about what drew Desdemona to the Moor are admitted to our minds as possibilities, along with the possibility that Iago's obscene images are the product of distorting personal hatred, envy, misogyny, and racism; once we see the lovers together we reject or reinterpret Iago's interpretation, although he goes on believing it. And we entertain other interpretative possibilities—if, for example, by the end of the Senate scene we fear that there may be dangers in this marriage of true minds, even without the active interventions of an Iago. If we admire

Desdemona for seeing the Moor's "visage in his mind," like the Duke and unlike the racist Brabantio and Iago, we resist Brabantio's view that his own daughter is externally fair but subtly duplicitous. Yet she *has* successfully deceived her father through all the months of a secret wooing when Othello and Cassio were secret visitors. To resist Brabantio's interpretation we must find some way of *not* "seeing" Brabantio as a tragically betrayed father who will soon die of a broken heart, and whose uncaring or unimaginative daughter can apparently forget her father's agony and humiliation when she tells Othello that the hand he is holding, "that gave away my heart," also "hath felt no age, nor knowne no sorrow" (3.4.45, 37). For example, we can "see" the sustained deception and elopement as an unavoidable necessity forced on Desdemona (like Jessica) by the father's harshness and bigotry, and "see" Brabantio himself as an autocratic Egeus playing out the ancient comic role of the impotently raging *senex iratus* who opposes the course of true love but fortunately has no eyes to see what is going on in his own house. Deception, intrigue, elopements and a furious father: these are stock items in comedy, and one part of Brabantio's agony—or that of the Poet in the *Sonnets* or of Othello when he thinks that he too is locked in an agonizing triangle—is the lacerating sense of the proximity of comedy, and derision. But if we stave off Brabantio's alarming view of Desdemona's deception by reinterpreting it more lightly, we shall not be prepared for the devastating effect on Othello of Iago's later reminder, "She did deceive her Father, marrying you." Where Desdemona speaks of seeing "Othello's visage in his mind" but cannot see her murderer's mind, Othello speaks of being free and bounteous to her mind but thinks she had it in her to become what she is not. Neither sees or knows the other's mind.

Within the seemingly firm framework provided by the Duke's or Desdemona's applications of the "fair/black" metaphor, Brabantio's final couplet asserts that his own daughter is not internally and externally fair, but externally fair and internally foul—just as Emilia reviles Othello as externally and internally foul. But, in all these applications of the metaphor, the mind or inner self is conceived in static rather than dynamic terms, as some stable entity or essence. Jarringly different applications of the metaphor then reveal the speaker: we "see" how Brabantio's judgment is distorted by his racism, Emilia's by her indiscriminating conviction that all men are "stomachs," Iago's by his undiscriminating conviction that all women are whores, and so on.

Yet to take (or see) "I saw *Othello's* visage in his mind" as a proof of Desdemona's virtue is already to consider it as a projection of her nature, not a perception of Othello's. That is how Montano regards Othello's loving misjudgment of Cassio's "infirmitie":

> Perhaps he sees it not, or his good nature
> Prizes the vertue that appeares in *Cassio*,
> And lookes not on his evills: is not this true?
> (2.3.133–35)

But here another difficulty appears, if *thinking well* of someone reveals the thinker: to fail to see virtue (like Brabantio), and to look for or on evils (like Iago), reveals a *bad* nature. What is most alarming in Brabantio's final couplet is not that opposing judgment of Desdemona, which we resist and reinterpret because we don't think or want to think like a Brabantio or an Iago, but the doubt about who has "eyes to see." The seemingly stable formations and applications of the "fair/black" metaphor, and the corresponding essentialist view of the self as a stable entity, are being exposed and opposed, within the play, to a sense of the unreliability of the observer as well as of what is to be seen, and a corresponding sense of the self as something dynamic and unstable, which includes everything we have it in us to become.

In these poetic-dramatic terms, giving the "faire" but shady Bianca *that* name—White!—is a good joke. But here we can profitably turn to the play in which Shakespeare reworks another story from Cinthio's *Hecatomitthi*—and names his deputy governor "Angelo." Both *Othello* and *Measure for Measure* were performed in 1604; there was a court performance of *Othello* on November 1 and of *Measure for Measure* on December 26. Like Othello, the highly principled Angelo reveals and, to his own horror, discovers what he has it in him to become, while Desdemona and Isabella are both self-committed idealists with no more experience than Othello and Angelo of the passions their plays will engage. Since both plays are so concerned with idealists who are isolated and exposed by their own high principles, and since both are based on stories in the *Hecatommithi*, we might expect to make something of that; but the overlapping between the plays has more to do with what Shakespeare brought to his reading than with anything in these stories. It is Shakespeare who makes Isabella a youthfully idealistic religious novice who appeals to the Sermon on the Mount, while the corrupt governor in Cinthio's story (as in his later play *Epitia*) is simply corrupt and altogether unlike the inhumanly chilly but highly principled young deputy whose collapse will give point to Isabella's appeal. The Sermon on the Mount is revolutionary both in theological and moral terms: theologically, because it internalizes external acts and those Mosaic ordinances which governed external acts; morally, because it is so much less concerned with actions and their consequences than with the inner state of the agent—with what we *all* have it in us to become. In these radically internalized terms, where the God who sees within may regard lustful thoughts as adultery or anger as murder (Matthew 5:21–28), the fact that Angelo doesn't succeed in raping Isabella and having her brother killed matters less than that revelation of what is *in* him—of what Hopkins called the "mind's mountains and cliffs of fall."

We *see* the fair white Cassio's noble, generously loving qualities in the harbor scene, when he expresses his vicarious joy at his beloved general's marriage or resists Iago's smutty assaults. These qualities or potentialities are real enough: they are there to be seen, living in Cassio as they do not live in Iago, just as nothing that happens in *King Lear* makes us doubt that there is an essential difference between Cordelia's nature and that of her sisters. But to talk of the "essential" is still dangerous, especially where "nature" is concerned, and this scene in *Othello* remorselessly shows why. What immediately follows shows how these real and admirable qualities are still only one part of Cassio's self, which is better conceived as a huge quarrelsome family or matrix of possible selves. Within minutes we are wincing at the most degrading exposures as we see how Cassio (like Othello) is "now a sensible man, by and by a Foole, and presently a Beast." What is exposed is not only the drunken collapse into blood lust that betrays Othello's trust, but also something unexpectedly sordid, petty, and nasty in Cassio which crawls into view when we (and Iago) see his conceit over his new rank or "Place" combining with his sense of himself as "a man of qualitie," and with a maudlin, Holy Willie–like religiosity:

> *Cassio.* Why this is a more exquisite Song then the other.
> *Iago.* Will you heare't again?
> *Cassio.* No: for I hold him to be unworthy of his Place, that do's those

things. Well: heav'ns above all: and there be soules must be saved,
and there be soules must not be saved.

(2.3.98–104)

Iago wouldn't like to hear that "The Lieutenant is to be saved before
the Ancient." In another sense he would, since this gives him a further
insight into his victim; he can then play on Cassio's shamingly stupid
self-conceit, persuading Cassio that what was "bestiall" was not really
him, so that Cassio owes it to himself not to be a "severe moraller." So,
even as Cassio speaks of how he can "frankly despise my selfe," that
word "frankly" shows his recovering self-esteem: he is ready to think
it rather fine that he can arraign himself so severely for what is in
"the devil drunkennesse." Later, we will see what unexpected nastiness
is in Othello, and, just as Cassio blames the devil in drunkenness, the
final scene shows Othello blaming the demi-devil who "ensnared"
him, and striving, above all, to sever the "monstrous Acte" from its
agent. Angelo doesn't do that in the last words *he* speaks:

> I am so sorrie, that such sorrow I procure,
> And so deepe sticks it in my penitent heart,
> That I crave death more willingly then mercy,
> 'Tis my deserving, and I doe entreat it.

(5.1.474–77)

The art that exposes such things is either very *cruel,* or challengingly *magnanimous:* cruel if we think it comes close to vindicating
Iago's reductive view of Cassio and Othello; magnanimous if we think
it takes an encompassing view, showing how the fair Cassio and the
black Othello both have it in them to be fair *and* foul. But this once
again engages the conflict between static and dynamic views of the
self. In his concern to establish what Othello really and essentially *is,*
Coleridge takes (and misquotes) Othello's own claim to be "not easily
wrought" as a *confirmation* that "the noble Moor" was "above all low
passions"—whereas the pardoning of Angelo is "horrible" and "baf-
fles the strong indignant claim of justice": "cruelty, with lust and damnable baseness, cannot be forgiven, because we cannot conceive them
as being morally repented of."[64] In this way the Christian Coleridge
deflects what is most disturbing in these plays, and also in the Sermon
on the Mount. For in so fiercely repudiating any suggestion that we
might see ourselves in Angelo, Coleridge sounds like Angelo: the

Pharisaic insistence on what "cannot be forgiven" combines with the sturdy emphasis on what "we cannot conceive"—or on what it is not in us to imagine might be in us. We may well ask, "Who has a breast so pure?"

But of course Shakespeare gives that question to Iago:

> Utter my Thoughts? why say, they are vild, and falce?
> As where's that Palace, whereinto foule things
> Sometimes intrude not? Who has that breast so pure,
> Wherein uncleanly Apprehensions
> Keepe Leetes, and Law-dayes, and in Sessions sit
> With meditations lawfull?
>
> (3.3.137–41)

Since the first Quarto version is different and in some respects clearer, it's worth quoting too:

> Utter my thoughts? Why, say they are vile and false:
> As where's that pallace, whereinto foule things
> Sometimes intrude not? who has a breast so pure,
> But some uncleanely apprehensions,
> Keepe leetes and law-dayes, and in Session sit
> With meditations lawfull?

This speech not only recalls *Measure for Measure* in its legal imagery; a more self-aware Isabella might have said something like this when she invokes the Sermon on the Mount in her most impassioned plea to Angelo. That Iago should be given these lines shows, in little, how Cinthio's story has been turned into a moral and interpretative torture chamber.

For in *Othello*, as in the other plays I have discussed, the complex design urges us to see farther than any of the characters—and farther than critical interventions in the debate about what Othello really and essentially is. Yet the design of *Othello* keeps catching us in a nasty twist, where it is as though the play helps Iago to exploit, and misrepresent, what the play is doing—whenever it summons our sense of the mind as something vertiginous, with cliffs of fall, and sets that against the wish to think of the mind or self in vulnerably simple ways, as something stable and readable. The interpretative uncertainty the *play* produces is alarming, but also potentially *liberating*, in the way that Duncan's lines in *Macbeth* are both alarming and liberating:

> There's no Art,
> To finde the Mindes construction in the face.
> He was a Gentleman on whom I built
> An absolute trust.
>
> (1.4.11–14)

The building metaphors interlock: to trust somebody involves trusting to one's own interpretative construction or reading of another mind's "construction," so that trust itself is constructed or "built" on insecure foundations. In knowing that and accepting the odds, Duncan is unillusioned rather than disillusioned; when he proceeds to place his trust in Banquo and Macbeth—laboring to make them full of growing—he knows what he is doing, and knows the risks. This makes Duncan both braver and more perceptive than the son who speaks in a confidently summary fashion of "this dead Butcher, and his Fiend-like Queene" (5.9.35): the complex design of *Macbeth* is constantly undermining tidy categories. But then in *Othello* interpretative uncertainty never afflicts Iago; he works to bring it about, so that he can exploit it.

Iago's tactic is to persuade others that something they had not thought was something they had not *wanted* to think—which then seems more plausible or compelling, or, as Iago puts it in a wonderfully chilling phrase, "proball to thinking" (2.3.338). So, as soon as Brabantio is persuaded to acknowledge the (to him) unthinkable possibility he had repressed, what was unthinkable "oppresses" him as a perceived truth: "This Accident is not unlike my dreame, / Beleefe of it oppresses me alreadie" (1.1.142–43). In the harbor scene Iago can persuade Roderigo to accept a strong misreading, which Roderigo initially rejects as preposterous, by playing on the gull's fear of being unworldly and unknowing. In 3.3, once Othello tries to make out in his own mind whatever "Monster" or "horrible Conceite" Iago has "shut up" in his mind, because it is "Too hideous to be shewne," Othello is *admitting* the "Monster": in being persuaded to give it imaginative house-room, he makes it his own. In 4.1, the appalled, bewildered Lodovico asks Iago,

Is this the Noble Moore, whom our full Senate
Call all in all sufficient? Is this the Nature
Whom Passion could not shake? Whose solid vertue
The shot of Accident, nor dart of Chance
Could neither grave, nor pierce?

(4.1.264–68)

Characteristically, Iago plays on this anxiety about whether the Senate could so have misjudged Othello's "Nature"—not by telling Roderigo "What I have seene and knowne," but by telling him to make up his own mind:

You shall observe him,
And his owne courses will denote him so,
That I may save my speech: do but go after
And marke how he continues.

(lines 278–81)

But the finely calculated effect of Iago's tormenting reticence is that Lodovico is persuaded that his and the Senate's earlier judgment of Othello's essential "Nature" *must* have been wrong: "I am sorry that I am deceiv'd in him."

In other words, Iago's tactic depends upon persuasion, not evidence, and is familiar enough in reductive psychoanalytical interpretations. As Wittgenstein observed of Freud, "the attraction of certain kinds of explanation is overwhelming" and in itself "an extremely interesting phenomenon," since it is "not a matter of discovery, but persuasion": "In particular, explanation of the kind 'This is really only this' . . . The idea of an underworld, a secret cellar. Something hidden, uncanny . . . It may be the fact that the explanation is extremely repellent that drives you to adopt it."[65] Iago is a brilliant opportunist; but then Shakespeare's play not only provides him with the opportunities he seizes, it—the play, or Shakespeare-as-Iago—works on us as Iago works on his victims, so that the real dramatist and the malign surrogate dramatist share the responsibility for what happens onstage *and* in our minds, as we struggle with "uncleanly Apprehensions."

So, the play not only exposes us to Iago's very "uncleanly" strong misreading of what brought Othello and Desdemona together, before we can determine that this is a misreading; the play also undermines, or makes uncertain, the basis for a correct and corrective reading, since the Senate scene introduces other "uncleanly" worries. In the harbor scene we know immediately that Iago's strong misreading of the behavior of Cassio and Desdemona is malicious and perversely contrived; but we start watching their behavior in an anxiously protective way, as if to consider what could be misrepresented—and then, in 3.3, see Desdemona behaving with Cassio in a way that we, like Othello, find hard to understand or explain. Similarly, although there is so much to make us resist Iago's reductive views of Othello or Cassio, his carefully staged demonstrations of what they are "really" like are alarmingly successful; and the play then makes it very difficult to sustain a view of Othello as the "noble Moor" or of Cassio as the honorable lieutenant (which is how he is described in the "Names of the Actors" at the end of the Folio, where Bianca figures as "a Curtezan"). Diagnostic accounts of Othello's essential "Nature," as deluded egotist or deluded Christian, are also difficult to sustain—though it is worth noticing how many antiessentialist materialists present essentialist readings. The difficulty could be liberating, if it helped to release us from over-simple views of the self as a stable essence; but in *Othello* the alternative view of the self as an ensemble of possible selves and potentialities isn't likely to register in positive or reassuring ways. The "Who has a breast so pure?" speech is given to Iago.

Considered in these perspectives, the play itself may be seen as a "horrible Conceite"—that is, as a sustained poetic-dramatic conceit in which the "fair/black" metaphor opens up the conflict between stable and dynamic models of the self. Similarly, in the second tetralogy, the richly developed contrast between the two Harrys involves a comparable clash between opposed ground-metaphors: the "chain of being" metaphor, which inevitably encourages the authoritarian idea of a chain of command by suggesting that the "body" (or commonweal) must be ruled by the "head," is opposed to another body metaphor involving the quarrel between the "head" and the "heart." Because the complex design in Shakespearean poetic drama usually involves a sustained and (in the seventeenth-century sense) *witty* poetic-dramatic conceit, it is not merely provoking, or arch, to speak of the play's "dramatic thinking": the thinking—about Othello, or Henry, or Shylock—takes place within that creative arena. Similarly, the poetic-dramatic presentation of Prince Hal's controlled descents into prose, or of Othello's uncontrolled collapses and more or less partial recoveries, depends upon metaphorical modes of representation: we don't understand these by going around with a notebook and listening for when real people speak verse or prose. To disregard the play's complex design and treat the constituents of poetic-dramatic meaning as mere ancillaries, considering the play as though it might as well have been written in prose, is like reading Da Ponte's libretto to find out what happens in a Mozart opera.

The New Historicist as Iago

Seeing Through Seeing Through

Let us recall again that first long speech of Iago's which "demystifies" Othello's aspiring, idealistic rhetoric and reveals it as the evasive, self-aggrandizing, and self-deceiving utterance of a man "loving his owne pride, and purposes."

> Three Great-ones of the Cittie,
> (In personall suite to make me his Lieutenant)
> Off-capt to him: and by the faith of man
> I know my price, I am worth no worsse a place.
> But he (as loving his owne pride, and purposes)
> Evades them, with a bumbast Circumstance,
> Horribly stufft with Epithites of warre.
>
> (1.1.8–14)

We hear this before we have heard the so-called Othello music, and it is important that we first hear Iago telling us what to listen for. *The Tragedie of Othello* can only start when we begin to fear that Othello's idealism may be vulnerable to this reductively materialist genealogizing of its "purposes"—purposes that, in Iago's derisive view, Othello successfully furthers by concealing not only from others but also from himself. Iago similarly assures Roderigo that Cassio's "Civill, and Humaine seeming" masks what is "most hidden":

a knave very voluble: no further conscionable, then in putting on the meere forme of Civill, and Humaine seeming, for the better compasse of his salt, and most hidden loose Affection. . . . A slipper, and subtle knave, a finder of occasions: that he's an eye can stampe, and counterfeit Advantages, though true Advantage never present it selfe. . . . A pestilent compleat knave. (2.1.238–44,247)

But then *The Tragedie of Othello* could not be a tragedy, in any serious or compelling sense, if Iago's reductive genealogies seemed unproblematically true: the play would be a protracted, painfully untragic exposure or unmasking. This produces a problem: given what happens, why shouldn't we suppose (however reluctantly) that Iago is *right* about Othello and Cassio?

One rather complicated answer is suggested by that astonishing *coup de théâtre* in the handkerchief scene, which couldn't occur in a prose drama:

Lye with her? lye on her? We say lye on her, when they be-lye her. Lye with her: that's fullsome: Hankerchiefe: Confessions: Handkerchiefe. To confesse, and be hang'd for his labour. First, to be hang'd, and then to confesse: I tremble at it. Nature would not invest her selfe in such shadowing passion, without some Instruction. It is not words that shake me this (pish) Noses, Eares, and Lippes. (4.1.35–42)

To see Othello's plummeting collapse into fragmented prose as a revelation of his "true" nature involves us in a profoundly paradoxical dismantling of the conventions and practices of poetic drama. At this late stage in the play Othello is the only major character who has never been heard speaking in prose: in poetic-dramatic terms that *measures* the catastrophic descent. If the verse "really" signifies pretense, the reductive unpacking produces a paradox like that which appears in *Troilus and Cressida* if we accept the force of Thersites' brutally reductive genealogies. This is not inconceivable, but it is all too like throwing away the ladder by which we have ascended. We no longer have any secure basis for grasping what is signified in a passage like this, where within a few lines the poetic-dramatic representation organizes a series of intricately related metaphorical contrasts (verse/prose, high/low, up/down, tuned/untuned, music/discords):

Othello.   Amen to that (sweet Powers)
   I cannot speake enough of this content,
   It stoppes me heere: it is too much of joy.
   And this, and this the greatest discords be
                  [Kissing her]
   That ere our hearts shall make.
Iago. [Aside] Oh you are well tun'd now: But Ile set downe the peggs that
make this Musicke, as honest as I am.

                                     (2.1.195–201)

A less elaborate answer is that Iago himself lets fall some very different remarks about Othello's "Nature," when he observes that

     The Moore is of a free, and open Nature,
     That thinkes men honest, that but seeme to be so,
                 (1.3.399–400)

or when he concedes (immediately before working himself up with
the fantasy that he has been cuckolded by the "lustie Moore") that

     The Moore (howbeit that I endure him not)
     Is of a constant, loving, Noble Nature,
     And I dare thinke, he'le prove to *Desdemona*
     A most deere husband.
                 (2.1.288–91)

Similarly, and almost poignantly, he remarks that Cassio "hath a dayly
beauty in his life, / That makes me ugly" (5.1.19–20). Such lapses
suggest how Iago himself cannot altogether believe in the truth of his
own reductive genealogizing: the "monstrous Birth" he determines
to bring "to the worlds light" is something he has "engendred," not
merely delivered like a critical midwife. He exposes something intricate and vulnerable in his own motives for insisting on his brutally,
willfully reductive accounts of human motives, accounts he *needs* to
believe. And the fascinatingly uncertain relation between Iago's inqui-
sitional unpackings and some need to protect and fortify himself is
apparent even in that first long speech. His account of Othello's
"pride, and purposes" reveals a great deal about his own, and shows
how he responds to other mens' successes. "I know my price, I am
worth no worsse a place": in insisting on his own "worth," he is also

consoling himself by asserting that he alone knows how to estimate true "worth"—unlike Othello when he preferred Cassio, and unlike all those who have been taken in by Othello. Like Thersites and even Falstaff, Iago prides himself on being a truth-teller, and the truths he tells are always reductive and unreflexive: in diminishing others, they protect his own self-esteem. He declares "I am nothing, if not Criticall," but one reason for being "Criticall" in his fashion is to ensure that he does not have to consider himself as "nothing."

The conditions of Iago's strength are also his weakness, and one of the more sustained moral and dramatic ironies in *Othello* turns on what is incapacitating in Iago's commitment to a materialistically reductive account of human motives. We don't need to see much of Othello to recognize what was misjudged in Iago's reliance on securing the patronage of three "Great-ones of the Cittie," or to see that Othello's conversion to Christianity matters to him in ways Iago cannot conceive. Before the end of the Senate scene it is clear to us that the attraction between Othello and Desdemona is idealistic, perhaps worryingly idealistic, but Iago goes on believing that it is perversely sexual. "I do know the State," Iago characteristically asserts, in explaining why the Senate will not dismiss Othello; the State does not dismiss him, but it does break off its urgent, "Post-haste" business to consider Brabantio's charges. The Iago who similarly proclaims "Not I for love and dutie" is incapable of foreseeing that his own wife may betray him, consciously risking and losing her own life, and prompted by nothing but love and duty.

The Iago who prides himself on being nothing if not critical would have enjoyed the concept of "critique." The opposite of being "Criticall" in Iago's sense is being credulous or idealistic—being artless, not subtle; being ardent, not cool; and being magnanimous, not malign. I take these terms from Dr. Johnson:

> The fiery openness of *Othello*, magnanimous, artless, and credulous, boundless in his confidence, ardent in his affection, inflexible in his resolution, and obdurate in his revenge; the cool malignity of *Iago*, silent in his resentment, subtle in his designs, and studious at once of his interest and his vengeance,[1]

Such considerations suggest why this play provides a vantage point from which to consider (I nearly said "critique") some of the most unsatisfactory or disturbing features of "the 'new historicism' of cultural materialism." I shall begin at the seamy end, with some specimens of a familiar and degrading form of Iago-like *ressentiment*. They need to be inspected—or flapped, as Pope flaps "Sporus," that "painted child of dirt, that stinks and stings"—not only because they deride and dismiss "humanism" in ways that make critical dialogue impossible, but because their own "appropriation" of materialism is an obstacle to the emergence of any more thoughtful and reflexive cultural materialism.

The Fear of Being Taken In

"'Materialism' is opposed to 'idealism'"; I take that seemingly straightforward statement not from a critical account of *Othello* but from "Cultural Materialism," the foreword to the "Cultural Politics" series edited by Jonathan Dollimore and Alan Sinfield.[2] The context makes a difference, and the sense of "materialism" narrows when the series' editors explain that "cultural meanings" are "always, finally, political meanings"—without any attempt to explain why political meanings are not always, finally, cultural meanings. Taking the latter view would involve recognizing what is metaphysical in their own "political" meanings, and what is odd about their conspicuously unreflexive, reactive assault on so-called essentialist humanism for not telling the Truth. So, for example, it would force Dollimore to think about what is at issue in the final chapter of *Radical Tragedy*, "Beyond Essentialist Humanism," where he rather casually suggests that Derrida "may be too fatalistic": "Derrida has insisted that metaphysics is so deeply rooted in our discourses that there is no getting beyond it (*Positions*, 21); perhaps in this he is too fatalistic. Nevertheless his assertion is strikingly apt for the history of the essentialist humanism which has pervaded English studies."[3] That "Nevertheless" is shameless: Derrida's "assertion" is "strikingly apt" for Them, if not true of Us. But it is also almost touching, as a measure of Dollimore's priestly faith that his own ideological commitments are not metaphysical, but true. As we saw in Chapter 1, Derrida is rigorous and unequivocal in his insistence that the politics of the Left, no less than the Right, is "fundamentally metaphysical." However, Dollimore doesn't want to, and in a more damaging sense can't afford to, engage with that. He doesn't want to, because he is content to discount any number of differences as long as the main marxoid "objective" is secured: "Anti-humanism and its declared objective—the decentring of man—is probably the most controversial aspect of Marxist, structuralist and post-structuralist theory" (249). He can't afford to, because this would expose the way in which the carefully fashioned ideological Self depends upon the ahistorical demonization of the "humanist" Other. So we are told, once again, "the materialist is opposed to the idealist"; but now the original proposition is part of a series of team-calls.

The same sense of a common cause appears in *Political Shakespeare*, the volume in this series which brought together American new historicists and British cultural materialists to represent "the 'new historicism' of cultural materialism." Another volume, *The Shakespeare Myth*, is conspicuously British, but its editor, Graham Holderness, is no less vigilantly aware of the need for "polemical stances" in "opposing the liberal-humanist hegemony."[4] Criticism wouldn't be enough. This book includes a number of interviews with "prominent cultural practitioners of Shakespeare," but it is emphasized that these interviewees are exhibits, not writers: "All of the writers in this book are alert to the fact that Shakespeare is today less an author than an apparatus" (204). One of these museum exhibits, Jonathan Miller, does challenge the curators by suggesting that a preoccupation with "the *political* dimension" is too often associated with a disregard for "the world and the life of the imagination" and that "search for the *mentalité* of a particular period" which distinguishes the "good ethnographer": "the reason why I admire the work of the French marxist historians of the *Annales* school, is that their marxism is beautifully assimilated to a broad view of what it was actually like to live out your life—and your imaginative life—at that time" (199, 202). I agree, and doubt that Greenblatt would find this appeal to ethnography offensive; but it enrages Eagleton in his combative "Afterword."

Eagleton begins by recalling his own early years as "a working-class student" in Cambridge (while observing his rule of silence on his years as editor of a Roman Catholic journal). He confides that Shakespeare seemed to matter not for his "eloquence," which was "what put me off" ("an excessive garrulousness for which the closest analogy seemed that endless middle-class gushing and twittering"), but because "Shakespeare showed me two things: first that language was power; secondly, that I had neither" (203). The Warton Professor of English Literature at the University of Oxford then provides this contemptuous genealogy of Miller's "liberal pluralism" and "bland Hampstead bohemianism":

> These are the very top dogs of the industry, the managing directors and executives of the whole shebang; and their collective ideological consciousness, all the way from strident elitism and abstract universalism to the depoliticising eclecticism of a Miller, makes for depressing reading. Depressing, but hardly surprising: for they did of course get where they are today partly because they hold precisely these views. (207)

Just as Iago's view of Othello betrays a great deal about Iago, this tells us less about Miller than about Eagleton. The theoretical preoccupation with "power" and "ideology" is revealed as a personal preoccupation with power and position, within the "industry": to "get where *they* are" evidently matters very much.

This disagreeably personal reflection on Eagleton's disagreeably personal explanation of the relation between Miller's views and material success seems in place (and not an Iago-like explanation of my own) for less limitingly personal reasons. Only the very naive or saintly could fail to see how contemporary theoretical and ideological disputes have an institutional setting, where they are practically and inevitably associated with other kinds of "contestation"—personal or group advancement, promotions, and patronage; on the other hand only the very cynical would think it sufficient to explain such disputes in that insultingly reductive fashion. Yet, as we have seen, cultural materialist accounts of what Holderness amiably calls the "reactionary or liberal-humanist" position all too often proceed in a reductive fashion that makes dialogue impossible. So, for example, in *That Shakespeherian Rag* Terence Hawkes favors the same kind of "explanation" as Eagleton, when he gleefully reviews the careers of Raleigh and Bradley, of Tillyard and Dover Wilson: Hawkes's "liberal humanist," like Nietzsche's Christian, expects to be very well paid.[5] One wonders what account Hawkes could offer of noninstitutional nineteenth-century Shakespeareans like Fleay or Furness; or, more pertinent, of Leavis's career, and of the relation between Leavis's critical beliefs and his worrying bank balance and modest house in Bulstrode Gardens. But here, once again, the critic's reductive account of human motives reveals more about his own. For Hawkes there are no critical Emilias.

As Hugh Grady explains in "situating" his own materialist account of twentieth-century Shakespeare criticism, "Marxist-influenced criticism, with its lengthy tradition of disclosing political and economic interests at work in texts which pass themselves off as 'value-free', 'objective', or 'disinterested', has been a major influence in the new interpretations, especially in Shakespeare studies."[6] Because this is true, it is all the more important to notice what can be disabling in a "tradition of ideology critique" not noted for reflexivity. Consider the kind of proposition I trust nobody would now contest: slavery is wrong. This is not Aristotle's view in the *Politics,* in which he argues that some are born to be slaves and others to rule over them: slavery is right because it is naturally ordained.[7] It plainly suited the Greeks to take this view, since the Greek state depended on slavery; but then, no less plainly, it makes a difference whether we suppose that (1) Aristotle supported the practice of slavery because it was in his or the Greek interest to do so, or that (2) Aristotle did not question or attack the practice because he *believed* that it was right and natural. The first explanation would be far more damaging to our sense of Aristotle's moral and intellectual integrity. But the difference between being *disposed* to favor the one kind of explanation rather than the other is scarcely less important. Somebody who inclined to the second explanation, preferring to think Aristotle wrong but not a moral blackguard, would be showing what Iago calls a "free and open nature"; the danger here is that of being taken in. Somebody who, with no more evidence, always favored the first kind of explanation—and even made it a principle in "ideological critique"—would be taking something more like Iago's reductively materialistic view of human motives; the danger here is that the fear of being taken in can also be incapacitating.

For a grimly amusing parallel in criticism we might consider the relation between the thesis of Arthur Marotti's influential essay "John Donne and the Rewards of Patronage" and the first of that essay's many footnotes.[8] Marotti's new historicist thesis is that Donne's "personally and culturally encoded literary idiom" reflects his "steady concern with competition, ambition, and career—in effect, with the realities and rules of patronage" (209). Marotti's Donne, like Tennenhouse's Shakespeare, is eager to please those in power; yet Marotti's own idiom submits to a bit of decoding. For example, when he writes that "although we think of him now primarily as a literary man who wrote first poetry, then sermons, Donne actually treated literature as an avocation rather than a vocation, as part of a style of life and career whose goals were the social prestige and preferment that successful exploitation of the patronage system would win" (208), the word "actually" is being set in a tendentious—logically blurred but slurring— relation to "although." Suppose somebody were to say, "Although we think of Wallace Stevens now primarily as a poet, he actually had a very successful career in insurance." Although that tells us nothing we didn't already know, it implies some need for a more suspiciously knowing view of what we thought we knew, as though what is *really* in question is something we hadn't been able to see or hadn't wanted to confront.[9] In each case the seemingly firm but tendentious "although . . . actually" fends off questions like Would it have been better for Stevens to have had an unsuccessful career in insurance? and Wasn't giving sermons part of the Dean of St. Pauls' vocation? In Donne's case "we" are to see not only how Donne's poetry and sermons were directed to the "goals" of "social prestige and preferment," but also how high-minded and unworldly "we" have hitherto been if we failed to see what Donne was "actually" up to. To take a more generous or mixed view of Donne's motives becomes critically disqualifying: the critic must be more knowing, more able to "see through" things and people, and here, as in *That Shakespeherian Rag* there is more than a whiff of Lytton Strachey.[10] But then what are we to think once this veil falls from our eyes and our eyes fall on that first footnote, telling us that "the research for this essay was completed on a John Simon Guggenheim Memorial Foundation fellowship in 1975–76"? I trust that Marotti himself would be *angered* by any suggestion that his reason for undertaking the research was "actually" to secure the foundation's patronage.

We should be suspicious of the hermeneutics of suspicion; here I invite the reader to reflect on whether, in reading that last paragraph, she or he registered any silent protest at the association of high-mindedness with *un*worldliness. From this it is but a short step to the Iago-like assumption that a grubby explanation must be more knowing. These examples of "ideological critique" resemble Iago's unpacking of Othello's "pride, and purposes," or of Cassio's "Civill, and Humaine seeming." I am not suggesting that critics should try to be unknowingly high-minded in Othello's all too problematic way. Othello wouldn't be a very good critic; as Iago observes, he is "unbookish," although he works hard and gets most of the play's classical allusions.[11] Rather, I am objecting to the routinely degrading, uncritical dogmatism of any "critique" that assumes that a reductively materialist genealogy is always in place and always more persuasive; the account of Sidney's obsessive concern with status in Greenblatt's brilliant essay "Murdering Peasants" would be less striking and persuasive if we thought this kind of account must always be true.[12] As Iago's wife shows him, the "Not I for love and duty" view of human motives and potentialities can be most ignorant where it is most assured. Eagleton, Marotti, Tennenhouse, and Hawkes also leave out "love and duty" and any conception of a commitment that wouldn't be self-serving—as if they would be ashamed to be caught looking *up* to anything or anyone. But that itself is shameful, and best understood in the terms of A. W. Schlegel's comment on the relation between Iago's cleverness and ignorance: "Accessible only to selfish emotions, he is thoroughly skilled in rousing the passions of others, and in availing himself of every opening which they give him: he is as excellent an observer of men as any one can be who is unacquainted with higher motives of action from his own experience."[13]

The Riverbed

As I observed earlier, if you believe that values are contingent it doesn't get you very far to show how so-called humanist values are culturally specific: that is just what values are, and what many so-called humanist critics also take them to be. The important question is what you think really important, and what kind of difference it then makes to affirm values one holds while recognizing their historicity. I want to address this complicated question by comparing the simple but powerful new historicist thesis in Clifford Siskin's *Historicity of Romantic Discourse* with Leavis's misguided attack on historicist readings in "Blake and Dickens: *Little Dorrit*."[14] The comparison will also help us to consider the seemingly sharp opposition—which I nonetheless take to be apparent rather than real—between Siskin's argument that we are "inside" Romantic discourse where we should not be, and Greenblatt's estranging insistence that we cannot but be "outside" Renaissance discourses.

Siskin is much concerned to historicize our present, and argues that precisely because the psychologized "reality" of "Romanticism" has helped to determine our own understanding, we are now disposed to treat historical concepts of self and behavior as natural truths. He is rightly alarmed by the ease with which a critic like Marilyn Butler can "slip," in a passage of only three sentences, from "movements" to "crossroads" to "periods" to "phases" to "styles" (129–30); his own more exacting historicizing strategy is well illustrated in his sixth chapter, in which he examines the debate about whether Jane Austen is a "Romantic" as "a test case for contemporary literary historians." After arguing that Austen, Wordsworth, and Charlotte Brontë had "much in common," Siskin explains that Wordsworth and Brontë could nonetheless reject Austen because for them a Romantic conception of "development" had come to be a given, or "truth of Nature"—and thus provides a "no more valid basis of comparison than death or taxes to us" (147). Consequently, Wordsworth could object to Austen because "her 'mystification' of the newly 'natural'" varied from his own, although "when we place ourselves outside Romantic discourse we see Austen's works, as well as Wordsworth's poems, within it." *The Prelude* and *Northanger Abbey* both illustrate literature's "generative and exemplary role in the recasting of what late eighteenth-century culture first takes to be human"; but it is also still a feature of our own literary history that it "(Romantically) posits innovation in terms of (creative) originality." One ironic consequence is that, when seen in these terms, the Wordsworth of the "Great Decade" becomes "the most blatant victim of that very myth of creativity *he* helped to articulate" (8).

This new historicist scrutinizing of the pastness of our present unsettles familiar issues and offers a powerful challenge to those who would take over, without historicizing, Romantic preoccupations with the self, its development, and its relations to non-human Nature. When Keats characterizes his own differences from Wordsworth by contrasting the "egotistical sublime" (where the subject is stable and the objects change) with "negative capability" (where the object is stable and the subject changes, or keeps losing its "identity"), the contrast conceals an affinity that Siskin thinks no less important: "the goal of all Romantic inquiries is 'sympathetic identification.'" In Thomas McFarland's quarrel with Harold Bloom, Haydon's famous account of Keats "glorying in the fields" was said to show how "experience" was more important to Keats than reading "prior poems" and Bloomian intertextuality; here too Siskin's questions are pertinent and disruptive. Is "glorying in the fields" testimony to Keats's "individual" and "unique" genius, or to that historical change which had generated "a new set of behaviours towards natural objects" within an entire culture, so that even mountain climbing became *normal*? "Does the 'intensity' of such behaviours generate the poetical, or does a particular historical concept of the poetical authorize and instigate being intense? . . . Is it not important to ask why Keats was out in the fields in the first place? And why his reactions were thought worthy of being recorded? And why they were recorded in the personal diary of another artist as evidence of artistic temperament?" (42).

To press Siskin's thesis a little harder we might ask to what extent Leavis's account of *Little Dorrit* fails, in Siskin's terms, to perceive its own historical relation to the Romantic and Victorian discourses it interprets. In Leavis's terms, that relation demonstrates the possibility of continuity within a culture: what matters for us in *Little Dorrit* is also what establishes the novel's relation to Blake's "London." Although Herbert Lindenberger has praised Siskin's book (on its back cover) for showing how "modern expositors" are "themselves unwittingly captives of the verbal practices of those they seek to interpret," Leavis would doubtless have protested (like some of the critics Siskin criticizes) that he was not an unwitting captive at all, but a willing and critical collaborator. Leavis's essay also provides a useful "test case," because it is so dismissive of historicist readings that are concerned with historically specific "social criticism" in Dickens's novel and that in Leavis's view only distract us from the "essential 'social criticism'":

> The problem ('social problem') with which Dickens's book challenges us in the Marshalsea isn't of a kind to which the abolition of imprisonment for debt has any relevance. This isn't to say that Dickens didn't in his innermost being cry out against the very idea of imprisonment for debt. The book does that. The fact that imprisonment for debt had been abolished before he wrote *Little Dorrit* only serves to make the spirit of his use of the Marshalsea the more unambiguous. All his early readers would know of the not distant actuality; and no one would for a moment suppose him ignorant of the abolition. (*Dickens the Novelist*, 222)

Here Leavis doesn't deny that Dickens is exposing a "stultifying irrationality": because "the debtor in prison is debarred from setting about earning the means of repayment," imprisoning debtors "represents starkly the most indefensible idea of retribution" (223). But for Leavis the "essential nature of his 'social criticism'" has rather to do with the affirmation of "life, which—this is the insistence—doesn't belong to the quantitative order, can't be averaged, gives no hold for statistics and can't be weighed against money": "life against money! It is the blasphemous iniquity of that, legally and righteously enforced, that Little Dorrit can't swallow: who can suppose that it's the money she cares about? Her protest is against the whole code" (224). Clennam's disapproval of this protest then shows that the code "clings still from his upbringing," despite his brave and determined break with his family and his repudiation of the belief that "what could not be weighed, measured, and priced had no existence." But although this analysis of Clennam is penetrating and convincing, it doesn't show why it is necessary or helpful to oppose "'social criticism'" (in disdainful scare-quotes, which function like tongs) to the "essential" criticism.

In fact, although the Marshalsea prison was closed in 1849, six years before Dickens began his novel, imprisonment for debt wasn't actually abolished until 1869—more than a decade after the novel's publication. In Shakespeare's lifetime the "stultifying irrationality" of imprisoning debtors was doubtless apparent, in its practical aspects, to many who found themselves in Ludgate prison or the Fleet; but their confinement was coercive rather than penal, and had little to do with any idea of retributive justice, since the modern conception of a term of imprisonment *as* the punishment for most crimes barely existed.[15] Leavis's own protest against the "whole code" and its "indefensible idea of retribution" embodies ideas about retributive justice and individual responsibility which evolved historically, but which he treats as givens, or natural truths. Consequently, his attack on historicizing readings seems particularly misconceived, because its own assumptive basis needs to be historicized and understood in relation to the emergence, in the late eighteenth and early nineteenth centuries, of new ways of thinking about imprisonment, punishment, the self and its development, and individual responsibility.

The larger significance that Leavis wants to isolate, by invoking "life" and emphasizing the novel's relation to Blake's "London," is embedded in those socially and historically specific topicalities which Leavis sees as merely distracting: the debate over imprisonment for debt; the introduction of limited-liability laws in 1855, which, if they had been enacted earlier, could have helped Dorrit and Clennam; those attempts at Sabbatarian legislation in the same year which gave the third chapter of *Little Dorrit* its pungent contemporaneity; the collapse in 1856 of the Tipperary Bank ("a certain Irish bank") and then the Royal British Bank, after nonfictional Merdles were profitably associated with those in public office; the appalling Crimean fiasco of 1854–55 and the scandalous attempts of Lord Aberdeen's administration to overlook the 1856 Report's findings (with its indictment of the "Commissariat" in which Mrs. General's husband worked). And for any contemporary reader who saw the parallel between Rowland Hill's struggles with a corrupt, self-interested bureaucracy and the fictional Daniel Doyce's struggles with the Circumlocution Office, this parallel would have given all the more force and substance to Dickens's ferocious satire on the Civil Service. That satire, indeed, is why James Fitzjames Stephen kept attacking the novel for its allegedly untruthful representations of the upper classes and British institutions. But when Dickens replied, he didn't insist, like Leavis, on an "essential" criticism; he insisted on the truthful way in which Doyce's fictional struggles paralleled Hill's struggles.[16] That Leavis should have wanted to discount what the illiberal Stephen so wanted to disprove or discredit seems especially ironic, and sad, if one remembers how Stephen—who once expressed regret that public opinion would no longer tolerate a death sentence for offences against property—was the formidably illiberal Establishment Enemy not only to Dickens but to John Stuart Mill, whose essays on Bentham and Coleridge Leavis edited and warmly admired.[17] But then, when Leavis refers to Doyce's "indefeasible 'responsibility towards something other than himself,'" that all too Lawrentian way of putting it makes Doyce sound like a disembodied precursor of Tom Brangwen in *The Rainbow* ("He knew he did not belong to himself"). Certainly Doyce is disinterested, but he expresses that stance in emphasizing the need to be responsible for oneself: significantly, when he insists that "you hold your life on the condition that to the last you shall struggle hard for it," he is responding to Clennam's despondent suggestion that he should give up in his battle with the Circumlocution Office. Leavis makes things more difficult for himself in giving the word "life" far too much rhetorical work to do, and in wanting to sever the immensely strengthening relation between "essential 'social criticism'" and historical actualities.

But he also works in this way with Blake's "London," depoliticizing a great revolutionary poem by ignoring what is topical and specific: for example, the relation between the soldiers in Blake's poem and the soldiers who were at that time garrisoned in St. James's Park in readiness for any attack on the monarchy—many of them conscripts who, like the sailors in Melville's *Billy Budd,* might have preferred, if they could only act as free men, to attack the very institutions they were obliged to defend. "London" is anarchic in a precise sense: Blake believes that the institutions of the Church, Palace, and Marriage (seen as an oppressive institution that legalizes love) should be destroyed, and that something better would emerge from the rubble. In suppressing Blake's "idiosyncratic" use of capitals—where their idiosyncracy is one obvious reason for keeping them—modernized editions also prevent the reader from noticing how, in this poem, Blake's wholly consistent way of capitalizing institutions and their victims (the "Palace," the "Soldier," and so on) posits a series of analogically malign cause-and-effect relationships that revolution would overthrow.

Blake's poem is socially and historically specific in many details, and nightmarishly surreal in others. This "London" is both the real city and a terrifying place of the mind, or underworld realm of Urizen ("your reason"), in which the cries are all heard synaesthetically: nobody *could* "hear how" the Chimney-sweeper's childish cry "appalls" the "black'ning Church," or "how" the hapless Soldier's sigh streams in blood down Palace walls, or "how" the youthful Harlot's cry blights with plagues the Marriage Hearse. This consistent use of synaesthesia works all the more powerfully because it is not immediately noticed, while Blake's use of the continuous present has a similarly surreal, intensifying effect. To refer to *blackened* churches would have been far less effective. As it is, *appall* keeps close to the original French sense of being made to grow pale *(apalir de),* while carrying the ecclesiastical associations with the *pall* covering an altar—or hearse. The churches are *paling* at the chimney-sweeps' cries even as their Portland stone is *blackening* with the pall of London's soot. The Shakespearean density of the poem's language (with the recalling of *Macbeth* in the final stanza) is also revolutionary, but in the old, rather than the new or emerging, sense of that word: it is a return or restoration, which bypasses and thoroughly rejects or breaks with "Augustan" notions of linguistic decorum. And in these ways the poem's emphasis on "mind-forged manacles" becomes all the more sinister and disquietingly mysterious: destroying oppressive institutions is one thing, and difficult enough—but what can unmanacle the mind that does its own policing?

That, I think, is the most important connection between this poem and Dickens's novel, which is similarly disquieting in showing how Clennam is still held fast by internalized, psychologized manacles, like the chain on the novel's title page or the chain he sees decorating his mother's Bible. Chapter 3 had provided a glimpse of Clennam as a "morally handcuffed" boy, packed off to church like the children in Blake's "Holy Thursday" poems. But the adult Clennam's predicament is worse: his bold attempt at self-emancipation has produced something self-defeating, and the final chapters show how, despite his consciously determined rejection of money values, Clennam's attitude toward money has been so thoroughly internalized that, when Amy offers him her money to secure his release, he feels bound to refuse. The "mind-forged manacles" work to ensure that his very attempt at integrity is infected from within: not only would he acquiesce to the final ruin of his own life in renouncing Amy, he would actively contribute to the ruin of her life—by attaching more importance to his reactive inversion of society's perverted money values than to her own love values.

Leavis wants to emphasize this Blakean aspect, or continuity, yet his own vitalist concern with "life" weakens his critical case by encouraging him to *oppose* the "essential" to what he sees as *merely* historical—and here Siskin's thesis does help to explain what is going wrong. Because Leavis himself considers the "idea of retribution" unhistorically, treating it as a given, or natural truth, even while he attacks historicist readings, his situation might be compared to that of a man standing in a bucket and trying to lift himself from the ground. But it is important to see what does not follow. My own disagreement is critical: I think Leavis's readings of *Little Dorrit* and "London" would be better readings if, instead of opposing the historically specific to the "essential," he had recognized how the relation is one of positive, provoking interdependence. That recognition would also have strengthened his account of the values and creative concerns he admires in these works and wishes to reaffirm, as *continuous* with our contemporary needs and concerns. Certainly, I wish Leavis were more circumspect in his talismanic use of terms like "life" and "essential"; but to see that usage merely as an example of "essentialist humanism" is to miss what matters, and make new shiny manacles out of French fashion accessories. That is, the critical disagreement couldn't justify the kind of slide seen in Hawkes's discussion of *Henry V* or Norris's discussion of *Othello*—the slide from anti-humanism (humanist values are contingent and wrong) into glib pococurantism (there are no grounds for declaring one reading better than another: a play like *Henry V* can be "made to" support any view). Sooner or later—as Norris later insisted, in the passage quoted in this book's prologue— some things seem really important, and this is "not a good time to be telling students that history is only what counts as such according to some present consensus-view, and that finally it all comes down to a struggle for power between various, more or less plausible narrative fictions."

Perhaps there are advanced theorists who, when they hear Milosz or Kundera speak of justice or truth, widen their eyes and murmur incredulously, "Where have they *been*?" Knowing where they've been makes it all the more important, in our present situation, to reaffirm some of the things Leavis is affirming in Blake and Dickens, including that concern with the self and individual responsibility which is, as Siskin usefully reminds us, a new and distinctive feature of Romantic discourse. Like most of us, Leavis associates the idea of imprisonment as the punishment with the idea that the punishment is retribution for an offense, but the first idea has evolved historically, and the second is not unproblematic in philosophical terms.[18] Nonetheless, seeing that Leavis's "idea of retributive justice" is culture-specific won't take us far if we think that all thinking about justice is historically and culturally bounded; it remains important to decide whether we want, say, Mill's ideas or Stephen's opposed ideas to prevail in our own society. Justice—and what, in democratic societies, we wish the law to do or not do in our names—is one of the few things every responsible person should think about, and one of the innumerable things literature helps us to think about. This need not involve a return to the foundationalist search for eternal or ahistorical truths that could direct us from behind. We can affirm a value, not as some part of the world's furniture that we have only to "read off," but as the sort of furniture (much of it secondhand) we want to see in a world we want to live in.

One disquieting feature of Siskin's historicist project is the way in

which his account of what it is to affirm a value threatens to undermine his project—for example, when he relies on words like "myth"
or "valorize" or "mystify," or refers to moving or placing ourselves
"inside" or "outside" a cultural "discourse" as though that were something we could do at will, when his thesis is that we have been "captives" of Romantic discourse. An analogy may suggest what is
disquieting. There is an important difference between the situation
of a Western musicologist who has become sufficiently inward with
Indian music and culture to recognize when a *rag* is being disciplined
by a *tal*, and that of a student for whom a classical sonata is as alien
and indecipherable as the Indian *rag*. Somebody who then persuaded
the student that these musical discourses are produced by the "inevitably political" workings of social, economic, and institutional power
would be teaching the student how to be more ignorant, which is a
familiar paradox in universities. A reader who really was "outside
Romantic discourse" would find *The Prelude* or *Northanger Abbey* indecipherable; she might observe that the natives have valorized these
works, but would have no more inward grasp of the values in question
than a tourist who finds Thai temples tatty but thinks he has seen
what the Thais see and value. Being "inside" a cultural discourse is
far more complicated than pseudoscientific talk of "mystifying" and
"valorizing" allows.

Wittgenstein addressed this issue in his 1938 lectures on aesthetics
when he asked, How can we understand what Buffon meant by a
word like *nette*, in his *Discours sur le style*? Wittgenstein's answer was
that Buffon makes "ever so many distinctions which I only understand vaguely but which he didn't mean vaguely—all kinds of nuances
like 'grand', 'charming', 'nice'."

> The words we call expressions of aesthetic judgement play a very compli-
> cated role, but a very definite role, in what we call a culture of a period.
> To describe their use or to describe what you mean by a cultured taste,
> you have to describe a culture. What we now call a cultured taste perhaps
> didn't exist in the Middle Ages. An entirely different game is played in
> different ages.
>   What belongs to a language game is a whole culture. In describing
> musical taste you have to describe whether children give concerts,
> whether women do or whether men only give them, etc. etc.[19]

Later he observes that "in order to get clear about aesthetic words you have to describe ways of living. We think we have to talk about aesthetic judgements like 'This is beautiful', but we find that if we have to talk about aesthetic judgements we don't find these words at all, but a word used something like a gesture, accompanying a complicated activity" (11). This observation looks back to the beginning of the lectures on aesthetics, where Wittgenstein begins by observing that "the subject is very big and entirely misunderstood as far as I can see," and then goes on to attack the traditional approach to aesthetics as a branch of epistemology concerned with the move from description to evaluation—as though the act of valuing were like deciding to put on an extra sweater. It also bears on Siskin's projected "history of norm change" and "formal features."

Indeed, Wittgenstein's challenge to traditional "aesthetics" extends to much contemporary literary theory that seeks a totalizing view and shows "contempt for the particular case." As Austen Quigley observes, "What so often happens when we apply our investigative metaphors is that 'seeing something in terms of X' degenerates into 'seeing something as X' and then finally into simply 'seeing X'. . . . What we need to establish is that there is a possibility of discovery even when what we see is constantly encountered in the context of what we are likely to see."[20] Siskin "sees X"; but in Wittgenstein's terms Siskin's "formal features" are abstract empty forms until they can be grasped in relation to "forms of living." Achieving anything more than a "vague" understanding of what *nette* meant to Buffon involves situating the word within different cultural practices and discovering what changing human needs and cultural potentialities it answers to—not by considering it as a "norm" or "ideal" (or transparent counter, unaffected by historical contingencies), but by seeing what life it led and what went on around it. Suitable English parallels for the Buffon example would be Donald Davie's discussion of the way in which concepts of "strength" and "ease" changed in the first half of the seventeenth century and reflected changing concepts of courtliness; or Jean Hagstrum's discussion of the topical and strategic way in which Johnson's concept of the "beautiful" mediated between Warton's "twin nerves of poetry," to accommodate Johnson's sense of Pope's greatness while allowing that Pope was neither "sublime" nor "pathetic."[21]

Johnson illustrates, perhaps better than any other critic, how critical judgments can be powerfully, but only internally, coherent. If we had read all of the *Lives of the Poets* except the "Life of Gray," predicting how Johnson would regard Gray would be an excellent test of how well we had grasped Johnson's values. But the coherence in question, which makes some prediction possible, is necessarily (not "merely") internal, and provides no Archimedean point from which to predict how Johnson would read *The Waste Land:* if Johnson had suddenly been transported to Eliot's London in a Wellsian time machine he would have found the cultural changes too bewildering to provide any vantage point for judgment, while if he had somehow lived on into our century, like Janáček's Elina Makropulos or one of Swift's Struldbruggs, he would no longer be responding as "Johnson." Moreover, although the exercise of critical intelligence and historical imagination can help us to grasp what is internally coherent in Johnson's criticism, and so help us make imaginative and critical sense of the map of seventeenth-century poetry he provides in the "Life of Cowley," we can't take over his values or use his map; in this literary terrain we use something that is still recognizably the alternative mapping provided in Eliot's essays. We may read Donne, George Herbert, and Marvell in un-Eliotic ways, but we read these poets rather than Cowley, Denham, and Waller; if and when we do read Cowley we remain unshaken in our belief that it is more important to read Donne.

Suppose we *could* somehow convince ourselves that Cowley is the best of the so-called metaphysicals (as Johnson unequivocally asserts), and that Waller and Denham were more significant poets than George Herbert or Marvell (whom Johnson never mentions); still, much more is in question than a miscellany of particular valuations. We could not but be aware that the particular valuations in question seemed idiosyncratic or incomprehensible to our contemporaries; the strain this produced would be at the furthest remove from Johnson's very positive sense of his own culture and its achievements. His sense of the significance of Waller and Denham is inseparable from his confidently informing sense of how they were preparing the way for the supreme achievements of Dryden and Pope; here his *Lives* have more in common with Giorgio Vasari's *Lives of the Artists*—the way in which Vasari takes Giotto or Cimabue to be trying and failing to do what Michelangelo supremely did. What is in question is not a random set but a network of related judgments—a "system," but in Wittgenstein's *anti*-foundational sense: "The child learns to believe a host of things. I.e. it learns to act according to those beliefs. Bit by bit there forms a system of what is believed, and in that system some things stand unshakeably fast and some are more or less liable to shift. What stands fast does so, not because it is intrinsically obvious or convincing; it is rather held fast by what lies around it."[22] This view of "beliefs" and their susceptibility to change led Wittgenstein to his famous, gravely beautiful river image, in which propositions describing a world-picture are considered as "part of a kind of mythology" and the riverbed itself moves, but more slowly than the waters: "The mythology may change back into a state of flux, the river-bed of thoughts may shift. But I distinguish between the movement of the waters on the river-bed and the shift of the bed itself; though there is not a sharp division of the one from the other" (94–97). "At the foundation of a well-founded belief lies belief that is not founded," Wittgenstein observes later in *On Certainty,* just after turning the foundational metaphor inside out: "I have arrived at the rock bottom of my convictions. And one might almost say that these foundation-walls are carried by the whole house. One gives oneself a false picture of doubt" (248–49).

Siskin refers to "myths" in a quite different way, which once again illustrates the difference between the claim that "cultural meanings" are "always, finally, political" and the claim that political meanings are always, finally, cultural. His projected "new literary history" will have no truck with "the myths of the Great Decade and six-poet Romanticism"; with "the central Romantic myth of the artist as creative genius" (*Historicity of Romantic Discourse,* 27); with "the Romantic myth of culture—a myth which assigns to a set of primary 'artistic' texts, and their 'creators,' the power of psychologically transcending the everyday without unduly interfering with it" (11); or with "the myth of the individual within that culture" (25). On this view, T. S. Eliot's account of the relation between changes in "sensibility" and "expression" in late eighteenth-century poetry would just show how Eliot was yet another captive of all these various Romantic "myths": "Sensibility alters from generation to generation in everybody, whether we will or no, but expression is only altered by a man of genius. A great many second-rate poets, in fact, are second-rate just for this reason, that they have not the sensitiveness and consciousness to perceive that they feel differently from the preceding generation, and therefore must use words differently."[23] But then just what is Siskin's idea of "myth" being opposed to? The Truth, or some alternative "myth" or political fiction? And if we reject or see through "the myths of the Great

Decade and six-poet Romanticism" should we be reading different poets, or reading the six poets very differently?

Siskin doesn't answer such questions, and when we see why, we see Iago in a chic beret. At the outset Siskin expresses his indebtedness to the writer whose stature is clearly not in question: "Like him, I assert that modern power is exerted not through the repression but the production of knowledge" (13). Foucault is the inspiration for the wish "to explore the politics of feeling in the inventing of the literary institution—specifically, how Literature was empowered as a discipline by the rewriting of moral imperatives into aesthetic ones" (12). Siskin presents a post-Foucauldian theory of cultural conspiracy which disregards the complexity of cultural negotiations with the past, and sees arguments about what is "really" great as "a blind": "When I use the Great Decade syndrome as a touchstone throughout this book, it is not to argue about what is 'really' great but to demonstrate how such arguments can be a blind to what is actually at stake: an understanding of the formal and conceptual limitations of different kinds of literary histories" (9). Siskin has no language in which to consider cultural continuities, since he regards those whose critical discourse reaffirms features of Romantic discourse as its captives. The following passage illustrates his usual strategy for deflecting evaluative issues: "Thus to avoid what I would argue is *now* a less valuable, as well as repetitive, fate of writing 'critical' developmental narratives to praise 'creative' developmental narratives, we do not need to evaluate differently (Akenside over Wordsworth), but to use the generic differences elided by such praise as a framework for historicizing both the text's features and procedures and our own Romantic origins" (18). This claim refuses to engage the very issues it raises. The "repetitive" character of criticism is certainly depressing, but Siskin wouldn't be involved in repetition if his own arguments were informed by a sense of what "now" seems *more* valuable. To say in this context that "we do not need to evaluate differently (Akenside over Wordsworth)" only makes matters worse: why *not* value Akenside over Wordsworth, and how does Siskin himself read Wordsworth? And what directs or animates a "new literary history" in which *complaints* about the "myths of the Great Decade and six-poet Romanticism" are accompanied by *assurances* that there is no "need to evaluate differently"?

Siskin wouldn't want to pursue the anti-foundationalist challenge in Wittgenstein's riverbed image, where any world-picture (including

Siskin's) is "a kind of mythology"—or in the much earlier, somber warning in the *Tractatus*, where Wittgenstein argued that "ethics and aesthetics are one and the same" because "in the world everything is as it is, and everything happens as it does happen: in it no value exists and if it did it would have no value."[24] Instead, Siskin makes the old-fashioned—and old historicist—assumption that he can describe without evaluating, insulate his "history of norm change" from questions of value, and concentrate on "formal features" without exploring "forms of living." He should know better, insofar as new historicism aligns itself with cultural anthropology: Greenblatt nicely observes in "Filthy Rites" that "ethnography is, in effect, the study of those who do not live by one's rules."[25] But Siskin prefers to dismiss "the myth of the individual" and "growth" without trying to get clear about alternatives to myth, the individual, and growth: "Rather than regarding it as a psychological truth, I argue that development is an all-encompassing formal strategy underpinning middle-class culture itself: its characteristic way of representing and evaluating the individual as something that grows" (12). Values, a fig! 'Tis in our disciplinary institutions, that we are thus and thus.

Othello 1980

The grace and sanity of this passage from Greenblatt's "Resonance and Wonder" should clear the air:

> To study the culture of sixteenth-century England did not present itself as an escape from the turmoil of the present; it seemed rather an intervention, a mode of relation. The fascination of the Renaissance for me was that it seemed to be powerfully linked to the present, both analogically and causally. This double link at once called forth and qualified my value judgments: called them forth because my response to the past was inextricably bound up with my response to the present; qualified them because the analysis of the past revealed the complex, unsettling historical genealogy of the very judgments I was making. To study Renaissance culture, then, was simultaneously to feel more rooted and more estranged in my own values.[26]

That is finely said, and, as so often with this critic, beautifully said. In giving this account of the "double link" and so explicitly dissociating himself from the second meaning of *historicism* supplied by his *American College Dictionary*—that is, "the theory that the historian must avoid all value judgments in his study of past periods or former cultures"—Greenblatt is recognizing what any genuinely critical historicism and historical criticism must recognize: both the impossibility of suspending our own value judgments, and the bracing possibility that learning what it is to feel "more rooted and more estranged" in our own values can help us towards a better understanding of our present.

If this were all that is at issue, it would be enough to suggest how Greenblatt's new historicism differs from British cultural materialist criticism, but not enough to explain the very different and hostile accounts provided by critics like Edward Pechter and Richard Levin, who are more worried by what British cultural materialist and American new historicist readings, including Greenblatt's, have in common. Here we might consider what Greenblatt has to say of the first meaning of "historicism," according to his *American College Dictionary*: namely, "the belief that processes are at work in history that man can do little to alter." This too, Greenblatt insists, is a position that "most of the writing labeled new historicist, and certainly my own work, has set itself resolutely against." For although new historicism "eschews the use of the term man," it actually insists on the importance of human agency. Indeed, "even inaction or extreme marginality is understood to possess meaning and therefore to imply intention":

> Every form of behaviour, in this view, is a strategy, taking up arms or taking flight are significant social actions, but so is staying put, minding one's business, turning one's face to the wall. Agency is virtually inescapable.
>
> Inescapable but not simple: new historicism, as I understand it, does not posit historical processes as unalterable and inexorable, but it does tend to discover limits or constraints upon individual intervention. Actions that appear to be single are disclosed as multiple; the apparently isolated power of the individual genius turns out to be bound up with collective social energy; a gesture of dissent may be an element in a larger legitimation process, while an attempt to stabilize the order of things may turn out to subvert it. And political valences may change, sometimes abruptly: there are no guarantees, no absolute, formal assurances that what seems progressive in one set of contingent circumstances will not come to seem reactionary in another. (164–65)

And this too is so well said that it might seem more difficult than ever to understand why, as Greenblatt goes on to observe, "new historicism's insistence on the pervasiveness of agency has apparently led some of its critics to find in it a Nietzschean celebration of the ruthless will to power, while its ironic and skeptical reappraisal of the cult of heroic individualism has led others to find in it a pessimistic doctrine of human helplessness" (165).

The reason for this quarrel, which for Greenblatt involves so much misrepresentation, becomes clearer when Greenblatt replies to the respective protests of the "Marxist" Walter Cohen and the "liberal humanist" Edward Pechter. Like many British cultural materialists, Cohen objects to new historicism's "liberal disillusionment" and the idea that "any apparent site of resistance ultimately serves the interests of power" and is "ultimately coopted"[27]—to which Greenblatt crisply replies, "Some are, some aren't." Pechter had expressed his reluctance "to accept the will to power as the defining human essence"[28]—to which Greenblatt replies by treating Pechter's less "plausible" protest as a quaint "liberal humanist" confession: "the very idea of a 'defining human essence' is precisely what new historicists find vacuous and untenable" (165).

The footwork is fleet, but too fancy. For example, it is clear that Pechter was actually attributing to new historicists a form of essentialism, not confessing his own. The effect of Greenblatt's ripostes, coming after that impressive general account of why the new historicist is opposed to received notions of "historicism," is to make his "Marxist" and "liberal humanist" critics seem rigid and reactionary, caught in older, outmoded pieties and unavailingly simple paradigms. It is the new historicist who then appears to be insisting, in a truly forward-looking way, on inescapably complex negotiations or modes of relation, exchanges and reciprocities, and arguing that the relation between a text and its contexts, or between the self and social system, are mutually generative. Yet of course that is Pechter's own position, and the basis of his objections to the theory of containment. To follow this startling comedy of reversals we must attend to the underlying logic and assumptive basis of Greenblatt's *readings*—for example, when he is explaining the "orthodox doctrine that governs Othello's sexual attitudes" or the "logic which governs the relation between orthodoxy and subversion" in the "Henriad."

When Greenblatt attempts to deflect Pechter's criticism by labeling it as "liberal humanist" and misrepresenting it as "essentialist," he aligns himself with the British cultural materialists. This is disappointing, yet consistent with Greenblatt's shifty response to the third and last definition of "Historicism" in the *American College Dictionary*: "veneration of the past or of tradition." He observes, shrewdly, that this third definition "sits in a strange relation to the second, but they are not simply alternatives," since the "apparent eschewing of value judgments was often accompanied by a still more apparent admiration, however cloaked as objective description, of the past." So far so good, but then comes this:

> One of the more irritating qualities of my own literary training had been its relentlessly celebratory character: literary criticism was and largely remains a kind of secular theodicy. Every decision made by a great artist could be shown to be a brilliant one: works that had seemed flawed and uneven to an earlier generation of critics bent on displaying discriminations in taste were now revealed to be organic masterpieces. A standard assignment in my student years was to show how a text that seemed to break in parts was really a complex whole: thousands of pages were dutifully churned out to prove that the bizarre subplot of *The Changeling* was cunningly integrated into the tragic mainplot or that every tedious bit of clowning in *Doctor Faustus* was richly significant. Behind these exercises was the assumption that great works of art were triumphs of resolution, that they were, in Bakhtin's term, monological—the mature expression of a single artistic intention. (*Learning to Curse*, 168)

Of course the target here is all too familiar, a lamentably uncritical part of the history of the academic-industrial "professionalization" of English studies. Yet even as Greenblatt appeals, so beguilingly and forcefully, to the reader's critical sense of what is, after all, "flawed and uneven" in *Doctor Faustus* or *The Changeling*, he is briskly passing over or disparaging those critics in an "earlier generation" who were *not* showing uncritical "veneration." The disparaging move comes when their critical activity and their readiness to scrutinize the "flawed or uneven" is said to show how they were "bent on displaying discriminations in taste."

The alternative Greenblatt then brings forward, with some parental pride, is certainly different:

> Here again new historicist critics have swerved in a different direction. They have been more interested in unresolved conflict and contradiction

than in integration; they are as concerned with the margins as with the center; and they have turned from a celebration of achieved aesthetic order to an exploration of the ideological and material bases for the production of this order. Traditional formalism and historicism, twin legacies of early nineteenth-century Germany, shared a vision of high culture as a harmonising domain of reconciliation based upon an aesthetic labor that transcends specific economic or political determinants. What is missing is psychic, social or material resistance, a stubborn, unassimilable otherness, a sense of distance and difference. New historicism has attempted to restore this distance; hence its characteristic concerns have seemed to some critics off-center or strange. (168–69)

But this is no cure for the ills Greenblatt describes; rather, it is a prescription for contracting a different disease. For the *critical* alternative to a criticism that is "relentlessly celebratory"—in a word, uncritical—is not a criticism that is relentlessly *un*celebratory, and that casually distinguishes between the "marginal" and the "central" as though making that distinction were not itself an exacting critical task. And the *critical* alternative to an undiscriminating academic industrialism that sets out to show how every work is "really a complex whole" is not a criticism that disdains to consider any work as a complex whole.

Of course a great work of art can be—as I argue *Othello* is—both a complex whole and "flawed" or "uneven," but Greenblatt's own alternative doesn't engage that possibility. Rather, its chosen vantage point, or preferred angle of perception, is diametrically and dogmatically opposed to that in Barbara Everett's *Young Hamlet,* where she suggests that being concerned with the plays' "truth to ordinary experience" does not necessarily entail some "lack of interest in historical context," since "it can be the very sense of a work's age that brings with it a sharper regaining of its modernity": "One of the hardest but most fascinating of all intellectual problems is how not to patronize the past. We err, certainly, by forgetting that the past is not the same as ourselves. But we may err even more by not remembering that the past probably has more in common with us than we think."[29] That idea of continuity in difference—of what Greenblatt called a "double link"—is what is missing in Greenblatt's own account of "what is missing," in which the emphasis falls so remorselessly on what is *estranging*—on "unassimilable otherness", "distance and difference": the new historicist E-effect.

Of course the idea that "powerful critics" can produce a definitively "whole reading" that exhausts the work of art is an "illusion," like "the assumption that great works of art were [always] triumphs of resolution" and "the mature expression of a single artistic intention," or like the idea that "every decision made by a great artist could be shown to be a brilliant one." These are easy, undefended targets, although we might notice how, even as Greenblatt dismisses that last idea, the idea of creative decisions enters by the back door. Yet this makes it more than ever important to remember that although there can be no "whole reading," we can try to keep faith with—and extend—our sense of the work as a more or less "complex whole."

That is one reason for reading criticism, or indeed for the kind of game I sometimes play with students: the texts of the play are closed, and the group then tries to reconstruct the sequence of scenes from memory; the rest of the session is then spent considering what those things we found it difficult or impossible to remember are doing in the play. The exercise regularly shows how much has been left out, or ironed out, when we think we know a play well enough to have a "line" on it (Richard Levin's "My theme can lick your theme" comes to mind).[30] The exercise can also be critically frustrating, in exposing our tendency to disregard what we cannot explain or make sense of (why Hamlet sends that letter to Claudius, for example), and it can be critically illuminating, if (as my experience suggests) students who in some sense know *Hamlet* well have difficulty in remembering where his soliloquies occur, or remember the third act of *Othello* as though it began in the third scene, without the scene with the Clown, Emilia's speech, and the short second scene. The tendency to forget how the "high" is interwoven with the "low," or when the so-called main plot gives way to a so-called sub-plot or "secondary" action suggests (again in my local experience) that we are no longer attuned to what I have called dramatic "rhyming."

Such an exercise is not like the "standard assignment" Greenblatt complains about, where the aim is "to show how a text that seemed to break in parts was really a complex whole"; rather, it brings home how often a text is a more or less complex whole, to which we are more or less adequate, and does this by revealing what is blocked out when we place an interpretative grid over the text and report on whatever shows through it. In that way it can expose and help to check any readiness to slide into what Richard Rorty calls "doxography": the "*half-hearted* attempt to tell a new story of intellectual progress by describing all texts in the light of recent discoveries," either by imposing "a problematic on a canon drawn up without reference to that problematic" or, conversely, by imposing "a canon on a problematic constructed without reference to that canon." This, Rorty observes, "is half-hearted because it lacks the courage to readjust the canon to suit the new discoveries."[31]

Much has happened since 1980. With hindsight, what now seems most prophetic in the penultimate paragraph of that remarkable and beguiling epilogue to *Renaissance Self-Fashioning* is the way it slides between what should be seen, and avoided, as equally false extremes:

> When I first conceived this book several years ago, I intended to explore the ways in which major English writers of the sixteenth century created their own performances, to analyze the choices they made in representing themselves and in fashioning characters, to understand the role of human autonomy in the construction of identity. It seemed to me the very hallmark of the Renaissance that middle-class and aristocratic males began to feel that they possessed such shaping power over their lives, and I saw this power and the freedom it implied as an important element in my own sense of myself. But as my work progressed, I perceived that fashioning myself and being fashioned by cultural institutions—family, religion, state—were inseparably intertwined. In all my texts and documents, there were, so far as I could tell, no moments of pure, unfettered subjectivity; indeed, the human subject itself began to seem remarkably unfree, the ideological product of the relations of power in a particular society. Whenever I focused sharply upon a moment of apparently autonomous self-fashioning, I found not an epiphany of identity freely chosen but a cultural artifact. If there remained traces of free choice, the choice was among possibilities whose range was strictly delineated by the social and ideological system in force.[32]

The first false extreme is that represented by the dream of "pure, unfettered subjectivity" and an "epiphany of identity freely chosen": let us call this idealistic dream "Othello"—recalling the Othello of Act 1, who has so triumphantly fashioned his own identity in converting to Christianity, serving a state that makes ambition virtue, and marrying Desdemona. The opposed, no less false extreme is that represented by the nightmarish view of the human subject as merely the "ideological product of the relations of power in a particular society": let us call this materialistically reductive and determinist nightmare "Iago." The personal drama that unfolds is also compellingly representative; let us call this drama or psychomachia *Othello 1980*, since its excitements are related to those in Shakespeare's sustained poetic-dramatic conceit.

This contemporary drama begins with Young Goodman's realization that he can no longer believe in "Othello"—the idealistic "epiphany of identity freely chosen." Unlike the "historicists" described in his *American College Dictionary*, the protagonist will not surrender his concern with value judgments and human responsibility, but realizes that the values he wants to affirm are all culturally specific and contingent. The distress this causes him perhaps suggests the lingering influence of some metaphysical notion that if the Truth is not Here, it must be Somewhere Else. This is what "Iago" can play upon, and in the paragraph's great central scenes—corresponding with Shakespeare's 3.3—we see the protagonist's fatal wavering. He continues to use phrases like "inseparably intertwined," even as he also starts referring to the "human subject" as an "ideological product." Having abandoned that impossible, silly dream of "pure, unfettered subjectivity," he now slides, despite himself, toward the nightmarish negative image of the "remarkably unfree." That word "remarkably" is itself remarkable, in the way it resists what is being asserted about the only remaining "traces of free choice." Yet if the "choice" is inevitably limited in its "range" by what is culturally and historically possible, if it is a Gadamerian condition of our perceiving anything that our perceptions cannot but be culturally and historically bounded, what is so remarkable or painful about that? We cannot think like fifth-century Athenians, for example, but just as they managed fairly well without any concept of free will we can live without the dream of "pure, unfettered subjectivity." But in *Othello 1980* the protagonist's pain is largely self-inflicted as he surrenders to "Iago": instead of exploring the relation between creative agency and what is ineluctably contingent, he insists on what is "strictly delineated" by a "system in force."

My *Othello 1980* conceit is not offered in a merely satirical spirit. *Renaissance Self-Fashioning* is a major critical work that speaks to our situation; the epilogue does that in a remarkable way because it is genuinely and richly dramatic. To describe man as a "cultural artifact" is not original in itself; Geertz had used that very phrase, years earlier, and it is not even, in the last decades of the twentieth century, very shocking. It would be far more shocking, in our situation, to try to deny Geertz's claim that "there is no such thing as a human nature independent of culture." In a passage Greenblatt quotes in his introduction, Geertz explains that what he means by "culture" is not "complexes of concrete behavior patterns—customs, usages, traditions, habit clusters," but rather "a set of control mechanisms—plans, recipes, rules, instructions . . .—for the governing of behavior."[33] The distinction Geertz proposes is rich in consequences and intellectually exciting, but there is no note of Nietzschean or Conradian anguish: God is not only dead, his grave is overgrown, and if anything about Geertz's tone shocks it is the absence of shock. The drama in Greenblatt's epilogue recovers that shock and *finds* us, in Coleridge's sense, because Greenblatt is so bravely candid and unacademic, and speaks very powerfully to all those who no longer believe in "Othello" but, for one reason or another, distrust "Iago." And the eloquence and power with which Greenblatt conveys his passionate hatred of human cruelty also seems to me unrivaled in contemporary criticism.

And yet—there is a yet—the psychomachia in his own epilogue exposes the contradiction that resurfaces in the readings of *Othello* or the "Henriad." When challenged by a Pechter or a Cohen, or when thinking in more amenably abstract terms, Greenblatt reaffirms his belief that a text and its contexts, a self and social system, are "inseparably intertwined"; he provides the basis for a "cultural poetics" and a genuine cultural materialism in providing that felicitous and compelling account of how studying the past both calls forth and qualifies our value judgments, making us feel "more rooted and more estranged." Yet the readings restage the psychomachia in a way that measures the difference between cultural poetics and new historicism. Again, we see the (very prominent) protagonist relinquishing "Othello," and, with something like Macbeth's fascinated, courageous horror, feeling and watching himself yield to the gravitational pull of "Iago." The *readings* of Shakespeare never convey what it might mean to "feel more rooted." Instead, their increasingly partial samplings of the Shakespearean text—which sometimes seem like the new historicist equivalent of the "soundbite"—constantly enforce the sense of being "more estranged": really to understand Shakespeare is to see that plays like *Henry V* and *Othello* are museum pieces.

In this way the readings present further variations on those exciting but false extremes represented in "Othello 1980." If we think that the past is neither the same as ourselves, nor "unassimilably" alien, the new historicist version of Them and Us is no less unsatisfactory than the anti-humanist version of Them and Us provided by the British cultural materialists. If we think that a text is neither independent of, nor wholly governed by, its contexts—just as the "self" does not transcend but is not altogether constituted by social system— then to replace that impossible dream of "free unfettered subjectivity" with the authoritarian nightmare of the self as "ideological product" is to refuse to wake up.

This is why we should be especially concerned to know what Greenblatt means—whether, or how far, he means what he says— when, in the opening pages of *Shakespeare Negotiations,* he affirms his continuing belief that "sustained, scrupulous attention to formal and linguistic design will remain at the center of literary teaching and study."[34] He goes on to refer to his own "vision" as "necessarily more fragmentary"; yet any suggestion that this is a disarmingly modest claim for the *supplementary* illuminations provided by studying the "borders" and "margins of the text" is dispelled by the quietly skeptical reference to the "presumed center of the literary domain" and the "satisfying illusion of a 'whole reading'"—that is, "the impression conveyed by powerful critics that had they but world enough and time, they could illuminate every corner of the text and knit together into a unified interpretative vision all their discrete perceptions." Greenblatt's "Resonance and Wonder" offers a suavely conciliatory but unconvincing defense of his "Invisible Bullets" essay, in which Greenblatt insists that his chief concern was to offer a "particularizing argument" about the second tetralogy, and not to argue in general or universal terms that "resistance is impossible" (*Learning to Curse,* 165–66). This addresses, and may appease, those whose own chief concern is with Greenblatt's ideological standpoint, but not those whose worries and protests have to do with the "particularizing argument" itself. Greenblatt is still disagreeing with (and rebuking) critics who suppose that "certain rhetorical features in much-loved literary works constitute authentic acts of political liberation"; but the tetralogy's "political" effect isn't what is at issue either, and once again there is a tacit assumption that the original audiences would have responded as a monolithic entity. What is of great interest in "Resonance and Wonder" is that Greenblatt seems genuinely perplexed and upset by the controversy "Invisible Bullets" provoked. This puzzlement measures the rift between his sense of what he is doing and what the readings do—or, in more general terms, measures the rift between Greenblatt's often inspiring conception of "cultural poetics" and new historicist practice.

This is why the seemingly sharp contrast between Siskin and Greenblatt—between the argument that we are "inside" romantic discourse when we shouldn't be and the argument that we can't but be "outside" Renaissance discourse even when we think we are not—is less sharp than it seems. Siskin doesn't rise above questions of value, he evades them, and presents a no less evasive theory of cultural conspiracy. Of course, any affirmation involves a suppression: a macho culture suppresses a "gentleman" culture, and vice versa, but regarding either as no more than a "blind" for suppressing the other won't be of much help in reading Borges or Dickens. Greenblatt isn't evasive in that way, and the idea of the "double link" affirms the possibility of continuity as well as difference; but in his readings the emphasis falls always on "distance and difference" and an estranging, "unassimilable otherness." The arcane and anecdotal historical component is no less estranging. Here, even though Leavis's attack on historicizing readings of *Little Dorrit* is critically misguided, the hermeneutical and methodological challenge he issued in 1953 to the bewildered F. W. Bateson (bewildered, because he had no effective reply) hasn't lost its problematic force and point, when considering new historicist ways of doing history: "'Context', as something determinate, is, and can be, nothing but [the literary historian's] postulate; the wider he goes in his ambition to construct it from his reading in the period, the more is it his construction (in so far as he produces anything more than a mass of heterogenous information alleged to be relevant)."[35] Moreover, when we consider Siskin's "alternative functions for criticism" or Greenblatt's equivocal distinction between the "margins" and the "center," the warning that Leavis added seems no less timely now: "If you propose to place the importance of literary criticism in some non-literary-critical function, you betray your unbelief that literary criticism really matters. And if you don't believe in literary criticism, then your belief that literature itself really matters will have the support of an honored convention, but must be suspect of resting very much on that" (180).

Such a warning, or appeal, would be unlikely to impress Stanley

Fish, who quite unequivocally insists that it is "right," and not in any way "a matter of scandal," to say that "the profession exists so that there may be a means of accreditation and advancement for people in the profession, and not out of any inner necessity and certainly not out of cultural need or the need of individual teachers."[36] And it seems unlikely that Fish's concept of "professionalism" would have impressed Wittgenstein, who urged Leavis to "give up criticism." Anti-foundationalism takes different forms, and Greenblatt's concern with "cultural poetics" and the "double link" is far closer to Wittgenstein's idea of the "river-bed" than Fish's numerous recyclings of the Wittgensteinian perception that "at the foundation of well-founded belief lies belief that is not founded." As Martha Nussbaum observes in her fine reply to Fish's essay: "The discovery that there is not a divine code fixed eternally independently of our existence and thought, the discovery that truth is to some extent or in some manner human and historical, certainly does not warrant the conclusion that every human truth is as good as every other." After relating Fish's version of anti-foundationalism to Gorgias's argument that there is no truth, only different and more or less successful forms of manipulation that allow no distinction between persuasion and force, Nussbaum comments:

> First, I think that it is only because we have for a long time, through the dominance of various kinds of formalism, lost the sense that literature deals with human matters of great importance that the Gorgianic turn could flourish as it does. For I have enough respect for Fish as a human being to conjecture (in ignorance) that in anything that really matters to him—politics, personal friendship and love, the rearing of children— he believes that there is a very important distinction between persuasion and force. (When Derrida was in jail in Czechoslovakia it was evident to all members of the profession what that distinction was.) Nor, I bet, does he think that in matters of child rearing the latest deliverances of pediatricians and child psychologists are criterial of truth and exempt from rational criticism; that in matters of love and sex the latest fads of sociology and sexology are criterial of correctness; and so on. Why is the literary profession and its subject matters treated so lightly, as if it were the one place where we could play around with these differences? Isn't it, too, about something real and really important?
>
> Second, the activity of justification I have described shows, I believe, one very important link between philosophy and literature. As we ask, concerning any belief, what its depth is for us (let us say, the belief in

the incommensurability of ethical values, or the beliefs about persons outlined above), we need to be imagining vividly what a life would look like both with and without that belief, allowing ourselves, in imagination and emotion, to get a sense of what the cost for us would be if we gave it up. To get that kind of understanding of possibilities, an understanding that is both emotional and intellectual, we need literature in philosophy; for literature can show us in rich detail, as formal abstract argument cannot, what it is like to live in a certain way.[37]

It hardly seems original, or contentious, to propose Shakespeare as the supreme example in our literature of a writer who is constantly and vividly imagining what lives are like with or without certain beliefs—imagining what it means to *be* an Othello or an Iago, a Henry or a Michael Williams.

Nor is it original, although it is more contentious, to propose that contemporary criticism should resist foundationalism, and work from a recognition that values are socially specific and historically contingent. Ever since its inception as a university discipline, "English" has been fending off attempts to annex it to history or philosophy. And there have always been unfortunates whose only paradigm of value is politics; that is not new either, although the enormous institutional and capital investment that looms behind Fish's conception of "professionalism" is unprecedented, and militates against critical dialogue. Too much is at stake, not least in the profitable business of marketing the "new" products of those who oppose "Western capitalism"; the approaches I have criticized are tenured into the next century. Yet what is sad and exasperating about "the 'New Historicism' of cultural materialism" is that it keeps offering different versions of "Iago" which work to prevent any sustained engagement with Shakespeare's complex designs, while at the same time deflecting the real challenge—the possible value and even, in our present situation, nobility—of any more reflexive and exploratory cultural materialism, or genuine "cultural poetics."

APPENDIX

Dashing Othello's Spirits

"I see this hath a little dash'd your spirits"
—Iago

Imagine a parliamentary stenographer scribbling furiously in the days before tape recorders. His job is to record politicians' speeches so that they can be written up and preserved in an official parliamentary record like Hansard. In delivering a speech the politicians frequently lose their thread, forget their grammar, dangle clauses, fail to finish sentences, or interrupt themselves with impromptu remarks or parenthetical swipes at a political opponent. When some dramatic break or swerve in the speech seems too uncertain to sort out there and then, the stenographer sticks in clumps of hyphens, partly as a signal to himself that he will need to sort this out later when "correcting" and "clarifying" his final copy for Hansard. But imagine, too, that this is a parliament where politicians customarily speak in verse, so that one of the things the stenographer has to do is record when they don't. He still uses his clumps of hyphens wherever he suspects, but isn't immediately sure, that a speaker is failing to sustain the verse line, or dropping into prose; he can work through his text later, to work out what was happening.

In the sixth of the appendixes to the New Arden *Othello* (London: Methuen, 1965), Ridley discusses a "typographical oddity in Q1 which perhaps merits some attention": "Some seventy times there occur three (occasionally four or two) successive hyphens (- - -). All but four of these 'triple-hyphens' are repeated in Q2 (though almost invariably by an ordinary 'em rule' (—), but only two are repeated in F" (224).

[258]

As Ridley observes, this unusual marking "seems to represent throughout something that the compositor had before him in his copy (i.e., the assumed transcript) and that he followed with considerable care"; yet the Folio dispenses with this "oddity," and its significance "is not always the same." Sometimes the successive hyphens are "just ordinary parentheses"; often they "indicate an interruption of speech" or "a change of subject"; and there are also cases where they seem to be "used to indicate the presence of hypermetrical syllables at the end of the line" (225–26).

Certainly, the significance of these hyphens is not always the same, any more than it is for my imaginary stenographer. In the terms of my analogy, the stenographer's notes are more like what we have in the Quarto, where the hyphens mark different kinds of distraction or disturbance; later, when preparing a fair copy for Hansard, which gives us something more like what we have in the Folio, the stenographer sifts through the cases to decide, and make clear, what was going on. In all those cases which involve the *possibility* of a rupturing of the verse line, the stenographer's concern is to resolve, not record, that doubt about what was happening, and to replace the hyphens with a less ambiguous and idiosyncratic marking. So, in many of these cases where the hyphens disappear in the Folio, the apparent disturbance is assimilated within a metrically regular verse line. In some other cases relineation seems to resolve the puzzle. In others the hypermetrical disturbance is real, not merely apparent, but again the stenographer dispenses with the idiosyncratic hyphens. Yet the Quarto's successive hyphens seem more systematic, and so more significant, than Ridley allows. They alert us to Shakespeare's interest in the dramatic potential of prosaic eruptions and disruptions within the verse line, and to the ways in which Othello's breakdown is being traced in poetic-dramatic terms.

The "typographical oddity" appears seventy-three times in the First Quarto, and a look at the nineteen instances in Act 1 suggests how it is doing different jobs but in an intelligibly systematic fashion. As earlier in this book, the act, scene, and line references in what follows are those of the Riverside text, which differs from both the Quarto and the Folio, since it is an eclectic text—like all modernized editions, and like the Oxford old-spelling edition. Where the comparison seems instructive, I have quoted the Folio text and that of two modernized editions, the New Arden and Sanders's New Cambridge (Cambridge: Cambridge University Press, 1984).

(1)   *Iago.* 1.1.55–56
    And such a one doe I professe my selfe,- - - - for sir,
    It is as sure as you are *Roderigo,*

    And such a one do I professe my self. For (Sir)
    It is as sure as you are *Roderigo,*

                                        (Folio)
    And such a one do I profess myself.
    For, sir,
    It is as sure as you are Roderigo,
                            (New Cambridge)

Here the Quarto hyphens signal the rupturing of the verse line, as Iago thinks of something further and rushes on. The New Cambridge commas and relineation make this awkwardly ponderous and unrushed. The parentheses around "Sir" in the Folio preserve the pace while giving a guide to intonation.

(2)   *Iago.* 1.2.153
    Marry to.- - - -Come Captaine, will you goe?

    Marry to—Come Captaine, will you go?
                            (Folio)

Generally the Folio eliminates the hyphens, but this is one of the two cases where it uses an em rule. Iago interrupts himself, when Othello returns. If Iago had gone on to name Desdemona, the line would have continued as an iambic pentameter; although what he says instead is iambic, it isn't assimilated, as many other cases are, to a regular verse line. This suggests that it is misguided for modern editors to offset Othello's "Have with you" (the New Arden offers "ha' with you") to the right, as though it completes a divided but regular verse line.

(3)   *Senator.* 1.3.17–19
    This cannot be by no assay of reason- - -
    Tis a Pageant,

To keepe us in false gaze: when we consider

> This cannot be
> By no assay of reason. 'Tis a Pageant
> To keepe us in false gaze, when we consider
>> (Folio)

> This cannot be,
> By no assay of reason. 'Tis a pageant
> To keep us in false gaze. When we consider
>> (New Cambridge)

> This cannot be
> By no assay of reason . . . 'tis a pageant,
> To keep us in false gaze: when we consider
>> (New Arden)

Once again the Quarto hyphens signal the presence of a hypermetrical phrase, slung between two regular pentameters; in a naturalistic way, they also suggest somebody thinking on the spot. The Folio lineation removes the hypermetrical phrase, while making the senator sound more fluent and decided, though not as definite as he seems in the New Cambridge text. The punctuation in the New Arden is a curious hybrid, neither Jacobean nor modern; the dots are uncomfortably reminiscent of Old Cambridge scandals like Quiller-Couch's edition of *The Tempest*, in which the stage directions bring in whizzing fireballs or tell us that Miranda is gazing out to sea at moments when her text is sprinkled with winsome dots.

(4)   *Duke.* 1.3.171–72
> I thinke this tale would win my daughter to,- - - -
> Good *Brabantio*, take up this mangled matter at the best,

> I thinke this tale would win my Daughter too,
> Good *Brabantio*, take up this mangled matter at the best:
>> (Folio)

Since the metrical stress on "to" completes the regular pentameter, it is clear that *too* is meant: the Duke completes his first sentence. The comma and hyphens then signal the moment when he turns to Brabantio, addressing him in a hypermetrical phrase which is again metrically stranded between two regular pentameters.

(5, 6) *Desdemona, Duke.* 1.3.246
And if my simplenesse.- - - -
Du. What would you- - - -speake.

T'assist my simplenesse.
Duke. What would you *Desdemona?*
(Folio)

In the Quarto the nicely observed naturalistic effect is assimilated into a metrically regular pentameter line: the bold but nervous Desdemona doesn't finish her sentence, and the Duke breaks in encouragingly. The Folio's substitution of "T'assist" for "And if" ensures that Desdemona does finish her sentence, and sounds less tentative, while the Duke's response is also smoother but more formal; but smoothing out the Quarto's naturalistic effects is metrically less smooth, since Desdemona's name won't fit into the line.

(7) *Othello.* 1.3.268–69
For she is with me;- - -no, when light-wingd toyes,
And feather'd Cupid foyles with wanton dulnesse

When she is with me. No, when light wing'd Toyes
Of feather'd *Cupid,* seele with wanton dulnesse
(Folio)

Again the Folio is smoother; "No" has a different force or emphasis when it follows "when she is with me" not "for she is with me," while the Quarto's "light-wingd toyes, *And* feather'd Cupid *foyles*" is less orderly than the Folio version. As so often, the Quarto is more naturalistic in suggesting that the character is thinking on the spot and hasn't sorted out his words and phrases as one would in a prepared or considered speech. We shall see later why it is important that the hyphens don't reappear in any speech of Othello's until well into 3.3, and do not here signal any metrical irregularity.

(8–14) *Iago.* 1.3.341–47

It cannot be, that *Desdemona* should long continue her love unto the Moore,- - -put money in thy purse,- -nor he to her; it was a violent commencement, and thou shalt see an answerable sequestration: put but money in thy purse.- - - -These Moores are changeable in their wills:- - -fill thy purse with money.

Further instances follow in this prose dialogue between Iago and Roderigo:

therefore make money,- - -a pox of drowning,

Thou art sure of me- - -goe, make money- - -I have told thee often

The Quarto punctuation is helpful, since it brings out the alternation and intonational difference between Iago's two voices, each with a different level or pitch: the voice that speaks of money is repetitive and unvarying, until that more emphatic shift from "put" to "fill," while the other voice is energetically expansive and explanatory. The Folio punctuation is more subtly inflected but also more demanding, since it doesn't underline that effect of a duet or counterpoint between two voices:

It cannot be long that *Desdemona* should continue her love to the Moore. Put Money in thy purse: nor he his to her. It was a violent Commencement in her, and thou shalt see an answerable Sequestration, put but Money in thy purse. These Moores are changeable in their wils: fill thy purse with Money.

(15)   *Iago.* (1.3.376)

Go to, farewell:- - -doe you heare *Roderigo?*

Go too, farewell. Do you heare *Roderigo?*
                                        (Folio)

Having dismissed Roderigo, Iago detains him; he isn't saying "go, do you hear?" and the line isn't verse. The hyphens signal the change of mind and intonation ("go- -no, wait a minute"); the Folio trusts the reader to see and hear what is happening without nursery-slopes assistance.

(16–19) *Iago.* 1.3.388–89, 394, 401–4
Ha's done my office; I know not, if't be true- - -
Yet I, for meere suspition in that kind [. . .]

A double knavery- - -how, how,- - -let me see,

And will as tenderly be led bit'h nose- - -as Asses are:
I ha't, it is ingender'd: Hell and night
Must bring this monstrous birth to the worlds light.

Once Iago is left alone at the end of the first act he speaks in verse, and the Quarto hyphens appear in three of his verse lines. However, only the third of these lines is metrically fractured. Here is the Folio, in which "She" is clearly a misprint for "He," and was corrected in the later Folios.

She ha's done my Office. I know not if't be true,
But I, for meere suspition in that kinde,

In double knavery. How? How? Let's see.

And will as tenderly be lead by' th' Nose
As Asses are:
I have't: it is engendred: Hell, and Night,
Must bring this monstrous Birth, to the worlds light.

As usual, the Folio dispenses with the Quarto hyphens, while distinguishing between the different kinds of disturbance: "As Asses are" is hypermetrical, whereas any disturbance or excitement in the first and second instances is still accommodated within metrically regular verse lines.

Of the nineteen instances of hyphens in Act 1, fourteen involve Iago. This isn't surprising, because the rapid, improvisational energy of his speech so frequently carries him into some metrical hinterland where what began as verse is either disrupted within the line or disrupted by a hypermetrical addition to the line. In other cases the Quarto hyphens appear to signal some disruption that threatens, but then turns out to be accommodated within, the verse line. Here are all the other lines where the Quarto uses hyphens in Iago's verse:

As my young mistris dog. - -Now my sicke foole *Roderigo,*
(2.3.51)

Why then let a souldier drinke.- - -Some wine, boyes,
(2.3.73–74)

O sweete *England,*- - -King *Stephen* was a worthy peere.
(2.3.88–89)

Then take thine owd cloke about thee.- - -Some wine ho.
(2.3.96–97)

Who's that that rings the bell? Diablo- - -ho,
(2.3.161)

Cassio my Lord? - -no sure, I cannot thinke it,
(3.3.38)

Be not you knowne on't, I have use for it:- -go leave me
(3.3.319–20)

God buy you, take thine office,- -O wretched foole,
(3.3.375)

Faith that he did- -I know not what he did
(4.1.32)

I am very glad to see you Seignior:- -welcome to *Cypres*
(4.1.220–21)

Another instance, which actually appears as prose in the Quarto but as a verse line in the Folio and modern editions, occurs at 4.1.48:

my Lord I say, *Othello,*- -how now *Cassio*

That and some of the other instances, like those where Iago interrupts his own song, wouldn't be worth remarking were it not for that general instability that distinguishes Iago's verse, and makes it difficult to determine in some cases whether a speech is in verse or prose.

Consider these two examples from the harbor scene. What is perhaps Iago's most menacing and metaphorically complicated aside is printed as verse in the Quarto (and begins by completing Othello's preceding half-line) and as prose in the Folio:

> O you are well tun'd now,
> But I'le set downe the pegs, that make this musique,
> As honest as I am.

[Aside] Oh you are well tun'd now: But Ile set downe the peggs that make this Musicke, as honest as I am.

Earlier in the same scene, another of Iago's speeches is verse in the Quarto and prose in the Folio:

> Come on, Come on, you are Pictures out adores:
> Bells in your Parlors: Wildcats in your Kitchins:
> Saints in your injuries: Divells being offended:
> Players in your houswifery; and houswives in your beds.

Come on, come on: you are Pictures out of doore: Bells in your Parlours: Wilde-Cats in your Kitchens: Saints in your Injuries: Devils being offended: Players in your Huswiferie, and Huswives in your Beds.

The important point here is not that we try to resolve this difference—as though one text were "right," where both are good—but that we see how often Iago's speeches enter this metrical hinterland. His verse is, as it were, regularly irregular: like that of the 1590s satirists, and even Donne in his looser *Satyres,* its forceful elisions and hypermetrical syllables show the meter being infected by the colloquial rhythms of excited speech—or show the meter being suddenly cheerfully smashed, or dashed, by the irresistible vigor of some sudden thought, like the hypermetrical "As Asses are." Iago is continually thinking on the spot, and seeing what can be done or said. The improvisational energy is characteristic, because this is how Iago is characterized in poetic-dramatic terms: this is what is being opposed to—and eventually untunes—Othello's "musique."

For that very reason we might *like* or be very much interested by the way in which the Quarto hyphens signal all those moments of doubt which the Folio resolves, say, between the metrically irregular

> And such a one doe I professe my selfe,- - - -for sir,
> (1.1.55)

and the metrically regular, but similarly improvisational,

> A double knavery- - -how, how- - -let me see,
> (line 394)

And we may then dislike the way in which modern editors tidy up Iago's verse, allowing external or mechanical considerations of metrical regularity to determine the choice between, say, the Folio's

> Christen'd, and Heathen) must be be-leed, and calm'd
> (1.1.30)

and the Quarto's

> Christian and Heathen, must be led, and calm'd,

where "be be-leed" includes a hypermetrical syllable, but is also entirely characteristic of Iago. And "be-leed" makes perfectly good sense—as the New Cambridge editor concedes, while nonetheless opting for Malone's emendation, "Christian and heathen, must be lee'd and calmed."

A longer quotation from the Folio text of this speech should also suggest what is lost in eliminating all those parentheses which, in the Folio though not the Quarto, show how one idea engenders another and—without slowing the exuberantly athletic pace of Iago's verse—call for correspondingly rapid shifts in intonation:

> Meere pratle (without practise)
> Is all his Souldiership. But he (Sir) had th'election;
> And I (of whom his eies had seene the proofe
> At Rhodes, at Ciprus, and on other grounds
> Christen'd, and Heathen) must be be-leed, and calm'd
> By Debitor, and Creditor. This Counter-caster,
> He (in good time) must his Lieutenant be,
> And I (blesse the marke) his Mooreships Auntient.
> (lines 26–33)

That, as a reading text, is far more subtly nuanced and suggestive than the Quarto, where the equivalent passage comes in the second half of an immensely long, lightly punctuated sentence:

As masterly as he: meere prattle without practise,
Is all his souldier-shippe: but he sir had the election,
And I, of whom his eyes had seene the proofe,
At Rhodes, at Cipres, and on other grounds,
Christian and Heathen, must be led, and calm'd,
By Debitor and Creditor, this Counter-caster:
He in good time, must his Lieutenant be,
And I, God blesse the marke, his Worships Ancient.

Look at what any modernized edition does with this speech, or with these two versions of this speech: in comparison with either the Folio or Quarto, the modernized version will be lumpish.

Here we might imagine our stenographer writing his memoirs, and recalling which politicians in his poetic parliament were most likely to slide into prose even when they were ostensibly speaking in verse. Iago, he recalls, was a constant offender. But on going through his working notes, he is struck by the way in which, even when speeches by Desdemona and Cassio made him resort to his hyphens at the time, the disturbance in question was never accompanied by a rupturing of the meter—until Cassio disgraced himself, and Desdemona was about to die. As for Othello—but we had better look at the simpler cases before considering that complex case.

The Quarto hyphens appear in five of Cassio's lines. Before he gets drunk there are three instances. The first merely registers an interruption and change of subject, and could be read as metrically regular if we want to allow for the conversational elision ("who's put in?"). The other two lines are metrically regular and, in context, engagingly "poetic" in their ardent enthusiasm.

Does beare all excellency.- - -now, who has put in?
(2.1.65)

A sennights speede- - -great Jove Othello guard,
(2.1.77)

And bring all *Cypresse* comfort,- - -O behold
(2.1.82)

And we might note in passing how in the prose dialogue that follows in 2.3, when Cassio resists Iago's smutty suggestions, Iago's prose is thoroughly prosaic where Cassio's seems about to lift into verse:

> *Cas.* She is a most exquisite Lady.
> *Iag.* And I'le warrant her full of game.
> *Cas.* Indeed she is a most fresh and delicate creature.
> *Iag.* What an eye she has?
> Methinkes it sounds a parley of provocation.
> *Cas.* An inviting eye, and yet me thinkes right moddest.
> *Iag.* And when she speakes, tis an alarme to love.
> *Cas.* It is indeed perfection.
> (2.3.18–28)

Once Cassio has yielded to Iago, drink, and the "beast" within, he has two more lines with hyphens. The first is prose, whether or not we think it an abortive attempt at a verse line:

> I have well approov'd it sir,- - -I drunke?
> (2.3.312)

The other instance also signals an awkward failure to sustain the verse line:

> I have made bold *Iago* to send in to your wife,- -my suite to her,
> Is, that she will to vertuous *Desdemona*,
> Procure me some access.
> (3.1.33–36)

The Folio softens the awkwardness without removing it:

> I have made bold *(Iago)* to send in to your wife:
> My suite to her is, that she will to vertuous *Desdemona*
> Procure me some access.

The awkwardness is presumably wanted, and registers Cassio's unease and embarrassment. It would have been easy to write something like this:

> I have made bold, Iago, to send your wife
> My suite that she'll to vertuous Desdemona
> Procure me some access.

The Quarto hyphens occur in seven of Desdemona's lines. But in six of these cases the disturbance in question is accommodated within the verse line, as though Desdemona isn't capable of metrical or indeed any kind of irregularity:

> And if my simpleness.- - - -
>
> (1.3.246)

> O but I feare:- - -how lost you company?
>
> (2.1.91)

> Come on, assay- -there's one gone to the Harbor?
>
> (2.1.120)

> O that's an honest fellow:-do not doubt *Cassio,*
>
> (3.3.5)

> Will not goe from my mind- -harke, who's that knocks?
>
> (4.3.31)

> My feare interprets then,- -what is he dead?
>
> (5.2.73)

The exception—in the Quarto, though not in the Folio—is a hypermetrical addition which suddenly bursts her verse line to make it accommodate a full, vehemently passionate denial:

> I never did offend you in my life- -never lov'd *Cassio,*
> But with such generall warranty of heaven,
> As I might love: I never gave him token.
>
> (5.2.58–60)

Othello's case is more complicated. His collapse into prose in 4.1 is all the more momentous because we have never heard him speak in prose, unlike the dangerously flexible, volatile Iago. But then, if prose is whatever is not, or not quite, verse, the Quarto hyphens trace a more gradual and subtle process of disintegration which begins where we would expect, in 3.3. Until then it is as though Othello were loftily confined within his strenuously aspiring poetic register: he seems incapable of speaking prose, or not-verse. We hear Desdemona and

Cassio speaking prose early on, though it is worth noticing that apart from their respective prose exchanges with the Clown (where to speak verse would be to stand on ceremony), they only descend to prose when in the company of Iago. Iago's own command of different registers is so complete as to allow that chillingly effortless, mocking parody of sustained Othello-like sonorities:

> Looke where he comes: Not Poppy, nor Mandragora,
> Nor all the drowsie Syrrups of the world
> Shall ever medicine thee to that sweete sleepe
> Which thou owd'st yesterday.
>
> (3.3.330–33)

As we have seen, the hyphens appear in only one of Othello's lines before 3.3, and in that case the meter is preserved:

> For she is with me;- - -no, when light-winged toyes
> (1.3.268)

The same holds true for the first example in 3.3:

> He did from first to last:- -Why does thou aske?
> (3.3.96)

The next instance is metrically ambiguous—a terrible tremor that shows Iago beginning to succeed in untuning the pegs that make Othello's music. Othello's agonized response to Iago's question, would he "behold her topt?"—

> Death and damnation- -oh
> (3.3.397)

completes a verse line, and his howl or moan may or may not be hypermetrical, since the *-ion* suffix can be pronounced as one syllable or two. But then, some fifty lines later, the next Quarto hyphens mark what we have so often heard in this play, but never before in Othello's verse—a hypermetrical phrase coming between two regular verse lines:

All my fond love, thus doe I blow to heaven,- -tis gone.
Arise blacke vengeance, from thy hollow Cell.

$$(3.3.445-46)$$

Eight lines later—after the frenzied cry, "O blood, *Iago*, blood"—
comes the hypermetrical "Never" and the two lines the Quarto offers
in the place of the Folio's Pontic sea speech. At this point Othello is
losing control in metrical as in other terms. The meter collapses in
his explosion, "Dam her lewd minks: O dam her," and although his
last line in this scene is printed as though it were still verse, there is
nothing to recall the "Othello music": "For the faire divell: now art
thou my Lieutenant."

Othello's verse, at least, tends to recover whenever he gets away from
Iago; we see or hear this in 3.4 and in the first part of 4.1, until Iago's
return brings on the precipitous collapse into incoherent prose, and
"a Traunce." When Othello degrades himself by spying on Cassio in
the handkerchief scene, he is locked into prose; after that the Quarto
hyphens reappear with increasing frequency. The next two instances
are equivocal, in that the first might still be a regular verse line with
an elision in "I will":

I will chop her into messes- - -cuckold me!

$$(4.1.188)$$

While in the second the Folio tells us (though the Quarto doesn't)
that Othello is reading from the official letter:

This faile you not to doe, as you will.- - -

$$(4.1.217)$$

But then comes another collapse, in which the bombardment of hyphens shows how the deranged Othello is now entirely unable to keep
control of himself or his verse:

I am commaunded here:- -get you away,
I'le send for you anon:- -Sir, I obey the mandat,
And will returne to *Venice:*- - -hence, avant,
Cassio shall have my place; and sir tonight
I doe intreate that we may sup together,
You are welcome sir to *Cypres,*- -goates and monkies.

$$(4.1.258-60)$$

Similarly, the remaining hyphens signal the difficulty, and in most cases the impossibility, of sustaining his verse line:

> Let me see your eyes- -looke in my face
> (4.2.25–26)

> To point his slow unmooving fingers at- -oh, oh,
> (4.2.54)

> Made to write whore on?- - -What, committed?
> (4.2.71)

> And will not hear't:- -what committed, -impudent strumpet,
> (4.2.79)

> Will you walke sir:- - -O *Desdemona.*
> (4.3.5)

> Thou teachest me;- -minion, your deare lies dead,
> (5.1.33.

> That he hath- - - -ud:death [used thee]
> (5.2.69)

> O strumpet,- -weepest thou for him to my face?
> (5.2.78)

> I would not have thee linger in thy paine,- - -so, so.
> (5.2.89)

Since the First Quarto and the Folio texts of *Othello* are now usually regarded as two independently authoritative Shakespearean versions, it seems more important than ever to notice how much method there is in the Quarto's use of hyphens. Of the five remaining verse instances I have not yet mentioned, two are metrically regular, while the others all involve further examples of hypermetrical additions to what would otherwise be metrically regular lines:

> *Montano.* Can hold the motties.- - -What shall we heare of this?
> (2.1.9)

Roderigo.   O dambd *Iago*, O inhumaine dog,- -O, O, O.
                                    (5.1.62)

Emilia.   I do beseech you that I may speake with you.-good my Lord.
                                    (5.2.101–2)

Emilia.   As ignorant as dirtt; thou hast done a deed- - -
                                    (5.2.164)

Lodovico.   The death of *Cassio;* to be undertooke- - -by *Roderigo.*
                                    (5.2.311)

The eight remaining instances of the Quarto hyphens all occur in
prose passages. Six occur in Iago's prose speeches, at 2.1.179, 2.1.217,
2.1.284, 2.3.29, 2.3.37, and 4.1.47 (which is prose in the Quarto, verse
in the Folio), and another in a prose speech of Cassio's (3.1.27); the
remaining instance occurs when Othello leaves the stage in Act 4, and
is so distraught that he addresses his wife in rough prose:

> Get you to bed, o'the instant I will be return'd, forthwith, dispatch your
> Attendant there,- -looke it be done. (4.3.7–9)

Our collecting of all those cases where the Quarto employs its hyphens should sharpen, not blur, our sense of the remarkable way
in which the play orchestrates the poetic-dramatic contrast between
Othello and Iago—and their developing proximity. In the first half
of the play, before the direct assault on Othello begins in 3.3, the
hyphens are used thirty-eight times, above all in Iago's speeches, with
twenty-three instances as opposed to Othello's one. In the second half
of the play the hyphens are used thirty-six times, but now twenty of
these instances occur in Othello's speeches, and only six in Iago's.

What Ridley tentatively—though very perceptively—singles out as
a "typographical oddity which perhaps merits some attention" is being
used as a fine though idiosyncratic instrument for recording different
kinds of disruption, disturbance, and disintegration. And contagion:
like Desdemona and Cassio, Othello falls into prose—falling much
later, and much further, when he is with Iago—and recovers metrically when he is not with Iago. But the hyphens show how the recoveries are always partial, and the final murderous collapse takes place

without Iago's presence—unless we hear that presence, and feel its gravitational pull, in Othello's ruptured verse.

The differences between the Folio and Quarto lineations are important; but both, in their different ways, are concerned to make metrical (or poetic-dramatic) sense of what is happening. Just as the Folio lineation removes Desdemona's one hypermetrical outburst, Othello's last hyphens disappear when "so, so" is presented as the start of a new verse line:

> I would not have thee linger in thy paine?
> So, so.
>
> Æmil. *within.* What hoa? my Lord, my Lord?
>
> *Oth.* Who's there?

That eliminates the hypermetrical irregularity, yet it should by now be clear that the Quarto isn't including the irregular line because it is casual or negligent about metrical matters: here as elsewhere, the hypermetrical addition is carefully marked, and the consistent use of hyphens manifests a strong, exploratory interest in what can be achieved or suggested through carefully scored disruptions within a verse speech. Although they present alternatives which are metrically very different, both texts are concerned with what is to be heard.

Indeed, it is sobering, and humbling, to reflect on what both the Folio and Quarto compositors expected readers to hear without seeing. They always set each new speaker's line immediately after the speech heading, where modern readers are more likely to *need* that modern typographical convention which shows when a line is divided between different speakers by offsetting to the right:

> So, so.
>   —What hoa? my Lord, my Lord?
>   —Who's there?

Since the so-called "accidentals" of punctuation affect what we hear or fail to hear—the verse's movement, pace, and intonation—the traditional distinction between substantives and accidentals becomes rather problematic. On the one hand, the distinction appears to deny that metrical movement is a constituent of poetic and poetic-dramatic meaning: accidentals are, as the *Concise Oxford Dictionary* states, what is "not essential in a conception," yet the way in which verse moves— who speaks it, and how—is very much part of the poetic-dramatic "conception," and it is also affected by so-called accidentals of punctuation. On the other hand, the enormous differences between the Folio and Quarto punctuation seem to justify the traditional distinction; as the New Cambridge editor puts it, the First Quarto and the Folio "represent two Shakespearean versions of the play"—not two essentially different plays. So what could we be losing, which is in any way essential, in reading a *modernized* text?

Here is the First Folio text of Othello's first extended speech, followed by the New Arden text:

> Let him do his spight;
> My services, which I have done the Signorie
> Shall out-tongue his Complaints. 'Tis yet to know,
> Which when I know, that boasting is an Honour,
> I shall promulgate. I fetch my life and being,
> From Men of Royall Seige. And my demerites
> May speake (unbonnetted) to as proud a Fortune
> As this that I have reach'd. For know *Iago,*
> But that I love the gentle *Desdemona,*
> I would not my unhoused free condition
> Put into Circumscription, and Confine,
> For the Seas worth. But looke, what Lights come yond?
>   (1.2.17–28)

> Let him do his spite;
> My services, which I have done the signiory,
> Shall out-tongue his complaints; 'tis yet to know—
> Which, when I know that boasting is an honour,
> I shall provulgate—I fetch my life and being
> From men of royal siege, and my demerits
> May speak unbonneted to as proud a fortune
> As this that I have reach'd; for know, Iago,
> But that I love the gentle Desdemona,
> I would not my unhoused free condition
> Put into circumscription and confine
> For the sea's worth. But look what lights come yonder.

Those differences that are "substantive" in the traditional sense arise because the New Arden is eclectic. So, Ridley prefers the First Quarto "provulgate" to the Folio and Second Quarto "promulgate," and both quartos' "yonder" to the Folio "yond," but doesn't prefer the quartos' "height" to "siege." In preferring "provulgate" Ridley observes that the *OED* "does not even recognize this word"; that isn't true, but the odd error doesn't destroy Ridley's appeal to "the *difficilior lectio* principle." *Provulgate* was certainly a rare word, whereas *promulgate* had been in use from 1530. Not only is it unlikely, as Ridley observes, that a compositor would have come up with such an unexpected word: this is just the kind of remote word Othello does use—like *agnize* and *portance*, which are unexpected, or *exsufflicate*, which according to the *OED* is not found outside this play. Such words help to characterise Othello, and what has been called the "Othello music"; they also suggest what Iago has in mind when he sneeringly refers to "horribly stufft" epithets and "bumbast Circumstance."

But what of those changes that involved so-called accidentals? Is the editor's decision to present what are five sentences in the Folio as one long, elaborately punctuated sentence less 'substantive," or less significant in relation to the poetic-dramatic characterization, than the decision to print *provulgate* rather than *promulgate?* It hardly matters whether *unbonneted* is spelled *unbonnetted*, but does it matter whether the word appears between parentheses?

I have already suggested that Iago's parentheses in the Folio affect our sense of the rapid pace of his speeches, yet even the recent Oxford old-spelling edition routinely removes all of the Folio's parentheses. The Quarto is far more sparing in its use of parentheses, and is generally very lightly punctuated; but that too preserves the pace, whereas the heavier punctuation in modern editions may be one reason why modern performances of Shakespeare usually take one or even two hours too long, even after the cuts. Stephen Orgel remarks in his important edition of *The Tempest* (Oxford: Clarendon Press, 1967) that for several years the play's "only life was in performance," since there was no published text (12); and it might be argued that we can't see parentheses in a performance. Yet actors had parts prepared from the company text—which existed!—and began by reading their parts; moreover, an experienced dramatist like Ben Jonson, who saw his own Folio through the press, wouldn't put parentheses in his scripts unless he thought they made a difference to delivery. I find the effect of reading "(unbonnetted)" is different from that of reading "unbonneted" and something I don't want to be deprived of. One might compare the effect of reading "(Lady)" or "(deare)" in a Renaissance seduction poem: to put such words between commas threatens to make the line slower and more ponderous, less suggestive of the advancing hand; whereas placing them in parentheses preserves the pace while calling for a quick intonational nuance or inflection, consonant with the speaker's own alertness to what he is saying and its likely effect. Without the parentheses Othello could simply be belaboring the point about his own worth; placed in parentheses, the word carries the possibility of a sudden lively thought, allowing us to hear not a sonorously sustained "song of myself" but the varying tones of a quick, complicated man whose apparent assurance also reveals irritation and anxiety.

Removing or adding commas clearly does affect the movement of a verse line, even though the difference isn't easily indicated in any system of metrical notation. The Folio commas after "Circumscription," "Confine," and "looke" affect the movement of the last two lines; similarly, although the difference between the Folio's

Which when I know, that boasting is an Honour,

and the New Arden's

Which, when I know that boasting is an honour,

is hard to measure, it is perceptible. Moreover, if we agree that the modernized punctuation gives greater emphasis to "Which" and less to "know," we confront a rather awkward paradox. The modernized punctuation is more attentive to logical and syntactical structure, but the Jacobean pointing is more concerned with delivery; yet that ought to concern us in reading a dramatic text or script. Not least in this case, where reducing the emphasis on "know" and putting it on "Which" makes it less easy to see or hear how the word *know* has an important structural and dramatic function in threading together different parts of Othello's speech: "'Tis yet to know;" "Which when I know"; "For know Iago." In 3.3 it is presumably an insinuating emphasis or crafty hesitation on that word in Iago's "My Lord, for ought I know" which prompts Othello's exasperated "What do'st thou thinke?"

Even as Othello speaks of what he knows but has chosen not to tell, his speech travels from the confidence of "Let him do his spight" to this curiously unexpected insistence:

> For know *Iago,*
> But that I love the gentle *Desdemona,*
> I would not my unhoused free condition
> Put into Circumscription, and Confine,
> For the Seas worth.

Why should Othello want Iago to know that? Here, another effect of modern punctuation—with its concern to clarify or "point" syntactic and logical (but not psychological) relationships—is to make this speech seem more elaborately composed and confidently consequential than it is in the Folio text.

At first Othello seems strikingly confident that his services will "out-tongue" a grave and reverend senator's "Complaints." But then he begins to speak of what the Senate itself has "yet to know," as though registering the unwelcome possibility that his past record and proud reticence may not suffice. If he is being charged with having reached so "proud a Fortune" by marrying a senator's daughter, he may well have to reveal, proudly, what in the past he has proudly chosen not to reveal—and is revealing now, as he chooses to confide in the man he had earlier chosen not to tell about the secret wooing. As he now braces himself to speak—if he must—of what the Senate has "yet to know," he reveals how this goes against the grain: *he* has "yet to know" that "boasting is an Honour."

This tension suggests why the Folio's "promulgate" is also, as Polonius would say, very good, and better than Ridley allows. He observes in his New Arden edition that "*promulgate* has a certain connotation of publication by official authority which is not particularly appropriate to Othello's hypothetical action as a private individual in presenting the common people *(vulgus)* with the facts" (16). But that picks up the division revealed in the reference to "boasting" and "Honour." If the "Services" are not enough, the authoritative publication of his "Royall" birth may be needed to persuade doubtful senators that he is neither an inferior nor a social climber; but this need in itself is demeaning, since it involves deferring to the senators by trying to increase their sense of his worth. Othello cannot escape this distasteful situation, because of his own new situation as a married man. The speech is proud, confident, forceful; yet the nervy Folio sentences and uncertain transitions allow glimpses of an underlying agitation, as it is borne in upon Othello that he *is* circumscribed and confined by his present situation. He cannot regret being a married man, since he loves Desdemona, yet his perplexed sense of being constrained now catches up another, ominously unfocused fear about the constraints of married life as he tells Iago what to "know": "But that I love the gentle *Desdemona,* I would not." We need to see how the speech arrives at this unexpected insistence, and here the Folio text is boldly dramatic and helpfully nuanced. As the New Arden turns five Folio sentences into one elephantine sentence, it also flattens out these inner tensions; partly because the modernized punctuation is more concerned with logical and syntactical relationships, the speech seems less dramatic but more weightily assured, less tense but more sonorously purposeful in its progressions.

But of course I have not acknowledged one real or apparent justification for that huge sentence in New Ardenese: the First Quarto presents the whole speech as one sentence. Moreover, the Quarto doesn't place "unbonnited" in parentheses, and in general uses parentheses very sparingly: there aren't any in Iago's first two long speeches, for example. And although the Quarto does place the comma after "know," not "when," in the fourth line, there are no commas after "circumscription" and "confine." The Quarto's status as an independently authoritative text is less in doubt now than it was when Ridley mounted his challenging textual arguments. I have argued that the Quarto hyphens are uniquely valuable and suggestive; in his own appendix on the "triple hyphens" Ridley hints, in his judicious way, that the "typographical oddity" is authorial, representing "something that the compositor had before him in his copy (i.e., the assumed transcript)," and something that a careless transcriber would not "take the quite needless trouble of inserting in his transcript." In short, it seems possible and even likely that the punctuation in the Quarto is more Shakespearean, where the finely nuanced punctuation in the Folio might be described as more Jonsonian. Once the missing phrase in the fourth line has been supplied from the Folio, should we prefer to read Othello's speech as the Quarto presents it?

Let him doe his spite,
My services which I have done the Seigniorie,
Shall out tongue his complaints, tis yet to know,
That boasting is an honour,
I shall provulgate, I fetch my life and being,
From men of royall height, and my demerrits,
May speake unbonnited to as proud a fortune
As this that I have reach'd; for know *Iago,*
But that I love the gentle *Desdemona,*
I would not, my unhoused free condition,
Put into circumscription and confine
For the seas worth.　*Enter Cassio with lights, Officers, and torches*
But Looke what lights come yonder.

Perhaps the stenographer analogy is still helpful, even if we think
that the Quarto punctuation brings us as close as we can get to Shakespeare's own. There is certainly nothing lumbering or elephantine
about the Quarto punctuation: here as elsewhere its ubiquitous commas provide information about delivery and pace, but that in turn
suggests why the effect of preserving the long sentence in the modernized New Arden version is quite different. As Ridley himself succinctly puts it, "Shakespearean" punctuation "was a dramatic tool, not
a grammatical one": "Shakespeare, that is, was writing for dramatic
delivery, while his editors re-write him for logical comprehension
from the page" (226). Yet the "re-writing" in a modernized text has a
thickening, retarding, and even a blurring effect, since the "modern"
punctuation is inevitably heavier, and inevitably anachronistic—neither Jacobean nor modern. Moreover, if we think of the Quarto punctuation as a *creative* stenographer's record of what he hears voices
saying in his head, it still doesn't provide as much analytical and direc-
tional guidance as readers may need if they are to hear what is happening.

If that is our first concern, it would not be contradictory or absurd
to prefer to read Shakespeare in the Folio version even when we
believed that some quartos, like the First Quarto *Othello* or the Second
Quarto *Hamlet,* bring us closer to the way Shakespeare punctuated
his text. The Folio remains indispensable, because it was so carefully
and lovingly prepared as a contemporary reading edition. Of all the
books in the language, it is the greatest treasure; yet it is not even
available in a modern reading edition. What is wanted is not another

expensive and bulky facsimile for scholars and antiquarians but an edited, user-friendly modern edition that prints *loue* as *love*, corrects misprints and agreed errors, gives important Quarto variants at the bottom of the page, offsets to the right when a verse line is divided between different speakers, and isn't too expensive for students and actors. In a brave new world, some high-minded Gideon would ensure that this is the book to be found in every hotel room.

Notes

PROLOGUE

1. Graham Bradshaw, *Shakespeare's Scepticism* (London: Harvester Press; New York: St. Martin's Press, 1987).

2. Hugh Grady, *The Modernist Shakespeare: Critical Texts in a Material World* (Oxford: Clarendon Press, 1991), 160.

3. See A. P. Rossiter, *Angel with Horns* (London: Longman, 1961); Norman Rabkin, *Shakespeare and the Common Understanding* (New York: Free Press, 1967); Wilbur Sanders, *The Dramatist and the Received Idea: Studies in the Plays of Marlowe and Shakespeare* (Cambridge: Cambridge University Press, 1968); Sigurd Burckhardt, *Shakespearian Meanings* (Princeton: Princeton University Press, 1968). D. C. Allen's review of Tillyard appeared in the *American Journal of Philology* 56 (1945): 434–36.

4. Stephen Booth, "The Value of Hamlet," in Norman Rabkin, ed., *Reinterpretations of Elizabethan Drama* (New York and London: Columbia University Press, 1969), 137–76; quotation on 138. Booth adds that in a culture so "shaped by the Platonic presumption that the reality of anything is other than its apparent self . . . it is no wonder that critics prefer the word *meaning* (which implies effort rather than success) to *saying,* and that in turn they would rather talk about what a work *says* or *shows* (both of which suggest the hidden essence bared of the dross of physicality) than talk about what it *does.*"

5. Jonathan Dollimore, "Shakespeare, Cultural Materialism, and the New Historicism," in Dollimore and Alan Sinfield, eds., *Political Shakespeare: New Essays in Cultural Materialism* (Manchester: Manchester University Press; Ithaca: Cornell University Press, 1985), 2–17; quotation on 5.

6. Empson's essay "Hunt the Symbol" originally appeared in the *Times Literary Supplement*, April 23, 1964; reprinted in William Empson, *Essays on Shakespeare* (Cambridge: Cambridge University Press, 1987), 231–43.

7. See Eagleton's afterword in Graham Holderness, ed., *The Shakespeare Myth* (Manchester and New York: Manchester University Press, 1988), 204. It is characteristic of Eagleton to call, so dramatically, for a "Caliban school of criticism" without asking whether it had been around for a long time. I discuss the relation between Robert Graves's and Ted Hughes's readings of *The Tempest* in "Visions of the Goddess," in *The Achievement of Ted Hughes*, ed. Keith Sagar (Manchester: Manchester University Press, 1984), 52–69. It's worth remarking—with Auden's "The Sea and the Mirror" also in mind— that poets seem to warm to Prospero less readily than do academics; the point here may be not that academic critics are more judicious but that in aspiring to be "authorities" they are more inclined to be authoritarian. None- theless, several so-called humanist readings also took a dissenting, critical view of Prospero, notably Harry Berger, "Miraculous Harp: A Reading of Shakespeare's *Tempest*," in *Shakespeare Studies* 5 (1969): 353–83; Clifford Leech, *Shakespeare's Tragedies* (London: Chatto & Windus, 1950), 142–58; and James Smith's 1954 reading, which Smith included in his *Shakespearian and Other Essays* (Cambridge: Cambridge University Press, 1974), 159–261. Im- portant anticolonial responses by writers such as George Lamming, Octave Mannoni, Aimé Césaire and Fernandez Retamar also appeared in these dec- ades or earlier, and are discussed in Alden T. Vaughan and Virginia Mason Vaughan, *Shakespeare's Caliban* (Cambridge: Cambridge University Press, 1991), 144–71. In other words, this was no barrenly conservative period in the history of *Tempest* criticism, and contemporary accounts of the discourses of colonialism are much indebted to it. However, what Eagleton appears to want in calling for a "Caliban school of criticism" is an unnuanced, bluntly confrontational and predictable critique. What he himself provides, in *William Shakespeare* (Oxford: Basil Blackwell, 1986), is, to be fair, very different: the play becomes a curiously cerebral and essentialist allegory, in which "Ariel and Caliban symbolize, respectively, pure language and pure body" and the "central fusion of body and language, as usual with Shakespeare, is mar- riage" (95).

8. See Malcolm Evans, *Signifying Nothing: Truth's True Contents in Shake- speare's Text* (Brighton: Harvester Press; Athens: University of Georgia Press, 1986), especially chap. 1. Although Evans is often subtle and rewarding, he produces his characterisation or caricature of "the" so-called humanist (or non-Marxist) response by ignoring earlier critics whose work anticipated his own and by lumping together remarkably different critics—as in his refer- ences to "*the* critical tradition of Eliot, Leavis and Tillyard" (252, my italics; compare 257), who allegedly all believe that Shakespeare's work 'emerges from and reflects the unity of 'a lost Elizabethan Utopia'" (252). In the terms of Rossiter's Joycean contrast between one-eyed and two-eyed vision, Evans

and Eagleton favor readings that are no less one-eyed than those of the critics criticized by Empson and Berger, only now everything is to be seen through the other, no less authoritarian, eye. This is too like having to choose between Hitler and Stalin.

9. Jonathan Dollimore, *Radical Tragedy: Religion, Ideology, and Power in the Drama of Shakespeare and His Contemporaries* (Brighton: Harvester Press; Chicago: University of Chicago Press, 1984).

10. Grady, *Modernist Shakespeare,* 159–60.

11. Ibid., 196: "In this insistence on clash and disunity which cannot be reduced to unity, we have perhaps the first sounding of a truly Post-modernist Shakespearian criticism; unfortunately Burckhardt took his own life before his achievement could be recognized." The implied relation between suicide and recognition is curious.

12. Rabkin, *Reinterpretations of Elizabethan Drama,* v–x.

13. Keith Brown, *Times Literary Supplement,* August 22, 1986, 917.

14. I discuss the issue of royal "hypocrisy" later, in Chapter 1.

15. Graham Holderness, Nick Potter, and John Turner, *Shakespeare: The Play of History* (London: Macmillan; Iowa City: University of Iowa Press, 1988), 4.

16. See John M. Ellis, *Against Deconstruction* (Princeton: Princeton University Press, 1989), 37–38, 141. "Derrida is, in fact, attacking a view of meaning that by now would have to be counted a very naive and uninformed one; for example, it has been dismembered in various ways, with varying emphases, by analytic philosophers such as Wittgenstein and others who have worked in his tradition, by linguists such as J. R. Firth, by anthropological linguists working in the tradition of Edward Sapir and Benjamin Lee Whorf, and by countless others. When, in 1966, Derrida began to denounce this kind of thinking as a *universal* error, he was demonstrating an extraordinary isolation from what had been happening for many years" (38).

17. Jonathan Dollimore and Alan Sinfield, "History and Ideology: the Instance of *Henry V,*" in John Drakakis, ed., *Alternative Shakespeares* (London and New York: Methuen, 1985), 206–27.

18. Dollimore, *Radical Tragedy,* 190–91. Some of the objections entered here were originally made in my review of this book, *Times Literary Supplement,* August 17, 1984, 924.

19. See Nicholas Brooke's Revels edition of George Chapman, *Bussy D'Ambois* (London: Methuen, 1964), 154.

20. Alan Sinfield, *Faultlines: Cultural Materialism and the Politics of Dissident Reading* (Oxford: Clarendon Press, 1992), 261; the extended version of "History and Ideology" appears on 109–42.

21. Dollimore and Sinfield, "Cultural Materialism," in *Political Shakespeare,* vii–viii; this foreword is variously modified in other volumes, like *Shakespeare Myth,* but the passages I criticize remain.

22. Sinfield, *Faultlines,* 299–300; Arnold Wesker, *The Merchant,* ed. Glenda

Leeming (London: Methuen, 1983). The first version of Wesker's play was performed in 1976, and his preface first appeared as an article in *Guardian*, August 29, 1981. For an excellent discussion of the way in which "the integrity of his intention is destructive of the dramatic qualities of his play," see John Lyon, *"The Merchant of Venice"* (New York: Harvester Press, 1988), 18–25. In the final chapter, James C. Bulman, *"The Merchant of Venice"* (Manchester and New York: University of Manchester Press, 1991) discusses Wesker's adaptation in relation to the Shakespearean play's performance history.

23. See John Elsom, ed., *Is Shakespeare Still Our Contemporary?* (London and New York: Routledge, 1989), 144; Ruth von Ledebur, "Reading Shakespeare's Merchant of Venice with German Students," in Hanna Scolnicov and Peter Holland, eds., *Reading Plays: Interpretation and Reception* (Cambridge: Cambridge University Press, 1991), 123–39.

Elsom's interesting collection presents the transcribed and edited proceedings of a public seminar staged at the Young Vic Theatre by the International Association of Theatre Critics. The "problem" of *The Merchant of Venice* was extensively discussed, and in ways that prompted a Russian critic, the late Alexander Anikst, to enter this quiet protest: "Shakespeare, I think, believed that we are cleverer than we really are. He expected us to go away from his plays and think about them, coming to conclusions that can't be expressed in easy formulas" (180). This made no impression on the Marxist critic Ernst Schumacher, who went on to insist that "so soon after the holocaust and the murder of six million Jews, it is impossible in my view to play *The Merchant of Venice*" (181). For Schumacher the play should not be performed since "Hitler used it, Goebbels used it, and it contributed directly to the extermination of the Jews, the 'final solution' of 1943" (143). Although Schumacher himself observed that this was "a typical use of Shakespeare in a false way," this did not affect his view that the play itself is anti-Semitic, and that both Shakespeare's play and Marlowe's *Jew of Malta* "came from" Lopez's execution (143). In fact, Lopez's trial and execution took place in 1594, whereas *The Jew of Malta* was acted in 1591–92 and Marlowe died in 1593; as for *The Merchant of Venice*, recent scholarship assigns it to 1597 rather than 1594, for the reasons summarized in Molly Mahood's New Cambridge edition (Cambridge University Press, 1987), 4–7. Moreover, like other critics who pursue a Lopez connection, Schumacher never asks why the Queen appointed a Jewish physician. Yet here, as Anikst saw, the real "problem" lies elsewhere, in that assumption that a drama or dramatist must be telling its audience what to think.

24. Elsom, ed., *Is Shakespeare Still Our Contemporary?*, 145 (Handelsatz) and 181 (Fried).

25. Chinua Achebe, "An Image of Africa: Racism in Conrad's *Heart of Darkness*," in *Hopes and Impediments: Selected Essays 1965–87* (London: Heineman, 1988; New York: Doubleday, 1989), 1–13.

26. One "liberal" reading that assumes that Shakespeare is sharply critical

of the play's Christians is A. D. Moody's monograph *"The Merchant of Venice"* (London: Edward Arnold, 1964). But Moody is too shrewd a critic to assume that any Christian (or Jewish) character must be seen as "the Christian" (or as "the Jew"); unlike Sinfield, he sees that the play presents a spectrum of anti-Semitic attitudes and a telling contrast between Shylock's and Jessica's attitudes to Christians. The 1984 Royal Shakespeare Company production, which Sinfield so admired, has stayed in my memory as the most stupid and vulgarly insensitive Shakespeare production I have ever seen. For example, Portia's wish that none of Morocco's "complexion" be among her suitors was expressed to a black Nerissa. The budget for the production would probably have sustained a good provincial company for more than a year, and, as so often happens in the RSC, worked against the drama: the huge life-size caskets were always visible, diminishing the contrast between Venice and Belmont, while the stage was cluttered with costly carpets and two Renaissance organs, which were constantly moved back and forth. This, in producing a play which is intelligently concerned with race and the use of riches!

27. Quoted in Elsom, ed., *Is Shakespeare Still Our Contemporary?*, 179.

28. Dollimore, "Transgression and Surveillance in *Measure for Measure*," in *Political Shakespeare*, 72–87.

29. Christopher Norris, *Deconstruction and the Interests of Theory* (London: Pinter Publishers, 1988; Norman: University of Oklahoma Press, 1989), 242. Norris cites Paul Hirst, "Althusser's Theory of Ideology," *Economy and Society* 5 (1976): 385–412.

30. See the letter from Sinfield, *London Review of Books*, March 7, 1991, 5, in that journal's long-running "Bardbiz" correspondence: "And why do the same misconceptions keep churning on through, month after month? For instance, why does Pratt elide cultural materialism and post-structuralism?" In *Modernist Shakespeare* Grady similarly protests that "to speak of Marxism in the singular has become misleading and almost indefensible" (5–6); but to speak of "humanism" in the singular *is* indefensible, and more misleading. Presumably Dollimore's elisions would be defended as strategic, in the manner of Michael Ryan's explanation, in *Marxism and Deconstruction: A Critical Articulation* (Baltimore and London: Johns Hopkins Press, 1982), of the use he makes of Derrida: "I have attempted to explain certain aspects of Derrida's work which can be used within critical marxism. This is by no means an exhaustive introduction, and, at times, it is not even an accurate account, because my purpose has been to interpret Derrida in a way that is politically useful" (xiv).

31. This proposition is discussed in my epilogue.

32. Graham Holderness, *Shakespeare's History* (Dublin: Gill and Macmillan; New York: St. Martin's Press, 1985), 148.

33. Terence Hawkes, "Wittgenstein's Shakespeare," in Maurice Charney, ed., *"Bad" Shakespeare: Revaluations of the Shakespeare Canon* (London: Associ-

ated University Presses; Rutherford, N.J.: Farleigh Dickenson University Press, 1988), 55–60.

34. Christopher Norris, *Deconstruction and the Interests of Theory*, 109–25; quotation on 124. This essay first appeared in *Alternative Shakespeares*, 47–66.

35. John Bayley, *The Characters of Love* (London: Constable, 1960); my quotations are taken from the 1968 Chatto & Windus paperback edition. The Leavis-Bradley dispute was extensively discussed throughout the decades Norris disregards: for relevant surveys, see Helen Gardner, "*Othello:* A Retrospect: 1900–1967," *Shakespeare Survey* 21 (Cambridge: Cambridge University Press, 1968), 1–12, and Robert Hapgood's chapter on *Othello* in Stanley Wells, ed., *Shakespeare: Select Bibliographical Guides* (Oxford: Oxford University Press, 1973), 159–70. Jane Adamson's discussion of this issue in "*Othello*" *as Tragedy: Some Problems in Judgment and Feeling* (Cambridge: Cambridge University Press, 1980) is probably the most searching; her whole book might be seen as a pioneering attempt to break free of the impasse created by Leavis's quarrel with Bradley and "sentimentalist" readings.

36. F. R. Leavis, "'Diabolic Intellect' and the Noble Hero: A Note on Othello," *Scrutiny* 6 (1937): 259–83; later collected in *The Common Pursuit* (London: Chatto & Windus, 1952), 136–59, as "Diabolic Intellect and the Noble Hero: Or the Sentimentalist's *Othello.*"

37. Jean Howard, "The New Historicism in Renaissance Studies," *English Literary Renaissance* 16 (1986): 13–43. For a devastating demolition of Terry Eagleton's similar idea of a monolithic eighteenth century, see Donald Greene, "An Anatomy of Pope-Bashing," in G. S. Rousseau and Pat Rogers, eds., *The Enduring Legacy: Alexander Pope Tercentenary Essays* (Cambridge: Cambridge University Press, 1988), 241–81. As for the medieval monolith, I doubt that this fantasy would survive an hour or two spent with Alastair Minnis, A. B. Scott, and David Wallace, *Medieval Literary Theory and Criticism c. 1100–1375: The Commentary Tradition* (Oxford: Clarendon Press, 1988).

38. Stephen L. Collins, "Where's the History in the New Literary Historicism? The Case of the English Renaissance," *Annals of Scholarship* 6 (1989): 231–48.

39. Rabkin, *Reinterpretations of Elizabethan Drama*, viii.

40. Thomas Kuhn, *The Structure of Scientific Revolutions*, 2d ed. (Chicago: University of Chicago Press, 1970), 172.

41. As Alexander Nehamas emphasizes in *Nietzsche: Life as Literature* (Cambridge, Mass., and London: Harvard University Press, 1985), Nietzsche continued to believe in the possibility and value of "good philology." Nehamas's second chapter, "Untruth as a Condition of Life" (42–73) explains why, in Nietzsche's terms, perspectivism does not imply that any interpretation is as good as another: the "free spirits" are those who "realize that all is in fact interpretation, and yet find in this realization not an obstacle to producing new ideas and values but a spur towards it" (5).

42. Stephen Greenblatt, "Towards a Poetics of Culture," in H. Aram

Veeser, ed., *The New Historicism* (New York and London: Routledge, 1989), 1–14. Earlier versions appeared in the Australian *Southern Review* 20 (1987) and Murray Krieger, ed., *The Aims of Representation* (New York: Columbia University Press, 1987).

43. Clifford Geertz, *Works and Lives: The Anthropologist as Author* (Stanford: Stanford University Press, 1988), 140.

44. Richard Taruskin, "The Pastness of the Present and the Presence of the Past," in Nicholas Kenyon, ed., *Authenticity and Early Music: A Symposium* (Oxford: Oxford University Press, 1988), 137–207.

45. Leonard Tennenhouse, *Power on Display: The Politics of Shakespeare's Genres* (London and New York: Methuen, 1986).

46. E. M. W. Tillyard, *The Elizabethan World Picture* (Harmondsworth: Penguin, 1963), 18.

47. Stephen Greenblatt, *Shakespearean Negotiations: The Circulation of Social Energy in Renaissance England* (Oxford: Clarendon Press, 1988), 21–65. For earlier, interestingly different versions of this essay, see *Glyph* 8 (1981): 40–61; Dollimore and Sinfield, eds., *Political Shakespeare*, 18–47; Coppélia Kahn and Peter Eriksen, eds., *Shakespeare's Rough Magic: Renaissance Essays in Honor of C. L. Barber* (Newark: University of Delaware Press, 1985), 276–302.

48. Stephen Greenblatt, *Renaissance Self-Fashioning: From More to Shakespeare* (Chicago: University of Chicago Press, 1980), 222–54.

49. Tennenhouse, *Power on Display*, 39.

50. Phyllis Rackin, *Stages of History: Shakespeare's English Chronicles* (London: Routledge; Ithaca: Cornell University Press, 1990), 55.

51. Jean E. Howard and Marion F. O'Connor, eds., *Shakespeare Reproduced: The Text in History and Ideology* (London: Methuen, 1987).

CHAPTER ONE

1. Stephen Greenblatt, *Shakespearean Negotiations: The Circulation of Social Energy in Renaissance England* (Oxford: Clarendon Press, 1988), 4–5.

2. M. Eddershaw, "Acting Methods: Brecht and Stanislavsky," in Graham Bartram and Anthony Waine, eds., *Brecht in Perspective* (London and New York: Longman, 1982), 128–44; quotation on 136.

3. Ann Jennalie Cook, *The Privileged Players of Shakespeare's London 1576–1642* (Princeton: Princeton University Press, 1981), 100. For a protest against Cook's picture of a homogeneous audience (or Greenblattian "collectivity"), see Martin Butler, *Theatre and Crisis 1632–1642* (Cambridge: Cambridge University Press, 1984), 293–306. As Janet Clare has more recently observed, in taking issue with Annabel Patterson's account of "conscious and collusive arrangements between authors and authorities": "playwriting is a commercial undertaking . . . the playwright has to take account of popular demands and taste" as well as "the likely response of the censor," and "the number of

cases of actual interference with texts by the censor and of post-performance intervention militates against a theory of a shared perception as applicable to theatrical censorship"; see Clare, *"Art Made Tongue-Tied by Authority": Elizabethan and Jacobean Dramatic Censorship* (Manchester and New York: Manchester University Press, 1990), xii. See note 49, below.

4. Leonard Tennenhouse, *Power on Display: The Politics of Shakespeare's Genres* (London and New York: Methuen, 1986), 106. Tennenhouse refers to Butler's book, but explains that for his "purposes the important point is less the exact socio-economic makeup of the audience and more the representations of the signs and symbols of state authority the stage mounted" (195). His thesis is "symbolic" and historicist, not historical.

5. Sally Beauman, *The Royal Shakespeare Company's Production of "Henry V"* (Oxford: Pergamon Press, 1976), 52. For a disquieting account of contemporary French dramatists' intense irritation or despair when directors kidnap and distort their plays, and the depressing effect this has had on new French drama, see Janice Berkowitz, "A Sense of Direction: The Author in Contemporary French Theater," *Modern Drama* 28 (1985): 413–30.

6. Quoted from Pennington's essay in the Brisbane program, and from the English Shakespeare Company press releases. I saw this production in Brisbane and reviewed it for *The Age Monthly Review* (October 1988): 20–22.

7. This point is made, usually very aggressively, by various British cultural materialists. See Graham Holderness, "Agincourt 1944: Readings in the Shakespearean Myth," *Literature and History* 10, no. 1 (1984): 24–45; Terence Hawkes, "Wittgenstein's Shakespeare," in Maurice Charney, ed., *"Bad" Shakespeare* (London: Associated University Presses; Rutherford, N.J.: Farleigh Dickenson University Press, 1988), 56–60. Earlier, in *That Shakespeherian Rag: Essays on a Critical Process* (London and New York: Methuen, 1986), Hawkes had gleefully compared the "siege mentality" of E. M. W. Tillyard's "well-known war effort, *The Elizabethan World Picture* of 1943," with John Dover Wilson's fear of the Bolsheviks and his insistence, in 1914, that Tsarism was Russia's form of democracy.

8. Michael Bogdanov and Michael Pennington acknowledge this connection in their interesting memoir, *The English Shakespeare Company: The Story of "The Wars of the Roses" 1986–1989* (London: Nick Hern Books, 1990), 27: "In a perceptive book, *Political Shakespeare*, edited by Jonathan Dollimore and Alan Sinfield, the contributors analyse the underlying radical political subversion contained in Shakespeare's work, a subversion that it is important to hold in mind, for example in attempting to scrape off the cloying mud of Olivier's propaganda *Henry V*, a film that involved the cutting of some one thousand five hundred lines in order to make the jingoistic cap fit."

9. Jonathan Dollimore and Alan Sinfield, "Cultural Materialism," in Graham Holderness, ed., *The Shakespeare Myth* (Manchester and New York: Manchester University Press, 1988), ix.

10. The duck-rabbit gestalt, which interested both Wittgenstein and E. H.

Gombrich, was first applied to *Henry V* by Norman Rabkin in "Rabbits, Ducks, and *Henry V,*" *Shakespeare Quarterly* 28 (1977): 279–96; this provided the basis for the chapter on *Henry V* in Rabkin's magnificently challenging *Shakespeare and the Problem of Meaning* (Chicago: University of Chicago Press, 1981), 33–62.

11. Stephen Orgel, ed., *The Tempest* (Oxford: Oxford University Press, 1987), 12. For an exemplary illustration of how much can depend on staging, see the discussion of different stagings of the scene in which Henry offers Williams money, in Robert Hapgood, *Shakespeare the Theatre-Poet* (Oxford: Clarendon Press, 1988), 138–44. The analogy from quantum physics has appealed both to Norman Rabkin, in *Shakespeare and the Common Understanding* (New York: Free Press, 1967)—a title that alludes to Robert Oppenheimer's *Science and the Common Understanding*—and to Philip C. McGuire in *Speechless Dialect: Shakespeare's Open Silences* (Berkeley: University of California Press, 1985); as McGuire puts it, the "transition from the possible to the actual, from multifaceted potentiality to single eigenstate, is a quantum leap, a leap into actuality out of an aggregate of potentialities" (137).

12. The script for Olivier's film was published and discussed in *Film Scripts One* (New York: Appleton-Century-Crofts, 1971), ed. George P. Garrett, O. B. Hardison, Jr., and Jane R. Gelfman; further details are provided in Harry M. Geduld, *Filmguide to Henry V* (Bloomington: University of Indiana Press, 1973). I am grateful to Anthony Brennan, who is himself preparing a book on *Henry V,* for providing me with precise details of the Branagh cuts before I was able to see the film and before Branagh published his script (London: Chatto & Windus, 1990). Branagh's cuts also made room for the interpolations—above all the ludicrously extended and sentimental battle scenes, which turn the film into an also-*Ran*. See note 14.

13. Interestingly enough, the film script suggests that the intention of this close-up was to focus, thrillingly, on the royal rings (133); the effect is more complicated, I think.

14. Gary Taylor, ed., *Henry V* (Oxford: Clarendon Press, 1982), 32. Apart from this, the only other bloodshed in Shakespeare's play is in 5.1, where Fluellen leaves Pistol with a "broken" and "ploodie" head and "cudgeld scarres" to come. Productions tend to play down what the text clearly indicates is a savage beating—while doing what they can to provide those thrilling battle scenes and onstage combats which Shakespeare, on this occasion, so pointedly *refuses* to provide. For an intricate, illuminating account of Shakespeare's treatment of battles in this and other plays, see Anthony Brennan, *Onstage and Offstage Worlds in Shakespeare's Plays* (London and New York: Routledge, 1989), 131–70 and 173–208.

15. J. C. Walters, ed., *Henry V* (London: Methuen, 1954), 78n.

16. The prominence and significance of rape imagery in this play is discussed in L. Wilcox, "Katherine of France as Victim and Bride," *Shakespeare Studies* 17 (1985): 61–76, and in C. L. Barber and Richard Wheeler, *The Whole*

Journey: Shakespeare's Power of Development (Berkeley: University of California Press, 1986), 218–21.

17. See Karl P. Wentersdorf's important article "The Conspiracies of Silence in *Henry V*," *Shakespeare Quarterly* 27 (1976): 264–87. In Holinshed the conspirators remain silent; it is Shakespeare who decides that they should speak, and in this puzzling fashion.

18. Harry Berger discusses the 'displacement" of the King's guilt in "What Did the King Know and When Did He Know It? Shakespearean Discourses and Psychoanalysis," *South Atlantic Quarterly* 88 (Fall 1989): 811–62: see especially 812–13, 853–58. In an earlier, interesting essay Berger had considered the "displacement" as "detextualization": "Sneak's Noise, or Rumor and Detextualization in 2 Henry IV," *Kenyon Review* 6 (Fall 1984): 58–78.

19. The fascinating relationship between Kurosawa's *The Bad Sleep Well* and *Hamlet* deserves a more extended discussion. However, a brief summary that substitutes the Shakespearean names for the Japanese should be enough to suggest how the echoes and far more complicated inversions of *Hamlet* are being used to distinguish the modern, corporate sickness from that in Denmark. Hamlet (Nishi) has discovered that his father was murdered on the orders of Claudius (Iwabuchi), the president of a large and powerful housing corporation. This Hamlet is thoroughly ruthless in his revenge, and dismisses the suggestion that he is becoming like what he is trying to destroy: as he tells Horatio (Itakuro), there is no other way of destroying Claudius, and to rely on the law would be a form of suicide since the processes of justice are controlled by Claudius and his political accomplices. When the film begins, Hamlet's revenge is almost complete: to gain the information he needs he has married Ophelia, who is the daughter not of Polonius (Moriyama) but of Claudius himself. Hamlet has become Claudius's son-in-law rather than stepson; Ophelia's brother Laertes (Tatsuo) is a playboy who, as the complicated plot unfolds, threatens both Hamlet and Claudius, as in Shakespeare's play. The first scene is a quite extraordinarily sustained tour de force, set in the corporation building where the lavish wedding party is taking place: this first recalls the second scene of *Hamlet* and then (before we can understand what is happening) turns into the "Mousetrap"—watched by the impassive, thoroughly controlled Hamlet, while the police and press wait outside. The most wrenching inversion comes when, after he has so cold-bloodedly married a woman he does not love, Hamlet falls in love with Ophelia, and confides in her. She unwittingly betrays his hiding place, and we never see Hamlet again. Horatio and Ophelia are powerless, and the devastating final sequence shows a suddenly obsequious Claudius telephoning an unnamed but *very* highly placed politician, assuring him that all is well, and arranging to take a holiday. There is a "wipe" and the title reappears: *The Bad Sleep Well.* Hamlet's Denmark seems hopeful in comparison.

Holinshed records that Henry V "slept verie little, but that verie soundly."

20. G. K. Hunter, "Truth and Art in History Plays," *Shakespeare Survey* 42 (Cambridge: Cambridge University Press, 1990): 15–24, 18–19.

21. Raphael Holinshed, *Chronicles of England, Scotland and Ireland*, 6 vols. (London, 1808), 3:132–33. As Phyllis Rackin usefully emphasizes in her important study *Stages of History: Shakespeare's English Chronicles* (London and New York: Routledge, 1990), the chronicles are the product of collaborative effort in which we hear a "plurality of voices": they "included the work of many writers—predecessors whose work was incorporated, successors who augmented the narratives after their authors' deaths, and collaborators at the time of their production" (23). See F. J. Levy's pioneering work, *Tudor Historical Thought* (San Marino, Calif.: Huntington Library, 1967).

22. See George T. Wright's comments on "squinting lines," which "produce an effect that no manner of printing so far devised can make clear to the reader"; Wright, *Shakespeare's Metrical Art* (Berkeley: University of California Press, 1988), 103.

23. For an excellent discussion of these issues, see Wentersdorf, "Conspiracies of Silence," especially 265–68, 280, 283. As Wentersdorf observes: "If Mortimer and his heirs are to be denied their rights to the crown on the ground that Mortimer is descended from Edward III in the female line, Henry V can scarcely proceed in conscience with his war to obtain the French crown on the basis of a claim likewise through descent in the female line," while "Cambridge and Scroop are challenging Henry V's right to the English throne on grounds at least as convincing as those justifying Henry's challenge to the French king."

The *King John* analogy is particularly interesting, in relation to Sigurd Burckhardt's arresting claim in *Shakespearean Meanings* (Princeton: Princeton University Press, 1968) that "what *King John* presents us with is a world in which authority is wholly untrustworthy" (138), and in which "he that holds his kingdom holds the law" (132). Several essays in Deborah T. Curren-Aquino, ed., *King John: New Perspectives* (London: Associated University Presses; Newark: University of Delaware Press, 1989) take up that challenge, as does David Womersley, "The Politics of King John," *Review of English Studies* 40 (November 1989): 497–515. But Burckhardt himself suggested that the latter history plays became "a kind of holding operation, with the work of discovery going on beneath the surface" (143); as far as *Henry V* is concerned, the important question is whether (as Marsha Robinson's essay in *King John: New Perspectives* assumes) the later play disregards the earlier play's challenging "discovery," and in this sense goes backward. This is what Annabel Patterson seems to think happened even between the Folio and Quarto versions of *Henry V*, since the Quarto eliminates so much of what I have called the historiographical challenge in the Folio; see Patterson, "Back by Popular Demand: The Two Versions of *Henry V*," in *Shakespeare and the Popular Voice* (Oxford and New York: Blackwell, 1989), 71–92, and the earlier version of this chapter in the 1989 volume of *Renaissance Drama*. However, since we do not know why these cuts were made, Patterson's argument reinforces the authority of the Folio text as the Shakespearean *Henry V.*

24. Alexander Leggatt, *Shakespeare's Political Drama* (London and New York: Routledge, 1988), 115.

25. "Thou art a blessed fellow to think as every man thinks," Hal wryly observes to Poins. "Never a man's thought in the world keeps the roadway better than thine" (*2H4*, 2.2.56–59). I do not want to deny that there were roadways; yet we should not assume that Shakespeare and every member of his audiences kept to them, or that establishing what they were and where they ran is a straightforward matter of consulting official maps—that is, discovering what those in authority said people should believe.

Would Elizabethans, for instance, have been repelled by the "incestuous" marriage of Claudius and Gertrude? Although nobody in *Hamlet* apart from the Ghost and Hamlet seem troubled enough to mention it, Harold Jenkins admits no doubt in his edition of Hamlet (London: Methuen, 1982): the relationship was incestuous, and repellent, because the Leviticus-based Elizabethan law condemned such unions. He doesn't explain why the *other* relevant biblical text considers the question when an unmarried brother *should* marry a deceased brother's widow; chap. 7 of John Scarisbrick, *Henry VIII* (London: Eyre and Spottiswoode, 1968) provides a magisterial account of the significance of these conflicting texts (Lev. 18.16, 20.21; Deut. 25.5) in relation to Henry's busy marital itinerary. As it happens, the corresponding Scottish law was, until very recently, still based on Leviticus: like the Elizabethan law, it made no distinction between sleeping with one's sister and with one's sister-in-law. The law was finally changed, since many Scots thought there was a difference, and thought it important; but Jenkins's argument about "the" Elizabethan audience would also oblige him to deny that contemporary Scots could think any such thing—until that moment when the law was changed, and suddenly they all thought and felt differently!

26. See Christopher Hibbert, *Agincourt* (London: Batsford, 1975), 33, and the telling discussion in Graham Holderness, Nick Potter, and John Turner, *Shakespeare: The Play of History* (London: Macmillan Press; Iowa City: University of Iowa Press, 1988), 63–67. Holinshed records that "soldiers were ransomed, and the towne sacked, to the great gain of the Englishmen," and warily mentions that others have made "mention of the distresses whereto the people, then expelled out of their habitations, were driven" (73–74); two thousand of the town's poor and infirm were expelled, and each was allowed to take no more than a small bundle and five sous.

Shakespeare's departure from his historical source material at this point is admittedly problematic. Some see it as evidence of a hagiographical determination to idealize power. In that case it's hard to understand why Shakespeare made Henry's speech so ruthless—and followed it with the governor's dignified and deflating speech, where the reason given for the surrender is the failure of reinforcements to arrive at the expected time. My own view is that the change is being assimilated to a long-range exploration of ends and means. The "Henriad" exposes short memories: many who would defend the Harfleur speech by arguing that Henry wanted to save lives would balk at defending Prince John's treacherous treatment of the rebels at Galtree, which also saves the lives of loyal soldiers. Moreover, in having Henry forbid looting, Shakespeare suggests the disquietingly ironic view that (as Hibbert's study confirms) the spoils of war were being reserved for the rulers and officers. Someone like Williams gets nothing at all, unless he accepts what the King and Fluellen give him; Pistol has to accept Fluellen's groat, but his obedience in butchering Le Fer means destitution. As ever, Shakespeare allows a view from the ranks—and a very topical one, since the frequently appalling situation of returning soldiers was something Cecil himself frequently bewailed, without being able to remedy it.

27. Edward Powell, *Kingship, Law, and Society: Criminal Justice in the Reign of Henry V* (Oxford: Clarendon Press, 1989), 233–34.

28. C. G. Cruikshank, *Elizabeth's Army*, 2d ed. (Oxford: Oxford University Press, 1968), chap. 2; Lindsay Boynton, *The Elizabethan Militia* (London: Routledge and Kegan Paul, 1967), chap. 6.

29. Peter Clark, *English Provincial Society from the Reformation to the Revolution* (Brighton: Harvester Press, 1977).

30. A similar pragmatic point might be made about *The Tempest* if, instead of basing our response on whatever general position we take in response to "post-colonial" critiques, we consider the particular characters who would dominate this particular island: Prospero, who will leave the island with no trace of regret once it has served his purpose, yet who is not simply an imperialist villain; Trinculo and Stephano, who have no sponsors; and Caliban, who cannot be considered merely as a dispossessed and much wronged "native" when he wants to rape Miranda and paunch Prospero with a stake.

31. Herbert Lindenberger, *Historical Drama: The Relation of Literature and Reality* (Chicago: University of Chicago Press, 1975), 78. The assumption that Shakespeare is speaking through the Chorus persists, for example in Dollimore and Sinfield's essay on this play, but it has also been challenged in several good discussions of the Chorus's role. See Anthony Brennan, "That Within Which Passeth Show," *Philological Quarterly* 59 (1980): 40–51, and Brennan's more recent chapter on *Henry V* in *Onstage and Offstage Worlds*, 173–208. See also Eamon Grennan, "This Story Shall the Good Man Teach his Son," *Papers on Language and Literature* 15 (1979): 370–82; Gunter Walch, "Henry V as Working-House of Ideology," *Shakespeare Survey* 40 (1988): 63–68. As Walch observes, "The Chorus is an integral part of Shakespeare's strategy not in spite of his information being unreliable, but because it is unreliable, and because what he does not tell us is more important than what he does tell us" (67).

32. Rossiter, *Angel with Horns*, 57; Burckhardt, *Shakespearian Meanings*, 193; Lindenberger quotes these critics in *Historical Drama*.

33. Brennan, *Onstage and Offstage Worlds,* 189.

34. Kenneth Branagh, *Shakespeare: Henry* 5 (London: Chatto & Windus, 1990), 11. Branagh declares the scene "resoundingly unfunny," without considering what the resonances might be if Shakespeare's complex design were regarded as anything more than a vehicle for the ego of actors with a crippling Olivier complex.

35. Quoted in Lindenberger, *Historical Drama,* 78.

36. Phillip Mallett, "Shakespeare's Trickster-Kings: Richard III and Henry V," in P. V. Williams, ed., *The Fool and the Trickster: Studies in Honour of Enid Welsford* (Ipswich and Totowa, N.J.: Brewer, 1979), 64–82; quotation on 80.

37. Brennan, *Onstage and Offstage Worlds,* 182.

38. William Kinderman, *Beethoven's Diabelli Variations* (Oxford: Clarendon Press, 1987). Part 1 traces the process of composition; Part 2 then provides an extended analysis, beginning with a discussion of Beethoven's late compositional style, from which my quotations are taken (63–67).

39. Richard Kearney, *Dialogues with Contemporary Continental Thinkers* (Manchester: Manchester University Press, 1984), 22.

40. Rabkin, *Shakespeare and the Problem of Meaning,* 61; E. H. Gombrich, *Art and Illusion: A Study of the Psychology of Pictorial Representation* (New York: Pantheon Books, 1960), 5–6. Julian Hochberg provides a brief, shrewdly skeptical appraisal of gestalt theory in Richard Gregory, ed., *The Oxford Companion to the Mind* (Oxford: Oxford University Press, 1987), 288–91.

41. Greenblatt, *Shakespearean Negotiations,* 62–63; see my prologue, note 47, for details of earlier versions of this essay, "Invisible Bullets." Greenblatt's modest reluctance to provide such bibliographical details is regrettable, since readers who first encounter the essays in volumes like *Shakespearean Negotiations* and *Learning to Curse* may simply fail to realize that whatever seems familiar and current is so only because the earlier versions had been so influential.

42. J. Hillis Miller, "The Triumph of Theory, the Resistance to Reading, and the Question of the Material Base," *PMLA* 102 (1987): 281–91; quotation on 283. Louis A. Montrose discusses the significance of Miller's presidential address in "Professing the Renaissance: The Poetics and Politics of Culture," H. Aram Veeser, ed., *The New Historicism* (London and New York: Routledge, 1990), 15–36.

43. Stephen Greenblatt, *Renaissance Self-Fashioning: From More to Shakespeare* (Chicago: University of Chicago Press, 1980), 257.

44. Joseph Conrad, *Nostromo,* Everyman Library ed. (London: Dent, 1957), 497. References to the "sustaining illusions" recur throughout Conrad, although I think their relation to Nietzsche has more to do with affinity (and similar responses to Schopenhauer) than with direct influence: see my "Myth, Ethos, and the Heart of Conrad's Darkness," *English Studies* 72 (1991): 160–72.

45. Clifford Geertz, *The Interpretation of Cultures* (New York: Basic Books,

1973), 5. The fertilizing relation between new historicism and Geertzian cultural anthropology is well represented in James Clifford and G. E. Marcus, eds., *Writing Culture: The Poetics and Politics of Ethnography* (Berkeley: University of California Press, 1987).

46. Clifford Geertz, *Islam Observed* (New Haven: Yale University Press, 1968; Chicago: University of Chicago Press, Phoenix ed., 1971), 97.

47. For a sharp and unconvinced appraisal of Greenblatt's more Foucauldian assumptions, see E. A. J. Honigman, "The New Shakespeare?" *New York Review of Books* (March 31, 1988): 32–35.

48. Greenblatt, *Shakespearean Negotiations*, 22. It is worth noticing, by way of anticipating more important differences, that British cultural materialists like Dollimore have tended to follow Keith Thomas in supposing that atheism was not unknown in the Renaissance. For Greenblatt, "there is no justification" for dismissing Machiavelli's or Montaigne's professions "of faith as mere hypocrisy"; in *Radical Tragedy*, Dollimore's account of Montaigne's essay "On custom" is very different, and even suggests that Montaigne's thinking is virtually "identical" with Althusser's (17)! That either critic should feel so certain about what goes on in "l'arrière pensée" is rather surprising.

49. For other examples of the (limited) strategies for "getting past" the censors, see Christopher Hill, "Censorship and English Literature," in *Collected Essays of Christopher Hill*, vol. 1: *Writing and Revolution in Seventeenth-Century England* (Brighton: Harvester Press, 1986), 32–71. In this fine essay Hill suggests that the ending of ecclesiastical control may have been "the most significant event in the history of seventeenth-century English literature" (40), and inclines to Glynne Wickham's view that "the decadence of Jacobean and Caroline drama was due in far greater measure to censorship than to the inadequacy of dramatists" (39). When the lid of censorship was lifted, briefly, in the early 1640s, Cromwell himself was appalled by what was revealed—including the memorable remark that the only heaven is woman, and marriage the only hell. This "late printing age" finished in 1660, with the restoration of censorship, ecclesiastical control, and other evils.

Again, it's worth noticing the contrast with British cultural materialists, who are much concerned with censorship. New historicist proponents of the theory of containment have no obvious line of defense against the criticism advanced by Anthony Dawson in "*Measure for Measure*, New Historicism, and Theoretical Power," *Shakespeare Quarterly* 39 (1988): 328–41: "If censorship was necessary, and from the point of view of the authorities it clearly was, then this fact alone suggests that there were rifts and faults in the apparently seamless strata of power, and suggests further that the argument about containment simply doesn't hold" (333). A further difficulty, as Stephen L. Collins shows, is that so few new historicists consider how the ideology of state power was still evolving in this period; see Collins, *From Divine Cosmos to Sovereign State: An Intellectual History of Consciousness and the Idea of Order in Renaissance England* (Oxford: Oxford University Press, 1989). Far from being static, or fully articulated, its history was complicated and dynamic; as both Collins and Edward Pechter (see note 52) complain, new historicist literary criticism too often treats its "historical" material (or anecdotes) as though history provided a stable referent untouched by historical process or human agency.

The most thoroughly documented discussion of the effects of Tudor and Stuart censorship on the drama is to be found in Clare, *"Art Made Tongue-Tied by Authority."* If this book does not put paid forever to the new historicist theory of containment, that will tell us the extent to which the professionalized study of "English," instead of resembling other disciplines where opposed theories and paradigms supersede each other in a structured way, now resembles an amusement park for protected species.

50. A direct avowal of atheism was in effect a criminal confession: atheism was *punished.* As for the distinction between the "unthinkable" and the "unprintable," I have twice had the misfortune to meet academics who thought blacks intellectually inferior but knew that to say this in print would be "unthinkable"—professional suicide. What would we think of a sociological study, based on printed evidence, which concluded that academic racism was "unthinkable" except when ascribed to others?

David Berman, *A History of Atheism in Britain: From Hobbes to Russell* (London and New York: Croom Helm, 1988) suggests that no direct avowal of intellectual atheism was published in England before 1782. To explain why this was preceded by some two centuries of anti-atheistical writing, in which theists repeatedly argued against atheism while at the same time denying that it existed, Berman applies the Freudian distinction between (conscious, deliberate) suppression and (unconscious, irrational) repression.

51. In his *Shakespeare's Soliloquies,* translated (from the German) by Charity Scott Stokes (London and New York: Methuen, 1987), Wolfgang Clemen suggests that a Shakespearean soliloquy might involve "a deliberate attempt to deceive others" (5), but he provides no instance. As far as I can see, such an attempt is never made.

52. Edward Pechter, "The New Historicism and Its Discontents: Politicizing Renaissance Drama," *PMLA* 102 (1987): 292–303. I am indebted to this important essay.

53. Stephen Greenblatt, "Towards a Poetics of Culture," *Southern Review* [Australia] 20 (1987): 3–15. (The essay is reprinted in *Learning to Curse,* 146–60).

54. For Harold Goddard's essay on *Henry V,* see his posthumously titled *The Meaning of Shakespeare,* 2 vols. (Chicago: University of Chicago Press, 1951), 215–68.

55. Sherman Hawkins, "Aggression and the Project of the Histories," in Norman Holland, Sidney Homan, and Bernard J. Paris, eds., *Shakespeare's Personality* (Berkeley: University of California Press): 41–65. Queen Elizabeth's remark is too frequently quoted out of context, and as though it were made shortly after, not months after, the private performance of Shake-

speare's *Richard II* on the eve of the Essex rising. There's no evidence that the royal displeasure on that occasion extended to Shakespeare, just as there's no evidence that the deposition scene was ever performed in Elizabeth's reign.

56. An "impossible object" is a drawing of a solid figure that cannot exist because it embodies self-contradictory elements. In his preface to Roger Penrose, *The Emperor's New Mind: Concerning Computers, Minds, and the Laws of Physics* (Oxford University Press: New York, 1989), Martin Gardner describes how the young Penrose discovered the "tribar," which he and his father, Lionel, then turned into the Penrose Staircase—the structure used by Maurits Escher in his lithographs *Ascending and Descending* and *Waterfall:* "One day when Penrose was lying in bed, in what he called a 'fit of madness', he visualized an impossible object in four-dimensional space. It is something, he said, that a four-space creature, if it came upon it, would exclaim 'My God, what's that?'"

57. Melvin Konner, *The Tangled Wing: Biological Constraints on the Human Spirit* (London: Weidenfeld and Nicholson; New York: Holt, Rinehart & Winston, 1982), especially 103–5; see also my comments in *Shakespeare Scepticism,* 156–58.

58. In a contemporary, rather than Shakespearean, context, the overtly anti-Christian stance taken by Greenblatt and a few other critics like Jonathan Culler is critically and morally courageous precisely because it is so unrepresentative of what the vast majority of Americans evidently believe. For pungent commentaries, see Gary Wills, *Under God: Religion and American Politics* (Hemel Hempstead: Simon and Schuster, 1992), and Culler, "Political Criticism: Confronting Religion," in *Framing the Sign: Criticism and Its Institutions* (Oxford: Basil Blackwell; Norman: University of Oklahoma Press, 1988), 69–84. The recent, unprecedentedly thorough survey of religious affiliation in the United States commissioned by the City University of New York suggests that no more than 8 percent of Americans are atheists or agnostics; 26.2 percent are Roman Catholic, while 60.2 percent are "other Christian" (predominantly Protestant) and only 3.7 percent belong to non-Christian religions including Judaism (2 percent). For an angry and sensibly frightened account of the Christian Right's infrastructure—including some 470 television stations, 1,300 radio stations, 300 periodicals, 6,000 Christian bookstores, 17,000 schools and 250 colleges, universities, and seminaries—see Ellen Messer-Davidow, "The Right Moves: Conservatism and Higher Education," in Betty Jean Craige, ed., *Literature, Language, and Politics* (Athens: University of Georgia Press, 1988), 54–83.

59. See Mary McCarthy, *Medina* (London: Wildwood House, 1973), 80–85.

60. C. S. Lewis, *English Literature in the Sixteenth Century, Excluding Drama* (Oxford: Clarendon Press, 1954), 230; Greenblatt, *Renaissance Self-Fashioning,* 136.

61. Steven Mullaney, *The Place of the Stage: License, Play, and Power in Renaissance England* (Chicago: University of Chicago Press, 1988), 52.

62. Mullaney emphasizes his indebtedness to Raymond Williams. The kind of model he finds attractive and useful in British Marxist criticism derives from Williams and E. P. Thompson; it is well represented by the following passage from the essay "Subcultures, Cultures, and Class," in Stuart Hall and Tony Jefferson, eds., *Resistance through Rituals* (London: Hutchinson, 1976), 12: "The dominant culture of a complex society is never a homogeneous structure. It is layered, reflecting different interests within the dominant class (e.g., an aristocratic versus a bourgeois outlook), containing different traces from the past (e.g., religious ideas within a largely secular culture), as well as emergent elements in the present. Subordinate cultures will not always be in open conflict with it. They may, for long periods, coexist with it, negotiate the spaces and gaps in it, make inroads into it, 'warrening it from within'." See *Marxism and Literature* (Oxford: Oxford University Press, 1978), chap. 8; Mullaney, *The Place of the Stage*, 15.

63. Frederick Crews, *Skeptical Engagements* (New York: Oxford University Press, 1986), 179.

64. Luc Ferry and Alain Renaut, *French Philosophy of the Sixties: An Essay on Antihumanism,* trans. Mary Schnackenberg Cattani (Amherst: University of Massachusetts Press, 1990), 19–20; originally published as *La pensée 68: Essai sur l'anti-humanisme contemporain* (Paris: Gallimard, 1984).

65. Collins, "Where's the History in the New Literary Historicism?" 241.

66. Jonathan Dollimore and Alan Sinfield, "History and Ideology: The Instance of *Henry V,*" in John Drakakis, ed., *Alternative Shakespeares* (London: Methuen, 1985), 206–27; quotation on 211–12.

67. Quoted from Derrida's interview with Richard Kearney in Kearney's *Dialogues with Contemporary Continental Thinkers: The Phenomenological Heritage* (Manchester and Dover, N.H.: Manchester University Press, 1985), 119–20.

68. Jonathan Dollimore and Alan Sinfield, in their foreword to *Political Shakespeare: New Essays in Cultural Materialism* (Manchester: Manchester University Press; Ithaca: Cornell University Press, 1985), vii–viii.

69. Catherine Belsey, *Critical Practice* (London: Routledge and Kegan Paul, 1980), 128. In Belsey's more recent book, *John Milton: Language, Gender, Power* (Oxford and New York: Blackwell, 1988), her insistence that readings "produce" meaning, and that books are not produced by autonomous individuals, produces a kind of two-tier system. She feels obliged to put Milton's name in scare-quotes, but not her own. To establish why it is so misleading to regard "Milton" or "Shakespeare" as an authoritative author Belsey would think it sufficient to cite Macherey, Althusser, and the other theorists she regards as genuinely authoritative authors.

70. Ted Hughes, "The summoner," *Cave Birds* (London: Faber and Faber, 1978), 8.

71. Dollimore and Sinfield are referring to Philip Edwards, *Threshold of a Nation: A Study in English and Irish Drama* (Cambridge: Cambridge University

Press, 1979). In his lively account of the spread of Tudor imperialism, Edwards assumes that *Henry V* must also be seen in these terms: "Shakespeare's story of what happened in France would be universally accepted as what was to happen in their own terms, especially in Ireland" (82). "Universally" begs one question, "accepted" begs another.

72. For M. T. Clanchy's criticism that Powell's *Kingship, Law, and Society* is too uncritically pro-Henry, and Powell's reply, see the *Times Literary Supplement*, March 23 and the correspondence column for April 7, 1990.

73. Machiavelli, *The Prince*, trans. Harvey Mansfield, Jr. (Chicago: University of Chicago Press, 1985), 71.

74. Taylor, ed., *Henry V*, 55.

75. So, to take a painfully gross example, in the 1984 RSC production Bardolph was garroted on stage by Exeter, in front of Branagh's Henry, and in Branagh's film there is a seemingly interminable hanging. As Branagh explains in *Players of Shakespeare*, vol. 2: *Further Essays in Shakespearean Performance*, ed. R. Jackson and R. Smallwood (Cambridge: Cambridge University Press, 1988): "Bardolph must die but not, I felt, without intense cost to the King" (1903). That is, the alleged dramatic point is not to make us more aware of the "intense cost" to Bardolph, but to give us plenty of time to concentrate on the silently agonizing Star. Branagh embellishes this starry fantasy in *Beginnings* (London: Pan Books; New York: Norton, 1990), solemnly explaining that the "cost to the King is enormous," so that "tears stain his cheeks" (71, 73).

76. Arthur Sherbo, ed., *Johnson on Shakespeare* (New Haven and London: Yale University Press, 1968), 565: "I know not why Shakespeare now gives the King nearly such a character as he made him formerly ridicule in Percy. . . . The truth is, that the poet's matter failed him in the fifth act, and he was glad to fill it up with whatever he could get." For an excellent reappraisal of Johnson's Shakespeare criticism, see G. F. Parker, *Johnson's Shakespeare* (Oxford: Clarendon Press, 1989).

77. Stephen Booth, "Syntax as Rhetoric in *Richard II*," *Mosaic* 10 (1977): 87–103.

78. Jonas Barish, *The Antitheatrical Prejudice* (Berkeley: University of California Press, 1983).

79. Beauman, *Royal Shakespeare Company's "Henry V,"* 56.

80. R. Jackson and R. Smallwood, eds., *Players of Shakespeare*, 2:104.

81. *Antony and Cleopatra*, 5.2.2: Cleopatra continues, "Not being Fortune, he's but Fortune's knave." In *Radical Tragedy: Religion, Ideology, and Power in the Drama of Shakespeare and His Contemporaries* (Brighton: Harvester Press, 1984), Jonathan Dollimore blocks out this play's perspectives on the littleness of power by arguing that Antony is worried about sexual impotence, and that Octavius Caesar is the sexually commanding figure. This argument may seem

strange until one sees that sex is really all about power, while power is what is really sexy.

CHAPTER TWO

1. Arnold Schoenberg, *Style and Idea* (London: Faber & Faber, 1975), 165; *Fundamentals of Musical Composition* (London: Faber & Faber, 1967), 1–2.

2. The double-time theory was first outlined by John Wilson ("Christopher North") in *Blackwood's Magazine*, November 1849; April, May 1850. For editorial discussions see note 22. It's worth remembering that Dr. Johnson had commended the unity of time: "Had the scene opened in Cyprus, and the preceding incidents been occasionally related, there had been little wanting to a drama of the most exact and scrupulous regularity."

3. I discuss Shakespeare's treatment of the Duke and Barnardine more fully in *Shakespeare's Scepticism* (London: St. Martin, 1987), 164–218.

4. Stanley Cavell, *Must We Mean What We Say?* (New York: Scribner's, 1969), 213–37. A. D. Nuttall's essay "Did Meursault Mean to Kill the Arab? The Intentional Fallacy Fallacy" (1968) is reprinted in Nuttall, *The Stoic in Love: Selected Essays on Literature and Ideas* (New York and London: Harvester Wheatsheaf, 1989), 191–202. See also W. K. Wimsatt and Monroe C. Beardsley, "The Intentional Fallacy," *Sewanee Review* 54 (1946): 468–88; reprinted in David Newton-De Molina, ed., *On Literary Intention: Critical Essays* (Edinburgh: Edinburgh University Press, 1976).

5. Ser Giovanni, *Il Pecorone* (1558), trans. in Geoffrey Bullough, ed., *Narrative and Dramatic Sources of Shakespeare*, 8 vols. (London: Routledge and Kegan Paul, 1957), 1:463–76; and in Theodore Spencer, ed., *Elizabethan Love Stories* (London: Penguin, 1968), 177–96.

6. See A. J. A. Waldock, *Sophocles the Dramatist* (Cambridge: Cambridge University Press, 1951), 11–24.

7. Harold C. Goddard, *The Meaning of Shakespeare*, 2 vols. (Chicago: University of Chicago Press, 1951), 1:96–101; A. D. Moody, *Shakespeare: "The Merchant of Venice"* (London: Edward Arnold, 1964), 30. For discussion of the polarized critical debate about Shylock, see Norman Rabkin, *Shakespeare and the Problem of Meaning* (Chicago: University of Chicago Press, 1981), 1–32.

8. John Palmer, *Political and Comic Characters of Shakespeare* (London: Macmillan, 1964), 429. Palmer's discussion first appeared in 1946.

9. John Russell Brown, "Love's Wealth and 'The Merchant of Venice,'" reprinted in *The Merchant of Venice Casebook*, ed. J. Wilders (London: Macmillan Press, 1969), 175.

10. See the discussion of apprehending and comprehending in my *Shakespeare's Scepticism*, 32–49.

11. Stephen Booth, ed., *Shakespeare's Sonnets* (New Haven: Yale University Press, 1977) explores countless instances: see, for example, the brilliant com-

mentary on Sonnet 8, lines 5–8 (145–46). There is probably no edition more provoking to readers who are in the habit of treating a poem as though it were a Reuters dispatch or message in code, and want to know what the poem is "really" saying.

12. For both readings, see Stephen Greenblatt, ed., *The Power of Forms in the English Renaissance* (Norman: University of Oklahoma Press, 1982), 72–73, 79; compare Greenblatt, *Renaissance Self-Fashioning: From More to Shakespeare,* (Chicago: University of Chicago Press, 1980), 231–32. As for Berger's account of draining, it may be worth remarking that people usually recover from making love, and sometimes feel better for it.

13. This relationship was picked up in Ninagawa's remarkable 1985 production of *Macbeth*, as I remarked in a review, *Times Literary Supplement* (September 13, 1985): 1004. After being brutally sliced from nave to chops by Macduff's samurai sword, Ninagawa's Macbeth gradually assumed, and died in, a fetal position.

14. Raphael Holinshed, quoted in Kenneth Muir, ed., *Macbeth*, New Arden ed. (London: Methuen, 1959), 179; for a discussion of Shakespeare's treatment of Duncan, see my *Shakespeare's Scepticism*, 244–50.

15. See Harold Jenkins, ed., *Hamlet*, New Arden ed. (London: Methuen 1982), 123. I discussed the critical shortcomings of this edition in "Hamlet in the Prison of Arden," *London Review of Books* 4, no. 16 (1982): 12–14.

16. See my discussion in *Shakespeare's Scepticism*, 115–17.

17. Norman Malcolm, *Ludwig Wittgenstein: A Memoir* (Oxford: Oxford University Press, 1967), 66: "Imagine that there is a town in which the policemen are required to obtain information from each inhabitant, e.g., his age, where he came from, and what work he does. A record is kept of this information and some use is made of it. Occasionally when a policeman questions an inhabitant he discovers that the latter does not do any work. The policeman enters this fact on the record, because this too is a useful piece of information about the man!" The parable was a response to the A. J. Ayer version of logical positivism, but it has a wider application.

18. Since Horatio has been specifically instructed to watch to see whether the King betrays his guilt, his comment "Half a share" (3.2.273) suggests some lingering uncertainty about the success of the Mousetrap.

19. Francis Meres's famous list of "the best for Comedy among us" includes Shakespeare and "Anthony Mundye our best plotter." Munday evidently relished the problem case of the Jew and his bond, and provided two versions— first as the author of *Zelauto* (1580) and then as the translator of Alexander Silvayn's *The Orator* (1596), where Declamation 95 concerns "a jew who would for his debt have a pound of the flesh of a Christian." *The Orator* is a lively and impressive work, above all because it repeatedly presents conflicts where both parties have a case, and refrains from adjudicating between them (or resorting to Portia-like tricks): all the interest is in the problem. Now that *The Merchant* is thought to have been staged in 1597, not earlier, it is more

likely that Shakespeare wrote his play after reading *The Orator*, which also contains problem situations analogous to those in *Measure for Measure* and *Pericles*.

20. Marvin Spevack, *A Complete and Systematic Concordance to the Works of Shakespeare*, 9 vols. (Hildesheim: Georg Olms, 1969–1980), 1:36–62.

21. See Ernst Schanzer, *The Problem Plays of Shakespeare: A Study of Julius Caesar, Measure for Measure, Antony and Cleopatra* (London: Routledge, 1963), 1–9.

22. See the discussions in M. R. Ridley, ed., *Othello*, New Arden ed. (London: Methuen, 1965), lxvii–lxx, and Norman Sanders, ed., *Othello*, New Cambridge ed. (Cambridge: Cambridge University Press, 1984), 14–17. These views are less skeptical than those in H. H. Furness, ed., *Othello*, New Variorum ed. (Philadelphia: Lippincott, 1886), 358–72.

23. Jane Adamson, *"Othello" as Tragedy: Some Problems of Judgment and Feeling* (Cambridge: Cambridge University Press, 1980), 7.

24. Richard Levin, "Shakespearean Defects and Shakespeareans' Defenses," in Maurice Charney, ed., *"Bad" Shakespeare: Revaluations of the Shakespeare Canon* (London: Associated University Presses; Rutherford, N.J.: Farleigh Dickenson University Press, 1988), 23–36.

25. See my epilogue, "Verdi and Boito as Translators," in James Hepokoski, *Giuseppe Verdi: Falstaff* (Cambridge: Cambridge University Press, 1983), 152–71. For a discussion of what *Otello* owes to the nineteenth-century continental understanding of Shakespeare, see Hepokoski, "Boito and F.-V. Hugo's 'Magnificent Translation': A Study in the Genesis of the *Otello* Libretto," in Arthur Groos and Roger Parker, eds., *Reading Opera* (Princeton: Princeton University Press, 1988), 34–59.

26. See the very searching chapter "Time and Continuity" in Emrys Jones, *Scenic Form in Shakespeare* (Oxford: Clarendon Press, 1871), especially 41–43 and 54–63.

27. Frank Kermode, introduction to *Othello* in *The Riverside Shakespeare*, ed. G. Blakemore Evans et al., 2 vols. (Boston: Houghton Mifflin, 1974), 2:1199.

28. See John Dover Wilson, ed., *Othello*, New Shakespeare ed. (Cambridge: Cambridge University Press, 1957), xxxi.

29. Harley Granville-Barker, "The Ambiguity in Time: A Parenthesis," in *Prefaces to Shakespeare*, 2 vols. (London: Batsford, 1972), 2:24–30, directs attention to the unobtrusive but numerous indications of time which suggest the passage of a day from early morning to after midnight. Their unobtrusiveness is what seems telling: the point is they seem to emerge, naturally and easily, from the dramatist's own sense of when things are happening. We need not suppose that they are deliberately, consciously inserted.

About half way through 3.3—which extends through the morning just as the "dilatory time" in 2.3 extends through the night—Desdemona appears to fetch Othello to "dinner," that is, the midday meal for which the "generous Islanders / By you invited" are now arriving (280–81). Evidently, this is not just dinner but an official dinner arranged by Othello (we might recall that glimpse of his earlier activities in 3.2 and of letters he has already written), and a dinner that is then being delayed through the rest of this agonizing scene. The solidity of specification appears in those incidental details: there is a sense that as this scenario evolved fleeting matters of detail were considered. (Many great works are not like that: we may wonder but will never know how Don Alfonso persuades a regiment to help him in *Cosí fan tutte,* or why Hamlet didn't see Horatio at his father's funeral.) A few lines later, when Desdemona innocently attributes Othello's "paine upon my Forehead" to lack of sleep—"Why that's with watching, 'twill away againe"—this confirms that Othello spent hours tending Montano; we might not notice the significance of that single word "watching," but it is waiting for us if we look for it. Othello leaves with Desdemona for the dinner; within moments Iago has the handkerchief, impatiently dismisses Emilia, and is about to rush off to plant it in Cassio's lodging when Othello unexpectedly returns. By now Iago knows that time is of the essence, and he would hardly let a week pass without helping Cassio to find that handkerchief and satisfying Othello's demand for "proofes"; here "double-timers" create and then fail to notice another problem, by imagining a period of a "long time" between 3.3 and 4.1. But in 3.4 Cassio enters with the handkerchief and Iago, who has evidently lost no time; and, as Furness noticed, the idea of an appreciable lapse of time between 3.4 and 4.1 is scotched when Bianca returns that handkerchief "you gave me even now" (4.1.149–50). Again, the point is not that we would notice the significance of that "even now" but that its unemphatic casualness (which makes it easy not to notice) suggests how the dramatist is writing from a sure sense of when important matters take place.

30. Barbara Everett discusses this in Everett, *Young Hamlet: Essays on Shakespeare's Tragedies* (Oxford: Clarendon Press, 1989), 208–24, as "one of the best-known and longest-unresolved cruces in the canon," and proposes that the Folio's "damn'd" (Q: "dambd") should read *limn'd.* Sanders's long footnote in the New Cambridge *Othello* takes up most of the page, while the Furness Variorum notes cover five pages.

31. Reported in the Variorum *Othello.*

32. Wilson, in the New Shakespeare *Othello,* dismisses any idea that a suggestion of "premarital incontinence" would have served Iago's purpose, or Shakespeare's (xxxii), since he sees "cuckoldry" as the issue. But of course one might think it remarkably interesting that the *Sonnets, Othello,* and later *The Winter's Tale* all explore a situation in which a man believes that he has been betrayed by the male friend he most loves with the woman he most loves. In *A Lover's Complaint* the situational "rhyme" also allows a greater distancing: now the "Poet" overhears the complaint of an innocent (not "Dark" or "blacke") maid who was seduced by a Bertram-like young man who uses sonnets as part of his seduction technique.

33. "Leavis, *Othello,* and Self-knowledge," *Dutch Quarterly Review* 9 (1979): 218–31.

34. T. R. Nelson and Charles Haines, "Othello's Unconsummated Marriage," *Essays in Criticism,* 33 (1983): 1–18.

35. See Lawrence J. Ross, "Shakespeare's 'Dull Clown' and Symbolic Music," *Shakespeare Quarterly* 17 (1966): 107–28; "The Meaning of Strawberries in Shakespeare," *Studies in the Renaissance* 7 (1960): 225–40; Linda Boose, "Othello's Handkerchief: The Recognizance and Pledge of Love," *English Literary Renaissance* 5 (1975): 360–74. Like Greenblatt, Ross and Boose consider details that might make us doubt whether the marriage ever is consummated, but without drawing that conclusion.

36. Greenblatt, *Renaissance Self-Fashioning,* 251. Although Greenblatt and Edward Snow are both concerned with Othello's "sexual anxiety," their accounts diverge sharply at this point; see note 47, below.

37. Boose is good on this; see note 35, above. François Laroque, in his absorbing discussion of Othello and the festive traditions, analyzes the charivari as one of the instances in which the play offers a "double perspective, alternately comic and tragic, derisive and pathetic"; see Laroque, *Shakespeare's Festive World: Elizabethan Seasonal Entertainment and the Popular Stage* (Cambridge: Cambridge University Press, 1991), 287–89.

38. See H. A. Mason, *Shakespeare's Tragedies of Love* (London: Chatto & Windus, 1970), especially chap. 2, on *Othello.*

39. See Kenneth Burke's discussion of the consubstantiality between Othello and Iago in Burke, *A Grammar of Motives* (New York: Prentice Hall, 1945), 413–14. This is taken up by Greenblatt and by Karen Newman. In Emilia's case, the salutary force and independence of her views of men are so engaging that there is some corrective point in noticing how they complement Iago's cynical misogyny. Burke recalls Coleridge's remark that *rivales* are "opposite banks of the same stream"; that remark is relevant here if we think there is now some danger of sentimentalizing Emilia's "crypto-feminism," remarkable though it is.

40. I discuss this passage further in the appendix.

41. S. N. Garner, "Shakespeare's Desdemona," *Shakespeare Studies* 9 (1976): 232–52. Martin Orkin (see note 43) quotes, and quite properly expects us to disapprove of, A. C. Bradley's suggestion, in *Shakespearean Tragedy* (London: Macmillan, 1960), 165, that "perhaps, if we saw Othello coal-black with the bodily eye, the aversion of our blood, an aversion which comes as near to being merely physical as anything human can, would overpower our imagination and sink us below not Shakespeare only but the audiences of the seventeenth and eighteenth centuries." This sentence concludes the first paragraph of a long, rewardingly complicated footnote. However, the offensive sentence is striking in a different way if we consider what precedes it: "I will not discuss the further question whether, granted that to Shakespeare Othello was a black, he should be represented as a black in our theatres now. I dare say

not. We do not like the real Shakespeare. We like to have his language pruned and his conceptions flattened into something that suits our mouths and minds. And even if we were prepared to make an effort, still, as Lamb observes, to imagine is one thing and to see is another" (ibid.). Taking Bradley's paragraph as a whole, I would say that it recognizes, in a remarkably complicated and even courageous way, that "the real Shakespeare" may be too strong for modern sensibilities, including his own. Bradley sees how the play administers a profound shock, which challenges the audience to overcome that shock by taking something more like Desdemona's view of Othello's "visage." Bradley's assumption that this challenge will be too much for a modern audience (in 1904) seems to me less damaging to the play's dynamics than, say, Barbara Everett's attempts to reduce the shock by arguing for a merely "tawny" Moor or Karen Newman's assumption (see note 44) that we know better than to be shocked by a black Othello. Bradley sees the challenge; Everett and Newman—and Coleridge—deflect it.

42. Bradley's quarrel with Lamb takes up the second paragraph of the footnote discussed in my preceding footnote, and is again worth quoting in full: "As I have mentioned Lamb, I may observe that he differed from Coleridge as to Othello's colour, but, I am sorry to add, thought Desdemona to stand in need of excuse. 'This noble lady, with a singularity rather to be wondered at than imitated, had chosen for the object of her affections a Moor, or black. . . . Neither is Desdemona to be altogether condemned for unsuitableness of the person whom she had selected for her lover' *(Tales from Shakespeare).* Others, of course, have gone much further and have treated all the calamities of the tragedy as a sort of judgment on Desdemona's rashness, wilfulness and undutifulness. There is no arguing with opinions like this; but I cannot believe that even Lamb is true to Shakespeare in implying that Desdemona is in some degree to be condemned. What is there in the play to show that Shakespeare regarded her marriage differently from Imogen's?" That last question is worth putting, but one answer—which Lamb was evidently considering, but Bradley refused to countenance—is that Imogen is alive at the end of her play, while Desdemona isn't.

43. For Coleridge, "it would be something monstrous to conceive this beautiful Venetian girl falling in love with a veritable negro. It would argue a disproportionateness, a want of balance, in Desdemona, which Shakespeare does not appear to have in the least contemplated"; T. M. Raysor, ed., *Coleridge's Shakespearean Criticism,* 2 vols. (London: Dent, 1960), 1:42. (Raysor questions the authenticity of this passage, "certainly in part and perhaps even as a whole.") It is easy to assemble such quotations, and they are angrily dissected by Martin Orkin in "Othello and the 'Plain Face' of Racism," *Shakespeare Quarterly* 38 (1987): 166–88. Barbara Everett's argument for a tawny "Spanish" Othello was originally developed in "'Spanish' Othello: The Making of Shakespeare's Moor," *Shakespeare Survey* 35 (1982), and is reprinted in Everett, *Young Hamlet,* 186–207. Apparently, when tawny Spanish Moors say "I am

black" (3.3.262) we should regard that as an unhappy exaggeration: poor tawnies don't know better?

44. See Karen Newman's vigorous and challenging essay, "'And Wash the Ethiop White': Femininity and the Monstrous in *Othello*," in Jean E. Howard and Marion O'Connor, eds., *Shakespeare Reproduced: The Text in History and Ideology* (London and New York: Methuen, 1987), 143–62. Newman cites Orkin's essay but doesn't explain why she disagrees with his comment that the racist sentiment in the play is "to an important degree confined to Iago, Roderigo and Brabantio" (168).

45. Granville-Barker, *Prefaces to Shakespeare*, 2:17. The shocked Dover Wilson found this "incredible": "True, they [Othello's lines] are spoken before the wedding night, but by this placing of them Shakespeare surely meant to emphasize what Othello has said already at 1.3.26ff."; Wilson, New Shakespeare *Othello*, xxii. As usual, the word "surely" signals wishful thinking.

46. Compare "Have you quit the mines? have the pioners given o'er?" (*Henry V*, 3.2.86–87) and "Well said, old mole? canst work i'the earth so fast? A worthy pioner!" (*Hamlet*, 1.5.162–63).

47. Edward Snow, "Sexual Anxiety and the Male Order of Things in Othello," *English Literary Renaissance* 10 (1980): 384–412. For Snow, the murder "involves a repetition and undoing of the sexual experience." As this suggests, his argument overlaps with Greenblatt's at many points (each acknowledges the other), but Snow objects to Greenblatt's emphasis on the Christian doctrine that supposedly governs Othello's sexual attitudes: "Greenblatt has an especially acute discussion . . . of the theme of confession in *Othello* and its bearing on the play's insights into the malign influence of Christian doctrine on human life. But it is important not to scapegoat Christianity in turn, making it (as Greenblatt seems to do) the 'cause' of sexual disgust" (384). The reasons for the objection are not altogether clear; Snow agrees about Christianity's "malign influence" but doesn't want to see that as the main "cause" of Othello's neurosis. We might also doubt whether Greenblatt's essay ever attributes the "insights" into Christianity's "malign influence" to the play itself. If he thought that, he would presumably offer a different reading, and not suggest in his conclusion that Shakespeare is less radical than Marlowe. He might even have reflected on the dangers in taking a dramatic character together with historical characters in his discussion of Renaissance self-fashioning.

48. F. R. Leavis, "Diabolic Intellect and the Noble Hero: or, The Sentimentalist's Othello," *The Common Pursuit* (London: Chatto & Windus, 1952), 136–59; originally published in *Scrutiny* 6 (1937): 259–83.

49. This is a delicate matter. An Englishman reading the essay cannot but notice it, as an American reader would notice if an English critic's radical reading of Melville ignored twentieth-century American criticism.

50. See Martin Elliott, *Shakespeare's Invention of Othello* (London: Macmillan;

New York: St. Martin's Press, 1988), which provides some remarkably detailed and perceptive "close" readings of Othello's language.

51. F. R. Leavis, "Measure for Measure," in *The Common Pursuit* (London: Chatto & Windus, 1952), 160–81.

52. Geoffrey Strickland, *Structuralism or Criticism? Thoughts on How We Read* (Cambridge: Cambridge University Press, 1981), 36.

53. See Michael Baxandall, *Painting and Experience in Fifteenth-Century Italy*, 2d ed. (Oxford: Oxford University Press, 1988), pt. 2.

54. For a magnificent study of these and related matters, see Peter Brown, *The Body and Society: Men, Women, and Sexual Renunciation in Early Christianity* (New York: Columbia University Press, 1988).

55. D. S. Bailey, *The Man-Woman Relation in Christian Thought* (London: Longmans, 1959), 137. The "Gawain-poet" was evidently unaware of the theological "state of play" when, in *Cleanness* (lines 697–708), he described God's pride in making sex so pleasurable: "Bytweene a male and his make such merthe schulde come, / Wel nygh pure Paradyse moght prove no better."

56. Ibid., 171–72; see also François Wendel, *Calvin: Origins and Development of His Religious Thought*, trans. Philip Mairet (Durham, N.C.: Labyrinth Press, 1988), 65, for the interesting memorandum where Calvin reflects, "I, whom you see so hostile to celibacy, have never taken a wife." The idea that celibacy confers a higher spiritual state than marriage was of course repudiated by many sixteenth-century humanists. In objecting to the way in which Greenblatt's cento of quotations elides important shifts of emphasis and concern, I am not denying that unease or hostility has characterized Christian teaching on sexual pleasure. Bailey suggests that "the first express recognition in theological literature of what may be termed the relational purpose of coitus" comes in Jeremy Taylor's *Rules and Exercises of Holy Living*, when Taylor allows that one of the proper "ends" of marital intercourse is "to endear each other" (208).

57. See Craig R. Thompson, *The Colloquies of Erasmus* (Chicago: University of Chicago Press, 1965), 86–87.

58. Kenneth Muir, *The Sources of Shakespeare's Plays* (London: Methuen, 1977), 182–96.

59. Even Sonnet 129 could be regarded as a conventional exercise along the lines of Sidney's poem on desire, "Thou blind man's mark," leaving room for a correspondingly conventional distinction between mere desire and true love—or, as D. H. Lawrence prefers to express it in *The Virgin and the Gipsy*, mere "appetite" and true "desire." I myself think this a diminishing view of the sonnet: its quasi-dramatic intensities suggest some more sudden and searingly disillusioned and comprehensive revulsion. But then, if its "intensities" don't "suggest" that to another reader, so that one reading has to be defended against the other, the narrative context doesn't confirm just what has precipitated this passionately unbalanced outcry—and so the poem's quasi-dramatic character becomes more problematic. In sharp contrast, the

standpoint for the operative ironies in Sonnet 130 appears to involve a confident, almost sunnily ironic appeal to nature and adult sexual experience: unless one supposes that the mistress is unpleasantly swarthy, with halitosis and thumpingly flat feet, it seems clear that this poem is mocking the unrealistic expectations of those whose only mistress is their Muse. In other words, whatever had happened to precipitate Sonnet 129 seems forgotten in the next poem, and this interpretative awkwardness is further compounded if we want to establish whether the tone of Sonnet 131 is closer to that of 129 than to that of 130.

This in turn suggests how attempts to reorder the *Sonnets* beg the very question of tonal ambiguity they are trying to resolve: so, John Padel, *New Poems by Shakespeare: Order and Meaning Restored to the Sonnets* (London: Herbert Press, 1981), has already decided how *he* reads Sonnet 129 when he puts it with Sonnet 140 and suggests that, even though Sidney's *Certain Sonnets* 31 and 32 had not yet been published, we "may infer that Sidney's sister had just shown them to Shakespeare and would at once recognize his feat of extempore emulation . . . on or about April 1597." We could take a quite different track if we were concerned with the close parallels between Sonnet 130 and Sonnet 21; nor does that rule out the possibility that either or both of these poems existed independently before Shakespeare himself decided to develop such parallels and "rhymes" in the 1609 Quarto.

60. Bullough, *Narrative and Dramatic Sources*, 7:240.

61. John Salway, "Veritable Negroes and Circumcized Dogs: Racial Disturbances in Shakespeare," in Lesley Aers and Nigel Wheale, eds., *Shakespeare in the Changing Curriculum* (London and New York: Routledge, 1991), 108–24, 116–17.

62. For a contrasting "materialist" account, see Kiernan Ryan, *Shakespeare* (New York and London: Harvester Wheatsheaf, 1989), 51: "The destruction of the love and lives of Othello and Desdemona lays bare the barbarity of a culture whose ruling preconceptions about race and sexuality deny the human right of such a love to exist and flourish." Ryan's engaging account seems committed to the idea that the play is intelligently exposing racist and sexual prejudice—despite his somewhat equivocal next sentence: "The modern significance and value of the play are rooted in this revelation." Why "modern"?

63. For a brilliant account of how metaphors involve us in a conceptual activity, see Mark Turner, *Reading Minds: The Study of English in the Age of Cognitive Science* (Princeton: Princeton University Press, 1991). Turner and George Lakoff discuss the conventional metaphor "Bad is black" in *More than Cool Reason: A Field Guide to Poetic Metaphor* (Chicago: University of Chicago Press, 1989), 184–85.

64. Raysor, ed., *Coleridge's Shakespearean Criticism*, 1:102. My comment on Angelo's last words may be thought too generous, or credulous, if we give weight to the Duke's later comment, when Claudio appears:

By this Lord *Angelo* perceives he's safe,
Methinkes I see a quickning in his eye:
Well *Angelo,* your evill quits you well.
(5.1.492–95)

On the other hand, it is not necessary to attach that meaning to Angelo's response. The Duke cannot know any better than we do whether Angelo feels a more disinterested relief on seeing that Claudio is alive still, when Isabella apparently registers no response at all; in that case, the Duke's markedly ungenerous interpretation of the "quickning" would reveal his own character, and the kind of resentful hostility toward Angelo which he betrayed in the play's third scene.

65. Ludwig Wittgenstein, *Lectures & Conversations on Aesthetics, Psychology, and Religious Belief* (Oxford: Basil Blackwell, 1966; reprint, 1983), 23–27.

EPILOGUE

1. Arthur Sherbo, ed., *Johnson on Shakespeare*, 2 vols. (New Haven and London: Yale University Press, 1968), 2:1047.

2. Jonathan Dollimore and Alan Sinfield, "Cultural Materialism," in Graham Holderness, ed., *The Shakespeare Myth* (Manchester and New York: Manchester University Press, 1988), ix.

3. Jonathan Dollimore, *Radical Tragedy: Religion, Ideology, and Power in the Drama of Shakespeare and His Contemporaries* (Brighton: Harvester Press; Chicago: University of Chicago Press, 1984), 253.

4. Holderness, ed., *Shakespeare Myth*, xiv.

5. Terence Hawkes, *That Shakespeherian Rag* (London and New York: Methuen, 1986).

6. Hugh Grady, *The Modernist Shakespeare: Critical Texts in a Material World* (Oxford: Clarendon Press, 1991), 5.

7. Aristotle, *Politics*, 1245a–b.

8. Arthur Marotti, "John Donne and the Rewards of Patronage," in Guy Fitch Lytle and Stephen Orgel, eds., *Patronage in the Renaissance* (Princeton: Princeton University Press, 1981), 207–34.

9. Charles Altieri, commenting on "the suspicious impulse now dominating literary criticism," says that "the most sensitive of the new historicists would also recognize their own suspicions as perhaps expressing a profound cultural shift which has made it difficult even to entertain seriously those questions which Stevens inherited from Romanticism. Yet too programmatic and generalized a commitment to these demystifying inquiries renders the critics more suspect than Stevens himself. What do they expect of poets, and why do they so rely on political critiques without confronting Stevens' deliberate rejection of the political order? Do they perhaps suppress out of embar-

rassment any need to take responsibility for their own idealizations? And might the commitment to suspicion derive in large part from their method having no language by which to take seriously what writers have to offer?" Altieri, "Why Stevens Must Be Abstract," in Albert Gelpi, ed., *Wallace Stevens: The Poetics of Modernism* (Cambridge and New York: Cambridge University Press, 1985), 86–118; quotation on 86.

10. Hawkes mentions his "early impulse to call the book *Eminent Shakespearians*"; *That Shakespeherean Rag*, ix.

11. In *Shakespeare and the Uses of Antiquity: An Introductory Essay* (London and New York: Routledge, 1990), Charles and Michele Martindale note that of the eleven classical references in the play six, and these the most substantial, are given to Othello (35).

12. Stephen Greenblatt, "Murdering Peasants," reprinted in *Learning to Curse: Essays in Early Modern Culture* (New York and London: Routledge, 1990), 99–130; on Sidney, see 114–19. Anne Barton objects to this essay, and to just about everything else in *Learning to Curse*, in "Perils of Historicism," *New York Review of Books*, March 28, 1991, 51–54.

13. A. W. Schlegel, *A Course of Lectures on Dramatic Art and Literature*, trans. John Black, rev. A. J. W. Morrison (London: Bohn's Library, 1846), 402.

14. Clifford Siskin, *The Historicity of Romantic Discourse* (Oxford: Oxford University Press, 1988); F. R. and Q. D. Leavis, *Dickens the Novelist* (London: Chatto & Windus, 1970), 213–76.

15. The first two chapters of R. B. Pugh, *Imprisonment in Medieval England* (Cambridge: Cambridge University Press, 1968) provide a good account of the earlier uses of imprisonment. Pugh distinguishes three kinds of imprisonment which, in the Middle Ages, often tended to merge—custodial (holding the prisoner until the Quarter Day Sessions or Assizes), punitive (punishment after conviction), and coercive (making the prisoner yield to his captor's will). Most crimes were punished by death, mutilation, outlawry, or cash compensation (all cheaper than imprisonment). Coercive imprisonment as a means of securing the payment into the Exchequer of debts due to the crown was widely practiced in the reign of Henry II, and a 1352 statute placed the common creditor in the same position as the crown, by giving the right to imprison the debtor's body until the debt in dispute was settled.

16. Stephen attacked *Little Dorrit* more than once; the relevant extracts from his *Edinburgh Review* article "The License of Modern Novelists" and from Dickens's "Rejoinder" in *Household Words* are reprinted in Alan Shelston, ed., *Dickens: "Dombey and Son" and "Little Dorrit"* (London: Macmillan, 1985), 118–23. Fitzjames Stephen's father, James Stephen, was Colonial Under-Secretary. In his biography of his brother, Leslie Stephen observes that the assault upon the Circumlocution Office seemed "especially offensive because 'Barnacle Tite,' and the effete aristocrats who are satirised in 'Little Dorrit', stood for representatives of Sir James Stephen and his best friends": Leslie Stephen, *The Life of Sir James Fitzjames Stephen* (London: Smith, Elder, 1895), 159. He

also recalls Carlyle's earlier and rather too pertinent use of the phrase "How Not To Do It" in his *Reminiscences:* "Colonial Office being an Impotency . . . (as Stephen inarticulately, though he never said or whispered it, well knew), what could an earnest and honest kind of man do but try to teach you how not to do it?" (50).

17. Liberals in Britain sometimes assume that the arguments in Mill's *On Liberty* play as important a role in contemporary judicial thinking as in their own. The alternative view, that the English judiciary's attitudes are still better represented by the powerfully illiberal assault on Mill in James Fitzjames Stephen's *Liberty, Equality, Fraternity* (London: Smith, Elder, 1873), is far more consistent with the evidence presented in John Griffith, *The Politics of the Judiciary* (Manchester: Manchester University Press, 1977).

18. See Peter Winch's essay "He's to Blame!" in *Wittgenstein: Attention to Particulars,* ed. Winch and D. Z. Phillips (London: Macmillan Press, 1985; New York: St. Martin's Press, 1989), 151–64.

19. Ludwig Wittgenstein, *Lectures and Conversations on Aesthetics, Psychology, and Religious Belief* (Oxford: Basil Blackwell, 1966; reprint, 1983), 8.

20. Austen Quigley, "Wittgenstein's Philosophizing and Literary Theorizing," *New Literary History* 19 (1988): 209–38; quotation on 228.

21. Donald Davie, *Purity of Diction in English Verse* (New York: Oxford University Press, 1953. Reprint, London: Chatto & Windus, 1967), appendix B; Jean H. Hagstrum, *Samuel Johnson's Literary Criticism* (Minneapolis: University of Minnesota Press, 1952. Reprint, Chicago: University of Chicago Press, 1967), chap. 7.

22. Wittgenstein, *On Certainty,* trans. Denis Paul and G. E. M. Anscombe (Oxford: Basil Blackwell, 1969), 144.

23. T. S. Eliot, "Eighteenth-Century Poetry," in Eliot, *Selected Prose,* ed. John Hayward (London: Penguin, 1953); this is a slightly abridged version of Eliot's introduction to *Johnson's London: A Poem and The Vanity of Human Wishes* (London: Etchell and Macdonald, 1930).

24. Ludwig Wittgenstein, *Tractatus Logico-Philosophicus,* trans. D. F. Pears and B. F. McGuiness (London: Routledge and Kegan Paul, 1961), 6.43, 6.41.

25. Greenblatt, *Learning to Curse,* 60. The subtitle, *Essays in Early Modern Culture,* suggests that Greenblatt has become more squeamish about using the term "Renaissance," which has references more literary and reformist than Greenblatt's own essays can easily accommodate. For a brief yet wonderfully fleet discussion of this, see the epilogue to Jean-Claude Margolin, *L'humanisme en Europe au temps de la Renaissance* (1981), trans. John L. Farthing, *Humanism in Europe at the Time of the Renaissance* (Durham, N.C.: Labyrinth Press, 1989).

26. Greenblatt, *Learning to Curse,* 167.

27. Walter Cohen, "Political Criticism of Shakespeare," in *Shakespeare Reproduced: The Text in History and Ideology,* ed. Jean E. Howard and Marion F. O'Connor (London and New York: Methuen, 1987), 18–46; quotation on 33.

28. Edward Pechter, "The New Historicism and Its Discontents: Politicizing Renaissance Drama," *PMLA* 102 (1987): 292–303; quotation on 301.

29. Barbara Everett, *Young Hamlet: Essays on Shakespeare's Tragedies* (Oxford: Clarendon Press, 1989), 1, 7.

30. See Levin's witty assault on the reductive tendencies of thematic criticism in *New Readings vs. Old Plays: Recent Trends in the Reinterpretation of English Renaissance Drama* (Chicago: University of Chicago Press, 1979).

31. Richard Rorty, "The Historiography of Philosophy: Four Genres," in Rorty, J. B. Schneewind, and Quentin Skinner, eds., *Philosophy in History* (Cambridge: Cambridge University Press, 1984), 49–76; quotation on 62–63.

32. Stephen Greenblatt, *Renaissance Self-Fashioning: From More to Shakespeare* (Chicago: University of Chicago Press, 1980), 256.

33. Clifford Geertz, *The Interpretation of Cultures* (New York: Basic Books, 1973), 44, 49.

34. Stephen Greenblatt, *Shakespearean Negotiations: The Circulation of Social Energy in Renaissance England* (Oxford: Clarendon Press, 1988), 4.

35. F. R. Leavis, "The Responsible Critic: Or the Function of Criticism at Any Time," *Scrutiny* 19 (1953): 162–83; quotation on 173.

36. Stanley Fish's 1985 essay "Anti-professionalism" is collected in *Doing What Comes Naturally* (Oxford: Oxford University Press, 1989), 215–46. Fish's concern with "professionalism" is no less evident when he discusses the rift between new historicist theory and practice; see Fish, "Commentary: The Young and the Restless," in H. Aram Veeser, ed., *The New Historicism* (London and New York: Routledge, 1989), 303–16. Fish argues that since doing history (or criticism) and theorizing about it are different "games" and "logically independent" activities, young and restless new historicists who worry about this are being unprofessional and even antiprofessional. His conclusion is that, instead of worrying, they should "sit back and enjoy the fruits of their personal success, wishing neither for more nor for less . . . in the words of the old Alka-Seltzer commercial, 'try it, you'll like it'" (316).

37. Martha Nussbaum, "Sophistry about Conventions," *New Literary History* 17 (1985): 125–40; quotation on 137.

Index

Subjects

All's Well That Ends Well: and habit of creative interiorization, 132

Antony and Cleopatra: Dollimore on, 301–2; on littleness of power, 144

Atheism: Berman on repression and suppression, 298; Greenblatt on, 83–85, 93–95, 297–99; Machiavelli and Montaigne, 297. *See also* Censorship

Audience: and Brecht, 35, 40, 45, 59; as "collectivity" (Greenblatt), 34–35, 59, 80–81, 84–95, 198; disagreement between Cook and Butler, 34–35, 289–90; divisions in, 32, 44–45, 50–53, 55–59, 109–11, 121–22; and modern directors, 15, 35–37, 290; as monolithic entity (theory of "double time"), 152–53, 163; Mullaney on, 96–98, 300; as queen (Tennenhouse), 28, 34–35, 95–96, 119, 290

Censorship, 34–35, 83–85, 91, 289–90, 297–98

Coercive dualisms: consciousness/social being determinant, 9–10; humanist/materialist, 7, 9, 11–12, 23–24, 30, 99–103, 111–12, 227–28; "humbug"/"official truth," 90, 94, 96; liberal/

dissident, 12–13; margins/center, 254; order/disorder, 101; subversion/containment, 80–83, 86–93, 98–99; text/context, 85–86, 98–99, 247, 254; "unfettered subjectivity"/self as "ideological product," 251–54

Critique. *See* Ideological critique

Cultural materialism. *See* Materialism

Cymbeline: and "negative capability," 38

Doxography, 250–51, 314

Dramatic "rhyming": as form of variational development, 76–77, 145–47. *See also* Sources; *titles of individual works of Shakespeare*

Either/or debates: and dramatic perspectivism, 20–23, 39, 60, 77–80, 115, 121–23, 133, 144, 284, 288, 290–91, 295; ideological recasting of characterological debates, 23, 90–95, 190–201

Hamlet: and *The Bad Sleep Well* (Kurosawa), 43, 292; and dramatic "rhyming," 64; H's letter to Claudius,

Hamlet (*cont.*)
  250; on honor, 79; and incest, 294;
  "Mousetrap," 136–38, 303
Henry IV (*Parts 1 and 2*): Greenblatt on
  different ways of being oneself,
  112–13; and lying 137; Mullaney on
  effect of Hal's initial appearance, 96;
  Rackin on "conservative" preference
  for second tetralogy, 30–31. *See also*
  Henry V: as poetic-dramatic conceit;
  Henry V: "self" as matrix of possible
  selves
Henry V: Branagh's version, 39, 59,
  62–63, 75, 122, 291, 295, 296, 301;
  critical debate reflected in English
  Shakespeare Company production,
  35–37, 91; Dollimore and Sinfield's
  anti-humanist reading, 10–11, 26,
  98–112, 295, 300; Greenblatt on
  containment of subversion, 34–36,
  80–98; Hawkes on the play as chaotic
  site, 18–23; Olivier's version, 18–20,
  37, 39–41, 44, 119, 182, 290–91; as
  poetic-dramatic conceit, 112–22,
  221–22; Rabkin on play as "duck-
  rabbit," 77–80, 90, 290–91; Rackin on
  what attracts "conservative" critics,
  30–31; Tennenhouse on play as
  "vehicle for disseminating court
  ideology," 27–30, 35, 37, 55, 95–96,
  107, 109–12
—complex design: authoritarianism of
  politicized readings, 35–39; as
  dependent on framing of discrepant
  perspectives, 34–46; effect of cuts
  (and interpolations) on structural
  dynamics, 39–41, 62–63, 75, 290–91,
  296, 301
—dramatic "rhyming": between
  Canterbury and King of France, 50;
  compared with three "rhymed" legal
  cases in *Measure for Measure*, 147;
  counterpointing of "high," "low," and
  "high/low" quarrels, 70–74; in first
  "low" scene, 67–70; in long-range
  "rhymes," 42–44, 84–85, 89–90,
  117–22; in rhyming of Chorus and
  Fluellen as amateur historians, 61–62,
  74–75; in structuring of Act V as a
  "rhyming" diptych, 63, 74–76, 108; in
  thefts of a pax, 40–41, 71
—historiographical challenge: absence
  of battle scenes, 291; compared with
  The Famous Victories, 146; and

conditions for conventional resolution,
  76–77; double time, 62–63; and
  dramatic perspectivism, 45–63,
  110–11, 123; effect of "Epilogue," 75;
  Harfleur, speech to and sacking of,
  42, 294–95; Irish campaign, 300–301;
  mythopeic concern with "Englishness,"
  36; nature of army, 57–58; rape
  imagery, 41, 108, 291–92; relation
  between Folio and Quarto texts,
  293–94; and use of chronicles, 32,
  45–47, 53, 62–63, 293; Yorkist
  conspiracy, 59, 104–5, 292–93
—"self" as matrix of possible selves:
  alienating effects of self-staging,
  113–18; Greenblatt's account of both
  as "hypocrites," 7, 42–43, 84–85;
  Hal's increasing isolation, 115–17;
  Henry IV and Hal each plans to "be
  my Selfe" as king, 112–13; "wooing"
  scene, 117–22
Henry VI: Rackin on contrasts between
  first and second tetralogies, 30–31, 50,
  75
Historicism, old and new: Greenblatt's
  account of differences, 245–51; and
  Leavis, 232–39; and Leavis-Bateson
  disagreement, 255; Miller on *annales*
  school, 228; need to historicize "new"
  historicism, 81–83, 86–87, 90, 296;
  and our present, 2, 92–93, 102,
  232–33. *See also* Materialism
Humanism: anti-humanism and
  materialist critics, 11–12, 17–18;
  associated with anti-Semitism, 11, 13,
  16, 286; in French "radicalizations" of
  German philosophy, 97–99; and
  genocide, 16, 106–8; and imperialism,
  10, 300–301; as monolithic ideology,
  2–8, 17, 21, 99–100, 111, 229,
  284–87; and patriarchal oppression,
  109–10; and race, gender, class
  exploitation, 11, 103, 111; and racism,
  103, 210–12. *See also* Materialism

Ideological critique: claims for, 1–8;
  hermeneutics of suspicion, 227–32; as
  a non-ideological account of ideology,
  11–12, 101–3, 111, 230, 239–40;
  Norris and Hirst on perceived failure
  of, 17, 287
Intention: Cavell and "Why this?"
  questions, 126–27; critics' evasion of
  issue, 29–31, 89, 193, 195, 211;

Intention *(cont.)*
  materialists' repudiation of concern
  with intention and authorial meaning,
  18–24, 30, 82–83, 103–4, 110, 300;
  reductive characterizations of
  Shakespeare's intentions, 9, 11–16;
  sources as guide to dramatic
  intentions, 30–32; Strickland on
  evaluation as interpretation, 194. *See
  also* Poetic drama; Sources

Julius Caesar: honor in, 79; marriage in,
  182; as problem play, 144

King John, 30; critical arguments, 293;
  French in, 50; Pandulph, 49
King Lear: blank verse as metaphor,
  179–80; Dollimore on play's
  repudiation of essentialist humanism,
  9, 11–12; dramatic "rhyming," 64;
  "essential" differences between sisters,
  216; Greenblatt's contrast between
  "subversion contained" and
  "containment subverted," 91; "milky
  kindness," 134; Tate's adaptation, 134;
  Tennenhouse on Cordelia dying to
  preserve patriarchal principle, 27,
  109–10

Love's Labour's Lost: compared with
  Sonnets, 203
Lover's Complaint: "rhyming" with *Sonnets*
  in 1609 Quarto, 305

Macbeth: Berger on "milk" as semen,
  134, 303; dramatic "rhyming," 41, 64;
  framing of discrepant perspectives,
  39; Greenblatt on onanism, 134; milk
  in, 134–35, 303–4; Mullaney on
  "complex design," 97; Ninagawa's
  production, 303; on the "Mindes
  construction," 122, 212, 219, 253;
  unseaming and Caesarean birth, 135,
  138, 303
Materialism: conflation of new
  historicism and cultural materialism,
  2, 7, 11, 28–29, 33, 97–101, 228; neo-
  Tillyardian approach, 7–18, 23–24,
  27–28, 32, 103, 107–10; new
  historicist E-effect, 28–30, 90, 95,
  245–47, 249, 252–57; "Them and Us"
  opposition, 28–30, 90, 93–95, 97,
  107–8, 110–12, 210, 254. *See also*

Historicism; Humanism; Intention;
  Poetic drama; Values
Measure for Measure: Angelo's last words
  and Duke's view of him, 217, 310–11;
  Claudio's atheism, 84; Dollimore on
  "reactionary fantasy," 16, 287;
  dramatic "rhyming," 140–48; dynamic
  conception of self, 122, 206, 215–16,
  218; exposure of Escalus, 73;
  Mullaney on "complex design," 97;
  transformation of sources, 125–26,
  132, 141–48, 215–16
Merchant of Venice: handling of time,
  128–30; Jessica's "lie," 130–34,
  137–39, 158; and *Jew of Malta,* 286;
  and *Measure for Measure,* 141, 143–44;
  Anthony Munday's interest in
  situation, 140, 303–4; Shylock and
  Emilia, 172; Shylock as "epicenter,"
  144–45, 214; Sinfield on anti-
  Semitism, 12–16, 285–86; welding of
  sources into poetic-dramatic conceit,
  132, 140, 146; and Wesker's *Merchant,*
  12, 285–86
Meter: as constituent of meaning,
  275–76
Midsummer Night's Dream: Egeus as *senex
  iratus,* 214; lovers' "shaping
  phantasies," 203
Modernized texts, xi–xii, 260–61,
  267–68, 275–82

New Historicism. *See* Historicism

Othello: Bayley on "initial fallacy," 20–23;
  Greenblatt on Othello as deluded
  Christian, 29–32, 128, 163–68, 178,
  190–201, 211, 247, 253, 308, 309;
  ideological recasting of either/or
  debates, 20–23, 190–201; Leavis on
  Othello as deluded egotist, 164, 178,
  190, 191–93, 229, 288, 308; Newman
  on "Elizabethan sex-race system," 183,
  209–12, 308; Norris on "humanist"
  readings, 18, 20–23, 25, 239; Salway
  on "cultural racism," 210–12; Snow on
  "sexual anxiety," 190–91, 200–201,
  306, 308; Verdi's *Otello* as apotheosis
  of 19th-century readings, 148–49, 304
  —black/fair metaphor: and conflict
  between models of self, 214–21; Iago's
  tactic, 219–21; and interpretative
  insecurity, 201–22; racism, 182–83,
  209–12, 306–8, 310; relation to

Othello (*cont.*)

Sonnets, 202–6; and "versions of Iago,"
223–58

—Cinthio's story, 125, 147, 168–90,
206–9; Othello's and Desdemona's
ages, 182–88; "rhymes" and contrasts,
147, 168–72; unconsummated
marriage, 128, 150–51, 163–68, 187,
305, 306, 308

—"double-time" theory, 125, 128, 131,
148–68, 302, 304–5; and audience as
monolithic entity, 152–53; and
confusion about Cassio's "To who?"
and Iago's "a Fellow almost damn'd in
a faire Wife," 156–58, 305

—poetic-dramatic charting of Othello's
collapse, 178–80, 270–75; differences
between Quarto and Folio as reading
texts, 258–64, 275–82; Quarto
hyphens, 258–82

Perspectivism: as framing of discrepant
perspectives, 38–39; gestalt-
experience, 38–39, 41–42, 78–80, 296,
306; in *Merchant*, 14–16; in *Othello*,
168–90; in second tetralogy, 38–45,
46–63, 112–24

Poetic drama: as complex design, 1–2,
14–16, 18–20, 22, 65–66, 75, 98,
139–48; as experiential process over
time, 80, 136; as function of verse and
prose registers, 178–80, 224–26,
265–76; as matrix of meanings, 15,
31, 45; as sustained poetic-dramatic
conceit, 121–22, 178–80, 221–22

"Renaissance": as term, 313

Richard II: Booth on dramatic and
theatrical character, 118–19; Elizabeth
I and the Essex rising, 91, 298–99;
Hotspur and *Henry IV*, 36; lying in,
137; Richard and Henry V as player-
kings, 75; Tennenhouse on, 27

Richard III: accelerated time in, 30, 149,
296

Sermon on the Mount, 207, 216–17

Sonnets: Booth on, 133, 204–5, 302–3;
interpretative uncertainties, 202–7,
309–10; situational "rhyming" with
Othello, Winter's Tale, and *Lover's
Complaint,* 161, 202, 305

Sources: compression of "romance" time
of Italian *novelle*, 125, 128–39,
148–68; departures from as guide to
dramatic intentions, 30–32, 125–39;
in reworking of Chronicles, 41, 45–47,
53, 55, 105, 117, 135–36;
transformations of Cinthio's story of
the Moor, 168–90, 201–22; variational
development, 139–48. *See also*
Dramatic "rhyming"; Intention

Tempest: Caliban as "epicenter," 144–45;
Caliban as Shakespeare's last Moor,
204; dramatic "rhyming," 64–67, 69,
75; Eagleton and Evans on "humanist"
readings, 5–6, 284; Empson's criticism
of Traversi and Kermode, 4–5, 7;
intractability of situation, 69–70, 295

Titus Andronicus: relation to black/fair
metaphor, 203

Tribars, critical, 91–92, 200, 299

Troilus and Cressida: Dollimore on play's
repudiation of essentialist humanism,
9–12; structural dynamics, 123, 224

Values: anti-foundationalist alternatives,
240–43, 255–57, 288, 311, 313;
cultural conspiracy theories, 6–7,
9–12, 244, 255; Greenblatt's concern
with "double link," 245–49, 252–57;
Siskin on being "inside" a culture,
239–40; as socially specific and
historically contingent, 16–17, 25–28,
232, 238–39; Wittgenstein on
describing a culture and "ways of
living," 241

Winter's Tale: contrast with sources, 127;
situational overlap with *Othello* and
Sonnets, 303

Names

Achebe, Chinua, 13, 286
Adamson, Jane, 20, 22, 148, 288, 304
Akenside, Mark, 244
Allen, D. C., 3–4, 6, 84, 283
Althusser, Louis, 17, 97, 287, 297, 300
Altieri, Charles, 311–12
Anikst, Alexander, 286
Aquinas, Thomas, 197
Aristotle, 230, 311
Auden, W. H., 2, 284
Augustine, Saint, 196
Austen, Jane, 233, 240
Ayer, A. J., 303

Bach, J. S., 109–10
Bailey, D. S., 309
Barber, C. L., 291–92
Barish, Jonas, 119, 301
Barton, Anne, 312
Bateson, F. W., 255, 314
Baudrillard, Jean, 26
Baxandall, Michael, 194, 309
Bayley, John, 20–23, 288
Beardsley, Monroe, 126, 302
Beauman, Sally, 290, 301
Becon, Thomas, 197
Beethoven, Ludwig van, 75–77
Belsey, Catherine, 103, 110, 300
Berger, Harry, 5, 134, 284, 285, 292, 303
Berkowitz, Janice, 290
Berman, David, 298
Blake, William, 232, 235, 237–39
Bloom, Harold, 233
Bogdanov, Michael, 37, 91, 290
Boito, Arrigo, 148–49, 304
Boose, Linda, 164, 306
Booth, Edwin, 157
Booth, Stephen, 3, 118–19, 133, 204–5, 283, 301–3
Borges, Jorge Luis, 255
Boynton, Lindsay, 57–58, 295
Bradley, A. C., 21, 148, 168, 177, 191, 229, 306–7
Branagh, Kenneth, 39, 59, 62–63, 75, 122, 296, 301
Brecht, Bertolt, 35, 40, 45, 59, 289
Brennan, Anthony, 61, 69, 74, 291, 295–96
Brontë, Charlotte, 233
Brontë, Emily, 148, 153
Brooke, Nicholas, 285

Brown, John Russell, 131–33, 138–40, 147, 302
Brown, Keith, 6, 285
Brown, Peter, 309
Bullough, Geoffrey, 302, 310
Bulman, James, 286
Bunyan, John, 84
Burckhardt, Sigurd, 3, 6, 60, 283, 285, 293, 295
Burke, Kenneth, 170, 191, 306
Burton, Richard, 116
Bush, George, 86
Butler, Marilyn, 233
Butler, Martin, 289, 290

Calvin, Jean, 192, 196–97, 309
Carlyle, Thomas, 313
Cavell, Stanley, 126–27, 191, 302
Césaire, Aimé, 284
Chapman, Edward, 9–10, 285
Chaucer, Geoffrey, 96
Cinthio, Giraldi, 125–26, 143, 148–49, 168–78, 181–86, 189–90, 201, 202, 206–8, 215–16, 218
Clanchy, M. T., 110, 301
Clare, Janet, 289–90
Clarendon, Edward Hyde, Earl of, 44
Clark, Peter, 58, 295
Clifford, James, 297
Cohen, Walter, 247, 253, 313
Coleridge, S. T., 168, 195, 200, 217–18, 306–7, 310
Collins, Stephen L., 24, 100, 288, 297–98, 300
Conrad, Joseph, 10, 13, 81–82, 253, 296
Cook, Ann Jellalie, 34–35, 289
Cowley, Abraham, 242
Crews, Frederick, 98–99, 300
Cromwell, Oliver, 297
Cruikshank, C. G., 57–58, 295
Culler, Jonathan, 299
Curren-Aquino, Deborah T., 293

Davie, Donald, 241, 313
Dawson, Anthony, 297
Denham, John, 242
Derrida, Jacques, 7, 26, 99, 101–2, 256, 285, 296, 300
Dickens, Charles, 232, 234–36, 238–39, 255, 312–13
Dollimore, Jonathan, 1–5, 7–11, 16, 23–24, 26–28, 37–38, 88, 98–112,

Dollimore (*cont.*)
  210, 283, 285, 287, 290, 295, 297, 300, 311
Donne, John, 121, 134, 242
Drakakis, John, 5, 10, 17, 26, 285, 300

Eagleton, Terence, 5, 17, 228–29, 284–85, 288
Eddershaw, M., 289
Edwards, Philip, 106–7, 300–301
Eliot, T. S., 115, 242, 243, 284
Elliott, Martin, 191, 308
Ellis, John, 7, 285
Elsom, John, 286
Empson, William, 4–5, 211, 284–85
English Shakespeare Company, 35–37, 91, 290
Erasmus, Desiderius, 10, 38, 197, 309
Evans, Malcolm, 5, 25, 284–85
Everett, Barbara, 157, 183, 249, 305, 307–8, 314

Ferry, Luc, 99, 300
Firth, J. R., 7
Fischer, Edwin, 20
Fish, Stanley, 26, 255–57, 314
Földes, Anna, 13
Foucault, Michel, 10, 27, 82–83, 96, 99, 244
Freud, Sigmund, 99, 177, 220, 298
Fried, Erich, 13
Furness, H. H., 229, 304–5

Gadamer, Hans-Georg, 252
Gardner, Helen, 288
Gardner, Martin, 299
Garner, S. N., 306
Gawain-poet, 309
Geertz, Clifford, 27, 81–82, 96, 252–53, 289, 296–97, 314
Giovanni Fiorentino, 128, 132, 143, 302
Goddard, Harold, 91, 131, 298, 302
Gombrich, E. H., 290–91, 296
Grady, Hugh, 2, 6–8, 24, 230, 283, 311
Granville-Barker, Harley, 184, 304–5, 308
Graves, Robert, 5, 284
Gray, Thomas, 241–42
Greenblatt, Stephen, 1, 2, 7, 26–30, 32, 34–35, 59, 80–98, 100–102, 107–8, 111–12, 128, 134, 163–68, 178, 190–201, 211, 228, 245–56, 288–89, 296–99, 303, 306, 312–14
Greene, Donald, 288

Griffith, John, 313

Hagstrum, Jean, 241
Haines, Charles, 164, 181, 306
Hall, John, 32, 41, 47
Hall, Stuart, 300
Handelsatz, Michael, 13
Hapgood, Robert, 288, 291
Harriot, Thomas, 32, 83, 86–87, 92, 98
Hawkes, Terence, 6, 17–23, 26, 229, 239, 287–88, 290, 311–12
Hawkins, Sherman, 91, 298
Haydon, Benjamin, 233–34
Hazlitt, William, 35, 87–88, 90–91
Heidegger, Martin, 99
Heller, Joseph, 81
Henry VIII, 94, 196
Hepokoski, James, 304
Hibbert, Christopher, 294–95
Hill, Christopher, 297
Hill, Rowland, 236
Hirst, Paul, 287
Hochberg, Julian, 296
Holderness, Graham, 1–2, 7, 17, 103–4, 228–29, 284–85, 287, 290, 294, 311
Holinshed, Raphael, 32, 41, 45–47, 53, 55, 292, 293
Honigmann, E. A. J., 297
Hopkins, G. M., 216
Howard, Alan, 35, 112
Howard, Jean E., 23–24, 33, 288–89, 304, 308, 313
Hughes, Ted, 5, 105, 284, 300
Hunter, G. K., 45–46, 293

Ibsen, Henrik, 144, 159

James, Henry, 94, 147, 241
Jenkins, Harold, 136, 294
Jerome, Saint, 196–97
Johnson, Samuel, 21, 63, 143, 147, 180, 195, 200–201, 226, 241–42, 302, 311
Jones, Emrys, 148–49, 304
Jonson, Ben, 98, 277, 280
Jordan, Winthrop, 211
Joyce, James, 8, 60, 98, 115, 122, 180

Kafka, Franz, 87, 92, 95
Kearney, Richard, 296, 300
Keats, John, 38–39, 147, 233–34
Kermode, Frank, 4–5, 92, 95, 151, 304
Kinderman, William, 76–77, 296
Knight, George Wilson, 191
Knights, L. C., 136

Konner, Melvin, 93, 299
Kott, Jan, 99, 101–2
Krauss, Werner, 12
Kuhn, Thomas, 6, 24, 288
Kundera, Milan, 239
Kurosawa, Akira, 43, 292

Lacan, Jacques, 99
Lakoff, George, 310
Lamb, Charles, 177, 307
Lamming, George, 284
Laroque, Francois, 306
Lawrence, D. H., 236, 309
Leavis, F. R., 21–23, 25–26, 164, 178,
    190–93, 229, 232, 234–39, 255, 288,
    308–9, 312, 314
Leech, Clifford, 5, 284
Leggatt, Alexander, 50, 294
Lem, Stanislaw, 95
Levin, Richard, 148, 246, 250, 304, 314
Levy, F. J., 293
Lewis, C. S., 94, 299
Lindenberger, Herbert, 60, 234, 295–96
Lombard, Peter, 197
Luther, Martin, 197
Lyon, John, 286

McCarthy, Mary, 94, 299
McFarland, Thomas, 233
McGuire, Philip C., 291
Machiavelli, Niccolo, 92, 116, 297, 301
Mahood, Molly, 286
Mallett, Phillip, 69, 91, 296
Malone, Edmond, 267
Mann, Thomas, 76, 131, 155
Mannoni, Octave, 284
Marcus, G. E., 297
Margolin, Jean-Claude, 313
Marlowe, Christopher, 30, 93, 248, 286
Marotti, Arthur, 230–32, 311
Martindale, Charles and Michèle, 312
Marx, Karl, 9, 99, 102
Mason, H. A., 169, 306
Melville, Herman, 237
Meres, Frances, 303
Messer-Davidow, Ellen, 299
Middleton, Thomas, 248
Mill, J. S., 236, 239, 313
Miller, J. Hillis, 81, 296
Miller, Jonathan, 228–29
Minnis, Alastair, 288
Montaigne, Michel de, 297
Monteverdi, Claudio, 205
Montrose, Louis A., 296

Moody, A. D., 131–33, 287, 302
Mozart, W. A., 109, 222
Muir, Kenneth, 201, 303, 309
Mullaney, Steven, 96–98, 100–102,
    299–300
Munday, Anthony, 140, 303

Nehamas, Alexander, 288
Nelson, T. G. A., 164, 181, 306
Newman, Karen, 183, 209–12, 306, 308
Nietzsche, Friedrich, 7–8, 26, 81–82, 86,
    99, 122, 247, 253, 296
Norris, Christopher, 17, 20–23, 25–27,
    239, 287, 288
North, Christopher. *See* Wilson, John
Nussbaum, Felicity, 256–57, 314
Nuttall, A. D., 126, 302

Olivier, Laurence, 18–19, 37, 39–41, 44,
    119, 182, 290, 291
Orgel, Stephen, 39, 277, 291, 311
Orkin, Martin, 306, 307
Osborne, John, 110

Padel, John, 310
Palmer, John, 131–33, 138–39, 147, 302
Parker, G. F., 301
Patterson, Annabel, 289, 293–94
Pechter, Edward, 85, 246–48, 253, 298,
    314
Pennington, Michael, 37, 91, 290
Penrose, Lionel, 92, 299
Penrose, Roger, 92, 299
Plutarch, 10
Poe, Edgar Allan, 39
Pope, Alexander, 68, 227, 241
Powell, Edward, 47, 57, 110, 295, 301
Puccini, Giacomo, 110
Pugh, R. B., 312
Pynchon, Thomas, 95

Quigley, Austen, 241, 313
Quiller-Couch, Arthur, 261

Rabkin, Norman, 3, 6, 24, 77–80, 87,
    90, 115, 191, 283, 285, 288, 291, 296,
    302
Rackin, Phyllis, 29–30, 289, 293
Ranke, Leopold von, 62
Reagan, Ronald, 27, 86–87, 93
Renaut, Alain, 99, 300
Retamar, Fernandez, 284
Ricoeur, Paul, 77–80

Ridley, M. R., 151, 153–55, 157, 161, 180, 182, 258–59, 277, 281, 304
Robinson, Marsha, 293
Rorty, Richard, 250–51, 314
Rose, Gillian, 26
Ross, Lawrence, 164, 306
Rossiter, A. P., 1–2, 6, 22, 60, 90, 97–98, 123, 283, 295
Royal Shakespeare Company, 35, 287, 290, 301
Ryan, Kiernan, 310
Ryan, Michael, 287
Rymer, Thomas, 177

Salway, John, 210–12, 310
Sanders, Norman, 154, 157, 304, 305
Sanders, Wilbur, 8, 99, 101–2, 283, 305
Sanger, C. P., 148
Sapir, Edward, 285
Sarracoll, John, 93–94
Scarisbrick, John, 294
Schanzer, Ernst, 144, 304
Schlegel, A. W., 232
Schoenberg, Arnold, 109, 125, 145–47, 302
Schopenhauer, Arthur, 296
Schumacher, Ernst, 286
Sidney, Philip, 232
Silvayn, Alexander, 303
Sinfield, Alan, 5, 8, 10–18, 23, 25–26, 28, 38, 98–112, 210, 227–28, 283, 285, 287, 290, 295, 311
Siskin, Clifford, 232–34, 238–41, 243–45, 255, 312
Smith, James, 284
Snow, Edward, 190–91, 200–201, 306, 308
Spencer, Theodore, 302
Spevack, Marvin, 144, 304
Stephen, James Fitzjames, 236, 239, 312–13
Stephen, Leslie, 312–13
Stevens, Wallace, 231, 311–12
Strachey, Lytton, 231, 312
Strickland, Geoffrey, 194, 309
Swift, Jonathan, 242
Synesius of Cyrene, 197

Taruskin, Richard, 27, 289
Taylor, Gary, 40, 116, 291
Taylor, Jeremy, 309

Tennenhouse, Leonard, 1–2, 27–30, 35, 37, 55, 95–96, 100, 107, 109, 112, 119, 232, 289
Thacker, David, 15
Theobald, Lewis, 185
Thomas, Keith, 191, 297
Thompson, Craig R., 309
Tillyard, E. M. W., 1–9, 11, 15–16, 19, 22–24, 28, 32, 85, 99, 101–2, 229, 284, 289, 290
Tolstoy, Leo, 180
Traversi, Derek, 4
Turner, Mark, 310

Vasari, Giorgio, 242
Vaughan, Alden T., 282
Vaughan, Virginia M., 282
Veeser, H. Aram, 26–27, 33, 288–89, 314
Verdi, Giuseppe, 144, 148–49, 179–80, 304

Wagner, Richard, 109, 135
Walch, Gunther, 295
Waldock, A. J. A., 128, 136, 302
Wallace, David, 288
Waller, Edmund, 242
Walters, J. C., 40–41, 290
Warton, Thomas, 241
Wendel, François, 309
Wentersdorf, Karl P., 110, 292–93
Wesker, Arnold, 12–14, 285–86
Wheeler, Richard, 291–92
Whetstone, George, 141, 146
Whorf, Benjamin Lee, 285
Wickham, Glynne, 297
Wilcox, L., 291
Williams, Raymond, 300
Wills, Gary, 299
Wilson, John ("Christopher North"), 131, 302
Wilson, John Dover, 37, 152, 159, 161, 170–71, 299, 304, 305, 308
Wimsatt, W. K., 302
Winch, Peter, 313
Wittgenstein, Ludwig, 7, 25, 137, 172, 220, 240–43, 285, 290, 303, 311, 313
Womersley, David, 293
Wordsworth, William, 233, 240, 244
Wright, George T., 293

Xystus, 197